The Genealogy of Disjunction

The Genealogy
of Disjunction

R. E. JENNINGS

New York   Oxford
OXFORD UNIVERSITY PRESS
1994

Oxford University Press

Oxford   New York
Athens   Auckland   Bangkok   Bombay
Calcutta   Cape Town   Dar es Salaam   Delhi
Florence   Hong Kong   Istanbul   Karachi
Kuala Lumpur   Madras   Madrid   Melbourne
Mexico City   Nairobi   Paris   Singapore
Taipei   Tokyo   Toronto

and associated companies in
Berlin   Ibadan

Published by Oxford University Press, Inc.,
200 Madison Avenue, New York, New York 10016

Oxford is a registered trademark of Oxford University Press

Library of Congress Cataloging-in-Publication Data
   Jennings, R. E. (Raymond Earl)   The genealogy of disjunction /
R. E. Jennings.
      p.   cm.
   Includes bibliographical references and index.
   ISBN 0-19-507524-2
   1. Disjunction (Logic)   2. Or (The English word)   I. Title.
   BC199.D56J46   1994
   160—dc20   93-11592

987654321

Printed in the United States of America
on acid-free paper

For Hugues Leblanc

Preface

Gilbert Ryle has remarked that the difference between philosophers and formal logicians is akin to the distinction between explorers of the moors and operators of tramways. The sensitive research logician may puzzle whether to accept the wayfarer's innocent admiration and wave back or to say something clever to disarm the social irony. For he is as likely as not to think of himself more on a footing with designers of tramways than with their operators, more on a social level with consultant to the corporation than with liveried employee. But the metaphor is more fundamentally misleading, and not intended as a slight. Much of the product of logical research has little anymore to do with secure inferential conveyance. Even the little light that might once have fallen fleetingly but usefully upon a ditch or a dead sheep shifts remorselessly ever toward the infrared. The vehicle is anymore only a logically possible tram.

Ryle's imagery is, however, vividly correct in one particular: logic in its usual presentation is a recent invention, in fact, not much older than the tram. And, even if neglectfully of some of the newer track, he rightfully regards logic as, like the tram, restricted in the manner of its service. But again, as it places the logician too close to the ground, the imagery locates his philosopher wrongly in a wild, not urban landscape. The philosopher's problem is not one of finding unfamiliar things to prod. His subject matter crowds him round. If it is perplexing, it is so not because it is alien, but because it is human and so familiar. The difficulty is that, at the level at which we want understanding, we do not understand the linguistic things that *we* do or how *we* do them. If a geographical image is sought, let it be the image of a cityscape filled with long evolved, albeit human contrivances, so far removed from their original materials and uses that, though everyday they serve our purposes, we can no longer fit their form to their function.

This book is an attempt to say how some of our logical vocabulary works in discourse. Its central subject matter is the word 'or', but the approach that it finally advocates it advocates for the study of other such vocabulary as well. 'Or' presents some curious and easily illustrated puzzles, that, possibly because they have not been recognized for what they are, have not been the source of entrenched philosophical doctrine. In this respect, 'or', unlike 'if', really is, to revert to something like Ryle's metaphor, virgin territory. There is yet time to save it from development, and from what seems to me to have been, in the case of 'if', the monopolistic application of wrong methods.

My own perplexities about 'or' were sown in 1964 by a reading of von Wright's *Logic of Preference* and provided some of the subject matter for two theses, an M.A. thesis at Queen's University written under the supervision of the late Jon Wheatley and a Ph.D. thesis at the University of London under the supervision of Bernard Williams. In the second, I proposed essentially the account of the puzzling conjunctive uses of 'or' that is further elaborated here, as well as the derivative account of the 'any/every' distinction that is the core of the one contained in this essay. But the punctuational explanation, as far as it had got, was unsatisfying inasmuch as it seemed unconnected with what I took to be the usual sentential uses that I simply assumed to be disjunctive. And there were other things to do. Several developments persuaded me to take it all up once again. The first was the large literature on 'if', a subject being called the logic of conditionals, that had never received the kind of simple-hearted scrutiny that had revealed so much that was perplexing about 'or'. The nearest to an analogous literature on 'or', as it seemed from the almost ostentatious isolation of academic philosophy, was pullulating within the confines of deontic logic under the heading of 'free choice permission'. It may be that no one had noticed essentially the same and odder features in the behaviour of 'or' throughout its uses in English, else there might have come into existence something calling itself the logic of disjunctions. News of the existence of a Counter-Earth in which linguists, with a much broader landscape in view, had been puzzling over the very problems that I had so long ago set aside reached me late in my application of CPR to older work. As might be expected, different starting points had yielded different emphases, though there had as well been some points of contact. In addition, the aims of the linguists were at an angle oblique to the aim of this essay: to try to say how we come to have a notion of logical disjunction. Much of the linguists' thinking about 'or', it seems, has had the truth-tabular '∨' as one of its light sources, so that the ideas of disjunction and set-theoretic union contribute perceptibly to its cast. So while I have tried to acknowledge points of contact and parallel developments, it has seemed best not to seem to be offering this essay as a response to current linguistic approaches, but to address myself to the philosophical problem I have set. Linguists by now are surely justified in assuming title to this portion of the moor and may, come to that, have their own ideas about which is Earth and which Counter-Earth. So I beg their indulgence as a former denizen if I seem to wander their marches in a stupor and to see the landscape as it was. Two recent developments within linguistics have seemed to confirm this course. The first is Victor Dudman's investigation of *if . . . then . . .* sentences which has brought us back from rhapsodic mythologizing about conditionals to something like simple systematic observation of *if*-clauses as adverbial modifications. The second is Laurence Horn's study of negation, which, in questioning the centrality of sentence-negation, provides a confirming datum to the view I shall put forward. Within this family of studies, as I hope to have demonstrated, 'or' deserves a volume to itself. If this work forestalls a wholly unwarranted development of logics of funny disjunctions, it will have served one of the purposes for its existence.

The second reason lies in the growing abundance of logic textbooks retailing wholly gratuitous (and with a moment's reflection, perfectly apparent) falsehoods about the relationship between the disjunction of propositional logic and the 'or' of English (and some of its counterparts in Latin), and that to no very important expository end. It seemed worthwhile to register the errors in an essay large enough to discuss a sufficiency of convincing examples and also begin a more plausible alternative account.

The third reason arises out of the second. As it seems from its fringe, emerging research in computer discourse generation is ill served by the prejudice, which the glib myth making of the logic texts tends to instil, that the central uses of 'or' and other 'logical' vocabulary of natural language are wholly to be accounted for by a truth conditional theory along the lines of formal semantics. To the extent that such research programmes are aided by possession of the right general principles, it seems worthwhile to try to pick out the regularities that a proper set of principles would codify and above all, to try to get right the vocabulary of the observation language. If an instructively oversimple slogan were to emerge from my efforts and be offered as amicular advice to discourse generation researchers, along the lines of the earlier 'Don't ask for the meaning; ask for the use', it would be 'Mainly we emit sounds'. In trying to understand, in a usefully general way, the sounds that we make, the pragmatic notions of discourse status and discourse adverbiality, however imperfectly formulated here, are likely to be more central than the notion of truth conditions, which after all applies only to theoretical entities of dubious origins whose relationship even to the narrow range of indicative speech that it is taken to explain is as tenuous as it is mysterious.

In the end, whether it has been worthwhile to write so long a book about so short a word is for the reader, not the writer, to say. But the writer, who best knows the reason for the work, is best placed to offer negative criteria of adequacy. One would be this: if the essay does not suggest strongly to the reader that a large part of our so-called logical vocabulary comes to its present uses from metalinguistic applications of the language of physical relationship, and that in much of its ordinary use it retains the kind of adverbiality that is claimed here for 'or', then I will have missed my mark. Second, if it does not demonstrate convincingly the worth of simply trying to sort out how the same logical vocabulary works in discourse, then it will have been insufficient means to one of its ends. No part of its task is to attempt a formal representation within logical theory, rather the reverse.

I am indebted to the late Jon Wheatley, who encouraged me to enter Philosophy and who supervised the earlier thesis, to Bernard Williams, who supervised the second, and the late Arthur Prior who examined it, to Risto Hilpinen, who encouraged me to take the project up again, or at the very least to publish the earlier work as an historical curiosity. In the course of writing and presenting to various forums what eventually became the present document, many colleagues have offered invaluable criticisms and advice and asked useful questions. Among them I should mention (in more or less chronological order) Rolf George, Max Cresswell, Peter Schotch, Jeff Pelletier, Johan van Benthem, Souren Teghrarian, Robert O'Toole, Hugues Leblanc, Michael Dowad, Robin Taylor, Charles Travis, Dorothy Edgington, Martin Hahn, Norman Swartz, and Mary Shaw. I especially wish to thank an anonymous Oxford University Press referee for useful truths about the state of the academic solar system and many detailed bibliographical and substantial suggestions.

Various agencies supported this work during its long history. They are, again in chronological order, the Ontario Ministry of Education, the Canada Council, the Commonwealth Scholarships Foundation and the British Council, the Social Sciences and Humanities Research Council of Canada and the Finnish Ministry of Education.

The manuscript was formatted and typeset with Borland Sprint and the Index was compiled using INDEXX.

R. E. J.

Burnaby, Canada
February, 1994

Contents

P A R T

1

The Story of 'Or'

1

Introduction

1.1 Preliminaries

This book is about the kinship of the English word 'or' and the logical connective ∨. The relationship is, I hope to show, not that of identity. It is not usefully illumined by metaphors that contrast civilian and military duties or adequately explained by contrasting eristic combat with drill. Neither is the connection that of rival or genial siblinghood of homebody and soldiering sibs. In fact, although it should illumine the place of 'or' in reasoning, an account of the connection will not dwell upon the civilian uses of 'or' that parallel the uses of ∨. Nor will such an account deal *primarily* with the use of 'or' as it occurs between indicative sentences, although it must connect those intersentential occurrences of 'or' with those in which it joins nouns, verbs, adjectives, adverbs, prepositions and so on. 'Or' is a sufficiently specialized part of speech that an account of its workings must sometimes be got at by contrasting its effect in particular occurrences with the effect of substituting the similarly specialized 'and', so this book must shed some reflected light upon that word as well. And finally since our interest in the doings of 'or' is a philosophical interest, it need hardly be said that we will consider 'or' also in relation to other vocabulary of natural language that has traditionally been or recently come to be regarded as meriting the attention of philosophers and philosophical logicians, in particular such constructions as 'If . . . then . . .', 'It ought to be the case that . . .', 'Necessarily . . .', and so on.

The question may be put baldly: Where does disjunction come from? It will seem a puzzling question to some, perhaps akin to such a question as 'Where does gravity come from?' The parallel is instructive. The notion of gravity represents a certain conception of an ensemble of relationships between physical bodies. In formulating the laws of gravitation Newton introduced novel elements to the language of physics. If the language he proposed offers us the best and final vehicle for expressing these relationships, then the question properly arises whether the laws which Newton expressed in that language are exactly true or nearly enough true for a limited range of calculations. If Newton has chosen for us the best of all possible mathematical idioms for expressing these relationships, and if the laws that he proposed express them exactly, then we may say, I suppose, that he discovered a real feature of the world, namely, gravity. If he did not choose the best of all possible mathematical idioms or if the laws he expressed in that idiom are not exactly correct, we are left with the question as to what his magnificent achievement was, and in particular, what gravity is, given that it is not a feature of the world after all. That question, the one that would remain even if Newton had not got it quite right, is the kind that I want to ask about the origins of disjunction. According to popular mythology, what Newton saw was that one of the physical relationships evident between a falling apple and the earth also holds between the moon and the earth, between the earth and the sun, and between every pair of massive bodies. And he found a mathematical function that provides an approximate measure of the relationship. What the precise connection is between that mathematics and the abstracted relationship for whose expression it was presumed a suitable vehicle is a posable question. Consider the parallel. The truth-functional notion of disjunction is, so far as we know, a recent invention, but in saying this we do not want to deny that even before the emergence of human speech our ancestors found themselves in situations where, faced with limited choices and finding some choices barred, they had the alternatives thrust upon them. We now sometimes describe their predicament in the language of disjunctive syllogism. But between their dilemmas and our formal description, there had to evolve a language in which *that* feature could be abstracted which makes that predicament structurally similar to others. As it happens, one of the idioms that have evolved for describing such conditions is a theoretical one involving notions such as truth and truth-bearing objects, disjunction, negation, and illation. But the natural idiom that that theoretical language has, for some purposes, displaced, is one which involves among other things, the use of compound sentences involving the word 'or'. So my question is: *how does there evolve a coordinating word having those properties of 'or' that* ∨ *is intended to capture?* Now the enthusiastic realist will no doubt prefer to say that gravitation exists independently of the theory, and that if there are discrepancies between the mathematics and the world, it is because the theory only approximately captures it; what is needed is mathematical theory that matches gravitational phenomena more closely. The same enthusiast, or a sib, will say that disjunction exists independently of the theory, that natural language expressed it with less than perfect crispness, that it is finally captured in the language of truth-functions. We may reply that had the theory of gravitation not been introduced, we would not have the vocabulary in which to frame the question; a similar rejoinder may be made about truth-functional logic and disjunction: if logical theory had not introduced the vocabulary of disjunction, we could not formulate the question. The point may be entirely one of intellectual style, the practitioner of one yearning toward belief in as much as possible, and the follower of the other content with belief in as much as necessary.

Is the 'or' that joins sentences and that finds its representative in the ∨ of truth-functional logic one with the 'or' which joins single words or phrases in lists within single sentences? The thrust of the account to be offered here is that the truth-functional character of 'or' and 'and', if they have such a character in their natural language habitat, is a character that they derive as a consequence of their playing a certain role in discourse, one best described as punctuational, or in a specialized sense of the word, *adverbial*. I shall argue that some of the features represented in propositional logic by familiar formal properties of ∨ and ∧ can be referred to, and could be inferred from, more general regularities in the uses of 'and' and 'or' that they possess even outside their propositional uses, and that these properties are essentially punctuational rather than truth-functional properties.

1.1.1 Disjunctions

The word 'disjunction' has had a varied career even within the present century, having meant, for some earlier authors, the denial of conjunction and having come to mean more recently what those same earlier authors would have called 'alternation'. The word is derived from the Latin *disiunctio* meaning 'separation' and has been inherited from a logical tradition traceable to the Stoics or possibly the later Peripatetics, although, as we shall see, its present applications represent a twentieth century innovation. Two binary truth-functions are currently labelled 'disjunction'. Both are semantically defined by truth tables that tabulate their graphs. The first, symbolized ∨ and called 'inclusive (or "non-exclusive") disjunction', is a function that takes a pair of truth values to the maximum of the pair. Its table displays a pair of sentence schemata, α and β, (the *disjuncts*) with all possible combinations of truth-values ('1' representing *true* and '0' representing *false*) and, for each combination of truth-values, the output value of the function, which is understood as the truth-value of the disjunction $\alpha \vee \beta$:

$$
\begin{array}{cc c}
\alpha & \beta & \alpha \vee \beta \\
1 & 1 & 1 \\
1 & 0 & 1 \\
0 & 1 & 1 \\
0 & 0 & 0
\end{array}
$$

We will sometimes refer to this function as 1110 disjunction.

In model-theoretic semantics where propositions are represented by sets of semantic markers called indices or points and sometimes thought of as possible states or worlds, the set of indices representing a sentence $\alpha \vee \beta$ is the union of the set of indices representing α and the set of points representing β. This semantic idiom takes up an idea that originated with George Boole (1854), that of regarding a proposition as, in effect, a property of semantic indices. Boole distinguished the *primary* propositions of categorical logic, which concerned relationships between classes of individuals, from *secondary* propositions, which consisted of primary propositions in logical combination. One important insight was that secondary propositions, like their primary constituents could be thought of as concerning relationships between and operations upon classes of items. Boole himself thought of secondary propositions as being about classes of moments. Thus, for example, a conditional 'If α, then β' would be true iff the the class of moments at which α is true is included in the class of moments at which β is true. He did not provide for inclusive disjunction in his informal semantic account, but we can see what it would be. In Boole's reading of the representation, the time during which $\alpha \vee \beta$ is true would be the time during which α is true taken together with the time during which β is true. There is a parallel, which we shall have occasion to mention again, between the logicians' semantic representation of 'or' as it joins sentences and their representation of 'or' as it joins terms. In both cases the semantics takes the *or*-construction to stand for a union of classes: in the former case, classes of moments or worlds or states, and in the latter, classes of objects.

A second 'disjunctive' truth-function, which we will symbolize by $\veebar$ is variously called 'exclusive disjunction', 'logical inequivalence', or 'logical difference'. $\veebar$ takes an input pair of distinct truth values to the value 1 and an input pair of equivalent truth values to 0. Its table is

$$
\begin{array}{cc|c}
\alpha & \beta & \alpha \veebar \beta \\
1 & 1 & 0 \\
1 & 0 & 1 \\
0 & 1 & 1 \\
0 & 0 & 0 \\
\end{array}
$$

Again, it will sometimes be convenient to refer to this as 0110 disjunction. The distinction between the two is sometimes marked in texts by saying that the former receives the value 1 when *at least* one of its disjuncts is true, the latter when *exactly* one of its disjuncts is true. This is a fair enough account when one bears in mind that both are binary truth-functions, so that there are always exactly two disjuncts. But, since both functions are associative (that is, 'A ∗ (B ∗ C)' is equivalent to '(A ∗ B) ∗ C', with '∗' indifferently understood as ∨ or $\veebar$), many textbook authors tolerate the harmless ambiguity occasioned by the omission of brackets. In this case, it is tempting to think of the resulting formula as a disjunction of three (or, in general, *n*) disjuncts. In this more relaxed idiom, no problems arise for the 'at least one' reading of ∨, but $\veebar$ can no longer be understood as 'saying' that exactly one disjunct is true. Consider the case of three 'disjuncts', and let them all be true. Then restore brackets in either of the two ways possible and the enclosed disjunction is false (since both of its disjuncts are true). But then exactly one of the official disjuncts of the resulting formula is true; thus the disjunction is true. In general, and speaking in this informal idiom, an exclusive disjunction, A, of any number of atomic disjuncts will be true if and only if an odd number of its disjuncts are true. The inductive proof (the only proof in this essay) is easily stated:

Proof:
The induction is on the number of 'disjuncts' of A. For convenience, we will regard a single atom as an exclusive disjunction of one disjunct. The basis of the induction is therefore clearly true, since A (itself an atom) is true if and only if the only one of its atoms is true. Now assume for the hypothesis of induction that the biconditional holds for every exclusive disjunction of fewer than *k* disjuncts, and suppose that A disjoins *k* atomic disjuncts. Then A is an exclusive disjunction of two exclusive disjunctions B and C, each of which has fewer than *k* atomic disjuncts. Now assume that A is true. Then exactly one of B and C is true. Without loss of generality we may assume that it is B. Then, by the hypothesis of induction, B has an odd number of true disjuncts, and C has an even number. But then, since an odd number added to an even number yields an odd number, A has an odd number of true disjuncts. Now assume that A is

false. Then either both B and C are true, or they are both false. Assume the former. Then, by the hypothesis of induction, each of B and C has an odd number of true disjuncts, and since an odd number added to an odd number yields an even number, A has an even number of true disjuncts. Assume the latter. Then, by the hypothesis of induction, each of B and C has an even number of true disjuncts. But again, an even number added to an even number yields an even number. Thus A has an even number of true disjuncts. That completes the induction. ∎

The infelicity of the idiom which generalizes exclusive disjunction to encompass n-ary exclusive disjunctions is made stark when we compare the case with that of material equivalence. Here one may in any case feel less inclined to adopt the informal idiom which would have us drop brackets and speak of more than two 'equivalents'. In this case, an inductive proof along parallel lines will establish that a material equivalence of any number of 'equivalents' is true if and only if an even number of its 'equivalents' are false. Consider a three-term equivalence of which two terms are false. Again equivalence is associative, so it does not matter where the brackets are placed, but let us consider the two possibilities. Either two false terms are bracketed or a true with a false. In the former case the bracketed equivalence is true, and since the third term is true, so is the whole formula. In the latter case, the bracketed equivalence is false, but so is the third term, so the whole formula is true. Thus three sentences would, in this idiom, be logically inequivalent (an odd number of them being true) if and only if they were logically equivalent (an even number of them being false), and so on for any odd-numbered set of indicative sentences. In general, any odd-numbered exclusive disjunction would be true if and only if the corresponding material equivalence were true, but any even-numbered exclusive disjunction would be true if and only if the corresponding material equivalence were false.

The point bears upon our study at a number of places, but is particularly important as an indication of how abrupt a division there is between the language of twentieth-century logic and its counterpart of so recent a period as the time of Boole (1815–64), for, as we shall see, although Boole was preoccupied with an exclusive disjunction, as distinct from the disjunction symbolized by ∨, ∨̲ does not capture his conception of exclusive disjunction. Moreover, it brings into focus how generally ill understood is the relationship between twentieth-century logic and what came before it, for even acute historians of the subject have missed the point, and modern textbook writers, when their attention falls upon the subject, usually write as though the two conceptions were one.

1.1.2 Logic and language

The caution of authors of introductory logic textbooks, selective as it is, does in many cases incline them to warn the tiro that the logical particles 'and' and 'or' of natural language do not necessarily coincide in sense with the logical particles ∧ and ∨ of formal systems they present. Whereas the constants ∧ and ∨ of propositional logic connect only well-formed formulae (wffs), the coordinating conjunctions 'and' and 'or' are capable of joining virtually any parts of speech. Some textbook writers mention that in ordinary English, the conjunction 'and' may carry information about order (consider *Sally got married and had a baby*) that is absent from wffs in ∧, for which we expect as theorems all instances of:

$$\alpha \wedge \beta \leftrightarrow \beta \wedge \alpha.$$

Others take the trouble to mention that in ordinary English 'and' has non-sentential uses that are independent of its use as sentence connective (*They amused themselves with Snakes and Ladders*). Others note that the English 'and' may carry an additional understanding of mutuality (*Fred and Sally got married*) absent alike (in most idiolects still) from *Fred and Harry got married* and from well-formed formulae in ∧. But textbook writers by and large seem tacitly to accept what many of us were taught in school: that sentences in which 'or' occurs between nouns or adjectives or other parts of speech are elliptical for sentences in which 'or' occurs between whole sentences. Reichenbach (1947) puts it as baldly as any:

> The fundamental operations used to construct molecular sentences out of atomic sentences are expressed by the words 'not', 'or', 'and', 'implies', 'equivalent'. We call them *propositional operations*. In conversational language some of these words are sometimes used to combine, not sentences, but words, such as 'Peter or William will go with you'. We consider this sentence form an abbreviation of 'Peter will go with you or William will go with you'.

Of course Reichenbach was not propounding this as a global theory, and the assumption is innocent enough for local applications. So there is no imputation even of complacency in labelling the universalization of his maxim the *ellipsis view*. It is unlikely that many textbook authors would wish to propound such a view. Apart from the passing observation that in English, 'and' and 'or' sometimes join words and in propositional logic ∧ and ∨ always join wffs, together with oftentimes erroneous advice about how to get from one form to the other, the subject of 'and' and 'or' as list connectives is not discussed in logic textbooks, even those written for philosophy undergraduates. A number of linguists have taken up the subject in the past two decades, notably Legrand (1975). But no recent philosopher, with the exception of Peter Geach (1962, Chapter 7 'The Logic of Lists') and myself (Jennings 1967) has attempted separate, systematic consideration to the inferential behaviour of 'and' and 'or' as they occur more frequently in discourse, joining non-sentential parts of speech. It is pointless to speculate in detail why logic so neglects these non-propositional uses of what it regards as logical vocabulary, but part of the reason must surely be the refined tidiness of propositional methods that provide an attractive explanatory model.

Now the connection between sentences containing *and*- and *or*-lists on the one hand and compound sentences with 'and' and 'or' on the other bears a beguiling likeness to *distributivity* properties found in formal systems; complacent acceptance of something akin to the ellipsis view may be merely a symptom of this beguilement. The illustrations which follow are all from propositional logic, but quantificational logic holds further parallel examples. Consider, for example, the biconditional

$$\vdash \Box\alpha \wedge \Box\beta \leftrightarrow \Box(\alpha \wedge \beta),$$

found in certain modal logics, which represents the (conjunctive) distributivity of necessity ($\Box$) with respect to conjunction ($\wedge$). That property is a composite of two others, represented in the two directions of the $\leftrightarrow$: the first (left to right) is the aggregration property; the second (right to left), in the logics in question, is a propositional consequence of the more general property of monotonicity of $\Box$, the property of preserving the order of provable implications. Contrast with this the (disjunctive) distributivity of possibility ($\Diamond$) with respect to disjunction ($\vee$) represented in the biconditional

$$\Diamond\alpha \vee \Diamond\beta \leftrightarrow \Diamond(\alpha \vee \beta),$$

the (disjunctive) distributivity of negation ($\neg$) with respect to conjunction, represented in the biconditional

$$\neg\alpha \wedge \neg\beta \leftrightarrow \neg(\alpha \vee \beta),$$

and the (conjunctive) distributivity of negation ($\neg$) with respect to disjunction, represented in the biconditional

$$\neg\alpha \vee \neg\beta \leftrightarrow \neg(\alpha \wedge \beta).$$

In formal contexts, the language of distribution is sometimes used even when a conditional but not a biconditional is a theorem. In this idiom we may say that necessity does not distribute over disjunction since

$$\Box(\alpha \vee \beta) \to \Box\alpha \vee \Box\beta$$

is not a theorem, and that possibility distributes conjunctively over conjunction, but is not aggregative, since

$$\Diamond(\alpha \wedge \beta) \to \Diamond\alpha \wedge \Diamond\beta$$

is a theorem, but

$$\Diamond\alpha \wedge \Diamond\beta \to \Diamond(\alpha \wedge \beta)$$

is not. Again, we sometimes speak of these distributional transformations as distributive properties of the conjunctions and disjunctions over which they are or are not allowed. We may say that $\wedge$ is conjunctively distributive with respect to $\Box$ and with respect to $\Diamond$, but that $\vee$ is disjunctively distributive with respect to $\Diamond$ though not with respect to $\Box$.

Adapting the language of distribution to the description of list-containing sentences and corresponding compound sentences, we can restate the ellipsis view as the view that there is only ever one equivalent distributional transformation for a sentence containing a list formed with 'or' and only one for any sentence containing a list constructed with 'and'. We shall see early on that this ellipsis view is false and that the distributive properties of lists are as varied and, in some respects, nearly as systematic as the distributive properties of disjunctive and conjunctive sentences.

The modal formulae cited show a systematic correlation between the distributive characteristics of $\Box$ and $\Diamond$ with respect to $\wedge$ and $\vee$, which are directly attributable to the duality of these pairs of connectives. The distribution formulae pertaining to $\Box$ ($\Diamond$) with respect to $\wedge$ ($\vee$) can be inferred from the distributive properties of $\Diamond$ ($\Box$) with respect to $\vee$ ($\wedge$), via the biconditionals:

$$\Diamond\alpha \leftrightarrow \neg\Box\neg\alpha$$

and

$$\Box\alpha \leftrightarrow \neg\Diamond\neg\alpha$$

together with De Morgan's Laws:

$$\neg\alpha \wedge \neg\beta \leftrightarrow \neg(\alpha \vee \beta),$$

and

$$\neg\alpha \vee \neg\beta \leftrightarrow \neg(\alpha \wedge \beta).$$

We shall want an account of 'or' that makes these beautiful symmetries explicable. But we shall see that the distributive properties of lists vary systematically with the kinds of environments in which they occur and that the distributive variations of *or*-lists are generally correlated with variations in the distributive properties of *and*-lists in the same environments. In fact, we shall find a kind of dualism in the distributivity of *and*- and *or*-lists like the correlation attributable to the duality of disjunction and conjunction. Since these distributivity properties are composed of inferrability relationships, it is important to understand these matters if we want to reflect in particular formalisms (modal, deontic, doxastic, and so on) the inferential regularities found in the corresponding phenomena of ordinary discourse. For the logical vocabulary proper to these theories, 'necessarily', 'possibly', 'ought', 'may', 'believe', and so on is to be found in the environments that distribute in this way or that over *or*-lists and *and*-lists. The distributive properties of a list for an environment containing an occurrence of, say deontic vocabulary, give rules of inference for ordinary deontic discourse that we may expect to find mentioned in a theory of deontic inference, and insofar as we think of deontic logic as the proper embodiment of such a theory, represented there as well. Or, to consider a concrete (non-deontic) example, it is worth asking what effect, if any, the fact that the list in *Mary wants Stilton or cheddar* is undistributive has upon the role that this sentence can play in a practical syllogism.

Our interest in lists formed with 'and' and 'or' is inseparable from our interest in the environments in which lists formed with 'and' and 'or' occur. Indeed, we shall see that the nature of the environment seems to determine the distributive properties that *and*- and *or*-constructions have, and that that environmental determination of distributive behaviour of *and*- and *or*-constructions of itself provides a taxonomy of list-embedding contexts that then requires explanation.

1.1.3 Lists

By list I mean any non-sentential string consisting of more than one expression generally of the same grammatical type, separated by one of the connective words 'and' and 'or'. The expressions joined in this way are the terms of the list.

The use to be made of 'list' and 'term' is not particularly technical, but some of our lists will be explicit in a way that English lists usually are not. Whereas in English, commas might separate all the members of the list (*Mary, Charles, and Wah went with me*), I will generally write the list more laboriously with all the members separated by the same conjunction (*Mary and Charles and Wah went with me*).

It is worth remarking in passing that this feature of lists in English must complicate a little any view that sentences with *or*-lists (or *and*-lists) are elliptical for disjunctions (or conjunctions). Two features of ordinary English practice must sometimes introduce at least a little indirection in the formal representation of such sentences. In the first place, in their usual treatment, $\lor$ and $\land$ are binary connectives, so that a string such as

$$p_1 \lor p_2 \lor p_3$$

would not be well formed. A disjunctive sentence obtained by distribution over a three-term list would have to be represented by a wff having one of the forms

$$(\alpha \lor \beta) \lor \gamma \,/\, \alpha \lor (\beta \lor \gamma)$$

that is, by a disjunction, one of whose disjuncts is itself a disjunction. By contrast, there is no syntactic ambiguity in the sentence

Either I shall be imprisoned or I shall be fined or I shall be sued.

We may order the terms suitably, but we do not understand the result as a disjunction with one disjunctive term, though we can indicate subsidiary disjunctions by parallel structure as

Either I shall be imprisoned or fined or I shall be sued

here grouping liabilities according to legal kind. Arguably this must be represented by a wff bracketing the first pair rather than the second, but since $\lor$ is associative, any information about the appropriateness of the English grouping is effectively lost anyway.

Again, the use of commas complicates the story slightly. In the quoted presentiment rewritten in the commate form:

I shall be imprisoned, fined, or sued

the ',' is understood as an 'or', and in general in lists, ',' may be regarded as anaphoric, taking the sense of whichever of 'or' or 'and' succeeds. There is nothing in principle to prevent our preserving the comma between sentences in the distributed form, but in practice we do not do so when the intended sense is 'or', possibly because the presumption is that successive main clauses are informationally additive, so that the delayed 'or' requires a confusing reinterpretation. Even so, we tend to preserve the comma when the intended sense is 'and' only when the resulting clauses are fairly short, otherwise preferring some combination of 'and's, semicolons, and full-stops.

1.1.4 Environments

Particularly in early sections I use the word 'environment' to mean just the rest of the sentence in which the list occurs. At times, we will want to talk generally about sentences containing *or*-lists or *and*-lists without reference to any specific sentence, and it will be convenient to have some biodegradable notation for doing so. We will use lowercase letters from the beginning of the alphabet with or without subscripts for noun phrases occurring as members of lists: 'a', 'a_1', 'a_2', 'a_3', . . .; 'b', 'b_1', 'b_2', 'b_3', . . .; 'c', 'c_1', 'c_2', 'c_3', . . .; and so on. Lists will be called *and*-lists when they use 'and' and *or*-lists when they use 'or'. I say that a list of the form 'a_1 or a_2 or a_3' is an *or*-list of A's; a list of the form 'b_1 and b_2 and b_3' I call an *and*-list of B's, using 'A', 'B' and so on as stand-ins for general terms either naturally occurring or made up. I use suspension dots to indicate an indefinite rather than an infinite continuation of the list. One further such disposable device will be the use of '$\underline{\lambda}(\ )$' to represent the environment of a list in the sense of 'environment' already mentioned. The character λ is to suggest τὰ λοίπα meaning 'the remaining part', and has nothing to do with the λ-calculus. Thus the expression '$\underline{\lambda}(a_1$ and a_2 and $a_3)$' represents an *and*-list occurring in some or other sentence.

Our interest is in the relation between a sentence consisting of a list occurring in a context '$\underline{\lambda}(\ )$' and a combination of sentences each of which consists of a member of the list occurring in approximately the same context (necessary grammatical adjustments having been made). I call the transformation that takes a sentence of the former sort to a sentence of the latter sort the *distribution of the context '$\underline{\lambda}(\ )$' over the list*. I call the sentence S' that results from the distribution of its context over the list as the *distribution of* S, and, if S is truth-conditionally equivalent to S', I say that the list of S is conjunctively or disjunctively distributive accordingly as S' is a conjunction or a disjunction.

We must further distinguish between those cases in which a list-embedding sentence is *equivalent* to its distribution and those cases in which the list-containing sentence merely *entails* its distribution, and distinguish both of these from cases in which the original list-containing sentence does not entail its distribution. Consider the sentence

(1)   Jennifer is heavier than Sally and Peter.

It may be given either of two readings: one (which we could call its agglomerative or combinative reading) according to which Jennifer's weight exceeds the combined weight of Sally and Peter, and another (which we might call its dispersive or severantive reading) that claims only that Jennifer is heavier than the other two severally. But on either reading, it entails the sentence

(2)   Jennifer is heavier than Sally and Jennifer is heavier than Peter.

On the second reading, (1) (roughly speaking) just means the same as (2). But even interpreted as meaning that Jennifer is heavier than *the other two put together*, (1) entails (2). For either (a) Sally or Peter has zero weight (in which case their combined weight is the same as the weight of one of them), or (b) their combined weight is greater than the individual weight of either of them and *is heavier than* is a transitive relation. Nevertheless, under this interpretation, although (1) entails (2), (2) does not entail (1). Here and in such cases we may say that in the context 'Jennifer is heavier than ( )' the list 'Sally and Peter' has undistributed sense on this reading. That is to say that the undistributed form conveys something that the distributed form does not. But it could be said to be weakly (conjunctively) distributive. There are no doubt a range of such cases. Some *and*-lists, in some environments will be not merely collective, as, 'Laurie and Richard' might be in 'Sally is no intellectual match for Laurie and Richard' but combinative as well. Thus 'bread and butter' in 'Sally was eating bread and butter'; if that is what Sally was up to, then she was eating bread and she was eating butter, but the inference of opposite sense would be unwarranted. Likewise, a weakly (disjunctively) distributive *and*-list would have undistributive (perhaps combinative) sense in a sentence that entails its disjunctive distribution. Consider

(3)   Jennifer is at least as light as Jennifer and Peter

which, assuming co-referential occurrences of 'Jennifer', entails the disjunction

(4)   Jennifer is at least as light as Jennifer or Jennifer is at least as light as Peter.

Finally, when a list is neither distributive nor weakly distributive, I say that it is *undistributive* with respect to its environment. For example, on the reading of the sentence

(5)   Jennifer is lighter than Sally and Peter,

that means roughly 'Jennifer's weight is less than the sum of the weights of Sally and Peter', the list 'Sally and Peter' is undistributive in respect of 'Jennifer is lighter than ( )'.

This classificatory scheme embraces phenomena of distribution of which we shall take no account. In particular, we are not interested in cases where undistributiveness is syntactically rather than or as well as semantically dictated. Thus, for example, lists can be undistributive but not combinative, as in

(6)   Jennifer is the lighter of Jennifer and Peter.

The list in (6) is undistributive because no acceptable sentence results from placing 'Jennifer' or 'Peter' in the environment 'Jennifer is the lighter of ( )'. The same applies to such an environment as 'Jennifer is between ( )'.

A word about weak distribution: in formal propositional settings, distributional *transformations* are substitutions between equivalent sentences. Accordingly, distribution can take place even in sentences embedded in other sentences. But no single operation corresponds to weak distribution. Sometimes the move from a sentence containing a list to a conjunction or disjunction that it merely entails is licensed by rules such as *Modus Ponendo Ponens* or Hypothetical Syllogism or Monotonicity. But clearly moves licensed by such rules as these can take place in embedded sentences only in special circumstances. Our interest in weakly distributive lists lies, not in their entailment of conjunction or disjunction, but in their *non-equivalence* with conjunction or disjunction, that is, in their having undistributed sense. Their significance is that they provide evidence for a claim that at present I state but do not defend:

> Environments in which *and*-lists are undistributive or have undistributive
> sense, are environments for which is needed alternative list-forming
> vocabulary which will cue a distributive reading.

We have already given examples of sentences embedding undistributive lists
that cannot be considered to contribute to the need for a distribution-cueing item.
But because some such sentences raise questions which we nevertheless must
answer, it will be as well to let a little discussion attend their exclusion from
consideration. P. F. Strawson, writing in the idiom of predications rather than of
lists in environments, has remarked that for some interpretations of '*f*', the
equivalence between a statement of the form '*x* and *y* are *f*' and a statement of
the form '*x* is *f* and *y* is *f*' does not hold.

> . . .'Tom and Mary made friends' is not equivalent to 'Tom made friends
> and Mary made friends'. They mean, usually, quite different things. Nor
> does such an equivalence hold if we replace 'made friends' by 'met
> yesterday', 'were conversing', 'got married' or 'were playing chess'. Even
> 'Tom and William arrived' does not mean the same as 'Tom arrived and
> William arrived'; for the first suggests 'together' and the second an order
> of arrival. (Strawson 1952, 80)

Strawson has included two sorts of sentences in which *and*-lists are undistributive: those that carry a suggestion of togetherness, and those that imply
mutuality. The sentence 'Tom and Mary met' is not equivalent to 'Tom met and
Mary met' because the former sentence carries a suggestion of mutuality and the
latter sentence does not. But the second sentence fails to make sense because the
verb 'met', as a grammatically transitive verb, requires a direct object. The
reason why the former sentence makes sense is that the compound subject
suggests that a direct object is understood, namely, 'one another'. Moreover, it is
unnecessary to include the words 'one another' precisely because the sentence
does not make sense unless what would be conveyed by these words is
understood. With other sentences such as 'Tom and Mary got married', in
contexts where they carry a suggestion of mutuality, the implicit modification
'to one another' is also understood, but neither the suggestion of mutuality nor
the understanding of the 'to one another' expansion is necessary in order for the
sentence to be understood as an English sentence. There are readings of the
sentence for which both suggestions are absent.

This raises the question whether distributive properties should be syntactically, semantically, or pragmatically understood: what is distributed, —
words, properties, or attributions? The sentence

Tom and Mary got married

implies the sentence

Tom got married and Mary got married,

but the former sentence, on the mutuality reading, attributes something that the
second sentence does not, and the totality of what is attributed to Tom (that he

got married to Mary) is not the totality of what is attributed to Mary (that she got married to Tom). What is attributed to each of them in the second sentence is the weaker property of having got married to someone. So although the words 'got married' are the same, what is attributed of them collectively is not what is attributed to them severally. The case may seem to be distinguished on that score from the combinative reading of the earlier example:

(1)   Jennifer is heavier than Sally and Peter

which implies the sentence

Jennifer is heavier than Sally and Jennifer is heavier than Peter,

in which what is attributed to Sally and Peter severally is what had been attributed to them collectively in (1). There might seem to be justification therefore for regarding the list 'Sally and Peter' as weakly distributive in (1), but 'Tom and Mary' as undistributive on the mutuality reading of Strawson's example. But consider that in some occurrences of (1) in which the referents of 'Sally' and 'Peter' are people whose approximate weights are known, (1) may well attribute to Jennifer a prodigious weight, while the distribution of (1) merely attributes an impressive one. So (1) attributes to Sally a weight less by the weight of Peter than Jennifer, and to Peter a weight less by the weight of Sally than that of Jennifer, while the distribution of (1) attributes to each of them only a weight perhaps slightly less than Jennifer's. Thus, if we consider attributive content, (1) is undistributive; if we consider its verbal form, it is weakly distributive. Much the same applies to Strawson's example on the mutuality reading. Nevertheless, whatever we say about the examples given, the same verbal forms, 'Jennifer is heavier than ( )' and '( ) got married' are to be distinguished in the manner in which they will naturally be taken to distribute over lists formed with 'or'. For 'Jennifer is heavier than Peter or Sally' will be taken to attribute severally to Peter and Sally a weight less than that of Jennifer. But 'Tom or Mary got married' will be taken, not as an attribution to either of them, but only as the claim that at least one of them got married.

The language of distribution, with the attendant notions of entailment and equivalence confidently introduced as though requiring no explanation, will seem to hearken nostalgically to an earlier philosophical era. But although we have adopted what is called 'the formal mode' in introducing distinctions among kinds of distribution over lists, ultimately the discussion must come around to phenomena of discourse. The language of distribution is intended only to enable us to consider how items of discourse will be understood on particular occasions or kinds of occasions of use. Again, the distributive properties of lists in environments are their distributive properties on particular readings, which are the appropriate or intended readings for particular occasions. On this account alone, it should not be anticipated that any of the examples so far given are intended to illustrate anything that we will eventually understand as the *formal* properties of lists. A context, even when there are no problems about fixing its meaning, may distribute naturally in one way over one list but in another over another. Thus

Jennifer is lighter than Sally or Peter

is naturally taken to mean

Jennifer is lighter than Sally and Jennifer is lighter than Peter,

but, assuming one Jennifer, replace the occurrence of 'Sally' by an occurrence of 'Jennifer', and the result, when the cloud of puzzlement has passed, must be given a disjunctive reading or be accounted false. There seems no very satisfactory grounds for insisting a priori that a particular distributive transformation will represent the correct reading of every occurrence of that sentence.

1.1.5 About implicatures

The question of what distributive properties a list has in a certain context is: 'What combination of "$\lambda(a_1)$", "$\lambda(a_2)$", "$\lambda(a_3)$", and so on, if any, would the sentence "$\lambda(a_1$ and (or) a_2 and (or) a_2 and (or) a_3 and (or) . . .)" be taken to be equivalent to if it occurred *on a given occasion of use?*' The problem is that within certain limits, we can influence the interpretation that list-containing sentences are likely to receive, regardless of the nature of λ. To give an obvious example, if we say '$\lambda(a_1$ and a_2) so $\lambda(a_1)$', we preclude an undistributive interpretation by implicitly claiming that 'a_1 and a_2' is at least weakly distributive. Alternatively, we can incorporate such information into the members of the list that the range of possible interpretations is limited. The sentence 'Tom and Mary got married' may normally carry a suggestion of mutuality, but the result of substituting 'Jim and Fred', 'Susan and Alice', or any list having more than two members, or a list of pairs of people who in fact did marry one another would not normally carry such a suggestion. Similarly, we preclude an undistributive interpretation of 'a_2 and a_3' in 'a_1 is heavier than a_2 and a_3', by replacing 'a_1', 'a_2', and 'a_3' with 'a_1 who weighs ten stone', 'a_2 who weighs nine stone', and 'a_3 who weighs eight stone', respectively. In much of this, a principle of conversational charity is at work which assumes an interpretation which seems to make claims non-contradictory or true, remarks relevant, utterances meaningful, arguments plausible, and so on, or not, depending upon knowledge of or prejudice about the speaker. There is, in short, an assumption that something like Grice's Cooperative Principle is honoured or at least exploited by the conversational contribution, along the lines that Grice's maxims of quantity, quality, relation, and manner prescribe (1989, 26ff.).

Now the admission that a reading is subject to cancellation (or preclusion) by additional conversational matter will seem to bring the reading under the heading of implicatures rather than meanings. So some explanation must be given for the near total absence of the language of implicature here, especially as 'or' provides one of Grice's central illustrative examples. Grice's introduction of implicatures was intended to obviate as far as possible the need for distinguishing different senses. In the case of 'or' in particular, he was able by this means to avoid postulating a strong sense of 'or' in which its use implied ignorance as to which of the sentences it joins is true. The idea is that the *meaning* of 'or' is given by the truth conditions of disjunction, and anything additionally suggested by its use is an implicature of a particular occasion of use—clearly not an entailment since capable of explicit cancellation by denial without contradiction. The device seems to provide adequate means for dismissing the claim that 'or' sometimes has an exclusive meaning as well as the claim that it sometimes implies ignorance as to solution. Any contrivance making for tidy austerity is not to be despised, and in both of the cited applications it is very welcome. However, its usefulness is less clear where the existence of a fundamental truth-conditionally specifiable meaning is precisely what is in doubt. Consider the example previously given:

Jennifer is lighter than Sally or Peter.

I have claimed that it is naturally taken to mean

Jennifer is lighter than Sally and Jennifer is lighter than Peter.

One might feel tempted to say that it really means

Jennifer is lighter than Sally or Jennifer is lighter than Peter,

and that the conjunction is an implicature that can be cancelled or forestalled by the addition of 'but I don't know which'. But if this is an implicature, it is different from the implicature of ignorance or of exclusivity of other examples in that this one can be fixed, that is, rendered uncancellable by the addition of some such as 'so it doesn't matter which one you choose for counterweight'. Of course, since cancellability is a defining characteristic of implicature, we take liberties in speaking of fixable implicatures. At the same time it is not a matter of what is *entailed* by the first clause of

Jennifer is lighter than Sally or Peter; so it doesn't matter which lets go.

It is rather a matter of what, in that setting, it is plausibly taken to say. To be sure, even on the conjunctive reading it implies a disjunction, but so does every conjunction, yet we do not say that disjunction is part of the meaning of 'and'. To insist that this case is different, since the operative word is 'or' is to beg the question.

Contrast with this an implicature of ignorance or of exclusiveness attendant upon some particular disjunctive assertion. These represent inferences drawn by the hearer on the basis of what seems pointedly not to have been said, and perhaps in tacit recognition of a Gricean maxim; they do not represent the extraction of information available in what has been said. So an implicature of ignorance could not be rendered ineffaceable by the addition of 'so don't ask me which'. Neither could an implicature of exclusiveness be fixed by the addition of 'so one is false'. If the preceding *or*-construction has a disjunctive reading, these are, for the speaker, simply unwarranted inferences. But when the choice lies between a disjunctive and a conjunctive reading, either can be fixed while the other is precluded by the choice of suitable cues. We may argue as follows: the disjunctive meaning of the sentence

Jennifer is the sister of Sally or Peter,

which is naturally taken to mean

Jennifer is the sister of Sally or Jennifer is the sister of Peter,

is mere implicature, since it is forestallable by stressing the 'or' and adding 'so either of them should know her birthday'. Notice that it is not the implication of the disjunction that is cancelled; it is entailed by the conjunction. What is forestalled is one's understanding the claim as disjunctive. That on a conjunctive reading the claim entails the corresponding disjunction is insufficient to secure the position that 'or' here has disjunctive meaning, just as it is insufficient to warrant that the meaning of 'and' is ever (even in part) disjunctive.

What we have said so far is sufficient to show that the conjunctive readings of *or*-lists, though subject to cancellation, are not mere implicatures in Grice's sense, and this is sufficient to excuse the absence of that terminology from this essay. We could, of course, adapt Grice's notion to define a notion of fixable implicatures; but that would take us so close to the idea of fixable senses as to vitiate Grice's innovation.

There are deeper reasons as well for avoiding the language of implicature. One is the very appositeness of that language for expressing any of an indefinitely large class of theses distinct from the ones I want to establish. For example, whereas Grice accepts 1110 disjunction as giving the fundamental or standard meaning of 'or', I shall want to claim that the core meaning of 'or' cannot be given truth-conditionally. So if, as Grice insists, implicatures are of instances of use rather than of propositions, it seems best not to invite misunderstanding by using the term.

1.1.6 Environments and predication

My aim is to try to provide, as nearly as possible, a pre-theoretical account of the origins of disjunction. So it is well to disown at the start an idea that my notation may suggest. The expressions '$\underline{\lambda}(a_1$ and a_2 and a_3 and $\ldots$)' and '$\underline{\lambda}(a_1$ or a_2 or a_3 or $\ldots$)' have the appearance of expressions representing predications. The adoption of the notation should not be taken for the adoption of a kind of analysis. Likewise '$\underline{\lambda}(a_1)$' represents no more than a sentence containing a proper name or description or other nominal expression. Here '$\underline{\lambda}(\ )$' is meant to represent a natural environment in which a list might occur in ordinary speech. I propose to ask whether the distributive properties of a list occurring in the environment '$\underline{\lambda}(\ )$' depend in part upon the nature of $\underline{\lambda}$. The predication reading prejudices the question. If every list-bearing sentence is uniformly describable as 'the predication of $\ldots$ (the content of $\underline{\lambda}$) of a_1 and a_2 and a_3 and $\ldots$', then we are licensed to regard the distributive properties of a list in a environment '$\underline{\lambda}(\ )$' as those of the same list in the context 'It is true as regards ( ) that $\ldots$'. But we can have no reason based upon practice to regard the distributive properties of lists occurring in such an artificial environment as 'It is true as regards ( ) that $\ldots$' as anything but constant. At one extreme, it is doubtful, for example, whether we would preserve the sense of

Mary would like Worth or Joy

into a representation of it as

It is true as regards Worth or Joy that Mary would like it.

The doubt, moreover, is not just the doubt that the sense of the original does not survive the translation. The reason why it does not is that the second seems to insist upon being taken as a predication, which the first seems not to be. But much the same seems to be true in cases where the predication reading in itself is not the source of the difficulty. Consider

It is true as regards Sally or Jennifer that Peter is shorter than she is

as an attempted representation of

Peter is shorter than Sally or Jennifer.

The former, already pedantic as a spoken form, also requires a prophylactic thump on the 'or' to prevent a disjunctive reading, a thump that might be administered to the same effect italically in the stilted philosophese that is its natural home. But then we would have introduced new technical vocabulary, namely the thumped '*or*' for use where the familiar unthumped 'or' would have the same effect in the more natural form. Since much of the argument depends for its force on claims about what might be the natural understanding or reading of certain sentences, it is as well not to suggest the possibility of a standard translation. Such standard translations are seldom natural, and, while they may be useful for the creation or motivation of formalism, they may also numb intuitions about what they represent. In this respect, we take the linguists as our model, and not those philosophers.

1.1.7 Distribution of sentence-forming operations

After such a protracted introduction of the vocabulary, it is time to confess that eventually we must dispense with the language of distribution as too clumsy an instrument to let us say what we want to say, even about the restricted domain of whole sentences from which it has been borrowed. In the meantime, we will rub along as best we can, using the language of distribution indifferently for the communication of contexts to terms of lists, and for the more familiar transformations of prefixings of conjunctions and disjunctions to conjunctions or disjunctions of prefixings.

As well as conjunctions and disjunctions of sentences, we can form lists of clauses. Thus, just as we can join some pair of sentences α and β with 'or' and prefix 'It is not the case that' to the result, producing

It is not the case that α or β,

we can also form the list of *that*-clauses 'that α or that β' and place the whole within the context 'It is not the case that ( )' to produce the equally acceptable sentence

It is not the case that α or that β.

We must then ask: Given a context and particular sentences α and a, how should the quoted sentence be understood? In particular, how is its meaning to be distinguished from that of the sentence

It is not the case that α and that β?

Again, as we can construct a conditional sentence having as its antecedent two sentences α and β joined by 'or' as

If α or β, then γ,

so we can also form a list of *if*-clauses and place that list within the context '( ) then γ' to obtain

If α or if β, then γ.

As before, it is proper to ask, for a particular α, β, and γ, how that sentence is to be understood and how its meaning is to be distinguished from that of

If α and if β, then γ.

In each case in which we have formed a list of clauses, the question about how the sentence is to be understood is in part the question about the distributive properties of a list with respect to its environment. In none of them is the answer automatically discovered by consideration of the corresponding truth-functional case.

I have one final misgiving about the vocabulary of distribution. I have proposed it for two applications: first for transformations of list-embedding sentences to equivalent whole compound sentences, and second for transformations of sentence-embedding sentences to equivalent compound sentences. In doing so, we have taken over the language of propositional logic, including the terms 'disjunction' and 'conjunction' and their cognate forms, as well as the notion of equivalence. But we must not acquire the impression that the behavior of 'or' in lists is to be explained in terms of the truth-functional equivalence of the parent sentence to one or the other of propositional disjunction or propositional conjunction. The truth-functional equivalence of list-embedding sentences to disjunctions and conjunctions of sentences embedding items of lists can be an explanation of the equivalences of English only if the logical notion of disjunction provides a satisfactory final explanation of the sentence-connecting use of 'or'. In particular, this would be to assume that every *or*-compound of indicative sentences is a propositional disjunction. Since part of what we want to understand is the behavior of 'or' as it joins whole sentences, we must not complacently assume that we already do. Nevertheless, we will persevere a little while with the language we have set out. We will soon enough find that in many cases the transformation of a sentence embedding an *or*-list to an equivalent *or*-joined pair of sentences cannot plausibly be called 'disjunctive distribution'.

1.2 Introduction to 'Or'

1.2.1 The relevance of history

The study of the logic of lists has a long history. It was an important part of the medieval theory of reference, and most of the technical terms of distribution introduced thus far have their counterparts in the terminology of the Schoolmen and their descendents into the modern era. For example, we find *enumeratio pressa* and *enumeratio laxa* meaning, though via different metaphors, essentially what we mean by undistributive *or*-lists and distributive *or*-lists respectively, in the logical writings of Arnold Geulincx (1624–69), as a part of his explanation of *acceptio particularis* and *acceptio confusa*. His examples, though in Latin, would not be out of place in this essay.

> Acceptio Particularis est Acceptio Disjunctiva cum Enumeratione Laxa. Sic accipitur *Homo*, cum dico: *Aliquis homo est doctus*; sensus enim est: *Vel Petrus est doctus vel Paulus est doctus etc...* Acceptio Confusa est Acceptio Disjunctiva cum enumeratione Pressa; sic accipitur *Navis*, quando dico: *Aliqua Navis est necessaria ad navigandum*, sensus enim est: *Vel haec navis, vel illa navis, vel ista, etc. est necessaria ad navigandum;* non autem sensus est, quem faceret Enumeratio Laxa: *Vel haec navis est necessaria ad navigandum, vel illa navis est necessaria ad navigandum, vel ista navis est necessaria ad navigandum, etc.*, quia falsum est (Land 1891, 216–217)

But no detailed historical account is to be offered here. The authors in the scholastic tradition wrote expositions of philosophical doctrines, and explications of technical concepts. Their interests were not, as ours are, essentially linguistic. So we shall from time to time refer to them to illustrate a historical claim, but not to describe or criticize their writings on subject matter that, though related, is not germane to our own project.

1.2.2 How much unity can we expect?

Our aims in this essay are to provide a unified account of the role of 'or' in discourse and to explain the relationship of its place in natural language to the nature of the propositional disjunction of logic. On the face of it, the proposal is, if at least prudently vague in its second agendum, noticeably ambitious in its first, considering only the apparent diversity of uses that we have seen so far. But there is time enough to assess how unified an account has been given when it *has* been given, and such vagueness as is going to dissipate will have drifted away. Nevertheless, we can at least indicate at the outset some of what our ambition does not encompass, before setting out to fulfill it howsoever inadequately.

It ought first to be considered that in English the sound 'or' has had historically—and even retains in local dialect—a diversity well beyond the range of uses already alluded to. Some of the diversity derives from the fact that etymologically there are several different words sharing that spelling, even setting aside the heraldic use of 'or' (from Latin *aurum* meaning 'gold'). The familiar conjunctive 'or' has a common ancestor with the German *oder* and the English 'other' and is derived from the Anglo-Saxon *oþer*. But it shares or has shared its spelling with two other English words. Now this essay is not about etymologies. Nevertheless, etymologies are data, and as for any data their relevance is a matter for assessment and judgment. So without prejudging their significance, let us have them before us in the form of more or less unprocessed dictionary extracts. The first set are from the *OED*.

1.2.3 'Or' meaning 'early'

The *OED* reports a homophonous 'or' that, in its adverbial use meant *early, at an early hour* and sometimes had the comparative sense *at an earlier time*:

> *c* **1330** R. BRUNNE *Chron.* (1810) 8 He sette þe Inglis to be þralle þat or was so fre.
>
> *c* **1300** *Havelok* 728 But or he hauede michel shame . . .
>
> **b.** In the following there appears to be confusion with the conjunctive *or ere* . . . for *or e'er or ever* but used simply as = ere, before.
>
> **1629** MILTON *Ode Christ's Nativity* 86 The shepherds on the lawn, Or ere the point of dawn, Sate chatting in a rustick row.
>
> **1811** WORDSW. *Ep. to Sir G.H. Beaumont* 95 And long or ere the uprising of the Sun O'er dew-damped dust our journey was begun. . . .
>
> **d.** with the addition of *ever*, e'er:
>
> *Ever* adds emphasis: *or ever* = before ever, before even, before .. at all, or in any way. . . . But, in many early instances, *or ever* does not perceptibly differ from the simple *or, ere* or *before* whence perh. the later spelling *or ere* . . . .
>
> **e.** *or ere*, for *or e'er*, or ever . . .
>
> **1605** SHAKS. *Lear* II. iv. But this heart shal break into a hundred thousand flawes Or ere Ile weep . . .
>
> **2.** Of preference: Sooner than, rather than . . .
>
> **1514** EARL WORCESTER in Ellis *Orig. Lett.* Ser. II. I. 244 Never man . . . better loved his wife than he did, but or he wold have suche a woman abought hur, he hadde lever be without hur . . .
>
> **3.** After a comparative or *other*: = Than. . .
>
> **1567** *Gude & Godlie B.* (S.T.S) 135 Rather or thow suld ly in paine.
>
> **1637-50** ROW *Hist. Kirk* (Wodrow Soc.) 500 The Marques of Hunteley obtained more subscriptions .. in the toune and shyre of Aberdeen and Bamff or any other.
>
> **4.** = Lest . . .
>
> *c* **1470** HENRY *Wallace* I. 272 That gud man dred or Wallace should be tane

Notice that the homonymous 'or', which in the positive is related etymologically to *ere*, meaning *early, at an early hour*, and which in its comparative use means *earlier, at an earlier time, sooner*, is synonymous in the latter sense with *rather*, which only later lost its meaning as the comparative of *rape*, meaning *early*, and came to be used to introduce a preferred *alternative* (*sooner* has retained both of these uses). One might well wonder what influence the presence of this homonymous 'or' may have had in the use of the conjunctive 'or' (or, come to that, the use of *rather*) for introducing an alternative, and compare the earlier redundant construction *or ere* (which could have had the emphatic sense *before ever*) with the modern construction *or rather*. Again, one might wonder whether the presence of the *ere*-related 'or', perhaps by having created a predisposition, accounts in any measure for the analogy in usage between *ever* and *or*-lists of occasions, or for the near related uses of 'or' and 'before' in

> Go before I lose my temper

and

> Go or I'll lose my temper.

It is unlikely that any evidence now available could persuasively show what influence the presence of adjacent homonyms might have played in the accumulation to 'or' of its diversity of uses at any given stage. Unfortunately, transitional spelling practices are of little use as such indicators, since they may well reflect only mistaken initial etymological assumptions about a practice already well established in spoken discourse.

1.2.4 'Or' meaning 'but'

According to the *OED*, a third etymologically distinct 'or' having the sense of 'but' (or 'now' as in 'Now children never are allowed to leave their nurses in a crowd') occurs occasionally in Middle English. The same word, though uncommon, is retained in modern French with this meaning. The following is extracted from *Le Petit Robert*:

> **OR** *adv.* et *conj.* (X[e]; lat. pop. *hora* pour *hac hora* « à cette heure »; Cf. Désormais, dorénavant, encore, lors).
> **I.** Adv. *Vx.* Maintenant, présentement.
> **II.** Mod. *Conj.* Marquant un moment particulier d'une durée ou d'une raisonnement. « *Or, un dimanche elle aperçut tout à coup une femme qui promenait son enfant* » (MAUPASS.).
> —— 'or' sert à introduire la mineur d'un syllogisme, un argument ou une objection à une thèse.

Again, we cannot now say how, if at all, that 'or' influenced the use of 'but' in

> I have no money but I spend it

in the reading on which it is replaceable by 'or'.

1.2.5 'Or' the conjunction

The conjunction 'or' derives from the Anglo-Saxon 'other' (compare German *oder*), whose homonymic descendent retains a sense closer to the common ancestor, although since the association with the absolute form is long since lost, it lacks any comparative kinship with the notion of unity such as its other German cousin *ander* bears to *ein*. The following extracts are from Skeat (1911):

Or (1) conj., offering an alternative. (E.) Short for *other, outher, auther,* the M.E. forms, which answer to A.S. *āhwæþer.* But this M.E. other took the place of A.S. *oþþe,* or.

Other, second, different. (E.) M.E. *oter,* A.S. ōþer, other, second. + Du. *ander,* Icel. annarr (for **anthar-*), Dan. *anden,* Swed. *annan,* G. *ander,* Goth. *anthar*; Lithuan. *antras,* Skt. *antara-* other. In Skt. *an-tara-,* the suffix is the same as the usual comparative suffix (as in Gk. σοφώ – τερον, wiser). Cf. Skt. *an-ya,* other, different.

The remaining extracts are from the *OED* article, including one that illustrates transitional spellings:

[A phonetically reduced form of the obs. OTHER *conj.,* which, when disyllabic, Ormin wrote *oþerr,* when monosyllabic and unstressed, *oþþr* before a vowel, *orr* before a cons. The e. midl. dial. had *or c* 1250; and *c.* 1300 'or' was in common use in north midl. and northern writers; though the fuller *oþer,* other, continued in use, esp. in the south, till late in the 16th c. 'or' is properly the conjunction, not the associated adv. . . . which continued to be *other,* or *outher* in modern standard Eng. *either* (i.e. *either . . . or*); though *or . . . or* also occurs . . . .

B. Signification.
 1 *generally.* A particle co-ordinating two (or more) words, phrases, or clauses, between which there is an alternative.
  Things co-ordinated may differ in nature, or quality, or merely in quantity, in which case the one may include the other, as in 'it will cost you a pound or thirty shillings', 'two or three minutes', 'a word or two'. The second member may also express a correction or modification of the first, which may be strengthened by expanding 'or' to *or even, or rather, or at least.* . . .

  b. When singular subjects (sb. or pron.) are co-ordinated by 'or', strict logic and the rules of modern grammarians require the vb. to be singular; but at all times there has been a tendency to use the plural with two or more singular subjects when their mutual exclusion is not emphasized.

   When the subjects differ in number or person, the rule is that the vb. should agree with the last or nearest, e.g. 'I or thou art to blame', 'I, or thou, or he is the author of it' (Lindley Murray); but such constructions are apt to seem stiff and pedantic, and are consequently avoided. The question of gender causes further complications—esp. the want of a 3rd pers. pron. of common gender. To say either 'if he or she has his friends with him' or 'if she or he has her friends with her' is apt to be misleading, while 'if he or she has her or his friends with him or her' is clumsy and pedantic, which is avoided by saying 'have their friends with them'; so 'your brother or sister will lend their aid'. These difficulties appear to have been felt at all times, and have sometimes been avoided by making the verb immediately precede or follow the first subject, and agree with it.

2 The alternative expressed by 'or' is emphasized by prefixing the first member, or adding after the last, the associated adverb EITHER, formerly OTHER or OUTHER . . .: e. g. 'you may have either an apple or a pear'; 'I could eat an apple or a pear either'.

The primary function of *either*, and so on, is to emphasize the perfect indifference of the two (or more) things or courses; e.g. 'you may take either the medal or its value' = the medal and its value are equally at your option, you may take either; but a secondary function is to emphasize the mutual exclusiveness = either of the two but not both . . . .

3 *Or . . . or* . . . .

4 After a primary statement, 'or' appends a secondary alternative, or consequence of setting aside the primary statement: = otherwise, else; in any other case, if not . . . .

1820 Keats *Eve of St. Agnes* But dares not look behind or all the charm is fled . . . .

5 *Or else* . . . .

6 'or' connects two words denoting the same thing: = otherwise called, that is (= L. *vel, sive*). . . . **1842** . . . right or off wheel; . . . left or near wheel . . . *Mod.* using a common or garden spade.

In the entry for *the* we find:

þe was an A.S. disjunctive used with *whether* later displaced by 'or' in that position.

1.2.6 The etymological puzzle

It is not proposed to conjure an account of 'or' that brings unity to all of the recorded uses of 'or'. Apart from the speculative comments previously offered, this essay has nothing to say specifically about the 'or' that means 'early' or 'earlier' nor anything specific to the use of 'or' for 'now', though the latter use, were it alive in English as it is (barely) in French, would fit our final accounting. Our interest lies in the family of surviving uses of the 'or' descended from the Old English ordinal 'other' meaning 'second', which persists in such modern constructions as 'every other day'. The significance of the descent, and that of 'else' from *alius*, which also meant 'other', must eventually enter our account, but must, while the plot otherwise unfolds, be imagined hanging from its cliff.

Why consider etymologies at all, even as clues? The answer is complex and has to do, in a much more general philosophical theatre of operations, with what belongs to excrescent explicans and what to underlying explicandum. The problem has its counterpart in the philosophy of mind, where such questions arise as whether an adequate theory of mind must explain intentions, or whether the notion of *intention* is rather a construct of the primitive theory that is to be overthrown. It may be that there, as here, the choice is an artificial one, and that the distinction between the language of observation and the language of explanation cannot be maintained. Nevertheless, it can do no irremediable harm if we err on the side of austerity in our conception of what constitutes the observable data. Hence the methodological slogan: 'Mainly we emit sounds'. The point of its adoption does not lie in the expectation that our explanations will be couched in a theoretical language of physics and phonology, but in the need to be reminded that whatever account we give of how some portion of language works, it must be consonant with some basic physico-phonological facts. We make the sounds that we make in the situations in which we make them because others have made the sounds that *they* made in the situations in which *they* made them. And we make the sounds that we make in the situations in which we make them in part so that others will be disposed to make sounds of a certain sort in certain situations, and so on. These are all rather banal pronouncements, but any theory that we give must be not merely compatible but also consonant with these truths. It must be consonant also with another fact: that in the course of the transmission of these skills, and in the changing circumstances of their use, mutations are introduced and preserved. Even if there were non-trivial general truths about what patterns of sounds were reproduced in what circumstances in a given epoch, most users would grasp only restrictions of those general truths. Such mutations as occur would not be conscious reformations of the larger generalizations, but at best conscious alterations of their restrictions. It seems better, therefore, to have an account which is diachronically plausible, than one which is, though synchronically quite general, nevertheless creationist rather than evolutionary in character. This I take to be the relevance of etymology. Its relevance does not depend upon there figuring in our explicit understanding of our vocabulary some knowledge of how it came to be deployed as it is. Nor does it depend upon our intentions being one with those of our distant linguistic forbears.

So the etymological data, though we have had the merest sampling, will nevertheless suitably serve to introduce the very general puzzle about 'or' that eventually our account must try to dispel. As Geulincx observed, disjunctions are not genuinely composite sentences in the sense in which conjunctions are; they do not present their parts as assertions in their own right or with the force that they would have elsewhere on their own.[1] From the point of view of logic, we must regard the sequence of utterances that yields an 'or'-construction as subtractive, as tending, by the addition of its subsequent clauses, to produce a weakening of what would otherwise have been taken for a stronger claim. Yet etymologically the vocabulary would seem to belie this logical tendency, since 'or'-words derive from *additive* rather than from *subtractive* ancestors. Crudely expressed, the question is: how do we come to say less by uttering words whose ancestors suggested more rather than less? More fundamentally, how does such a construct as the disjunctive one gain purchase on our understanding?

---

1. *Disjunctiva non est tam proprie Enunciatio Composita quam Copulativa [conjunctive statement]; quia Disjunctiva non servat partes suas integras et idem in ipsa valentes, quod alibi et seorsim posetae valerent* (Land 1891, 240).

2

What Does Disjunction Do?

> The disjunctive judgment is regarded by modern logicians as expressing the real aim of Thought more fully than the previous forms: for it implies the existence of a systematically connected world.   H.W.B. JOSEPH

2.1 The Puzzle According to Russell

Bertrand Russell, though he confessed no puzzlement in the matter and did not consider the historical question at all, nevertheless put, in his William James lectures, what is in fact the most general puzzle about 'or' in philosophically more familiar terms. The context is a discussion of the transition from the primary, observation language to second-order language:

> We pass from the primary to the secondary language by adding what I call "logical words", such as "or", "not", "some", and "all", together with the words "true" and "false" as applied to sentences of the object-language. (Russell 1940, 20)

It is the absence of the logical words 'without exception' from the object-language that raises our questions.

> But how about "or"? You cannot show a child examples of it in the sensible world. You can say: "Will you have pudding or pie?" but if the child says yes, you cannot find a nutriment which is "pudding-or-pie". And yet "or" has a relation to experience; it is related to the experience of choice. But in choice we have before us two possible courses of action, that is to say, two actual thoughts as to courses of action. These thoughts may not involve explicit sentences, but no change is made in what is essential if we supposed them to be explicit. Thus "or", as an element of experience, presupposes sentences, or something mental related in a similar manner to some other fact. When we say "this or that" we are not saying something directly applicable to an object, but are stating a relation between *saying* "this" and *saying* "that". Our statement is about statements, and only indirectly about objects. (Russell 1940, 73)

In Russell's account, "or" corresponds to a state of hesitation.

A dog will wait at a fork in the road, to see which way you are going. If you put crumbs on the window-sill, you can see birds behaving in a manner which we should express by: "Shall I brave the danger or go hungry?" . . . I think that animals in a state of hesitation, although they do not use words, have something more or less analogous to a "propositional attitude", and I think any valid psychological explanation of the word "or" must be applicable, with suitable adaptations, to any behaviour that shows hesitation. (84)

And again:

Inanimate matter, when subjected to two simultaneous forces, chooses a middle course, according to the parallelogram law; but animals seldom do this. No motorist, at a fork in the road, goes across the fields in the middle . . . either one impulse completely prevails, or there is inaction. But the inaction . . . involves conflict and tension and discomfort . . . .

Thus when someone asserts "p or q", neither p nor q can be taken as saying something about the world, as would be the case if we asserted one of the alternatives; we have to consider the state of the person making the assertion. When we assert p, we are in a certain state; when we assert q, we are in a certain other state; when we assert "p or q" we are in a state which is derivative from these two previous states, and we express this state, not as something about the world. Our state is called "true" if p is true, and also if q is true, but not otherwise . . .

But, it will be objected, if we know "p or q", surely we know something about the world? To this question we may answer *yes* in one sense and *no* in another. To begin with the reasons for answering *no*: when we try to say what we know, we must use the word "or" over again. We can say: in a world in which p is true "p or q" is true; similarly if q is true: in our illustration of the fork in the road, "this road goes to Oxford" may express a geographical fact, and then "this road or that goes to Oxford" is true; similarly if that road goes to Oxford; but there is no state of affairs in the non-linguistic world which is found when, and only when, this road *or* that goes to Oxford. Thus the straightforward correspondence theory of truth, which is valid in the primary language, is no longer available where disjunctions are concerned. (85)

That is Russell's statement of the core of the puzzle about 'or'. His summation in his chapter 'Language as Expression' is:

Hesitation may be observed in animals, but in them, one supposes, it does not find verbal expression. Human beings, seeking to express it, have invented the word "or". (210)

The simple mythic terms of that explanation may not be intended to be taken at face value. His explanation for the presence of 'or' in the language, and presumably, since he does not refer only to English-speaking human beings, for the presence of 'or'-like words in other languages, is the evolutionary one that there are 'occurrences which make the word useful'. But his account of those occurrences is that they are subjective. 'In order to express a hesitation in words, we need "or" or some equivalent word' (210).

Russell is thinking of 'or' exclusively in those uses that, at least in declarative instances, most closely approach the ∨ of propositional logic. It is perhaps not surprising that, restricting attention to that narrow range of uses, he should have settled upon the account that he has given, expressed in the language of suspended motor impulses. He gives an account of negation in similar terms, this time mentioning inhibited motor impulses. Had he raised questions of compositionality, he would have been forced to consider negations of disjunctions, and this would certainly have greatly complicated his account or led to a complete reformulation. As it is, his account of the workings of 'or' does not give an explanation of any of its conjunctively distributive occurrences. The paragraph in which he makes his claim that the only occurrences that demand the word 'or' are hesitations is introduced by the sentence:

> I suggest that there is a difference between the word "or" and such words as "hot" or "cat".

Only two sentences after that paragraph we find the observation:

> It [hesitation] may be observed, for instance, in a bird timidly approaching crumbs on a window-sill, or in a man contemplating a dangerous leap across a chasm in order to escape from a wild animal.

Now it is true that *these* occurrences of 'or' do not *demand* 'or'. He might have used 'and' instead. So on that ground it is unfair to offer them as counterexamples to a claim about why 'or' is needed. But it is a fair presumption that, had he raised questions for himself about compositionality or attended to any conjunctively distributive *or*-constructions, even as he was composing his remarks, he would have been inclined toward a subtler account. As it is, all such occurrences are left unaccounted for by his explanation.

2.2 Grice's Go

More recently, also in the name of William James, Paul Grice has gone over the same ground. Grice's genetic speculations about 'or' are, like Russell's, part of an attempt to say more generally what the logical particles do in language and thus why they came into it. The former is important to the latter, one might suppose, since what the particle does provides the reason for its incorporation. Now, without digressing from the exposition of Grice's account, this is perhaps the moment to sow a plausible doubt about this method. Both Russell and Grice seem prematurely to rule out the possibility that the particle was brought into the language for another purpose now not considered its principal one, and that the serving of that purpose suggested, inspired, or made possible the use that the particle is now correctly or incorrectly supposed mainly to serve. In any case, Grice's mooted genetic account of 'or' is founded upon his account of what he takes to be its main use:

> A standard (if not *the* standard) employment of "or" is in the specification of possibilities (one of which is supposed by the speaker to be realized,

though he does not know which one), each of which is relevant in the same way to a given topic. (Grice 1989, 68)

His proposed model has the particles 'not', 'and', 'or', and 'if' entering the language in that order, which is the approximate order of their primitiveness. The device of negation enables us to deny whatever we are able to assert. The inferentially pallid conjunctive particle makes it possible to deny the totality of a succession of assertions without knowing, or at least committing ourselves to, which elements of the succession defeat the succession as a whole. In the case of a two-element conjunction, its mere denial insists that one of the three possibilities corresponding to the 0 rows of its truth table is realized. This matches the standard use of 'or', which is then introduced as a representation of the cognitive state of the person who knows that a conjunction is false but does not know which of the three possibilities is realized. The same cognitive state can be occasioned independently of negated conjunctions, as when in gradually refining our answer to some 'W'-question, we begin with a long disjunctive answer, inexact in the measure of the number of its disjuncts, and gradually, by *modus tollendo ponens*, achieve a shorter disjunction and more exact answer. This use of 'or' depends upon our having non-truth-functional grounds for asserting the disjunction. A disjunction cannot comfortably be substituted for its truth-functionally equivalent negated conjunction of negations, when that additional cognitive requirement is not met. Grice's example:

> A: "He didn't give notice of leaving and didn't pay his bill."
> B: . . . .
> B: (*after a conversational gap*): "It isn't true that he didn't give notice and didn't pay. He did both" (or did the first though not the second).

But the following would not be comfortable:

> B: "He either did give notice or did pay his bill. Indeed he did both things."

Here the specified conditions (such as addressing a 'W'-question) are lacking, and the use of "or" is unnatural. (69)

The example is not conclusive. On logical grounds the first reply is as odd as the second, since it also consists of a weak assertion rendered otiose by a succeeding stronger one. And the former may owe its greater legitimacy to its being also a metalinguistic denial of A's claim, repudiating that form of words as formulating a true account of the third person's behaviour.

Setting aside the expression of cognitive states, since either a disjunction or a truth-functionally equivalent negated conjunction of negations might be used to represent it, Grice must answer the question why there should be an 'or'. He fields two possible explanations. The first is economy in typography and in the number of concepts explicitly mentioned. The second invokes his operating assumption that the central place of disjunctions lies in the gradual refinement of answers to 'W'-questions. It also invokes what he calls a 'pointering' principle, which hypothesizes in this case a preference at each stage of the refinement for a formulation in unnegated forms if the anticipated ultimate refinement is unnegated, and for a formulation in negated forms if the anticipated ultimate refinement is negated.

Grice takes it as an adequate general characterization of the fundamental function of the disjunctive particle that it is an element in a procedure that:

(i) Seeks total or partial progress in the solution of 'W'-questions.
(ii) Deploys a method which is by its nature eliminative.
(iii) And so involves a pattern of argument in which there are two premises, one essentially disjunctive, the other nondisjunctive (or if disjunctive only accidentally so).
(iv) Requires that the logical quality (affirmative, negative, doubly negative) of the nondisjunctive premise be contradictorily opposed to that of one of the components of the disjunctive premise. (74)

A detailed response to Grice must lie in my own positive account, but I can indicate some of its points of vulnerability as a general account of 'or'. First, it conflates, without argument, the function of sentential *or*-compounds with that of disjunction. Second, it assumes that every instance of sub-sentential coordination with 'or' is adequately represented by some sentential compound. Third, it assumes that all *or*-compounds of non-indicative sentences are in some way derivative from indicative compounds. As in Russell's account, we need only look to the account itself to find instances of 'or' to challenge it. In Grice's case, consider only the following:

. . . they look at it in different lights and say such things as *It is a light green now* or *It has a touch of blue in it in this light.* Strictly (perhaps) it would be correct for them to say *It looks light green now* or *It seems to have a touch of blue in it in this light . . .* (44)

An ulterior conversational purpose may be either to provide a step on the way to an elimination of one disjunct (by modus tollendo ponens), leaving the other assertable (there being no advance idea which is to be eliminated), *or* to have a limited number of alternatives for planning purposes (in which case the elimination of all disjuncts but one by modus tollendo ponens *may* be unnecessary). (68)

But even if we restrict our attention to clearly disjunctive uses of 'or', introducing constructions in which it occurs cannot help but have consequences that truth conditions by themselves cannot explain. The case is sufficiently made if we consider what would be the narratival effect of replacing a non-disjunctive construction with a truth-conditionally equivalent disjunctive one. Consider a real example:

His stetson lay on one of the twin beds, some women's clothes on the other. (MacDonald 1964b, 119)

Evidently, supposing that the context had differentiated the beds by distance, the first portion of the sentence might be truth-conditionally equivalent to:

His stetson lay on the nearer twin bed or on the farther.

But the replacement of that first portion by the truth-conditionally equivalent alternative would produce a profound alteration of the narrative. It would be a puzzling, even narratologically nonsensical amendment of the text. Moreover, the puzzlement does not arise from the fact that in the replacement the narrator would not be telling us which bed had the stetson. He does not tell us in the original either. And if the latter implicates that he does not know or does not remember, why should it do so if the former does not? Grice's maxims do not serve, in that respect, to distinguish the two. The answer may be the simple one that the information as to which bed held the stetson is *conspicuously* absent from the amendment; its absence has become part of the narrative. It may be that, reading the former, one simply places the stetson on one of the beds, some readers on one bed, other readers on the other (the narrative will support either), but that, reading the amendment, one would be conscious of not having been told on which twin bed to locate the stetson and conscious, were one to imagine it on either of them, that one's choice of beds would have been an arbitrary one. Again, it may be that in the amendment, one assumes that the withheld information is significant, since the narrator seems to have been at pains to disclose its non-disclosure. Cueings figure in the selection of text beyond matters of quantity or maxims that regulate by truth-conditional distinctions.

Again, to raise questions about the connection between ignorance or hesitancy and the uses of disjunction is to circumscribe the inquiry artificially by excluding from consideration all the uses of 'or' that are not clearly disjunctive. Or perhaps it is to fail to notice that in literature they are by far the more common. Consider:

> Tom said: "I don't want to hurt anybody. I never did. Or maybe I did, I don't know." (MacDonald 1964b, 201)

or

> He made a noise in his throat which might have been a sob, or a growl of pain. (MacDonald 1958, 4),

which represent two slightly different uses of 'or', the former a tentative retraction of a prior claim, the second the venturing of an alternative construal. But except for those of the component sentences, truth conditions are not central to our understanding of these uses of 'or'. Indeed, if we are to have a truth-conditional account of the second example, we must treat it as a conjunction, not as a disjunction. Not all uses of 'or' are, like the clearly disjunctive uses, anticipated occurrences, and for many of these it is difficult to envisage an adequate account that does not have them somehow registering realizations on the fly.

2.3 Antecedents of Russell's Formulation

The nature of disjunction and its place in human cognition, and accordingly the character of 'or' and its role in inference, was a controversial matter while those philosophers still dominated the teaching of logic who conceived of the subject, after Boole, as an attempt to formulate the laws of human thought. Among these were H.W.B. Joseph[1] and Sydney Herbert Mellone[2], whose *Introductory Text-book of Logic* in its eighteenth edition was still in use in many universities at the time of the Russell's William James lectures. Russell's language of motor impulses is a neurophysiological updating of the earlier language of thought and judgment. His distinction between first-order and second-order language carries still an echo of Boole's distinction between primary and secondary propositions, the former being, in Boole's scheme and those of his successors, the categorical judgments of traditional logic and the latter, the combinations of primary propositions in conjunctions, disjunctions, hypotheticals, negations, and so on. His suggestion that 'or' represents a state of hesitation takes up in altered form a theme of earlier writers having to do with the character of disjunction in *individual* as contrasted with *general* propositions. The puzzlement about the role of disjunction in particular judgment is closely akin to Russell's puzzle about disjunctive desserts:

> The disjunctive judgment also raises a metaphysical problem, when we ask what real fact corresponds to it. 'Plato was born either in 429 or 427 B.C.' cannot state the actual fact about Plato: he was born definitely in one year, not merely in one or other; it is because *we do not know* in which, that we state an alternative, and there was no alternative in the event. Here, therefore, the disjunctive proposition seems rather to express the state of our knowledge than the state of the facts. (Joseph 1916, 188)

The metaphysical puzzle does not, however, arise for general propositions:

> On the other hand 'Number is either odd or even' seems to express a disjunction in the facts; and the species of the same genus are a kind of real disjunction. (188)

> It is a fundamental error to suppose that the disjunctive judgment expresses mere ignorance as to which of two predicates belongs to a given object. (220)

and, in explanation:

> Only on the basis of a knowledge of elementary geometry could we say that any section of a cone by a plane *must* be either a circle, or an ellipse, or a parabola, or a hyperbola, or two intersecting straight lines, or a single straight line . . . although the disjunctive form leaves partly indeterminate the particular reference which is predicated,—so that on this side it may be used to express ignorance,—yet, when it is correctly used, it implicitly refers an individual (A) to a *system*, and implies at the same time knowledge of the general nature of the system and the individual's place in it. If, in ordinary conversation, the disjunctive form is used to express *mere* ignorance and nothing more, it is incorrectly used; for it means, "I do not know whether A is B or C or something quite different."

---

1. 'Logic, then, is the science which studies the general principles in accordance with which we think about things, whatever things they may be' (1916, 3).
2. '. . . To study logic is to think about thought' (1905, 1).

He concludes with a claim on behalf of the community of logicians of his time, a claim that would likely startle and perplex undergraduate logicianers of this generation:

> The disjunctive judgment is regarded by modern logicians as expressing the real aim of Thought more fully than the previous forms: for it implies the existence of a systematically connected world. And in all real thinking we are seeking to connect facts together by means of general principles into a system. To understand this is to grasp the main clue to the solution of some of the most vexed questions of Logic. (381–382)

This exaltation of disjunction, which was characteristic of logic writers to the degree that they were influenced by the Idealist tradition of Hegel and Lotze, may be referred, in the genealogy of English logic texts, to Bernard Bosanquet's *Logic or the Morphology of Knowledge*, published in 1888, the title of which, in light of Mellone's later estimation, may give some clue to the place that it accords disjunction. Bosanquet's account of disjunctive judgment contrasts it with conjunction:

> A conjunctive judgment, or conjunction of judgments with an identical subject, can always be made disjunctive by wilful abstraction. A diamond is carbon, and crystalline, and very hard, and highly refractive. But if we limit the underlying identity, the nature of the stone, by the several conditions under which it exhibits these several predicates, then each of these predicates may be regarded as not conjoined with but exclusive of the other attributes enumerated. A diamond may be considered either merely as an element, or merely as a transparent substance exhibiting crystalline structure, or in its power of scratching other hard substances, or in its effect upon light.[3] This is disjunction—arbitrary and subjective, if we please, but still disjunction. Any distinguishable attributes may be regarded as reciprocally exclusive by our simply refusing to attend to more than one of them at once. (Bosanquet 1911, 322-323)

Alternatively, disjunctive judgment may originate 'with the discovery of an error in a generic judgment':

> '*Cereus* is a night-flowering plant'. 'No: *Cereus grandiflorus* is a night-flowering plant, but there are a hundred species of *Cereus*, and not all are night-flowering'. Such considerations would force upon us the disjunction, '*Cereus* blossoms either at night, or in the early morning, or &c., &c.' (323).

What these and other sources have in common is that they are all 'merely different ways of giving utterance to the interest which attaches to some pervading identity and compels us to pursue it throughout its modifications. Such an interest . . . environs every genuine judgment, and makes it an element in a system' (323). This 'pervading identity' within which the disjuncts represent more specific determinations is characteristic of Bosanquet's idea of genuine disjunction. 'By true disjunction I mean a judgment in which alternatives falling under a single identity are enumerated, and are known in virtue of

3. Notice that the embedded *or*-list is conjunctively distributive with respect to its context.

some pervading principle to be reciprocally exclusive, and to be exhaustive' (323). Disjunctions that fail to meet these requirements were, for Bosanquet, 'nothing but imperfect examples'. Among these was a close kin of the sort of disjunction for the expression of which Russell claims human language gave birth to 'or'. These are

> troublesome cases often taken as the true instances of Disjunction, which may be called 'Disjunctions of ignorance'. The essence of these is that they refer to an individual (actual or supposed) and not to an individuality, and consequently express doubt or indecision rather than knowledge. (324-325)

The operative distinction here seems to lie between mere pointing and defining description. Thus, his first example, 'A triangle is either isosceles, scalene, or equilateral,' which merely picks out a triangle without indication of what triangularity is, he claims to be 'a mere corollary from the true disjunction, which is, "A three-sided plane figure as such must have all of its sides equal, or two only equal, or all unequal"'. Again, the judgment 'Being an Oxford man, he is either a University College man or a Balliol man, or &c.' is a particular inference from the true disjunctive judgment which is generic in character, namely, that *all* Oxford men are members of . . . , where the space is to be filled with an exhaustive *or*-list of Oxford colleges. This genuine disjunctive judgment expresses knowledge of the collegiate character of the university. Disjunctions further still from the ideal are ones from which the original ideal disjunction is even more difficult to reconstruct.

> With disjunctions of this type we must class the commonest of all expressions of doubt or ignorance. 'He is either angry or jealous,' 'He has either measles or scarlet fever'. These, like the above, differ not in principle but only in perfection from the ideal disjunction. What operates is something we know, and know to contain the specified alternatives. We do not however specify our knowledge in detail—it may consist in a content hard to define—and we merely point to the concrete individual, in whom it is embodied and from whom it takes its interest. About this individual, as his complete state goes beyond our knowledge, the judgment takes the shape of doubt . . . (325)

For Bosanquet as for Mellone, but not for Russell or for other later logicians for whom the new language of propositional logic had displaced the idiom of subject and predicate terms, disjunctions were fundamentally about classes of things, not individuals. One other class of degenerate disjunctive judgments takes them to be about individual points of time. Bosanquet introduces it as a basis for the supposed exclusiveness of disjunction, but the example recurs in later discussions under other headings, and his discussion illustrates the primacy of classes in his account:

> The denial of coexistence in time, which appears in some disjunctions to be the principal meaning, is a corollary from the nature of the disjoined contents, not a result of the present tense employed as a vehicle of presentation. 'A railway signal shows to the same side either a red, or a

green, or a white light.' Now of course this judgment informs us that at any given moment of time we shall only see one of the three lights. But to interpret the judgment as if it essentially referred either to the moment at which it is made or to 'any given moment' is a fallacy . . . the judgment means that the nature of a railway signal is to show one light to the exclusion of another and the other to the exclusion of the one. From the nature of the case they exclude one another in time and in spatial direction. But the present of predication is coextensive, in its reference, with the nature of the signal, and does not refer especially or exclusively to the moment at which the judgment happens to be pronounced, nor even hypothetically to 'any given moment'. (326)

Now, as we have remarked, Bosanquet's interest is in the 'morphology of knowledge'. It was an essential feature, therefore, of the *ideal* disjunctive judgment as he understood the notion, that it could not fail to be true. 'We must . . . consider exclusively the perfect disjunction as a form of knowledge' (326-327). This characteristic of the disjunction of Bosanquet's conception accounts in part for Mellone's estimation of the centrality of disjunction in logic as he and his predecessor conceived it. It is evident that that earlier notion of disjunction differed fundamentally from the propositional notion of 1110 disjunction, which, by the time of the William James lectures, had all but superseded it, even from the 0110 truth-function that came to be called exclusive disjunction, and we shall eventually have to ask how they differ in relation to the 'or' of English. But one such difference may be remarked now in passing: that it was an expectation of Bosanquet's use of disjunctive ascriptions to classes that each of the disjuncts of the ascription should be witnessed in the class to which the ascription was made. Thus for example, '*A*'s are either *B* or *C*', if it is a true disjunctive judgment, represents a state of affairs in which some of the *A*'s are *B*'s and some are *C*'s and there are no *A*'s which are neither. It would exclude the case in which all of the *A*'s were *B*'s and none of them *C*'s. The quantificational construal of such a sentence which merely attributes to every individual *A*, in effect, the disjunctive property of being a *B* or a *C*, has no such implication, since every *A* could have that property by being a *B*, and none by being a *C*.

The idealist conception of disjunction resurfaces in a 1929 symposium in which J. D. Mabbott attempted a reassessment and defence of an idealist account of negation according to which it lacks objective reality. In Mabbott's treatment, a distinction is attempted between teleological negation and eliminative negation, the former being the character of judgments that register the failure of an individual to realize one's expectation for it, as in 'Number Three cannot row', and the latter of judgments that eliminate one disjunct of a set of disjuncts which taken together constitute a system or individuality in Bosanquet's sense, as in 'The signal is not red'. On Mabbott's account, 'the whole force of a genuine negation is eliminative and therefore rests upon a true disjunction'(Mabbott et al. 1929, 72). 'The aim of the negative judgment, then, is its own annihilation, and in completed knowledge, no trace of it survives.' (73). In obedience to the idealist notion that genuine disjunction is generic, he must insist:

Negative judgments . . . involve absolute falsehood, because they presuppose the disjunctive judgment in a particular form. "This railway signal (around the next corner) is either red or green." Here we have doubt and indeed error, for a disjunctive character, "either—or," cannot belong to a particular, but only to a universal. . . . Here we have a conflation of two undeniable facts. "This is a railway signal," and "Railway signal as such is either red or green." The step we take in conflating them brings in doubt because it is forced upon us by our own ignorance. It is definitely false, for at this moment the signal round the next corner is not "red or green"; it is green. (73)

In his reply, Ryle swaps Mabbott's (now bivalent) railway signal for Mrs. Smith's (multivalent) hat and restates Mabbott's position in the millineric idiom:

. . . "Mrs. Smith's hat is not green" presupposes, you say, that Mrs. Smith's hat is some-colour-or-other, *i.e.*, "Mrs. Smith's hat is not green" is nonsense unless it is true that the hat is *either* red *or* blue *or* green *or* yellow . . . But that is just the point. It is *not* true. A particular hat can not have a disjunctive colouring or hover between alternatives. If it is *e.g.*, blue, then it isn't any other colour, and so there is no "either-or" about it at all. (90–91)

Ryle's own position is that 'to predicate a determinable of a particular is not to ascribe *indeterminateness* to its character, but to ascribe to it the *sort* of determinateness that it has got . . .' (91)
He goes further:

. . . when I assert "Mrs. Smith's hat is some colour or other," *i.e.*, is either red or blue or green or yellow . . . not only am I not making the false or nonsensical assertion that it has an indeterminate colouring, but I am not even asserting or implying that my state of mind is indeterminate (in the popular sense, of course, of "undecided"). I may know which colour her hat actually is, and still the disjunctive sentence may express something that I know, namely, something rather general *about* the colour of her hat. (91–92)

Ryle then draws a consequence for Mabbott's position that for philosophers outside the idealist tradition, and more accustomed to the language of truth conditions, must seem to clinch the matter against the idealist position:

And I am so convinced that there are genuine disjunctive propositions about particulars, that I accuse Mr. Mabbott's theory, according to which ascription of an "either-or" to a particular is an ascription of indeterminateness to it, of implying that the proposition "Mrs. Smith's hat is either red or blue or green or yellow . . ." is exactly equivalent to its contradictory "Mrs. Smith's hat is *neither* red *nor* blue *nor* green *nor* yellow . . ." (92)

Ryle's positive account is worked out with another example:

I judge at Reading, say, "That train is going either to Swindon or to Oxford"; and I do so without necessarily implying that the engine-driver, the passengers, the signal-man or even I myself are in ignorance or doubt which its route actually is. Ordinarily, of course, I would not bother to *make* the statement if I was not in some doubt, since if I could identify its route it would be superfluous to mention such non-individuating facts about it. But facts do not cease to be facts or cease to be known when it becomes superfluous to mention them. The proposition, "The route of that train is either the Oxford route or the Swindon route," is not, therefore, a proposition about anybody's ignorance or indecision . . . Disjunctive propositions about particulars . . . are in fact descriptions not directly of the particulars but of characters of the particulars. (92) .

Of the contribution of the third of the symposiasts to the discussion of disjunction and negation, I draw only one thread for the eventual fabric of our account of 'or'. This is the observation that far from establishing the priority of disjunction over negation, Mabbott has illustrated, in his exposition, the indispensability of negation for the view of knowledge that the idealists wish to advance. His remarks are directed against the thesis 'that non-teleological negation occurs only as part of a process of elimination, and that it is always preceded by disjunction.'

That this thesis can hardly be right is shown by the very way in which it is expressed. The very use of the word "only" (and how can it be avoided?) is enough to betray it. When I say, "A *only* occurs as part of B," I must mean, "A does *not* occur except as part of B." "Only," in spite of its positive form, is obviously a negative adverb; and we may accordingly suspect that Mr. Mabbott is engaged in the eminently philosophical pastime of sawing off the bough upon which he sits.

A similar doubt besets us when we hear from Mr. Mabbott and others that negation is "subjective." For if we ask for an elucidation of this obscure saying only two answers seem possible, and both have "nots" in them. The first is, "Negative characteristics do *not* really exist though they seem to us to exist." The second is "Negations would *not* exist if minds did *not* exist." (104–105)

From our point of view, the most telling application of this line of criticism lies in noticing the place of negation in the account of disjunction itself:

. . . every disjunction *includes* within itself a number of negative propositions. The proposition "S is either A or B" *includes* within itself the proposition that A is not identical with B. That A is not identical with B is part of what is *meant* by the statement "S is either A or B." That S is not A cannot, I suppose be directly intuited. (If it could, Mr. Mabbott's view would be destroyed in another way.) It must therefore be inferred. But how?

Obviously from some positive characteristic which we find S to possess, *e.g.*, the characteristic E; but equally obviously this is not enough. We must know that E and A are incompatible. But this is simply the knowledge that "No E is A." (106)

An equally telling point against the view that disjunction is conceptually prior to negation would not require the acceptance of the exclusivity of ideal disjunction as the idealists conceive of it. The exhaustiveness of even non-exclusive disjunctions equally requires negation for its explication. For to recognize that a set of alternative predicates exhausts the possibilities for the individuals of a subject class is to say that for such individuals there are *no* additional possibilities. Parallel remarks could be made about the exhaustiveness of propositional disjuncts, but we shall save these for a later discussion.

In 1934 Mellone published a second text, *Elements of Modern Logic*, and it is instructive for gauging the altered positions of competing forces in academic logic at that time to compare it in one or two respects with his earlier work. We might first consider his account of what logic is. In the earlier text, the definition, except for the provisional one already mentioned, is postponed to a point late in the exposition, and when it comes is prolix and obscure, for all the exposition that has intervened:

> We have said that Logic deals with the principles which regulate valid or correct thought, and upon which the validity of the thought depends. We may call them *postulates* of knowledge, because without them not only science but everyday thought cannot even begin to work. If they are untrustworthy, every fabric of knowledge falls to pieces, for they are the general bonds of connection which hold it together, and only through them has our knowledge such coherence as it now possesses . . . The chief object of Modern Logic is to state these principles as completely and systematically as possible, in the light of the idea that the general activity of thought may be compared to the activity of a living organic body. (Mellone 1905, 363–364)

Contrast with that, the definition of *Elements*: Logic is the systematic investigation and study of the principles of valid reasoning; in other words, of the principles on which the validity of reasoning depends (14). Included among the purposes claimed for his first book was

> to show the open door leading from the traditional doctrine into the more modern and more strictly philosophical treatment of the subject. The book is intended to stop short of giving what is supplied in Professor Bosanquet's *Essentials of Logic* (not to mention larger works), but to lead on naturally to that and to a serious study of "Modern Logic". (1905, v)

When the same metaphor recurs in the preface to the second text, the open door leads rather 'to a study of "Modern Logic"—that is, of Logic as the subject stands at the present time' (1934, ii). Bosanquet finds mention in an addendum of the second (1945) edition of the text after the section devoted to a classifica-

tion of propositions that Mellone has based, 'with slight modifications of terminology, on the work of Bertrand Russell and W.E. Johnson.' He adds:

> From the point of view of the philosophical theory of knowledge, an
> elaborate classificatory system of the forms of logical Judgment has been
> worked out by Bosanquet, *Logic*, Vol. 1., Ch. V., VI., VIII. Bosanquet's
> work is historically important, in reference both to its antecedents in
> German thought and its influence on the study of Logic in England and
> America during the last fifty years. (1945, 83)

2.4 Logic, Language and History

Philosophers interest themselves in the study of logic partly out of a desire to
abstract and represent the inferential structure of portions of natural language
within a mathematically well-behaved system. But throughout its history logic
has served a second purpose, which has shaped its development. Its inventors,
whether philosophers or mathematicians, have also wished to conduct some of
their own inferential and analytic transactions in the stable currency that its
language provides. It is therefore fair to assume that the language of logic, at
least insofar as philosophers have mixed their labours with it, has for that reason
never quite achieved independence from philosophical outlook. It is accordingly
a reasonable working principle to avoid the assumption that it has. But it would
also be a mistake to assume too readily that philosophers are perfectly self-
conscious about the relationship between the logical practices of their age and its
broader philosophical outlook. It is true at least that, however much we protest
the contrary thesis, we do not really know what we will become persuaded of
next, let alone what our successors may come to think. It may be true of logical
values, as it seems to be true of ethical ones, that even if they are relative, it is
important that they not be widely thought to be so. As in the case of ethical
outlook, there is plenty of evidence in past changes to ground some such
generalization. But there is a strong disinclination to see the past from the side
rather than from the front. We more happily see our practice as consummation of
earlier than as fodder for later.

Now logical practices of the later twentieth century have got beyond the
fatuities of Hamilton and the metaphysical anxieties of Bradley and Bosanquet
that created about the subject an atmosphere of mystery and secular sanctimony.
But they have done so by embracing an independent formalism that lets the earlier worries be ignored. It has been left to linguistic philosophers and linguists to
diagnose the confusions of earlier writers and to burst the metaphysical *bulles*
that they inspired. In the meantime, the new formalism has created its own
presumptive mythology, particularly about its relationship to natural language,
and made work in its turn for the linguists. Matters are somewhat complicated
by the fact that the language of present-day logic, including the language of
quantifiers and truth-functions, has by now undeniably become an annex of
human language, and has proved itself a remarkably useful annex to boot,
certainly in philosophy and linguistics.

Of course, textbook writers and logic instructors issue plenty of disclaimers as
to what the formalism captures of ordinary language. It is, as we have remarked,

frequently pointed out that the 'and' of English can carry a suggestion of order or of mutuality or of combination absent from the connective ∧, and that the → of the formal system is a merely skeletal notion of a conditional. But they clearly feel that large tracts of natural language are by their nature truth-functional and that those areas are well enough represented by the truth-functional vocabulary of the propositional calculus. De Morgan's equivalences, for example, seem at least to parallel the behaviour of negating particles with 'and' and 'or' in English.

As we have had occasion to notice, the practice of logic has a sociological history. The truth-functional logic that is the foundation of the philosophical hopes of many was not the lucky product of a first attempt. The very notions of what a logic is and what it is for are the product of a long evolution. For this reason, it is not easy for a logician of one generation to assess the efforts of his predecessors. As a historian of logic, Bocheński is well acquainted with the difficulties and the attendant temptations:

> Earlier varieties are not simply predecessors of contemporary logic, but deal in part with the same or similar problems though from a different standpoint and by different methods. Now it is hard for a logician trained in the contemporary variety of logic to think himself into another. In other words, it is hard for him to find a criterion of comparison. He is constantly tempted to consider valuable only what fits into the categories of his own logic. Impressed by our technique, which is not by itself properly logic, having only superficial knowledge of past forms, judging from a particular standpoint, we too often risk misunderstanding and even under-rating other forms. (1970, 17)

The difficulties are the greater and complacency the more attractive when logically trained philosophers try to understand human language. For it is the product of a long and heterogeneous development, and it may occur to us that the confluences of dialect and the linguistic miscegenation lie ripe for the sort of garage sale clean-out and general tidying up that a well-understood calculus of truth-functions makes possible. Even Wittgenstein's conversion between *Tractatus* and *Philosophical Investigations* that so spectacularly reversed his understanding of language in relation to logic, is a testimony to the difficulty of the task. For though logic had now a more constricted role ('to say that a proposition is whatever can be true or false amounts to saying that we call something a proposition when *in our language* we apply the calculus of truth-functions to it' 1953, para. 136), it is really the multiplicity of language games that shrinks logic's place:

> How many kinds of sentences are there? Say assertion, question, and command; there are countless kinds: countless different kinds of use of what we call "symbols", "words", "sentences". And this multiplicity is not something fixed, given once for all, but new types of language . . . come into existence, and others become obsolete and get forgotten. (para. 23)

His avowed aim to turn the whole investigation around never leads him to question logic's credentials within that part of language that he takes to be its proper sphere. Although he has sloughed off his former preoccupation with indicative uses of language, he nowhere attaches any significance to the evident fact that the natural counterparts of logical connectives occur as well in a multiplicity of language games. He nowhere enquires into the connections among the uses of the so-called logical particles 'or', 'and', 'not', and so on in non-indicative language games.

Curiously enough, he seems to recognize the problem: 'The ideal, as we think of it, is unshakable . . . It is like a pair of glasses on our nose through which we see whatever we look at. It never occurs to us to take them off' (para. 103).

He has managed to pry off the spectacles to look at language and has persuaded other philosophers to do likewise (though to be fair, Wittgenstein had himself issued the prescription). But even if we are persuaded to take off our specs from time to time, the glasses themselves seem for him to remain the same; and he seems to have countenanced their resumed use for the study of logic itself and that part of natural language that is logic's province.

Wittgenstein's altered viewpoint ought to have suggested the prediction that disjunction would be found not to have been a primordial feature of language. He might have confirmed its value by tracing its consequences for an evolutionary development of disjunctive uses of 'or' out of uses in other language games. Such a picture could be set in contradistinction to the creationist accounts of Russell and Grice, according to which 'or' was introduced into the language as a disjunctive connective. The evolutionary picture is one according to which the truth-functional disjunctive uses of 'or' (and truth-functional uses more generally) were a kind of contrivance made up of more primitive regularities that persist in language and are not themselves truth-functional or even particularly logical in character. The final account of the origins of disjunction is, at least in its effect, a realization of Wittgenstein's aim, since it will show how the logical uses of 'or' have been sponsored by specific non-logical requirements of linguistic practice. It will, that is, have 'turned things around'.

3

The First Myth of 'Or'

Barmecide asked Shac'abac, a poor starving wretch to dinner, and set before him an empty plate. 'How do you like your soup?' asked the merchant. 'Excellently well,' replied Shac'abac.   ARABIAN NIGHTS

3.1 Modern Sources

"If there is anything as certain as death and taxes, it would appear to be the conviction of English-speaking logicians that purely truth-functional exclusive 'or' exists in English." Thus began a short article in *Mind* in 1971 entitled 'The Myth of the Exclusive "Or"' (Barrett & Stenner 1971, 116), which was to change forever the way logic textbooks are written.

We were the practice of philosophy more like that of, say, molecular biology, I might have begun this chapter in some such fashion. But progress in philosophy is not so easily yielded up by its practitioners. No medal was struck. Solemn mention of the topic of the exclusive 'or', which had become a grand tradition in the previous generation, far from falling decently into disuse, was to become a liturgical office that virtually all authors of *Copi Coporum* logic textbooks of the next generation would take upon themselves to intone over the tiro:

The word "or", in everyday language, possesses at least two different meanings. (Tarski 1941, 21)

Now the English word "or" is ambiguous and has at least two distinct meanings. (Basson & O'Connor 1960, 22)

The connective "or" has in ordinary English two distinct but related senses, which it is important to differentiate. (Ambrose & Lazerowitz 1962, 31)

The English word "or" can be ambiguous. (Rescher 1964, 178)

In everyday language, the word 'or' is used in two distinct senses. (Suppes 1957, 5)

Like 'and', the English disjunctive word 'or' is often used truth function-
ally. But unlike 'and', the connective 'or' has two truth functional uses.
(Massey 1970, 9)

In colloquial discourse, "or" is used in two ways. (Lambert & van
Fraassen 1972, 23)

This connective ['or'] is subject in ordinary discourse to conflicting
usages. (Quine 1972, 10)

However, in ordinary usage, the English word 'or' is ambiguous in that it
is commonly used to express two different meanings. (Baum 1975, 160)

However, the word *or* actually has two common uses in ordinary language
. . . (Georgacarakos 1979, 45)

The problem is that "or" is ambiguous. (Nolt 1984, 325)

The word "or" has two distinct meanings in English. (Salmon 1984, 40)

In English there are two different ways of using the word "or." (Barker
1985, 86)

The word "or" in English has two meanings. (Hurley 1985, 242)

There are two different senses of this connective ["or"] in common use.
(Kahane 1990, 22)

There are, then, two distinct truth-functional interpretations of 'either p or
q'. (Harrison 1992, 40)

It is unclear what significance one ought to attach to the distinction, apparent
among the quoted claims, between 'senses', 'meanings', 'interpretations', 'uses'
and 'ways of using'. Clearly there is room for a separation, but it seems clear
that the mention of *or*'s alleged double life has become little more than a conventional automatism of the genre, and to try to make much of such fine-grained
variations is almost certainly to try to reap a nicety where none was sown. There
are, moreover, sectarian divisions over what the different senses (uses,
meanings) are to be called, and these divisions are not significantly correlated
with the kind of distinction it is claimed to be:

These [senses] are given the special designations "exclusive" and "nonexclusive". (Ambrose & Lazerowitz 1962, 31)

'or' is equivocal in a way that ∨ is not. (Brody 1973, 95)

These senses are the *inclusive* sense of "or" and the *exclusive* sense of
"or." (Manicas 1976, 71)

In contrast to the inclusive sense of *or*, there is also an *exclusive* sense of *or*. (Georgacarakos 1979, 46)

One sense is the *nonexclusive* . . . The other sense in which 'or' is sometimes used [is] called the *exclusive*. (Quine 1972, 11-12)

One, the exclusive sense . . . The other sense of the term "or" is called its inclusive sense, or sometimes its *nonexclusive* sense. (Kahane 1990, 22)

Cutting across the differences of nomenclature, there are apparent divisions over what the distinction between the two senses amounts to, some introducing modal vocabulary into their account of the inclusive sense:

Sometimes when we say "*p* or *q*," what we mean is "*p* or *q* but not both." This is called the *exclusive* sense of "or." More often when we say "*p* or *q*," we mean "*p* or *q* and perhaps both." This is called the *inclusive* sense of "or." (Barker 1985, 86)

The inclusive sense means "either . . . or *and possibly both*." The exclusive sense—the "stronger" of the two—means "either . . . or *but not both*." (Manicas 1976, 71)

The force of "or" in the first case is: "one or the other but not both"; the force of "or" in the second case is "one or the other and perhaps both". The latter case is sometimes expressed as "and/or". The use of "or" in [the first case] is called the *exclusive use* of "or"; that in [the second case] is called the *inclusive use* of "or". (Lambert & van Fraassen 1972, 23)

"Or" is used *inclusively* when it means "one or the other and possibly both." It is is used *exclusively* when it means "one or the other but not both." (Hurley 1985, 242)

The English word *or* can be used both 'inclusively' as in [example], which does not rule out the possibility that . . . both, and 'exclusively' as in [example] . . . (McCawley 1981, 33)

and others not:

On one reading it means "either . . . or . . . *but not both*." On this reading, which is called the exclusive sense of "or," if both disjuncts are true the whole disjunction is false. On the other reading, which is called the inclusive sense, if both disjuncts are true so is the whole disjunction. This reading is sometimes expressed by the hybrid "and/or". (Nolt 1984, 325)

In one sense (known as the *exclusive* sense) it means "one or the other but not both." . . . The other sense (known as the *inclusive* sense) is often rendered by the expression "and/or" . . . (Salmon 1984, 40)

In the so-called *non-exclusive* sense, the disjunction of two sentences is true if at least one of the sentences is true . . . When people use 'or' in the *exclusive* sense to combine two sentences, they are asserting that one of the sentences is true and the other false. (Suppes 1957, 5-6)

. . . it can be used in either an *inclusive* sense, represented by the phraseology "either . . . or——, or both," or an *exclusive* sense, represented by the phraseology "either . . . or——, but not both." (Rescher 1964, 178)

Compound sentences formed by combining sentences by means of 'or' are called *disjunctions* or *alternations* . . . An inclusive disjunction is true if at least one of its two components is true; otherwise it is false . . . An exclusive disjunction is true if exactly one of its two components is true; otherwise it is false. (Massey 1970, 9)

The exclusive use of *or* implies that one and only one of the alternatives will hold. The inclusive *or* implies merely that at least one will hold. (Govier 1988, 198)

with others using modal words in their account of the exclusive sense:

How can we tell whether a disjunction is exclusive or inclusive? The question to ask in each case is this: *"Does the asserter regard the disjuncts as incompatible?* If your answer is yes, then treat the disjunction as exclusive; if your answer is no, then treat the disjunction as inclusive. This is not always an easy question to answer; since the asserter's intention would ultimately settle the issue, it may at times be simply impossible to answer [a *non sequitur*] . . . Sometimes the meanings of the disjuncts are such as to make them obviously incompatible, as in "George is in Chicago or in Houston" and "It's either Tuesday or Wednesday." In such cases, we are safe in regarding the disjunction as exclusive providing we can assume that the speaker or writer *knows* that the disjuncts are incompatible, and not merely that they are in fact incompatible. (Vernon & Nissen 1968, 73)

with yet others giving two accounts of each, one with modal language and one without:

The inclusive 'or' is used to assert that either the first disjunct or the second disjunction *or both* may be true . . . An inclusive disjunction is true if the first, the second, or both disjuncts are true; it is false only if both disjuncts are false . . . The exclusive 'or' is used in sentences where either the first disjunct, or the second disjunct, *but not both*, may be true. An exclusive disjunction is true if and only if the first disjunct is true and the second is false, or the first disjunct is false and the second disjunct is true. . . An exclusive disjunction is stronger than an inclusive disjunction, since for it to be true an extra condition has to hold—namely, that both disjuncts cannot be true. (Baum 1975, 160–161)

The operator 'or' forms compounds called *disjunctions*. A disjunction asserts of the statements it connects, called *disjuncts* that *at least one disjunct is true*. The operator 'or' in truth-functional logic is called the *inclusive* 'or' because it includes the possibility that all disjuncts are true. . . . On the other hand, the word 'or' in our language is sometimes used *exclusively*, that is, such that it excludes the possibility that more than one of the disjuncts may be true at the same time . . . The exclusive sense of 'or' is 'one or the other but not both'. (Johnson 1986, 174)

A sentence composed with two other sentences connected by 'or' is a *disjunction* . . . A sentence such as ['Helen is the winner or Mary is the winner'] is frequently, however, understood in the exclusive sense namely, as asserting that either Mary or Helen is the winner *but not both*. Our discussion of disjunctions in this section has addressed only the *inclusive* sense, because it *includes* the possibility of both disjuncts being TRUE. . . . Often, however, we want to exclude the possibility of both disjuncts being TRUE. Sometimes this possibility is excluded automatically: if you ask someone what today's date is and the reply is "It's either the 21st or the 22nd," you know it can't be both. This is an example of an *exclusive* disjunction. (Schagrin 1985, 52-5, 78)

. . . when two statements are compounded by the statement connective '____or____', the disjunction of the two statements is formed. . . . When a person asserting a disjunction intends to exclude the possibility that both disjuncts are true, then the disjunction is an *exclusive* disjunction. The disjoining word 'or' is used in its exclusive sense here, that is, to mean 'either____or____but not both'. . . . The word 'or' also has a *nonexclusive* sense, the sense of the legal word 'and/or' and of 'either____or____or possibly both' which is used to form *nonexclusive disjunctions*. (Resnick 1970, 28)

A compound proposition composed of two propositions connected by the word 'or' is called a disjunction, and its component propositions are called disjuncts. There are two kinds of disjunctions. Sometimes the word 'or' is used in an exclusive sense to mean 'either . . . or . . . , perhaps both'. Other times it is used in an exclusive sense to mean 'either . . . or . . . , but not both' . . .

> RULE: An inclusive disjunction is true if and only if at least one of its disjuncts is true. (Simco 1982, 6-7)

Apart from the differences in the details of their accounts of the distinction, there are differences in their estimates of the relative frequency with which 'or' occurs in the two senses:

... the English word 'or' nearly always connects sentences the joint truth of which is excluded on the basis of their content or on the basis of certain background assumptions. (Mates 1953, 75)[1]

Inclusive uses of "or" preponderate. (Hacking 1972, 92)

More often when we say "*p* or *q*," we mean "*p* or *q* and perhaps both." This is called the *inclusive* sense of "or." (Barker 1985, 86)

Because of the extreme rarity of the exclusive 'or' in English, logicians habitually translate 'or' as '∨' not ≠. (Richards 1978, 84)

If we want to establish indisputable instances of the exclusive use of 'or', we must imagine circumstances in which the person who uses 'or' has the positive purpose of denying, explicitly within the given statement, the joint truth of the components. Such examples are rare, but they exist. (Quine 1972, 11)

But in what is perhaps the more frequent use of "or", in which alternatives are presented—this or that but not both—the possibility of more than one alternative being true is *in fact* excluded, without its being conceptually impossible that more than one should be true. . . . We now come to a further and less common use of "or", that is sometimes indicated by the expression "and/or" . . . its nonexclusive usage. (Ambrose & Lazerowitz 1962, 31–32)

Cases of the exclusive sense of "or" occur, though less often. (Barker 1985, 87)

Natural language *or* is generally EXCLUSIVE in the sense that at least and at most one disjunct must be true. (van Dijk 1977, 63)

Finally we should notice that there is some disagreement about how the exclusive sense of 'or' is, or should be, reliably cued in English:

Almost any sentence which contains an "or," either alone, paired with an "either," or in the form "or else," can be symbolized as [an inclusive] disjunction. (Klenk 1983, 53)

To make it clear that *p* and *q* are exclusive alternatives, people sometimes say "*p* or *else q*." (Kelly 1988, 222–223)

In order to avoid misunderstandings, it would be expedient, in everyday as well as in scientific language, to use the word "*or*" by itself only in the first [non-exclusive] meaning, and to replace it by the compound expression "*either . . . or . . .*" whenever the second [exclusive] meaning is intended. (Tarski 1941, 22–23)

---

1. Mates takes this as a reason to doubt whether there is an exclusive sense of 'or'.

If an inclusive interpretation is possible but not desired by the speaker, the explicit exclusive disjunction *either . . . or . . .* must be used. (van Dijk 1977, 64)

Two functions (q V r) and (q ⊻ r) in propositional logic are called inclusive and exclusive disjunctions and mean respectively "q or r" and "either q or r" in everyday language. (Chi 1969, 77)

Apart from the tangle of views on the exclusive/inclusive distinction represented in most of the foregoing quotations, we find in some texts outright and in others near rejections of the distinction:

The standard logical definition of "or" (in "*P* or *Q*") is "Either *P* or *Q* or both" . . . But suppose I say, "He's in New York or he's in San Francisco." Surely I can't imply "or both" if I have any idea where New York and San Francisco are. . . . It is sometimes said that the "or" of "He's in New York or he's in San Francisco" is a "strong 'or'" implying "but not both." Are there really two different "or's" in English? Or is the "but not both" just something understood by the hearer?

If we can distinguish between what a statement (in itself) means from what kinds of expectations or beliefs it arouses, we can see that "but not both" is not a part of the meaning of the statement but rather part of the expectations or beliefs surrounding the statement. Since we all know someone can't be in both New York and San Francisco, the temptation is to think that the "or" is different. But this isn't sufficient evidence to think that the "or" is different. "Today he is in Toledo or in Detroit." Since Toledo is a relatively short (about one and a half hour) drive from Detroit, he could be in both today. (Yanal 1988, 109–110)

The sentence "It's raining, or the ground is wet" is true when and only when at least one of its simple clauses is true. Similarly, the symbolic sentence "(R ∨ W)" has the value *t* when and only when at least one of its disjuncts has the value *t*. Hence, "or" corresponds to CL's vel. The correspondence is so complete that, if the principal operator in an English sentence is "or", we call the sentence a *disjunction*.

Some people are reluctant to believe that an English disjunction is true when *both* its disjuncts are true. To see what lies behind this reluctance, suppose that a friend says, "I owe you a dinner; I'll take you out on Tuesday or Thursday." Plainly your friend doesn't plan to take you out to dinner on *both* days, and some people infer from this that—contrary to what we have said—the disjunction "I'll take you out to dinner on Tuesday or Thursday" is *false* when both of its disjuncts are true.
. . . In effect your friend made *two* statements . . . It is the first of these statements together with some obvious assumptions about your friend's generosity, that carries the implication that your friend will take you out to dinner only once. By itself, the disjunction . . . leaves open the possibility that your friend *will* take you out twice . . . Here—as in all other cases—a disjunction is true when one *or both* of its disjuncts are true. (Rubin & Young 1989, 94)

There are two different types of disjunction, the "strong" or "exclusive" disjunction and the "weak" or "nonexclusive" disjunction . . . English contains operators of both sorts. The most obvious example of a strong disjunctive operator is the expression 'or . . . but not both' . . . Similarly, the most obvious example of a weak disjunctive operator is the expression 'or . . . or both' . . .

But some operators are ambiguous or indifferent as to the strong/weak distinction. The word 'or' is a case in point . . . Nevertheless, there are conceivable circumstances in which 'or' might be used to form a strong disjunction. . . .

The character of the disjuncts does *not* dictate the sense in which a disjunctive operator is being used . . . the *fact* that both disjuncts *cannot* be true in no way shows that the *operator* explicitly denies their conjoint truth; and in the second place, the fact that both disjuncts *cannot* be true would seem to indicate . . . a perfect place to employ *weak* disjunction. . . .

Second, the expression 'either . . . or' is *not* equivalent to 'or . . . but not both'. . . . the function of 'either' . . . is to serve as a kind of bracket. (Tapscott 1976, 27–28)[2]

Since the English word 'or' nearly always connects sentences the joint truth of which is excluded on the basis of certain background assumptions, it is hard to decide whether this word occasionally has an 'exclusive' sense, as some logicians have asserted, or always has an 'inclusive' sense analogous to that of '∨'. (Mates 1965, 75)

The 'conceivable circumstances' to which Tapscott refers may well be those also cited by other authors and referred ultimately to Tarski. We may call examples of this class 'quality time' (qt) examples:

Consider the following . . .

(1) Either we will go to the movies or we will go to the beach.

. . . Sentence (1) expresses the statement that we will go to the movies or to the beach but not to both, and that statement is false if we go to neither or to both. (Brody 1973, 95)

Cases of the exclusive sense of "or" occur, though less often. If a father says to his child in a tone of refusal, "I'll take you to the zoo, *or* I'll take you to the beach," then one can accuse him of having spoken falsely if he takes the child both places. (Barker 1985, 87)

Such examples are rare, but they exist. In an example given by Tarski it is supposed that a child asks his father to take him to the beach and afterwards to a movie. The father replies, in a tone of refusal, "We will go either to the beach or to the movie." Here the exclusive use is clear; the father means simultaneously to promise and to refuse. (Quine 1972, 11–12)

---

2. Tapscott acknowledges Quine as the source of the (first) second point.

Tarski's actual example is less clear:

> If . . . a child has asked to be taken on a hike in the morning and to a theater in the afternoon, and we reply:
>
> *no, we are going on a hike or we are going to the theater,*
>
> then our usage of the word "*or*" is obviously of the second [exclusive] kind since we intend to comply with only one of the two requests. (Tarski 1941, 21)

The complication lies in the presence of the 'no'. For it is either an explicit denial of the conjunction, in which case to take the 'or' to be exclusive is to take the parent's position to have been overspecified,[3] or it is a refusal to be committed, in which case we need feel no temptation to take the 'or' as exclusive.

It may be of interest to future scholars to pick these expository threads from the prose of the textbooks and trace them back to the professorial frock coats from which they were drawn. I venture, on that score, only the comment that the experience of such scholars trying to gain an understanding of twentieth-century propositional logic by examining the texts will not be entirely unlike that of a twentieth-century scholar trying to sort out the logical doctrines of the Stoics. It may well be, for example, that the appearance of modal vocabulary in some early discussions of disjunction has no more doctrinal significance than it does in the discussions of present-day texts. There may be a common doctrine, but it is naïve to suppose that therefore one ought somewhere to find a clear statement of it.

What are the material conclusions? Disregarding the mooted example of Tarski, it seems that of the authors surveyed, Quine, Mates, and Tapscott come closest to a reasonable account. There is sufficient historical warrant for calling both the 1110 and the 0110 truth-functions 'disjunctions', and the labels 'inclusive' (or 'nonexclusive') for the one, and 'exclusive' for the other are a plausible way of marking the distinction. Moreover, there are English constructions that, for purposes of schematization, could be regarded as approximations of each. As Copi says, 'Where precision is at a premium and the exclusive sense of "or" is intended, the phrase "but not both" is usually added' (1961, 240). Klenk offers: 'An example of this might be the following: "John wants to be a lawyer or a physician, but not both"' (1983, 54), and if by this they mean just that such a construction approximates the 0110 truth-function, then well and good, but in that case it is the 0110 truth-function intended, not an exclusive sense of 'or'. If the exclusion rider is explicitly added, then the inclusive 'or' would do, and the use of the adversative 'but' conversationally implies that the 'or' thus qualified *is* rather of the 1110 variety. None of this warrants the claim that there is such a thing as an exclusive disjunctive meaning or sense or use of 'or' in English. Again, if the sentences joined by 'or' cannot both be true, then the matter is over-specified when it is claimed that 'or' there has an exclusive sense. When the disjoined sentences are not mutually exclusive, one must tell whether the possibility of their joint truth is being mooted either by the context

---

3. This is *merely* a complication, since we might well say without pleonasm 'No, we will not do both'.

or by intonation or by stress, but in this case again the inclusive 'or' will do. As for the Tarskian examples, if the parent must adopt a tone of stern refusal and come down upon the 'or' with an italicizing thump in order to convey exclusivity, then it must be explained why it is the 'or' rather than the tone and the thump that carries the rider of exclusion. But here, there might be contrived a case for a distinctive (since italicized or stressed) use of 'or'. Then again, if the parent does not make the exclusivity explicit by *some* means or other, there are no grounds for saying that he has managed to use 'or' in any but whatever the ordinary sense of it would be in the context, and there are obvious grounds for denying that the meaning of what we utter is ever a matter of intention or will-power alone.

The matter ought to be settled simply and finally by considering the characteristics of 0110 disjunction and asking whether there is a class of uses of 'or' realizing those characteristics in natural language. One such feature is its binarity, which, for the sake of well-formedness requires the insertion of parentheses, yielding:

$$(\alpha \veebar \beta) \veebar \gamma$$

or

$$\alpha \veebar (\beta \veebar \gamma)$$

and not tolerating

$$\alpha \veebar \beta \veebar \gamma.$$

Is there a scope-explicit use of 'or' in English for which we observe this requirement by rejecting the form

$$\alpha \text{ or } \beta \text{ or } \gamma$$

in favour of the form

$$\text{Either either } \alpha \text{ or } \beta \text{ or } \gamma$$

$$\text{either } \alpha \text{ or either } \beta \text{ or } \gamma?$$

Unfortunately, the fact that we reserve no such 'or' is of itself no final clue. For both $\vee$ and $\veebar$ are associative operations. So even if their binarity requires that we regard 'α or β or γ' now as having eight possible readings corresponding to the eight possible combinations of $\vee$, $\veebar$, and parenthesis placings, some of those will be entirely benign, because both operations are associative.

More telling is the question whether there is a use of 'or' that, when more than two indicative sentences are strung together with it, with or without scope indication, gives the whole construction the force of the claim only that there is an odd number such that that number of the conjoined sentences are true. Does a sentence of the form 'α or β or γ' ever mean 'Either exactly one or all three of: α, β, γ is true'? To this question the answer is surely that there is no more such an 'or' in English, than there is a use of 'if and only if' in English that gives to the construction of the form 'α if and only if β if and only if γ' the meaning 'None or exactly two of α, β, γ are false'. The most that can be argued is there is a use of 'or' that coincides with $\underline{\vee}$, as there is a sense of 'if and only if' that coincides with $\leftrightarrow$, *on the two-sentence case.*

Put the matter the other way round. Suppose we were to replace Tarski's example with one in which a child has asked to be taken on a hike in the morning, to a zoo in the afternoon, and to a cinema in the evening and we reply, under Tarski's direction, and with whatever tone of voice his simpler example required:

> *No, we are going on a hike or we are going to the zoo or we are going to the cinema,*

will it be alleged that the meaning of 'or' is unchanged from the original example? Setting aside the objections raised earlier, we may observe that if the intention of the reply is to refuse to satisfy more than one of the requests, then either the meaning of 'or' has undergone a change in the modification, or the meaning of 'or' in the original example was not that of 0110 disjunction.

3.2 The Sign of the Beast

How would we tell, of an occurrence of 'or', that it was an occurrence of an 'or' whose meaning was exactly or approximately captured by $\vee$? Barrett and Stenner propose a useful test (1971, 117). Since the truth table characteristic of $\vee$ differs from the truth table characteristic of $\underline{\vee}$ in having a 1 in the first row where the other has a 0, a convincing example would have to be a false *or*-compound of two true indicative sentences. Call this 'the 101 requirement'. Evidently such an example would carry more authority than an example that alternates two incompatible sentences, whose incompatibility suffices to preclude an assignment of 1 to both. Heaven knows that there is room enough here for confusion to set in. In the first place the notion of *logical* form does not apply straightforwardly to sentences of natural language; indeed, we may say that a sentence has no logical form independently of a specification of a formal language of representation. Certainly, there is no such thing as *the* form of a sentence independently of a theory that dictates selection of some particular language of representation over all others. Even then, whether it is suitable to call that form 'the *logical* form' of the sentence presumably depends upon whether the purpose of the representation is logical rather than linguistic or something else. Even when the relativity of the stock of available logical forms is admitted, which of the forms we assign to a sentence depends upon which of the inferences in which the sentence can figure we wish to have represented.[4] Now with a little good will we can fill in these numerous blanks for the cases at hand. What the authors may have in mind in alleging examples that do not satisfy the 101 requirement is this: since the language of representation is incapable of preserving the sub-sentential structure of the component sentences of their examples, the impossibility of assigning 1 to both component sentences must be conveyed somehow by constants. What vitiates the conclusion that

---

4. In fact, textbook authors frequently write of 'translating' an English sentence into a formula of a propositional language. But they clearly have in mind only a representation that preserves at least those structural features of the sentence whose inferential significance can be exploited in the language of representation.

(roughly) 'or' means $\underline{\vee}$ in such a case is that $\underline{\vee}$ is not required for the representation of such sentences. Let the first component sentence be represented by A and the second by B; then that exactly one of them is true is expressible in a propositional language having for connectives only $\neg$ and $\vee$, in particular, by the formula '$\neg(\neg A \vee B) \vee \neg(\neg B \vee A)$' or in a propositional language having $\wedge$ as well, by the formula '$(\neg A \wedge B) \vee (\neg B \wedge A)$'. To be sure, if the propositional language has the connective $\underline{\vee}$ as well, then both of those formulae are deductively equivalent to the formula 'A $\underline{\vee}$ B'. But the natural language sentence does not require representation by a formula in which the principal connective is $\underline{\vee}$. Moreover, the question arises whether, since the impossibility of assigning 1 to both components is a consequence of *their* meanings, the representations with $\vee$ are not (to introduce a frequently encountered desideratum) a little closer to the English.

3.2.1 Intentional spoor

Having said so much about purported cases in which the components are incompatible, it must be admitted that many of the more perplexing examples of the textbooks are ones whose components are not incompatible but seem to be thought to be by their authors. Thus, Hurley's alleged example (1991, 293):

> The Orient Express is either on track A or [on] track B.[5]

If this sentence is the exclusive disjunction of the obvious component sentences, it follows from it that track A is not identical with track B. Or consider the alleged example of Kegley and Kegley:

> John is at the play, or he is studying in the library.

of which they remark, 'There is no mistaking the sense of *or* here: John cannot be in both places at once'. (Kegley & Kegley 1978, 232) If their example is an example of exclusive disjunction, we may infer from it that the play is not being performed in the library, that the theatre is not in the library, that John is not swotting in the stalls between acts while his companion fights her way to the bar to fetch the drinks. Again, consider Kahane's (1990, 22)

> Art took the makeup exam on Tuesday or on Wednesday.

If this sentence is the exclusive disjunction of 'Art took the makeup exam on Tuesday' and 'Art took the makeup exam on Wednesday', then it follows from it that the makeup exam did not last two days or come in two instalments and that Art did not take the makeup exam twice. Such examples give rise to the suspicion that the authors advancing them accept some such view as that we can discover what instances of sentences mean by discovering the intentions of their utterers. This must be part of the account of how we discover what is meant by occurrences of sequences of sounds such as 'The bank has fallen', provided that, unlike the oracular 'DOMINESTES' ('Domi ne stes' [Do not stay home] or 'Domine stes' [Master, stay]),[6] the ambiguity is not what was intended. But

5. I have repeated the preposition for parallel structure.
6. Cited in Crystal, 1987 p. 63.

while this might be a means of discovering what is meant by the speaker, it can be a means of discovering what the occurrence of the sentence means only if the intended meaning is within the range of meanings available for the sequence of sounds to mean. Thus, for example, when Clarence Thomas said, 'I have never done anything that could be mistaken for sexual harassment', he may just have been engaging in careful speech, but he may have meant to exclude one of the cases that would have made that sentence true, namely that any sexual harassment in which he had engaged had been perfectly transparent, that is, that if anyone had taken anything that he had done for sexual harassment, that person would not have been mistaken. He may merely have misspoken or misunderstood the meanings of the words he used, but no intention he may have had would be capable of making that instance of that sentence mean 'I have never done anything that could be *taken* for sexual harassment.' Similar observations might be made of his 'I unconditionally and uncategorically deny it' (uttered in response to a reported allegation) except that in this case, since the adverbs conflict, one may presume that he misspoke. As applied to the question whether 'or' on occasion means $\underline{v}$, we may say that speakers' intentions can yield instances of 'or' requiring representation by $\underline{v}$, only if that meaning lies within the range of things that 'or' can mean. That is what is in question.

3.2.2 Inferential spoor

Kahane seems to suggest that the meaning of an instance of 'or' can be discovered by noting how the sentence in which it occurs figures in inference:

> . . . a sentence whose major connective is an *exclusive* "or" asserts that (1) at least one of its disjuncts is true (as do disjunctions formed by the inclusive "or"); and (2) *at least one disjunct is false.* Thus there is a sense in which the whole meaning of the inclusive "or" is only part of the meaning of the exclusive "or". So if we symbolize an exclusive use of the word "or" by "∨", we lose part of its meaning. Surprisingly, in many arguments in which the exclusive "or" is used, no harm is done if we symbolize the "or" by "∨". The validity of these arguments depends on the part of the meaning of the exclusive "∨" that it shares with the inclusive "or", namely the part that asserts at least one disjunct is true.
>
> But there are some arguments for which this is not the case. An example is the argument

1. Art took the makeup exam on Tuesday or Wednesday (*T* or *W*).

2. Art took the makeup exam on Tuesday (*T*).

/∴ 3. Art did not take the makeup exam on Wednesday (~*W*).

If the inclusive "or" is used to symbolize the "or" in the first premise of this argument, then the resulting argument will be invalid, since it will state that

1. Art took the makeup exam on Tuesday or Art took the makeup exam on Wednesday or Art took the makeup exam on Tuesday and on Wednesday.

2. Art took the makeup exam on Tuesday.

$/\therefore$ 3. Art did not take the makeup exam on Wednesday.

But the original argument is valid. The trouble is that the "or" in the original premise is the *exclusive* "or", and this time the additional claim made by the exclusive "or" cannot be omitted. We must not only assert that Art took the makeup exam on at least one of the two days, stated in symbols as $T \vee W$, but must *deny* that he took the exam on both days, stated in symbols as $\sim(T \cdot W)$. Thus we should symbolize the first premise as $(T \vee W) \cdot \sim(T \cdot W)$. (Kahane 1990, 23–24)

Now the idea of *the form of an argument* presents at least as many difficulties to the commentator as the idea of *the form of a sentence*. Every n-premiss argument has at least one invalid form, namely $P_1, \ldots, P_n/ \therefore Q$. An argument is valid iff at least one of the forms that it has is a valid one. So we can easily make up valid arguments even of the form: $P \vee Q, P/ \therefore \neg Q$. An argument of the form $P \vee \neg P, P$; therefore $\neg\neg P$ is also of the previous invalid form, but valid in virtue of the latter. But also valid is an argument of the form P; therefore $\neg\neg P$, and, by monotonicity, any argument that merely adds a premiss. Kahane's claim that the earlier argument is valid may be false, but if we accept the stipulation that it is valid, then we are bound to cast about for a valid form. If we treat the claims that Art wrote the exam on Tuesday and that Art wrote the exam on Wednesday as incompatible, then the validity of the argument would follow from the validity of the argument from T to ~W. Indeed, since 'T' and 'W' are constants, we can take T; therefore ~W to represent a singleton valid form. On the assumption that the argument is valid because the alternatives are incompatible, the first premiss can be represented by '$T \vee W$'. If we take the stipulation of validity to be a stipulation rather about the intentions of a fictional inferential agent (to steal a rose from the ethicists' garden), then if we insist upon taking the first premise to have its ordinary force, we are bound to represent the form as Kahane claims. But if our concern is just, at any cost, to make a valid argument of a fictional character's eccentric sayings, then we need not take even the ordinary force of the first premiss to be intended, and can represent its form as $T \mid W$. Unless there are independent grounds for supposing that 'or' sometimes requires representation as $\underline{\vee}$, the requirement of validity alone does not, in this instance, arbitrate between $\mid$ and $\underline{\vee}$ as its representative. To insist that the latter is indicated is to apply a principle of least eccentricity or of maximum charity. There is employment here for Thomson's minimally decent Samaritan.

3.2.3 Whence the illusion?

Two distinguishable classes of what might be called 'parental' uses of 'or' have been advanced in the textbooks as satisfying the 101 requirement. We find, on the one hand, the qt examples of the Tarski type in which a parent, in response to a request for a succession of activities, A and B, predicts with a tone of refusal, finality or frozen disdain something of the general shape:

We will do A *or* B.

On the other hand, we find warnings of the general character:

Either you do A, or B will happen.

In connection with qt pronouncements we find such explanations as that 'we intend to comply with only one of the requests' (Tarski 1941) or that 'the father means simultaneously to promise and to refuse' (Quine 1972) which locate the exclusivity in the speaker's intentions, or that we can be accused of having spoken falsely if we lay on both activities (Barker 1985). In connection with the second, warning, class of examples, we find such explanations as that the recipient of the warning 'would be rather upset' if he did A and B happened anyway (Rennie & Girle 1973), or as that B cannot fairly happen if the recipient does A (McKay 1989).

The illusion of exclusivity seems to be engendered differently in the two classes of examples. In the qt examples, the effect of stressing the presence of 'or' in the pronouncement may plausibly be understood as being to stress the absence of 'and', so that the use of 'or' is naturally taken as a pointed refusal to use 'and' instead. Now in certain contexts of use, a stressed refusal to say that A may count as an implicit denial that A, and a pointed refusal to commit oneself to a course of action, a refusal of the course of action. If there is an implicit denial of conjunction here, certainly if there is an implicit negation, then it is of the same family as the genus of Laurence Horn's *metalinguistic negation* ('a device for objecting to a previous utterance on any grounds whatever, including the conventional or conversational implicata it potentially induces, its morphology, its style or register, or its phonetic realization' 1989, 363). If there is a negation here, its genus could be thought of as that of stillborn twins of those in Horn's list; each takes the form of the labelled avoidance of an utterance to which the corresponding exception might otherwise be taken. There is a difference between doing a thing and doing one thing rather than another. If a portion of an utterance is so labelled, by stress or parenthetic enfoliature (' "or", I say, "or" dammit! . . .'), it might be describable as a kind of pre-emptive negation. So to find a negated conjunction in such uses of 'or' might be merely to treat such occurrences as instances of negation raisings. But such is the indirection that it would be something akin to a raising from the dead. Grice's maxim of quantity may be sufficient to explain the apprehended *négatité* (recalling Sartre on experiencing the absence of Pierre), and the inference to 'not both' may be grounded in the assumption that the speaker has made the strongest claim warranted by the facts as he knows them. But the character of the inference remains mysterious. That 'both' is not part of the claim does not of itself implicate that 'not both' is, and the assumption that the speaker has made the strongest claim he can that is warranted by the facts does not lead us, except in particular cases, to suppose that nothing stronger is true. In particular, even if exactly one of the disjuncts is true, then something stronger is true, namely, the conjunction of the true disjunct with the negation of the false one. Even an exclusive disjunction has more than one solution, and is itself equivalent to the non-exclusive disjunction of them.

In warnings, different forces are at play. To warn someone away from dangerous ground is often, perhaps usually, to indicate as well a zone of relative safety. So in McKay's example ('You will eat your dinner or you will be punished' 1989, 29) the warning that not eating dinner represents danger loses its point if eating dinner does not represent safety. Similarly in the example advanced by Rennie and Girle ('Either you put your toys away or you get no ice 1973, 31) the point of the utterance as a warning is lost if it does not direct the child both away from an icecream-less course and onto an icecreamy one.[7]

Pelletier (1978, 66) makes the useful observation that even if the second disjunct of:

> Either you eat your dinner or I'll spank you! (Quoted from Thomason 1970)

is strengthened as in:

> Either you eat your dinner or I'll spank you if you don't!

or as in

> Either you eat your dinner or I'll spank you for not eating it!

we do not thereby produce a sentence that is false if both disjuncts are true. Pelletier's argument for the former invokes but does not depend upon a particular semantics for the conditional. If the conditional is material, then the disjuncts are incompatible and the example therefore impotent. Curiously, Pelletier offers such an argument against the second alteration. But clearly a person can be punished for uncommitted offences. Either way, the second does not yield the required example.

In the case of warnings, we can test the robustness of the intuition that a $\underline{\vee}$ representation is required by performing a thought experiment much as we did with the Tarski example. Consider McKay's example with the dinner-eating clause analysed into its constituents, say, eating the peas and eating the potatoes. Then we might rework the warning as

> You will eat your peas and you will eat your potatoes or you will be punished.

Now if the effect of the original was to hold out the threat of punishment unless all of the dinner is eaten, this ought to be equivalent to

> You will eat your peas or you will be punished, and you will eat your potatoes or you will be punished.

But the two forms are not equivalent if the 'or' requires a $\underline{\vee}$ representation; for that conjunction will be false if the child eats the peas and is punished for not having eaten the potatoes, but the other exclusive disjunction (you will eat your potatoes or you will be punished) will in that case be true.

---

7. I am indebted to Robin Taylor for suggesting this way of putting the point.

Another useful suggestion of Pelletier's relies upon the fact that the negation of $\alpha \vee \beta$ is $(\alpha \wedge \beta) \vee (\neg\alpha \wedge \neg\beta)$. We ought therefore to be able to test our intuitions for a given purported example by considering what would make its negation true. There are difficulties with the test in practice, mainly arising from the general instability of sense under additions of negations. Three of the purported instances which Pelletier cites have the additional difficulty that they cannot themselves be represented as disjunctions of any sort, and although Pelletier correctly observes that the sentences obtained by a natural insertion of negating elements into the examples would not receive the required reading, his transformations cannot plausibly be regarded as their negations.

Along similar lines, denials of *or*-statement in favour of its *and*-counterpart might be thought to speak for the exclusivity of the rejected 'or':

Jackie ate her peas or her potatoes.
Jackie didn't eat her peas *or* her potatoes; she ate her peas *and* her potatoes.

But this is a metalinguistic negation in Horn's sense, rejecting not the truth of the disjunction, but the offering of it as an adequate account of what Jackie has eaten.

3.2.4 The Diners' Club

That is the first myth, that there is, in English, a use of 'or' that must be represented by $\vee$ in the language of propositional logic. Although an account of the origins of disjunction must obviously deal with the question if only to set it aside, and although one would wish to see it eradicated from textbooks, our main interest in the myth is not in its falsity, but in a puzzle that its falsity raises: if there has not come to be a truth-functionally exclusive use of 'or', how has there come to be an exhaustive use, and how does there come to be a disjunctive use of 'or' at all? But this puzzle we must set aside for consideration after other matters have been dealt with. Secondarily, however, it is important to dispel the myth of exclusive 'or' because it reinforces an assumption which we shall have to reject, that one or the other of the two competing truth-functions 0110 and 1110 must be *central* to an account of the role of 'or' in English. And the idea that 'or' sometimes incarnates one of them and at other times the other has spawned a mythogeny, which, for its hindrance of an understanding of 'or', is even more deserving of the deep six. The first of these lies in two related classes of examples adduced as evidence for the elusive 0110 'or'. The former class draws from the practices of child management that have already yielded up such a rich store. The second, the 'blue-plate' examples, reflect the austerities of affordable dining. Their general drift will no doubt yield up data as useful and intriguing for the social historian as for the historian of the logic textbook. But they evidently represent a compelling illusion and provide a lively illustration of Wittgenstein's 'spectacles' theme. Copi argues:

When a mother succumbs to her child's teasing and gives permission to take "a cookie or a piece of cake", it would be a backward or disobedient child who helped himself to both. (1961, 240)

R.C. Jeffrey:

> . . . when a child is told he may have candy or icecream. . . . Here the qualification "but not both" is tacitly understood. (1967, 10)

T.J. Richards:

> So how can we find a clear-cut case of the exclusive 'or'? Imagine a boy who asks for icecream *and* strawberries for tea. He is told as a sort of refusal: 'You can have icecream *or* strawberries for tea'. Here there is no doubt: not both may be had. (1978, 84)

Kalish, Montague, and Mar:

> When a parent who is attempting to limit a child's consumption of sweets says 'icecream or cake', the intent is to exclude the option of eating both icecream and cake. (1980, 55)

H. Pospesel:

> A mother who says "you may have an icecream sandwich or a Popsicle" is very likely excluding the case where the child gets both. (1984, 96)

Trudy Govier:

> A restaurant menu telling you that:
>
>> Jello or icecream is provided as a free dessert with your meal.
>
> is not telling you that you are allowed to have both. Here *or* is used exclusively . . .
>   You can express exclusive disjunction perfectly well using the symbols of propositional logic. Let's see how this works for the Jello and icecream case:
>
> Let *J* represent "You may have Jello for dessert."
>
> Let *I* represent "You may have icecream for dessert." The menu is stating:
>
> $$(J \vee I) \cdot - (J \cdot I)$$
>
> That is it allows one or the other, not both. (1988, 198)

Robert Baum:

> . . . when a customer in a restaurant asks the waiter 'What dessert comes with this dinner?' and the waiter answers 'You can have cake or pie,' he almost certainly means that the customer is entitled to either cake or pie for dessert, but not both. In this situation, 'or' is being used in the *exclusive* sense. (1975, 161)

Bergmann, Moor, and Nelson:

> Suppose the following occurs on a menu:
>
>> With your meal you get apple pie or chocolate cake.
>
> . . . if someone orders both apple pie and cake, the waiter is likely to point out that either cake or pie, but *not* both, come with the dinner. (1990, 24-5)

(We may call this the argument from confection.)

R.J. Fogelin on the entrée:

> "You may have chicken or steak" probably means that you cannot have both. (1982, 159)

By contrast, Robert M. Johnson offers:

> 'You may have mustard or relish on your hot dog' allows that you may have one or the other *or both*. (1986, 174)

and (one fancifully imagines, presiding Barmecide-like over the host of wistful diners) I. Copi in his more junior text:

> Where a restaurant lists "salad or dessert" on its *table d'hôte* menu, it is clearly meant that for the stated price of the meal, the diner may have one or the other *but not both*. (1961, 240)

McCawley makes a parallel observation:

> . . . *On the $1.25 lunch you can have either a soup or a dessert* . . . grants you permission to take one or the other but does not grant you permission to take both a soup and a dessert for your $1.25. (1981, 33)

Wesley C. Salmon retorts:

> In one sense (known as the *exclusive* sense) ['or'] means "one or the other but not both." This is the meaning it has on a menu in the phrase "soup or salad," used to tell what comes with the entree. (1984, 40)

In summation, G. Georgacarakos issues a manifesto:

> An example of a statement making use of the exclusive sense of *or* is the following:
>
>> Dinner at this restaurant includes either soup or salad
>
> This statement informs the customer that the price of dinner will include either soup or salad but not both. Accordingly, we should expect that this statement will be false not only if both the atomic statements *Dinner at this restaurant includes soup* and *Dinner at this restaurant includes salad* are false, but also if both are true . . . Hence the compound statement *Dinner at this restaurant includes soup or dinner at this restaurant includes salad* is an exclusive disjunction of the exclusive disjuncts

> *Dinner at this restaurant includes soup* and *Dinner at this restaurant includes salad.* (1979, 46)

Patrick Hurley has added the example only in his fourth edition, and so may be imagined as having arrived late to the feast, observes:

> You can have either soup or salad with this meal.

> The sense of [this statement] excludes the possibility of both alternatives being true. (1991, 293)

and (one imagines), turning to the senior students sitting along the wall, Copi says:

> A different sense of 'or' is intended when a restaurant lists 'tea or coffee' on its *table d'hôte* menu, meaning that for the stated price of the meal, the diner may have one or the other *but not both.* (1979, 11) [8]

Ian Hacking interjects:

> But now consider the statement:

> > Adam wants coffee or tea

> Do you suppose that Adam wants *both* coffee and tea? . . . Most people would expect Adam to be pleased if he got coffee or pleased if he got tea but surprised, perhaps revolted, if he got both. (1972, 92)

Ambrose and Lazerowitz return to Copi's theme:

> Menus presenting the alternatives of tea, coffee, or milk obviously are intended to permit one choice, and at most one, though clearly it is not conceptually *impossible,* or inconceivable, that a person should have more than one. "I will give you my coat or my umbrella" is another instance of the use of "or" in which it is factually excluded that both are true. (1962, 31)

Peter T. Manicas, responding to the offer of a coat or an umbrella, remarks:

> The following two statements illustrate the difference:

> > 1 The door to the cafeteria is locked on windy or on cold days.
> > 2 Willy is in class or he is at the ball game.

> In statement 1 the use of "or" strongly suggests the inclusive sense. That is, 1 suggests that the door is closed on windy days, that it is closed on cold days *and* that it is closed on windy *and* cold days. This, however, is not perfectly clear. (1976, 71)

Manicas, in explicitly inferring what ought to be its disjuncts from his alleged inclusive disjunction, is *ipso facto* recognizing that the example is not a disjunction. His test is adopted by Kegley and Kegley:

8. Implicit in Copi's formulation is the recognition that a customer with sufficient ready cash might be allowed both beverages.

The inclusive sense of *or* is the case in which we intend to admit the possibility that both disjuncts are true. Thus in asserting the disjunction "School is automatically closed on foggy days or on holidays," we suggest that school is closed on foggy days, that it is closed on holidays, *and* that it is closed on foggy holidays. (1978, 232)

3.2.5 Further examples

Other authors adduce examples from concessive contexts other than the *restaurative*, sometimes as examples of exclusive, sometimes for inclusive uses of 'or'.
Patrick Suppes:

When people use 'or' in the *exclusive* sense to combine two sentences they are asserting that one of the sentences is true and the other is false. This usage is often made more explicit by adding the phrase 'but not both'. Thus a father tells his child, 'You may go to the movies or you may go to the circus this Saturday but not both'. (1957, 6)

Nicholas Rescher:

These two very different senses of "or" are illustrated by the following sentences: *Physicians or the wives of physicians are eligible for membership; A member will pay the annual membership fee by February 1, or his membership lapses as of that day.* (1964, 178)

Morton L. Schagrin:

. . . if a college advisor tells you that you can major in the sciences or the humanities, this might mean that you have to choose which one area to major in. But it might mean that you can have a double major. In the first case, the advisor's offer was an exclusive disjunction; in the second case the offer was an inclusive disjunction. (1985, 78)

Robert Paul Churchill:

An example of an exclusive disjunction would be the statement that one was willing to go to a dance or to a movie, *but not to both.* This would be asserted as

I will [go either][9] to a dance or to a movie but not to both.

Another way to express the same statement would be

I will go to a dance or to a movie but I will not go to both a dance and a movie. (1990)

Hacking again:

---

9. Order reversed for parallel structure.

There are even clearer examples of *P* or *Q* but not both. If a schoolboy is trying to get out of some homework and miss a day at school because of his grandmother's funeral, his teacher might say:

> You will be allowed to miss a day of school *or* you will be excused homework.

> Has the boy been authorized to miss school *and* avoid his homework? . . . Most people, including the teacher, would say he has been allowed to do one or the other, but not both. (1972, 92)

Others still draw their examples from contexts generally admonitory, as, for example, R.L. Purtill:

> An example of an exclusive disjunction would be "Either pay your registration at the cashier's office or mail in a cheque to the registrar". (1979, 76)

Patrick J. Hurley's example of inclusive 'or':

> For example, "or" is used inclusively in the statement "Anyone who owns a car or a truck needs insurance" . . . it is intended that anyone who owns a car *and* a truck also needs insurance . . . (1985, 242)

Lambert and van Fraassen:

> Hale[10] wanted liberty or he wanted death

> The force of "or" . . . is: "one or the other but not both". . . . The use of "or" . . . is called the *exclusive use* of "or". . . . (1972, 23)

Now what is of interest about these examples is that none of them is an exclusive *disjunction* at all. Purtill's example is not even an indicative sentence. But the earlier parental and restaurative examples, though they are indicative, and although context or background information or intonation or stress may make them exclusive, are not disjunctive. I do not mean that the 'or' does not join sentences; that is also true. But even allowing for the ellipsis, they are not disjunctions of any sort. If they are to be represented by a propositional formula, the formula must be a conjunction, not a disjunction.

The point is an obvious one once made. To say to a diner, 'You may have tea or coffee' is to give the diner to understand that he may have tea, and also to give him to understand that he may have coffee. If we understand the waiter's utterance as a statement of fact rather than as a granting of permission, the fact that it states is a conjunctive one, namely, that the diner may have tea and the diner may have coffee. That conjunctive fact is compatible with the diner's not being permitted both tea and coffee. That is, the waiter could, without contradiction, say, 'You may have tea. You may have coffee. But I am afraid that you may not have tea and coffee.' Much the same can be said of the parental examples, with allowances for their being instances of grantings of permission rather than

10. The sentiment is sometimes attributed to Patrick Henry.

statements of fact.[11] To say to a child, 'You may take a *chausson aux pommes or a mille-feuilles'* is to give the child permission to take a *c.a.p* and to give the child permission to take a *m.-f.*; once again this is compatible with denying permission to have one of each. The denial may be made clear by intonation or context, rather than explicitly; nevertheless when the ellipsis is removed and, if needs be, the resulting sentence is taken as an assertion rather than a permission, it is a conjunction, not a disjunction. Even if an implicit 'but not both' is somehow conveyed, it can make the sentence an exclusive *disjunction* only if the sentence, on its normal reading, is a disjunction of some sort. But in the restaurative examples, even the one (relish or mustard) in which the rider is claimed absent, the sentence is not a disjunction of any sort. Were it in fact a disjunction, no permission would have been conveyed, because the addressee would not have been told what he was allowed to do. In fact, even when we say, as we might in English, 'You may have tea or you may have coffee', where the 'or' joins whole sentences, if the larger context makes clear that permission is being given, we interpret the sentence as a couple of permissions, not as a disjunction, and even in this case, though the 'or' be resoundingly italicized to exclude permission to have both, the sentence remains a pair of permissions. Both this and the ellipsis must be equivalent to successions of permissions to work at all as formulae for giving permission.

If we content ourselves with a truth-conditional account of such sentences, we can express the facts of these constructions in the language of distribution. In the sentence

You may have tea or coffee

the list 'tea or coffee' is a conjunctively distributive list; 'or' has this role in the context 'You may have ( )', because in that context a list formed with 'and' would receive a reading on which it was undistributive or had undistributive sense. That is, a list formed with 'and' would be understood as granting permission only to have both, or as granting permission to have either or both. The role of 'or' in this setting is to form an explicitly distributive list.

It is easy to see how the illusion arises that sentences embedding conjunctively distributive *or*-lists are genuine instances of a 0110 disjunctive 'or'. Although when they are regarded as statements of permissibility, it is plain that

You may have A or B

is truth-conditionally equivalent to

You may have A and you may have B

nevertheless, as *instruments* of permission, they would be significantly different in that even if it does not forbid having both, the first sentence, more explicitly than the second, withholds permission to do so. That difference disappears when forbiddance is made explicit. Even as instruments of permission there is nothing to choose between

11. The distinction is not an unimportant one, but the allowance has to be made even if the authors of the examples are to be granted them as instances of exclusive disjunctions. We can afford to set it aside for the moment.

You may have A or B, but you may not have both

and

You may have A and you may have B, but you may not have both.

But the truth-conditional equivalence between

You may have tea or coffee

and

You may have tea and you may have coffee

is a puzzle that the received views of the linguistic sources of logic are powerless to dispel. And the retrospective confidence that the 1110 and 0110 truth-functions may be applied as templates to discover which of the two 'or's the occurrence represents, itself represents a curious logical solecism. Those authors who are impressed with the capacity of the formula 'You may have this or that' to convey, if suitably intoned, disallowance of having both, fail to notice the misfit of the second template. Others, recognizing the capacity of the formula to give permission to have this *and* permission to have that, fail to notice the misfit of the first. Thus, according to van Dijk:

> INCLUSIVE DISJUNCTION is used in those cases where the facts are compatible and where the assertion is made that at least one item of a series has been or can be realized, as in:
>
> [30] Harry went to school in Cambridge or he studied in Oxford.
> [31] You may have an orange or you may take a pear. (1977, 64)

The one sees a logical implication where none is; the other fails to see that, despite its apparent form, in having in this instance said 'A or B', one has said A and one has said B.

That such sentences may bear, explicitly or by intonation or by contextual implication, the qualification 'but you may not have both' is a consequence of the non-aggregativity of environments with the modal auxiliary 'may'. That one may φ and one may ψ does not imply that one may φ and ψ. The same holds for 'may' in its alethic, as distinct from its deontic, uses. That it may be that α and it may be that β, does not imply that it may be that $\alpha \wedge \beta$. Thus Robert M. Johnson's mooted example of exclusive disjunction:

The baby may be a boy or a girl (1986, 174)

comes under the same strictures. On its most natural reading it says

The baby may be a boy and the baby may be a girl,

which may equally well be expressed by

The baby may be a boy or it may be a girl,

which although it consists of two sentences joined by 'or' is no kind of disjunction, since it implies that the baby may be a boy and it implies that the baby may be a girl. But as in the genuinely disjunctive cases, the fact, if it is one, that being a boy precludes being a girl vitiates rather than strengthens the claim that the 'or' demands here an exclusive reading.

The same fate attends some putative examples involving a concessive or volitional 'will' as distinct from a predictive 'shall', as in Churchill's example:

I will [go either] to a dance or to a movie but not to both.

If, as he proposes, it is to be read as an expression of willingness rather than as a prediction, then it is to be read as:

I will go to a dance; I will go to a movie; but I will not do both,

meaning

I am willing ('will agree') to go to a dance; I am willing ('will agree') to go to a movie; but I am not willing ('will not agree') to do both.

Substitute 'shall' in Churchill's example:

I shall [go either] to a dance or to a movie but not to both

and the conjunctive reading is lost. This feature of certain uses of 'will' is not lost on all the authors surveyed here. Hodges remarks:

There are a few unusual sentences in which or means something more like and, and it should be translated to '∧':

Uri Geller can read your mind, or he can bend your spoons. (1977, 96)

Vernon and Nissen make a similar point involving a conditional use of 'will':

. . . not all either-or statements are disjunctive statements. Suppose you are trying to decide whether you ought to hire Smith or Jones to do a plumbing job. You ask a friend, who says, "Either Smith or Jones will do a good job." This can be translated as "Either Smith will do a good job or Jones will do a good job." It is clear in this case that your friend is claiming that *both* of these component statements are true. Consequently, what we have here is a conjunctive statement. We must keep in mind, then, that a compound statement is not disjunctive merely because it is an either-or statement; it may be a conjunctive statement "in disguise" so to speak. (1968, 72)

We may add what they do not: that as in the other cases, the question may arise whether Smith *and* Jones would do a good job, and require a distinct answer.

Again, certain general claims involving 'or' will more naturally receive a conjunctive reading than a disjunctive one. So Manicas's exercise:

Fertilizer or rain increases growth,

which his answer key represents by 'p ∨ q' would on its natural reading be better represented by the form 'p ∧ q', although it might be expressed equivalently by the sentence 'Fertilizer increases growth, or rain increases growth' which nevertheless is not a disjunction, but merely an expression of alternative ways in which growth is increased. The question that arises and is presumably to be answered in the affirmative is the question whether a combination of rain and fertilizer does or does not increase growth. The 'but not both' qualification is not the exclusive property of disjunction.

There is a further observation that, since it is made in a textbook, may be mentioned here but discussed later. It is raised by McCawley and applies to Ambrosian and Lazerowitzian menus presenting the alternatives of tea, coffee, or milk, though the details of the application must remain for a time unclarified. McCawley's point depends upon the feature of exclusive disjunction discussed previously, that an n-term exclusive disjunction once disambiguated is true if and only if an odd number of its constituents are true:

> For example, *On the $1.25 lunch you can have french fries, boiled potato, or mashed potato* does not invite you to take one or three but not two of the alternatives: it simply invites you to take one. (1981, 78)

I restrict myself to one remark and one meta-remark. The remark is that if the menu entry contemplated by Ambrose and Lazerowitz is to be construed as a disjunction of some sort or other, then for the reason McCawley gives, it cannot be construed as an exclusive disjunction in the 0110 sense. The meta-remark is that the remark is otiose, since such an entry could not receive the reading that Ambrose and Lazerowitz require and be construed as a disjunction of any sort. We will postpone to a later discussion the rejection of some further ways in which McCawley's observation might be taken to apply to similar instances.

If we restrict ourselves to the alimentary examples cited, we may see that there are really three kinds of examples present, which, it may be, are properly thought of as one, but that might better be distinguished and separately considered. They are: (a) those of the general type:

> *With your meal (or 'for the price', etc.) you may have* A *or* B

and (b) those of the general type

> *With your meal (or 'for the price', etc.) you get* A *or* B

and (c) those of the general type

> A *or* B *is included in the price of the meal.*

The relationship between the first and the second is analogous to the relationship between 'I am willing to do A or B' and 'I will do A or B' on a non-predictive reading. Just as in this case, the author of the remark can be held to account for not doing A or B only under certain circumstances, outside of which he can reply 'Had I been asked, I would have', so the (b) author has not spoken falsely if the customer has neither A nor B. The fiduciary relationship between restaurant and diner is most succinctly expressed in the type (c) examples. A pie chart explaining where, proportionately, the price of the meal goes, would allocate a slice to an item which we might call the A-*or*-B-item. The general term 'A-or-B' comprehends two categories of things: A's and B's. The customer may choose which, but (so far as we know from what we have been told) the restaurant does not undertake to reduce the price if the customer takes neither. Now (a) type remarks with the modal 'may', are, as we have already remarked, most naturally read as a succession of permissions, or statements of permissibility. Offered in explanation of a menu entry or a policy, they tell the customer that he may have A *and* that he may have B. And again, although it does not tell him that he may have both, and perhaps pointedly refrains from so telling him, neither does it explicitly forbid his having both. The (a) type cases come under a more general class of 'puzzling' uses of 'or' introduced in the last chapter and to be considered again later. The (b) and (c) type cases represent a distinct though related category of uses, which will also recur in this work. For the moment let us call these last cases the *menu* 'or'. The coinage is intended to suggest a broader context that includes the use of the term 'menu' in computer interfaces, in particular, those screen menus in which the user is invited to move a highlight to a single item and press '⏎'.[12] The menu (the menu sections in the *restaurative* case) represents a stage of a generic procedure, a stage that may be occupied by any one of some array of items, and from among which the user or the diner must choose. Its properties distinguish it from 0110 in that it is of unfixed 'arity'; that is, it may combine without association any finite number of alternatives, and may be understood as having a quasi-quantificational sense, summed up by 'exactly one of'. Examples abound which are of the same general sort as the *if*-clause of Philip Marlowe's

If it's her neck or yours, she'll spill (Chandler 1942, 511)

or

If it's soup or salad, I'll have soup.

3.2.6 An observation for later reference

Authors of books about language, this author included, must use language to talk about language, so we may examine what they do as well as what they say. Here, gleaned from the textbooks, are three instances of a common use of 'or' that is not straightforwardly explainable as either an inclusive or an exclusive disjunctive use, namely the 'if . . . or if . . .' construction. Baum gives as a clear example of an inclusive disjunctive 'or', the one occurring in the sentence:

Tom dreamt about sex last night or Tom dreamt about food last night

---

12. The difference between menus in which a single item is highlighted and those in which any number can be highlighted may be regarded merely as a matter of expressive economy. An unrestricted screen could be replaced by one listing all sublists of a base list, and permitting only single-item selections.

and says of it:

> ... the above sentence is true either if Tom dreamt about sex last night, or
> if Tom dreamt about food last night, or if Tom dreamt about both last
> night. (1975, 160–161)

Hacking, giving what he takes to be an example of exclusive disjunction, asks
the reader to consider the statement

> Adam wants coffee or tea

and observes:

> Most people would expect Adam to be pleased if he got coffee or pleased
> if he got tea, but surprised, perhaps revolted, if he got both. (1972, 92)

Rescher, in the course of his claim that 'either . . . or___' has two senses,
himself uses 'either . . . or___' in what he can only regard as a third:

> ... it can be used in either an *inclusive* sense, represented by the phraseol-
> ogy "either . . . or___, or both," or an *exclusive* sense, represented by the
> phraseology "either . . . or___, but not both." (1964, 178)

Simco, justifying her rule for the truth conditions of inclusive disjunction,
observes:

> ... an inclusive disjunction of the form $p \vee q$ is true if p is true, or if q is
> true, or if both p and q are true. (1982, 7)[13]

It is simply a fact of language that the form 'A if B or if C or if D' has, as it
normally does, the reading as a succession of three conditionals: 'A if B; A if C;
A if D'. No truth-functional account of 'or' or 'if' provides a direct explanation
of this distributive phenomenon. An indirect explanation such as that it borrows
its meaning from the related form 'A if B or C or D' must meet the difficulties
raised elsewhere, namely, that its normal reading as a succession of conditionals
cannot be satisfactorily explained *on truth-functional grounds*, at least in the
same logical breath as the non-monotonicity[14] and non-contrapositivity[15] of the
conditional are more generally maintained.

3.3 A Historical Interlude: Boole's Rule

We have implied that the illusion of an exclusive disjunctive 'or' in English has
been reinforced, perhaps has arisen, from the presence in English of conjunctive

13. The rule does not, as she implies, follow from this fact, but only from this together with the fact
that it is not true otherwise.

14. To maintain that the conditional is non-monotonic is to deny that 'If B then C' can be inferred
from 'If A then C' together with 'A follows from B'; a favourite example notes that the conditional
'If you soak the match overnight and you strike it, it will light' does not follow from the conditional
'If you strike the match it will light'. Or consider the inference 'If Fred carries his passport, he will
be admitted without query; therefore if Fred carries his passport and wears only a false beard, he will
be admitted without query'.

15. The conditional contraposes iff 'If not-B, then not-A' follows from 'If A, then B'.

uses of 'or' to form explicitly distributive lists. In particular, one feature of such lists may well contribute to the *trompe-l'œil*, namely that such constructions fail, sometimes pointedly, to claim any additional undistributed sense. One fact of English that this points up is that expressions formed with 'and' no less than expressions formed with 'or' may be subject to questions about exclusivity. It may be a matter of interest to us that this fact was already well known to George Boole in 1847 and a matter for serious theoretical speculation.

> Speaking generally, the symbol + is the equivalent of the conjunctions "and", "or", and the symbol −, the equivalent of the preposition "except". Of the conjunctions "and" and "or", the former is usually employed when the collection to be described forms the subject, the latter when it forms the predicate, of a proposition. "The scholar and the man of the world desire happiness", may be taken as an illustration of one of these cases. "Things possessing utility are either productive of pleasure or preventive of pain", may exemplify the other. Now whenever an expression involving these particles presents itself in a primary proposition, it becomes very important to know whether the groups or classes separated in thought by them are intended to be quite distinct from each other and mutually exclusive, or not. Does the expression, "Scholars and men of the world" include or exclude those who are both? Does the expression "Either productive of pleasure or preventive of pain", include or exclude things which possess both these qualities? I apprehend that in strictness of meaning the conjunctions "and", "or", do possess the power of separation or exclusion here referred to; that the formula, "All x's are either y's or z's", rigorously interpreted, means "All x's are either y's but not z's or z's but not y's". But it must at the same time be admitted, that the "*jus et norma loquendi*" seems rather to favour an opposite interpretation. (1854, 55–56)

What may seem striking to the present-day reader of Boole is that he is free of the prejudice that unhesitatingly associates 'and' with intersections and 'or' with unions. It is tempting to say, with the benefit of hindsight, that he failed to see the analogy that led to later reforms of his work in accordance with De Morgan's principles of duality. It is true that the achievement of the comparative elegance of propositional logic required a fundamental redeployment of the basic constituents of Boole's representation. But Boole's approach was at least in this one respect closer to the unrefined data of natural language. His logical point of departure was nineteenth century syllogistic, and his linguistic focus was upon the representation of lists of general terms. It was from that conceptual raw material that he developed his algebra of classes, from which he then fashioned what we should regard now as the immediate ancestor of one standard semantic representation of propositions, namely, as classes of moments. The starting point of later theorists was of course the work that Boole had already done with the intriguing propositional portion of the work in place. From Boole's own vantage point, he could still see what it has grown more difficult for later logicians to regard as significant: that in the formation of lists in natural language 'and' and 'or' complement one another in what may be regarded as the same role. For our own purposes, we may restate the regularity which Boole is alleging here as

Boole's Rule

And-lists of general terms represent unions in the subject place; *or*-lists of general terms represent unions in the predicate place.

As a claim about distribution (in our sense rather than that of syllogistic), the effect of the rule may be seen in a restatement: *and*-lists of general terms are conjunctively distributive in the subject place; *or*-lists of general terms are disjunctively distributive in the predicate place. The rule can serve at best as a first rough approximation, or rather as a hint that there is a rule of some sort governing this or adjacent territory, even if this is not quite it. As we have seen, the presence of modals can make *or*-lists conjunctively distributive in the subject place as well. Recall Rescher's 'Physicians or the wives of physicians are eligible for membership.'

A distinguishable matter is Boole's preoccupation with the separative capacities of the conjunctive particles. His misgivings about the pervasive non-exclusive use of 'or' extended as well to those of 'and'. He insists: 'In strictness, the words "and," "or," interposed between the terms descriptive of two or more classes of objects, imply that these classes are quite distinct, so that no member of one is found in another'(32–33). Doubtless he has felt the oddness of such a sentence as 'Both cats and mammals have hearts' or 'The survivors were either women or humans' and the preference for the more natural 'Both cats and other mammals have hearts' and 'The survivors were either women or other humans'. In any case, he seems to regard as the more important fact that, as he claims, 'and' and 'or' have the power of separation or exclusion.[16] His insistence upon separation is really an insistence upon a preliminary preparation of natural language sentences as a part of their representation in his algebra: 'Remembering, however, that the symbol + does possess the separating power which has been the subject of discussion, we must resolve any disjunctive expression which may come before us into elements really separated in thought, then connect their respective expressions by the symbol +'. That is to say that the +, together with concatenation and − make it possible to make exclusiveness explicit, and the manipulations of the formalism require that classes explicitly constructed out of others be represented as unions of disjoint subclasses.

> And thus, according to the meaning implied, the expression, "Things which are either x's or y's," will have two different symbolic equivalents. If we mean "Things which are x's, but not y's, or y's but not x's." the expression will be
>
> $$x(1 - y) + y(1 - x).$$
>
> . . . If, however, we mean, "Things which are either x's, or, if not x's, then y's," the expression will be
>
> $$x + y(1 - x)$$

---

16. Boole's account is questionable. Whether the classes are intended to be disjoint from one another has to do with whether, in Boole's example, the speaker supposes that a true scholar could be a man of the world, not with the sense of 'and'. Post Wittgenstein it is difficult to support a view that a rigorous interpretation could be factually required and nevertheless opposed to normal usage.

This expresses the admissibility of things which are both x's and y's at the same time. It might more fully be expressed in the form

$$xy + x(1 - y) + y(1 - x)\}.$$

We have in this requirement yet another variation on an already varied theme. Boole's '+' is not in itself to be construed as a function that takes classes to the union of their differences. Rather it takes classes to unions of classes; it is the algebra that does not permit us to consider any but unions of disjoint sets.

Finally we must remark that, as Boole explicitly speaks of 'two or more classes', his conception of the relation that 'or' signifies when understood strictly cannot be understood as analogous to that of 0110 in any but the two element case. His representation of *or*- and *and*-lists of general terms and later his representation of propositional disjunction understands no fixed *arity*. Thus the class of x's, y's, z's is not represented by

$$z(1 - (x(1 - y) + y(1 - x))) + (x(1 - y) + y(1 - x))(1 - z)$$

which has the value 1 when exactly one of, or all of, x, y, and z do, but by

$$x(1 - y)(1 - z) + y(1 - x)(1 - z) + z(1 - x)(1 - y)$$

which has the value 1 exactly when exactly one of x, y, z does. The natural kinship of Boole's notion of exclusive disjunction is rather with what we have called the menu 'or' than with 0110.

Writing a quarter of a century earlier than Boole, Archbishop Whately, whom De Morgan would later refer to as 'the restorer of logical study in England' (Heath 1966, 237), had been quite clear that the question of exclusivity was a question about the disjuncts, and not about the meaning of 'or'. The following is taken from Whately's *Elements of Logic*, a standard English logic textbook of that earlier generation:

> Observe, that in these examples (as well as in most others) it is implied not only that one of the members (the categorical propositions) must be true, but that only one can be true; so that, in such cases, if one or more members are affirmed, the rest may be denied; (the members may then be called exclusive:) *e.g.* "it is summer, therefore it is neither spring, autumn, nor winter;" "either A is B, or C is D; but A is B, therefore C is not D." But this is by no means universally the case; *e.g.* "virtue tends to procure us either the esteem of mankind, or the favour of God": here both members are true, and consequently from one being affirmed we are not authorized to deny the other. Of course we are left to conjecture in each case, from the context, whether it is meant to be implied that the members are or are not "exclusive". (1834, 113–114)

If there was some original suggestion that has prompted so many reported urban sightings of 0110 disjunction, it is by now a little difficult to trace, but one feels that it cannot antedate the cataloguing of the sixteen binary truth-functions in the late nineteenth and early twentieth centuries. Nevertheless, there have been cognate exchanges about the nature of genuine disjunction among the major figures of British nineteenth century logic. Sir William Hamilton seems to have been among the early champions within the idiom of categorical logic, of the view that genuine disjunctions are necessarily exclusive, and John Stuart Mill, whose outlook was both more enlightened and more liberal, argued eloquently for the contrary position. Hamilton was alone in wishing to restrict disjunctions of categoricals to pairs having the same subject term, but assumed that the *form* of such propositions precluded that the predicate classes should have a non-empty intersection. In fact, he seems to have taken this as a proper expression of the Law of Excluded Middle. Mill claims that the restriction embodies an error of fact, though whether about the application of *Tertium non datur* or about the meaning of 'or', he does not make clear. In any case, as a counterindication of the theoretical usefulness of the stipulation he characteristically provides an ingenious argument whose validity both is indifferent to the restriction and cannot be demonstrated within a purely categorical logical theory.

> Very important consequences may sometimes be drawn from our knowledge that one or other of two perfectly compatible suppositions must be true. Suppose such an argument as this. To make an entirely unselfish use of despotic power a man must be either a saint or a philosopher; but saints and philosophers are rare; therefore those are rare, who make an entirely unselfish use of despotic power. The conclusion follows from the premises, and is of great practical importance. But does the disjunctive premise necessarily imply, or must it be construed as supposing, that the same person cannot be both a saint and a philosopher? Such a construction would be ridiculous. (1867, 409)

In the same passage Mill introduces his much cited counterexample to Hamilton's assumption that the disjunctive form denies the compatibility of its disjuncts: 'If we assert that a man who has acted in some particular way, must be either a knave or a fool, we by no means assert, or intend to assert, that he cannot be both'. Though undoubtedly telling equally against the myth of 0110 'or', it is important to bear in mind that Mill's criticisms were directed against an assumption within the tradition of categorical, not propositional logic. And as the debate proceeded into the early part of the twentieth century, it was not so much a debate about the meaning of 'or' (though respondents seemed sometimes to present it that way) as about the nature of disjunctive judgment. It was not purely a linguistic exchange, but rather one of those curious theological debates that arise from time to time among philosophers in which they argue about a technical term of earlier coinage, not with a view to uncovering the intentions of the coiner, but as though to discover some absolute meaning independent of actual use. In this case, it seems to have been assumed, on whatever evidence, that we are subject to disjunctive judgment, but recognized that we did not really know what that amounted to. Even that is a mild oversimplification, for the opponents of the exclusivist line frequently argued about the meaning of 'or'; it was the exclusivists, particularly the idealists, Bradley and Bosanquet, who stirred so many words into the metaphysical brew with such energy and to so little effect. And as it became clear in the course of the debate that intelligent colleagues seemed to persist in not admitting the exclusiveness, there crept into the language of the exclusivist party a hint that logic would replace an admittedly prevalent but imperfect conception of disjunction with one that their opponents of the moment would eventually recognize as superior. Bradley's reaction to Mill's example:

> When a speaker asserts that a given person is a fool or a rogue, he may not *mean* to deny that he is both. But having no interest in showing that he is both, being perfectly satisfied provided he is one, either *b* or *c*, the speaker has not the possibility *bc* in his mind. Ignoring it as irrelevant, he argues as if it did not exist. And thus he may practically be right in what he says, though formally his statement is downright false; for he has excluded the possibility *bc* (1922, 1: 121)

But his argument is one of metaphysical prudence:

> And it is not always safe to be slovenly . . . About the commonest mistake in metaphysics is the setting up of false alternatives. If we either admit *bc* as a predicate when *b* and *c* are discrepant, or exclude *bc* when *b* and *c* are compatible, we are liable to come to most false conclusions. (131–132)

And his own reconstruction flies in the face of the earlier formalist claim:

> It is false that the alternative "either rogue or fool" does never exclude the possibility of both. It is a common thing to make this mistake. When we try to guess a man's line of conduct, we first lay it down he is fool or rogue, and then afterwards, arguing that he is certainly a rogue, we conclude that his conduct will be deliberately selfish. But unfortunately the man has been a fool as well, and was not in any way to be relied on. It is often impossible to speak by the card, but still inaccuracy remains inaccuracy. And if we do not mention the alternative "or both," when held to our words we certainly exclude it. (132)

However unclear his actual argument, it is clear at least that Bradley is here talking principally about disjunctive judgments and only derivatively about the theoretical item defined by a truth table. And his points seem to rest upon the phenomenological distinctness of the disjuncts in relation to evidence and their use as grounds of subsequent deliberation. His own example seems to have us drawing, from the second disjunct, conclusions that require also the falsity of the first. Understood as an argument about truth conditions, the idea would seem to be that because we draw this conclusion, we must have rejected the first disjunction in opting for the second. And we want to object that this does not require that the original claim was really either rogue and not fool or fool and not rogue, only either (a) that our later assumption was really that he was a rogue and not a fool or (b) that our conclusion that his conduct would be deliberately selfish was insufficiently grounded. But Bradley's philosophical understanding of judgment is not reducible to the idea of the assignment of truth-value to a sentence, but is rather the placing of a proposition in a certain nexus of understanding. In the case in point, it is the acceptance of a disjunction as an explanation, and subsequently one of its disjuncts, on the same basis, as the ground of a set of assumptions. His being a rogue is one contemplated explanation; his being a fool is the other. The explanation according to which he is both is not contemplated. The acceptance of one alternative as the explanation would be wrong, that is, could lead to error if, as it turned out, it was really a combination of the two.

It is fair to say that, as between Mill and Boole on the one side, and Bradley and Bosanquet on the other, Mill and Boole came closer to the truth about the everyday use of 'or', but it would be wrong to see the tussle as about the answer to any question of which they shared a clear understanding. It was certainly not about whether ordinary language 'or' ever or usually or always requires 0110 representation. If Bradley was wrong, he was wrong on a much larger scale. In the philosophical sweepstakes, he was backing the wrong kind of horse; Ryle would perhaps say 'a tram horse'. Bradley does not stray so far from his own conception of disjunction as later writers do from theirs when he offers a conjunctive 'or' as an illustrative example:

> If, in drawing up a rule, I lay down that "the number of tickets being limited, each person shall be entitled to a red ticket or a white one," it is at once understood that the alternatives are incompatible. A ticket means here obviously one *at most*. But, if I say "No one shall be entitled to pass within this enclosure except the possessor of a white or red ticket," I should hardly be taken to exclude the man who was qualified by both. A ticket means here one *at least* . . . But in both cases "or" means exactly the same. In the second, as in the first, it is rigidly disjunctive. (132)

Bosanquet, who refers his readers to Bradley's discussion of Mill's example, as showing 'decisively that we never *really* mean to take into consideration under our judgment the conjunction of the alternatives specified in our "Either"——"or" ' (1911, 324) gives his own example, which indicates that his understanding of disjunction is not truth-conditional.

> 'To go by train you must have either a first, second, or third class ticket.' A man may of course buy all three, if he pleases; but the possession of them does not constitute a fourth case of liberty to go by the train. He goes by the train in virtue of one or other, though he may change carriages at every station if it amuses him. The conjunction of all three tickets forms no separate alternative as a particular way of going by train, and therefore is rightly disregarded in the disjunction. It is not indeed implied that 'If he has a first-class ticket he has not a second or third', but it is implied that 'If he goes in virtue of a first-class ticket he does not go in virtue of a second or third'. (324)

The present-day reader who has grown up with truth-conditional methods will detect here and in Bradley's discussion little more than a frustrating muddle. Certainly the question as to what unifies their examples is tricky and possibly unanswerable, since no sufficiently systematic theory has ever been born of their stirrings. But we can point to elements of a truth-functional account of disjunction that offer a parallel they might have accepted. In particular, Bosanquet's remark in the course of the discussion we have been citing, that 'any disjunction in which the alternatives are not reciprocally exclusive must of necessity fail to be exhaustive—the case in which any of them are conjoined being *casus omissi*' seems to suggest that we come close to illustrating his point if we contrast the perfect disjunctive normal form of '$\alpha \vee \beta$' with that of '$\alpha \veebar \beta$', that is,

$$(\alpha \wedge \beta) \vee (\alpha \wedge \neg\beta) \vee (\neg\alpha \wedge \beta)$$

with

$$(\alpha \land \neg\beta) \lor (\neg\alpha \land \beta)$$

respectively. Bearing in mind that $(\neg\alpha \land \beta)$ does not do justice to the notion of the judgment that β, and that $(\alpha \land \neg\beta)$ does not do justice to the notion of the judgment that α, both of these forms do provide representations having exclusive disjuncts. Under the assumption that 'or' is always to be understood exclusively, plainly an allegedly loose non-exclusive use of 'or', when set out as a collection of properly exclusive disjuncts, will always require an extra disjunct that is not explicitly mentioned in the original, and so is not exhaustive of the exclusive alternatives contemplated in the judgment it expresses.

The idealist account of disjunction can be and was criticized on its own terms. Its insistence upon exclusivity drew fire in *Mind* (from G.R.T. Ross) in 1903 as the complacence of later textbook writers would invite challenge in the same journal sixty-eight years on. One difference is perhaps that Bosanquet read Ross.

3.3.1 Myths of time

So entrancing is the myth that more recent writers claim to find it in theorists much earlier than Boole or Whately or think it remarkable when they do not. Consider G.H.R. Parkinson's account of Leibniz on the nature of propositions:

> It now remains to discuss what Leibniz says about the disjunctive proposi-
> tion—that is, about propositions of the form '*p* or *q*', where '*p*' and '*q*'
> stand for propositions. It is a commonplace of modern logic that the word
> 'or' and its equivalents can be used to join propositions in either of two
> ways, generally described as the 'exclusive' and 'non-exclusive' senses of
> 'or'. When 'or' has the non-exclusive sense, a proposition of the form '*p*
> or *q*' is true if at least one of the propositions '*p*' and '*q*' is true. If 'or' has
> the exclusive sense, then a proposition of the form '*p* or *q*' is true if one
> and one only of the propositions '*p*' and '*q*' is true. Leibniz does not show
> himself to be aware of this distinction, but the disjunction that he defines
> is clearly of the exclusive sort. This is the proposition, 'Either God is one
> or none', which he declares to be the same as 'If God is not none, he is
> one, and if God is not one, he is none'. Strictly, it is the second part only
> of this proposition which defines 'Either God is one or none'; the first part
> defines the equivalent proposition 'Either God is none or one'. (1965,
> 34–35)

It is unclear how the argument is to be parsed. On one reading, the weight of it seems to rest upon the incompatibility of the (understood) disjuncts: 'God is one' and 'God is none'. This, as we know, tells us nothing about the meaning of 'or'. If Leibniz's statement of the equivalence is taken at face value, then it conforms more or less exactly to a possible form of definition of non-exclusive disjunction. Again this tells us nothing, because we know nothing about the conception of the conditional that Leibniz had in mind, if in fact he had anything determinate in mind at all. Since on Leibniz's view the disjuncts are *necessarily* exhaustive, an argument parallel to the argument from their necessary disjointness to exclusive 'or' would invite us to some necessary 'if . . . then . . .' connection, and the 'or' would then be some intensional disjunction, whether exclusive or non-exclusive. It may be that the pleonastic character of the definition has suggested to Parkinson that Leibniz was striving for—even if he did not achieve—a definition of exclusive disjunction. But in fact Leibniz is merely following the practice of Joachim Jungius in explicating incomplete disjunction by providing a list of equipollent conditional forms. And the definition, taken at face value, does not support the view that he was striving to explicate any kind of exclusive disjunction. There is, as well, external evidence that this is so, for he gives what amounts to an equivalent definition elsewhere without the additional unnecessary clause:

> Demonstratur etiam ex his omnem propositionem aut veram aut falsam esse. Seu si L est non vera, est falsa.[17]

where the use of *seu* makes it reasonably clear that the second sentence is an explication of what the former sentence claims to have been proved. But, again, even if a case could be made that Leibniz had in mind some sort of exclusive disjunction, no more specific claim could be made than that he had in mind some notion of exclusive disjunction that coincides with 0110 disjunction in the two argument case.

So compelling is the illusion that the theory of truth-functions conjures, that historians who permit themselves may be mesmerized into attributing an understanding of 0110 disjunction to their predecessors even in the face of an exposition explicitly at odds with it. Thus Parkinson claims that Leibniz ought to have known of the distinction because Joachim Jungius did. But Jungius gives an account of *disjunctiva completa* and *disjunctiva incompleta* that, at length and in detail, exposes a quite different notion, and one without fixed arity: 'Disjunctiva in eo Copulatae similis est, quod et *pluribus quam duobus* membris constare potest, neque membra habet *ordine* differentia' (1957, 104) and one the truth of which requires that exactly one of its members be true: 'Ideo *Connexis aequipollet* non tantum ex uno membro sublato, reliquum, vel reliqua *potentibus*, sed etiam ex uno posito reliquum vel reliqua *tollentibus'* (104) His most detailed example illustrates both of these features:

> Item haec, *Rosa aut arbor est, aut herba, aut frutex,* aequipollet hisce *sex* connexis,
>
> > *Si rosa est arbor, neque frutex, neque herba est,*
> > *Si rosa est frutex, neque arbor, neque herba est,*
> > *Si rosa est herba, neque arbor, neque frutex est,*
> > *Si rosa non est arbor, vel frutex, vel herba est,*
> > *Si rosa non est frutex, vel arbor, vel herba est,*
> > *Si rosa non est herba, vel arbor, vel frutex est.* (104)

---

17. *Generales Inquisitiones de Analysi Notionum et Verifitatum* in Couturat 1966, 365.

Moreover, it is abundantly clear from his account that his understanding of complete disjunction is that it is constituted by a relationship among its disjuncts, which, in the two member case, is such that they can be neither simultaneously true nor simultaneously false. It is not the account of a logical form: '*Disjuncta Completa* est, cujus Affirmativa ita se habet, ut membra nec simul esse, nec simul non esse queant' (104). In fact, in the case of incomplete disjunction, one species, that of *tantùm ponens*, permits more than one or even all disjuncts to come to be true: vel etiam unum è pluribus necessariò esse significat, ita tamen ut permittat, utrumque vel omnia simul esse; (104) His example is of a doctor who tells a sick man that he will take his medicine or die, knowing that even if he takes the prescribed draught, he will eventually die. 'Ut si medicus dicat aegroto, *Aut bibes hunc haustum, aut morieris* . . . Scit enim Medicus, posse eum et bibere, et tamen mori.' The other, *tantùm tollens*, is such that its members cannot all be true, but they can all come to be false: 'membra non possunt simul esse, possunt tamen simul non esse'.[18] The relationship does not emerge solely, nor does it require representation, in indicative clauses. Among his examples of incomplete disjunction *tantùm ponens* is the imperative form,

$$\text{ἢ πίθι ἢ ἄπιθι}$$

with its Latin equivalent,

Aut bibe, aut abi.

(Drink or go away), and the participial form, *Vel pugnandum, vel cedendum.* Clearly, this is not an exposition of truth conditions for sentences corresponding to different senses of *aut*. When Jungius claims that *ambigua est omnis Disjunctiva, quia per easdem particulas, et* completè-disjunctiva *et utraque* Subdisjunctiva *effertur,* he is not claiming that the truth conditions are different on different occasions. Rather he is pointing out that, whether such a sentence is true or false, one cannot tell merely from the presence of *aut* or *vel* or ἢ, which of the several relationships holds between the items that it joins.

We owe to Peirce and Schroeder the important idea that Boole's operation + be permitted to replace Boole's derivative notion of disjunction as the union of relative complements, and although Boole's preoccupation with the exclusive conception of logical addition more probably arose from actuarial interests than from an immersion in logical traditions, this shedding of the exclusive understanding in favour of the non-exclusive has, for some authors, assumed the significance of a rite of passage, marking the emergence of a fundamentally transformed discipline. It is a curious thing, then, that anyone should see the difference between the older conception and the new as merely the difference between the adoption of one of the sixteen binary truth-functions as primitive rather than another, or as a difference in the sense of 'or' with which it is preoccupied. But so startling is the light of the new era that the former gloom may seem now so nearly impenetrable, and its denizens so confused that their doctrines, recast, become a colourful expository foil for our own. Thus, for

---

18. Ibid. His example: *Aut sedet Titius, aut ambulat*, potest enim etiam *jacère* vel *accumbere*, vel *stare*.

example, we find, 'Traditional logic books, from the *Port Royal Logic* down, have taken for granted that *either . . . or* meant *one and only one of the two.* In symbolic logic we have abandoned the tacit acceptance of this meaning' (Langer 1967, 348). But if we examine the account of disjunction in the *Port Royal Logic* we find an account different from that of twentieth century symbolic logic but also different from that of the *Logica Hamburgensis* of thirty years before. The conception of disjunction that Arnauld sets out there is one of opposing cases admitting no middle ground:

> *La vérité de ces propositions dépend de l'opposition nécessaire des parties, qui ne doivent point souffrir de milieu; mais, comme il faut qu'elles n'en puissent souffrir de tout pour être nécessairement vraies, il suffit qu'elles n'en souffrent point ordinairement pour être considerées comme moralement vraies. C'est pourquoi il est absolument vrai qu'une action faite avec jugement est bonne ou mauvaise, les théologiens faisent voir qu'il n'y en a point en particulier qui soit indifférente; mais quand on dit que les hommes ne se remuent que par l'intérêt ou par la crainte, cela n'est pas vrai absolument, puisqu'il y en a quelqu'uns qui ne se remuent ni par l'une, ni par l'autre de ces passions, mais par la considération de leur devoir; et ainsi, toute la vérité qui y peut être est que ce sont les deux ressorts qui remuent la plupart des hommes.* (Arnauld & Nicole 1662, 2d pt, Ch. IX)

It is clear that Arnauld's conception of disjunction is such that a disjunction is contradicted by a claim that denies the absence of a third possibility or middle ground.

> *Les propositions contradictoires aux disjonctives sont celles où on nie la verité de la disjonction; ce qu'on fait en Latin comme en toutes les autres propositions composées, en mettant la négation à la tête:* Non omnis actio est bona vel mala*; et en français:* Il n'est pas vrai que toute action soit bonne ou mauvaise. (Ch. IX)

Far from representing a doctrine about the meaning of 'or' (or *ou* or *aut* or *vel*), Arnauld's account of disjunction, like that of Jungius, is a doctrine about a kind of relationship. It has certain affinities with a relationship of opposition, but, if we may take Arnauld's account at face value, that relationship of opposition is itself to be understood as the exclusion of other possibilities. To be sure, Arnauld may have been confused or misled by the normal understanding of the contradictories, which would naturally have been taken to admit some third possibility. But there is no warrant in his account for an interpretation that attributes a particular meaning rather than a particular use to the French and Latin counterparts of 'or'.

3.3.2 A last gasp

The origins of the myth may lie rather in the manner in which modern first-order logic overwhelmed syllogistic than in the shift of paedagogic attention to the truth-functional idiom. The Fregean breakthrough consigned to relative obscurity more particular anti-syllogistic strategies taking form elsewhere along a broad front, among them that of Augustus De Morgan. De Morgan wanted to generalize the categorical form itself, to produce a syllogistic of abstract relation.

De Morgan saw, as many of the dominant logicians of his day could not, that the validity of syllogisms depended not so much upon the presence in premisses and conclusion of the particular copula verb 'is', as by its properties of symmetry and transitivity, properties that the copula shares with other relations.

> The word 'is,' which identifies, does not do its work because it identifies, except in so far as identification is a *transitive* and *convertible* notion. (1846, 80)

There was, he thought, no justification for the rather protestant notion of form under which, in his time, the logical establishment had been labouring.

> The only relations admitted into logic, down to the present time, are those which can be signified by *is* and denied by *is not*. All other relation is avoided by the dictum that it shall be of the form of thought to consider the related predicate as *the* predicate, and the judgment as a declaration or denial of identity between this and the related subject. (De Morgan 1862, 428)

Thus, the sentence '3 is greater than 2' is represented by a sentence that takes '3' as its subject, and 'things greater than 2' as its predicate. According to the prevailing conventions, even the equality ('A = B') of mathematics was considered to be material whereas its logical cousin, identity ('A is B') was taken to be formal. De Morgan saw the matter from a higher plane of abstraction. Taking as example the two syllogisms 'A = B, B = C, therefore A = C' and 'A is B, B is C, therefore A is C' (contemporary logicians would not happily have applied the term to both) he observes:

> What is the difference between the two syllogisms above? In the first case the mind acts through its sense of the transitiveness of '*equals*:' in the second, through its sense of the transitiveness of '*is*.' Transitiveness is the common form: the difference between *equality* and *identity* is the difference of matter. But the logician who hugs identity for its transitiveness, cannot hug transitiveness: let him learn abstraction. (79n)

The same convention that regarded all relation except that of identity as of matter rather than form was the more stultifying for having no clear foundation in theory or utility. The established logicians, in particular, Sir William Hamilton and his academic progeny had no explicitly articulated account of *form* other than the threadbare reach-me-down inherited from metaphysics. Mathematics, by contrast, had long since worn unselfconsciously essentially the concept of *form* now common to philosophical and mathematical logic. It was only these encounters with mathematics that brought philosophical logic to a fitting. Since the categorical forms of syllogistic were the only forms that philosophical logicians were equipped to recognize, their demonstration of the logical correctness of the former quoted schema, if it is *logically* correct, requires the extraction of its logical form. That demands a translation into properly categorical form. It must become: All A's are things identical to B's, All B's are things identical to C's; therefore all A's are things identical to C's. But in fact the resulting argument is not a valid syllogism since it has four terms rather than three: A's, things identical to B's, B's, and things identical to C's. But the argument is obviously a valid argument, whose validity ought to be demonstrable on the same terms as its nearly identical categorical counterpart. De Morgan's more abstract notion of form would comprehend both:

> I maintain that there is no purely and entirely *formal* proposition except this:—'There is the probability α that X is the relation L to Y.' Accordingly I hold that the copula is as much materialized when for L we read *identity*, as when for L we read *grandfather*. (218)

A system that did justice to the analysis of thought, De Morgan maintained, would encompass all combinations of relations in judgment and inference. It would embrace such arguments as 'A = B, B < C, therefore A < C', which depends upon the monotonicity of one relation along another, as well as those that depend upon transitivity, which is the monotonicity of a relation along itself. For illustration, compare the enthymematic force of the comment 'Any *fool* knows that' with that of '*Any* fool knows that', taking the italic as emphasis. Both express disgust at one's ignorance; one's knowing ought to have been inferable from one's intellectual capacities. But the second is the more insulting, since, although it mitigates culpability, it seems to do so through a suggested missing premiss to the effect that its audience is a fool. The former, the less insulting though less exculpating, suggests that one is a little better than a fool. The former is an enthymeme in the traditional syllogistic sense. But the latter is an enthymeme only in the broader De Morgan sense, since its formulation involves both the identity and the relation of comparative intellectual capacities. De Morgan's generalization would also allow for any argument that depends upon any inferentially significant relational property. In this much enlarged setting, the traditional syllogistic is seen to codify, howsoever adequately, only a particularistic fragment of the whole: 'the ordinary canons of syllogism do actually embrace *every* case in which one relation only is used, and that relation transitive and convertible' (215). De Morgan's proposed generalization might have provided the means of making clear the minimal demands of exclusive categorical disjunction upon the truth-functional disjunction of the new propositional idiom. If 'X or Y' names the union of two mutually exclusive and jointly exhaustive classes of objects, then of the two sentences 'a is an X' and 'a is a Y', assuming, of course, that a is the right kind of thing, exactly one will be true. But this can be explained as a consequence of a property of identity, as we see when we restate the two sentences as 'a is identical to some X' and 'a is identical to some Y'. If we think of identity as a relation, then we think of it as a relation that is the graph of the identity function. But not every relation is the graph of a function, and if R is not, then the two sentences 'a is R to some X' and 'a is R to some Y' will neither exclude one another nor exhaust a's possibilities: a may be a brother to a man and a brother to a woman, just as a may be an only child. In a logical idiom that does not restrict itself to categorical judgments, the insistence, for whatever philosophical purposes, upon exclusive classes of objects would not of itself require a corresponding insistence upon exclusive disjunction.

Whatever may have been the origins of the dogma, whether in Idealist or Boolean or earlier initiatives, its persistence seems to be attributable to the prevalence of confident theoretical assumptions which are almost certainly by-products of twentieth-century logic. One of them is the assumption that the semantics for the connective vocabulary of natural languages can and should be given truth-conditionally. Another is the assumption that, in particular, the literal or otherwise fundamental meanings of natural 'logical' vocabulary are those provided by the truth conditions of the connectives of classical propositional logic. The former assumption has persisted even among theorists who, like the relevantists and paraconsistentists, have wished to supplant classical logical methods; the latter has persisted even among those who, like Grice, are ready to accept that human speech is regulated by considerations other than conditions of truth and falsity. As I hope will become apparent in later chapters, a unified semantic account of *or*, and a uniform semantics of natural language connectives more generally must depend upon an abandonment of both assumptions.

4

The Puzzle about 'Or'

" . . . They're going to present a paper that may or may not reveal the truth about what happened to him."

Rawlings breathed heavily into my ear. "May or may not? And what might that be? Or not?" SARA PARETSKY

4.1 Conjunctive 'Or'

4.1.1 Introduction

In this chapter and the next we consider a puzzle about the word 'or' and some proposed solutions. The puzzle is the one introduced with the attempted examples of exclusive disjunction offered by the textbook authors. One of the solutions, the last, suggests a theory of the linguistic origins of disjunction, and of other logical vocabulary as well, and although we shall ultimately have reason to abandon the solution in such a narrow form, a broadened version of that theory is ultimately what this essay has to offer.

4.1.2 Disjunctive preferences

In *The Logic of Preference* (1963, 26), von Wright claims that 'disjunctive preferences are conjunctively distributive'. He rests this fundamental prohaeretic principle on linguistic facts of the following general sort. If someone claims

(0) I prefer shiitakes or truffles to morels or oysters,

then we can infer from this that he prefers shiitakes to morels *and* he prefers truffles to morels *and* he prefers shiitakes to oysters *and* he prefers truffles to oysters. If we symbolize the states characterized by his eating shiitakes, his eating truffles, his eating morels, and his eating oysters by p, q, r, and s, respectively, and the relational expression 'is preferred to' by P, we can, Von Wright would claim, represent this person's preference by the formula

$$((p \lor q) P (r \lor s)) \leftrightarrow ((p P r) \land (q P r) \land (p P r) \land (q P r)).$$

Von Wright's principle engenders puzzlement at two levels. We naturally recall theorems of propositional logic that bear a passing structural resemblance:

$$((p \lor q) \to r) \leftrightarrow ((p \to r) \land (q \to r))$$

and

$$\neg(p \lor q) \leftrightarrow (\neg p \land \neg q)$$

and that are also in accord with the way in which 'if . . . then . . .' and various negating devices behave in ordinary English:

(1) If you drop it or throw it, it will break

means roughly the same thing as

(1′) If you drop it, it will break and if you throw it, it will break.

And

(2) I won't drop it or throw it

means roughly the same thing as

(2′) I won't drop it and I won't throw it.

But in these cases, the explanation that we offer for the equivalences is a truth-functionally compositional one, cast in terms of the truth and falsity conditions for sentences composed with 'or', 'if . . . then . . .' and 'not'. In particular, we want to say, a sentence composed with 'or' will be false if and only if both component sentences are false, which explains the equivalence of (2) and (2′). Again, the truth of either of 'you drop it', 'you throw it' will make the *if*-clause of the conditional true, and so by the truth conditions for the conditional, it will make the *then*-clause true. The theorems of propositional logic are interpreted in such a way as to be provided with an analogous account. The contrast lies in the absence of any such compositional account of 'or' and the vocabulary of preference. Furthermore, the available truth-functional account seems to justify the intermediate recasting of (2) as

It is not the case that I will drop it or I will throw it

in which the 'or' joins sentences rather than verb phrases, while the recasting of 'shiitakes or truffles' as 'I eat shiitakes or I eat truffles' allows *P* to be treated as a propositional connective but gains no explanatory advantage. In short, in the standard propositional cases, our understanding of the behaviour of the English vocabulary and the propositional connectives can be given a truth-conditional basis. In the case of the preference statement and the distribution principle, the justification of the latter is only its accordance with the former; they have no common truth-conditional explanation. So the fundamental puzzle is this: Why should

(0) I prefer shiitakes or truffles to morels or oysters

mean

(0′) I prefer shiitakes to morels and truffles to morels and shiitakes to oysters and truffles to oysters?

4.1.3 Other examples

No sooner is the question registered than one sees that other examples seem to represent the same puzzling phenomenon. Why is the comparative construction

(3) Gloria is older than Chloë *or* Phoebe

taken to mean

(3′) Gloria is older than Chloë *and* Gloria is older than Phoebe

while the non-comparative construction

(4) Gloria is the sister of Chloë *or* Phoebe

is taken to mean

(4′) Gloria is the sister of Chloë *or* Gloria is the sister of Phoebe?

Why is the formula

(5) You may have tea *or* coffee

taken to mean

(5′) You may have tea *and* you may have coffee?

How do we explain the distributive difference between (3) and (4)? For that matter, how do we describe it? Since it seems to be the context $\lambda(\ )$ which makes the difference, it may be tempting to cite distributional rules for contexts. Accordingly, our notes will show that the rules for distributing the context 'a is heavier than ( )' as, for example, in

(6) Kimberley is heavier than Jack or Bob

are different from those for distributing 'a is related to ( )' as in

(7) Kimberley is related to Jack or Bob.

Whereas some relational expressions, the former among them, will be on the list of those conjunctively distributive over adjacent disjunctive lists, other relational expressions, 'a is related to ( )' among them, will turn up on the list of contexts disjunctively distributive over similar lists. Let us set this apart:

Some relational contexts are conjunctively distributive over *disjunctive* lists; other relational contexts are disjunctively distributive over *disjunctive* lists.

According to this description, some relational expressions have the one property and others have the other; the expression 'is preferred to' just happens to have the one it does. There are two difficulties with this formulation. The first is that having given it we are bound to explain why some relational expressions have this property and others do not. The distributive puzzle has merely been displaced. The second is that we should have to justify the assumption that every list formed with 'or' is a *disjunctive* list. This would prove difficult since we would have only its distributive properties and the presence of 'or' to go by. Where the list is conjunctively distributive, we have only the presence of 'or'. In this an or-list differs fundamentally from a propositional disjunction. In the latter case, there is a reliable property independent of distribution to justify the label 'disjunctive', namely, the truth conditions of the sentence. Lists have no truth conditions.

A third, less vexing difficulty is that if conjunctive distribution over adjacent *or*-lists is a property of certain relational expressions, then it is a property that they sometimes have and sometimes do not. We can invent contexts in which the distributive properties of these relational expressions are other than what they would normally be. We can say, for example, 'Kimberley is heavier than either Jack or Bob but I can't remember which' or (somewhat less plausibly) 'Kimberley is related to *either* Jack or Bob; so if as you claim, any relative will do, it doesn't matter which you choose'. The fact that these sentences are acceptable English, however unliterary, shows that conjunctive distribution over adjacent *or*-lists is neither an inalienable feature of the relational expression 'is heavier than' nor an unattainable one for the expression 'is related to'.

4.1.4 Some suggestive connections

One consideration seems to indicate that at least as satisfactory an explanation can be got by regarding the distributive peculiarity of (6) as a result of a special, idiomatic, conjunctive use of 'or'. It is that in contexts in which it is clear that the two referred to are Jack and Bob, we can say, instead of (6), 'Kimberley is heavier than either of them'. In affirmative contexts at least we could not, without a change of sense, say 'Kimberley is related to either of them' rather than (7). The fact that the sentence 'Kimberley is ***** *** either of them' means the same as 'Kimberley is ***** *** Jack and Kimberley is ***** *** Bob', whether we substitute 'related to' or 'heavier than', and this in spite of the fact that 'Kimberley is related to Jack or Bob' would not normally receive this reading, suggests that the equivalence in the second is a consequence of the presence of the expression 'either of them' rather than of the presence of the expression 'is heavier than'. This in turn prompts a new description of the distributive puzzle, at least for *or*-lists that are two items long:

> In some contexts an *or*-list 'a or a'' has a grammatical significance akin to the grammatical significance of expressions of the form 'either A' while in others it does not.

Considered in isolation, this fact suggests that it is misleading to describe the discrepancy as a difference in rules for the distribution of different relational expressions over adjacent *disjunctive* lists. In effect, it suggests quite a different picture: sometimes *or*-lists are disjunctive in sense, and other times not. Let us restate the puzzle at once in more neutral terms that do not restrict us to lists of two items:

> For some relational expressions, adjacent *or*-lists are usually disjunctively distributive; for other relational expressions, *or*-lists are conjunctively distributive.

Remembering that not only the relational expressions 'is heavier than' and 'is related to' are distributive over the list expressions in these sentences but also the whole of the remainder of each sentence, we can state the facts of the case using the 'λ' notation introduced earlier:

> Some sentences representable as '$\lambda(a_1$ or a_2 or . . .)' are taken to be equivalent to sentences of the form '$\underline{\lambda}(a_1)$ or $\lambda(a_2)$ or . . .', others as e-quivalent to sentences of the form '$\underline{\lambda}(a_1)$ and $\underline{\lambda}(a_2)$ and . . .'.

The redescription represents a major shift of perspective. In its original statement, as a difference in the distributive properties of different relational expressions, it is difficult to see what sort of explanation can be given of this distributional discrepancy. Restated as a difference in the distributive properties of *or*-lists, we can ask why it should be necessary that in some contexts an *or*-list be conjunctively distributive? Why is there a need for (which may just be to say 'why should there have come to be') a conjunctively distributive *or*-list in the context 'Kimberley is heavier than ( )'? Is there a need?

The context 'Kimberley is heavier than ( )' and the context 'Kimberley is related to ( )' differ in this respect: when a list of the form 'a_1 and a_2' occurs in the context 'Kimberley is related to ( )', it is not possible to construe the resulting sentence other than as being equivalent to the conjunction of 'Kimberley is related to a_1' and 'Kimberley is related to a_2'. However, when an *and*-list occurs in the context 'Kimberley is heavier than ( )', this could be construed as meaning something like 'Kimberley's weight exceeds the combined weights of a_1 and a_2'. Although this last implies that Kimberley is heavier than a_1 and Kimberley is heavier than a_2, the two are clearly not equivalent. Kimberley's weight can exceed that of a_1 and that of a_2 without exceeding the combined weight of a_1 and a_2. Using the terminology introduced in the previous chapter, in the context 'Kimberley is heavier than ( )', an *and*-list could be interpreted as having an undistributed sense, although the logic of the relational expression 'is heavier than' precludes an interpretation of the *and*-list as being undistributive. But the distributive properties are not just consequences of the essential mathematical properties of comparative weightiness. Rather, the properties of comparative weightiness sometimes require us to frame a sentence about this property in such a way as to force the reading that we want. Sometimes they do not. For example, although an *and*-list 'a_1 and a_2' occurring in the context '( ) are heavier than a_3,' *could* receive an undistributive reading, here the number of the verb countervails, making the undistributive interpretation uncertain in the absence of other reinforcing contextual clues. To settle the reading in some contexts, we may have recourse to some such device as 'taken together' or 'severally'. Nevertheless, the difference between the list-centred description and the context-centred description of distribution is evident in this example. The latter finds relevant explanatory data for some failures of conjunctive distribution over *and*-lists but not for conjunctive distributions over *or*-lists.

The distributive asymmetry of *and*- and *or*-lists is roughly paralleled by an asymmetry between 'both' and 'either' constructions. Contrast the pair

(8) Kimberley is heavier than both of them
(9) Kimberley is heavier than either of them

with the pair

(10) Kimberley is related to both of them
(11) Kimberley is related to either of them.

In (8) 'both of them' is capable of a combinative reading; 'either of them' in (9) is not. Both (8) and (9) are idiomatically unexceptionable. But neither (10) nor (11) is capable of a combinative reading. Then again, (11) is idiomatically suspect in simple declarative use.

4.2 Attempted Solutions

4.2.1 A prod tentative

All of this suggests some lines along which a solution to the puzzle about conjunctively distributive *or*-lists might be sketched. It suggests that there is a connection between (a) the possibility of an undistributive reading of *and*-lists or a reading that attributes an undistributed sense and (b) the conjunctive distributivity of a substituted *or*-list in that context. Without supposing that we have thereby satisfactorily said what the connection is, much less that we have explained its broader significance, we may venture an initial tentative prod at the puzzle. It will be unsatisfactory to say simply that the conjunctive distributivity of *or*-lists in certain sorts of contexts has evolved as a means of precluding misinterpretations, even though the possibility of error in some cases may make it seem highly desirable that there should be some essentially—or at least explicitly—distributive construction for such contexts. 'Evolved how?' one will ask, 'and from what?' Nevertheless, if in some contexts the *and*-list has a natural reading as undistributive or has undistributed sense, and in these contexts an *or*-list is, as a matter of idiom, normally understood as conjunctively distributive, then it is a reasonable conclusion that the function of the conjunctively distributive *or*-list and, one may therefore assume, at least the reason for its retention in the language, is this:

> The conjunctively distributive *or*-list provides a conjunctively distributive list that is not *capable* of an undistributive reading or a reading that attributes to it an undistributed sense.

According to such an account, in contexts where no such explicitly distributive construction is required, since *and*-lists there are conjunctively distributive, *or*-lists retain their disjunctively distributive reading. Thus for example, the context

'Kimberley is related to ( )' is not a context in which an *and*-list could be interpreted as being undistributive or as having undistributed sense, so (this account
would let us infer) this is a context in which a special distributive conjunctive
construction is not required; accordingly, in this context an *or*-list normally
receives a disjunctively distributive reading.

4.2.2 Preferences again

The relational expression 'is preferred to' is such that in the context '( ) is
preferred to a_3' and in the context 'a_3 is preferred to ( )', an *and*-list would
normally be interpreted as being undistributive. A person who prefers bread and
butter to dry rolls probably does not prefer butter to dry rolls. Likewise, one can
prefer dry rolls to bread and butter without preferring dry rolls to bread.
Therefore, according to the account, expressions of preference represent a
context in which an explicitly conjunctively distributive construction is required
or, if one prefers, one that is conjunctive in effect rather than combinative. *Or*-
lists provide such a construction. Hence, 'a_1 or a_2 is preferred to a_3' means 'a_1 is
preferred to a_3 and a_2 is preferred to a_3'.

On such an account, the fact that the preference can be recast in a form that
makes its verb phrases explicit *in whole sentential clauses* is irrelevant to the explanation of its distributive behaviour. The representability of preference as a
propositional attitude is only indirectly relevant to its distribution over 'or'. But
the requirement that verb phrases be understood or that verb phrases are an
essential ingredient of our understanding of preferences makes combinative
preferences expected and renders *and*-lists in statements of preference especially
susceptible to combinative readings. In fact, preference statements are, precisely
because of their implicit verb phrases, more plausible examples than the more
vivid but fanciful illustrations involving combined weights. The combinative understanding of an expressed preference for beer and sausages to tea and
sandwiches does not understand the preference as of one appalling pottage to
another, but rather of one complex activity to another, of drinking beer and
eating sausage to drinking tea and eating sandwiches.

4.2.3 Some pitfalls

We have already made the point that to look for a simple causal relationship
between the presence in the language of contexts in which *and*-lists are undistributive and the presence of conjunctively distributive *or*-lists would be
naïve given even as much as is known about the development of language. Quite
apart from the fact that the origins of such idiomatic constructions are usually
very distant, they are seldom if ever the result of individual or collective
decision. Explanations are therefore unlikely to take the form of reasons for the
coming into being of a construction. They are more likely to resemble evolutionary accounts; that is, they will take the form of reasons for the survival of
particular forms of speech and will be couched in the language of opportunism
and advantage. In general, it is surmised, when pairs of constructions survive in
language despite the fact that they sometimes have the same function, the reason
why they survive is that sometimes, as well, their functions are different.

Whatever explanation for the presence of conjunctively distributive *or*-lists we find in the suggested direction, it is likely to be an explanation along evolutionary lines. In the history of language as in the history of life forms, we may take it as a rule of thumb that it is wrong to try to establish simple explanatorily useful connections between abstracted synchronous forms; this is the stuff of design theories. Rather, one must choose as large a synchronous diversity as possible and look for a diachronic account that sees its parts evolving dynamically in relatively minute mutual reactions to local variations. No more can a reliably detailed story be reconstructed for human language than for the population of earthly life forms. But, again as a rule of thumb, we can be guided in the sort of hypotheses that we venture by the thought that whatever large-scale account we give must be consistent with the fact of some such underlying developments, as well as with such flimsy historical evidence as can be brought to bear.

Now, this essay is intended as a philosophical investigation rather than as an exercise in philology. The aim is to provide an account of the behaviour of 'or' in English and its relationship to the ∨ of propositional logic, as a means to a better understanding of both and as a vantage point from which to view more broadly the relationship between discourse and logic, reasoning and inference, correctness and truth. But the subject matter, human language, must provide some sort of check upon what we say, and one's confidence in the authority of one's own tongue and ear must be tempered by others' opinions and informed by what others actually say and have said. So some of the evidence is philological and historical. Moreover, as the story that I am trying to tell is the story of the 'or' of logic as well as of English, the brief forays into philology and history are in part the philology and history of philosophy, and there are few philosophical works to which this is entirely alien. Logicians often know little and understand less of the history of their discipline than is expected of philosophers in general, and it is worthwhile to be reminded how at once difficult, illuminating, and suggestive the work of one's predecessors can be when not viewed merely as feeble scuttlings up the evolutionary mountain to one's own.

Much as a unified account is desirable, even a superficial historical investigation reveals that whatever unity there is arises from diverse sources in earlier forms of this and other languages, and the same forms out of which the present ones have evolved have also spawned others and stayed on themselves in generalized or specialized or ancillary functions. There is much to contend with and much to be considered at once.

This sort of account should not be regarded as invalidated by the failure of the correlations it adduces to be perfectly universal. The use of language is seldom an entirely unconscious activity. So knowledge or opinion about its workings affects the way that we use it and ultimately how it works. Theories intended to describe how language is have a tendency to find prescriptive applications and, though born false, may die true. After all, just to the extent that reasonableness can be taken as evidence of the actuality of a conjectured rule of usage, it can also provide a reason for the same rule's adoption. Apart from the influence of theory, the affected and frivolous illiteracies of one age or class become the solemn orthoepy of another. (Consider only the American pronunciation of 'herb', descendent of an affectation long forgotten in British speech.) We cannot tell to what extent the use of 'or' in the practice of English is shaped by what understanding or prejudice students have acquired from their logic instructors. (An attempt in the next chapter to counter what would have been misinformation propagated by authors of logic textbooks may already be too late, the misinformation having made itself true.) Finally, for all of these reasons, we cannot regard ourselves as well placed to dismiss, as illiterate usage, counterexamples to whatever theory we favour. If the corroboration of actual use is what we want for our theories of discourse, then, among competing theories we must accept the one that satisfactorily explains more data. So any failure of universality, even if ultimately it can be explained away, clearly requires some mention and clearly complicates whatever story we finally tell.

4.2.4 Some apparent counterexamples

Any theory that accounts for distributivity of *or*-lists by the distributivity of *and*-lists must account for, or at least acknowledge, both of the obvious kinds of counterexamples: (a) contexts in which an *and*-list is undistributive but in which an *or*-list would not be conjunctively distributive, and (b) contexts in which an *or*-list would be conjunctively distributive yet in which an *and*-list could not be undistributive. Consider the first sort first. There are contexts where an *and*-list is undistributive and an *or*-list is unlikely English, as for example after spatial 'between',

$$a_1 \text{ is between ( ).}$$

Or-lists are sometimes found as objects of non-spatial 'between' as in mixed or compressed constructions such as

He had to choose between Sinatra, Tony Bennett, Mel Tormé, Peggy Lee or Bobby Darin. (Wambaugh 1990, 46)

He couldn't decide between a chaise or a hammock. (129)

where the expected completion of the phrase is overridden by the desired indication of presented alternatives. Thus, presumably, are new idioms forged. But here the *or*-list, once admitted, must behave like the *and*-list that it has supplanted. Other contexts in which such a correlation could not hold are those in which what is predicated of 'a_1 and a_2' must apply uniquely to some one object or collection of objects, so that an *or*-list must distribute disjunctively, as, for example,

$$a_1 \text{ is wholly owned by ( ).}$$

By contrast, *or*-lists occurring adjacent to comparative adjectival or adverbial expressions are normally conjunctively distributive despite the fact that in many such contexts an *and*-list could not possibly be construed as being undistributive or as having an undistributed sense. The comparison

(12) Claudia is more considerate than Monica or Sophia

will be read as

(13) Claudia is more considerate than Monica and Claudia is more considerate than Sophia,

but the sentence

(14) Claudia is more considerate than Monica and Sophia

must look for some such reading as one assuming shared responsibilities and corporate considerateness, or must be taken for the same claim as that of (12). We might, of course, in an access of juvenile exuberance, find ourselves claiming that Claudia is more considerate than Monica and Sophia put together, but the force of this more rhapsodic version is usually just that she is *very much* more considerate than the others.[1] It does not mean, for example, that the acts of consideration of Monica and Sophia would map onto a paltry proper subset of those of Claudia. However we take it, it is the expression 'put together', not 'and', which bears the weight of the reading. In any case, in this context, an 'or' would make no sense at all. In sentences containing comparative adjectival or adverbial expressions, *or*-lists are idiomatically more secure than *and*-lists. If the explanation that we applied to earlier examples represented the whole and final story, we would expect *and*-lists to be idiomatic and distributive in comparisons and *or*-lists to be disjunctively distributive.

That there are exceptions to the rule does not, of course, establish that there is *no* connection of the sort that the rule adumbrates, at least between the presence of contexts for which *and*-lists are undistributive and the presence of conjunctively distributive *or*-lists. It may only be that the scope of the rule has been too optimistically predicted. After all, some of the counterexamples were contexts in which a conjunctively distributive list is not possible, so not required. If there is a connection, then the claim that this is so rests upon the presence of contexts in which *and*-lists are undistributive and which in addition require a conjunctively distributive construction, and the rule applies only to such contexts. It must be borne in mind that if there are distributive rules, they are not such as to guide a mechanical rearrangement of words, but the way in which an arrangement of words is to be understood. If we conceive of distributivity as a matter of the permissible rearrangements of the terms of a sentence, then a distributivity marker such as 'severally' would actually defeat its own purpose. The *and*-list of the sentence

(15) Jones and Repford are to be held severally responsible

for example, would have to be accounted undistributive since the sentence is not equivalent to

(16) Jones is to be held severally responsible and Repford is to be held severally responsible.

Again, the fact that *or*-lists are conjunctively distributive for contexts containing comparative adjectival or adverbial expressions where *and*-lists would not be construed as being undistributive or as having an undistributed sense does not disprove the claim. It need only be taken to indicate that the use

---

1. It may of course be an essay at literal irony. Compare 'You're better looking than the two of them put together' or 'You're nothing if not a man of wit'.

of *or*-lists as conjunctively distributive constructions has become generalized beyond need.

4.2.5 The grammaticological account

It is a view likely to appeal to logicians and to logically trained philosophers that comparisons, since they seem universally to distribute conjunctively over *or*-lists might contain implicit negative elements.[2] Thus a sentence of the form

> a is heavier than b

is equivalent to the sentence

> b is not as heavy as a.

On this view, the sentence

> a is heavier than b or c

could be translated into

> It is not the case that b or c is as heavy as a.

This sentence is equivalent to

> It is not the case that b is as heavy as a or c is as heavy as a,

which is equivalent to

> It is not the case that b is as heavy as a and it is not the case that c is as heavy as a,

which finally is equivalent to

> a is heavier than b and a is heavier than c.

Thus on the assumption that the comparative sentence contains a concealed negation, the conjunctive distribution over *or* is explained as the distribution of negation over a disjunction resulting from disjunctive distribution over an *or*-list.

The solution combines elements of what could be called the received grammatical and received logical views: (a) that sentences with *or*-lists are elliptical for sentences joined by 'or',[3] and (b) distribution of contexts over sentences

---

2. This seems to have occurred to Arthur Prior. In reply to the discussion in Jennings (1967), and the suggested solution, he counter-suggested (in conversation May 1967) the hidden presence of negation as a possible explanation of conjunctive 'or'. I replied with the examples given here.

3. This assumption, for coordinations more generally, may be found discussed and rejected in Dik 1968, 72ff. The assumption, which Dik calls the 'reduction postulate', is that 'any sentence containing a coordination could be transformationally derived from underlying "sentence"-structures not containing coordinations.' For a historical account, see chapter 6 of that work. We shall see ample evidence that the principle is false, but our own discussions of related topics lie at an oblique angle to Dik's.

joined by 'or' lies within the province of logic and, where possible, is to be explained by reference to standard interpretations of logical connectives, $\lor$ in combination with some others. In the schematic example we considered above, the other connective was negation, but it might be any other of the distributively right sort. When the other connective or connectives are truth-functional, the distribution will fit into the standard logical framework; when it is some non-truth-functional connective, the logician's task is to set out the principles that completely axiomatize it with respect to some plausible class of models, or otherwise remark upon its characteristic behaviour in relation to logical vocabulary already familiar. Let us call this approach the *grammaticological approach*. A grammaticological account of distribution over *or*-lists depends upon our being able to understand the list-containing sentence as a sentence-embedding sentence. Let us say that, on this approach, list-containing sentences are taken to be *sententially paraphrasable*. We can represent the moves supposed implicit in distribution with modifications of schemata introduced earlier. On the grammaticological approach, a sentence

$$\underline{\lambda}(a_1 \text{ or } a_2)$$

is sententially paraphrasable as a sentence having the structure

$$\mu(v(a_1 \text{ or } a_2))$$

where

$$v(a_1 \text{ or } a_2)$$

is the embedded sentence, and '$v(\ )$' is a context of the kind for which '$\underline{\lambda}(\ )$' was introduced; that is to say, a sequence of words that together with a suitable list will form a sentence, but it is, by the grammatical principle, a context understood to distribute disjunctively over *or*-lists. The '$\mu(\ )$' is a context of a different sort, forming a sentence when supplied with a sentence, which is to say that μ represents a sentence-forming operator that distributes conjunctively over propositional disjunction. Schematized, the transformation goes as follows:

$\underline{\lambda}(a_1 \text{ or } a_2)$	[original]
$\mu(v(a_1 \text{ or } a_2))$	[paraphrase]
$\mu(v(a_1) \lor v(a_2))$	[g-distribution
$\mu(v(a_1)) \land \mu(v(a_2))$	[l-distribution]
$\underline{\lambda}(a_1) \land \underline{\lambda}(a_2)$	[paraphrase]

(the 'g' standing for 'grammatical', and 'l' for 'logical'.) Some such representation will yield von Wright's distribution principle for preference, taking

a is preferred to b or c

as

It is not the case that b or c is liked as much as a.

The implicit verb phrases permit the sentential paraphrase, the result of which is represented as

It is not the case that its being the case that φb ∨ φ'c is liked as much as its being the case that zf″a.

Here we discover that the two-place sentential operator 'Its being the case that . . . is liked as much as its being the case that . . .' distributes disjunctively over a lefthand propositional disjunction. The result of this distribution is the negated disjunction:

It is not the case that
[(its being the case that φb is liked as much as its being the case that φ″a)
∨
(its being the case that φ'c is liked as much as its being the case that φ″a)].

By De Morgan's Law, we distribute the negative prefix over the disjunction to obtain:

[It is not the case that
(its being the case that φb is liked as much as its being the case that φ″a)]
∧
[It is not the case that
(its being the case that φ'c is liked as much as its being the case that φ″a)].

and so finally

Its being the case that φ″a is preferred to its being the case that φb
∧
Its being the case that φ″a is preferred to its being the case that φ'c.

Now it must not be assumed, because we have found a representation of the equivalence, that we have an account of it, that is, an explanation of the English equivalence represented, and for that matter we must not content ourselves with a representation that claims to *discover* distributive principles as problematic as the one we set out to represent. In this example, we have had to accept disjunctive distribution of 'Its being the case that . . . is liked as much as its being the case that . . .' over a lefthand propositional disjunction. What, apart from the desired outcome of the representation of preference, could be the justification for this claim? If we consult the normal reading of English sentences involving 'like as much as', we find that a sentence such as

(17) I like sleeping as much as eating or drinking

would normally receive the reading

(17') I like sleeping as much as eating and I like sleeping as much as drinking.

Had we set ourselves to provide a representation of that distributive characteristic by postulating an implicit negation, we would have been led to the 'discovery' of the disjunctive distribution of preference over disjunction.

Beyond the problems entailed by making implicit negations explicit, the grammaticological account faces difficulties with those explicit negations that, in some positions, make no difference to the distributivity of comparisons.

Just as

a is very much heavier than b or c

receives a conjunctive reading, so does the negative

a is no heavier than b or c

namely,

a is no heavier than b and a is no heavier than c.

A related difficulty with the concealed negation view is that it renders inexplicable the equivalence of comparative sentences containing *and*-lists to propositional conjunction in cases where the distributive correlation fails. However implausible is an undistributive interpretation of the sentence

(18) Claudia is more considerate than Monica and Sophia,

it is equally improbable that the sentence

Monica and Sophia are not as considerate as Sophia

would be read undistributively, for unless the context '( ) are as considerate as Sophia' can be shown not to distribute conjunctively over 'Monica and Sophia', the sentence as a whole will be equivalent to propositional disjunction. For these reasons, we cannot assume at this point that the grammaticological account postulating 'implicit negation' obviously provides any *ultimate* clues, but we must not too hastily reject the view that propositional logic has a place in an account of how conjunctively distributive *or*-lists historically come to us.

4.2.6 Analogical accounts

The search for a *unified* account of 'or', in this setting, amounts to finding an account that does not force us to postulate different meanings of 'or' in distributively different environments. To this end the sentential uses seem to provide a useful and worthy model. The illusion of unity persists even if in some cases the basis for choosing what distributive properties to assign a newly minted logical operation such as preference remains slightly mysterious. This is because, however logical operations distribute over disjunction, the intended *meaning* of ∨ remains constantly what is given by its truth condition, and in some instances, negations, *if*-clauses, and so on, seem to contribute to the explanation for the equivalence. So the temptation to treat every non-sentential use of 'or' as elliptical for a sentential use, and to explain conjunctive distribution by implicit negatives is understandable. Understandable too is the temptation to overlook the little difficulties that suggest an imperfect fit. The systematic character of distribution in those sentential cases, justified and explicable as it is by reference to the truth and falsity conditions of disjunction, might be thought to provide a different sort of explanation for the distributive character of *or*-lists. For the truth-conditionally explicable cases may have satisfied in some central cases just the kind of distributive correlation suggested earlier, and thus to have given rise to an idiom that only later became general beyond the explanatory capacities of truth-functionality.

Such an analogical account conceives the development of conjunctive 'or' in three stages: first, the truth-conditionally forced distributivity of propositional connectives; second, the surface correlation of non-distributive 'and' with conjunctively distributive 'or'; and third, the exploitation of this surface correlation in environments which sometimes require an agglomerative reading and sometimes a dispersive one. Certainly there are points of similarity between the logic of lists and the logic of propositions that give the idea of an idiom generalized from truth-functional cases a measure of plausibility but also illustrate the benefits of having an independent truth-functional account of 'or' for sentential cases. If distributivity were the sole determinant of disjunctivity construction, then, for example, we should have to put an inconsistent interpretation on ∨ in formulae of the form

$$(\alpha \vee \beta) \rightarrow (\gamma \vee \delta)$$

since this formula is equivalent to the formula

$$(\alpha \rightarrow (\gamma \vee \delta)) \wedge (\beta \rightarrow (\gamma \vee \delta)),$$

but from it we can derive only

$$((\alpha \vee \beta) \rightarrow \gamma) \vee ((\alpha \vee \beta) \rightarrow \delta)$$

and not the formula

$$((\alpha \vee \beta) \rightarrow \gamma) \wedge ((\alpha \vee \beta) \rightarrow \delta).$$

Again, the form

$$\neg(\alpha \vee \beta)$$

is logically equivalent to the form

$$\neg\alpha \wedge \neg\beta,$$

while the form

$$\neg(\alpha \wedge \beta)$$

does not imply

$$\neg\alpha \wedge \neg\beta.$$

Could we disregard the truth conditions for disjunction, then in view of the difference in distributional properties, we should have to say, although '$\gamma \vee \delta$' is a disjunctive expression, '$\alpha \vee \beta$' must represent a special conjunctive construction both when it occurs negated and when as an antecedent. Finally, consistency would demand that we introduce a new symbol to replace ∨ in these places and wherever anything is conjunctively distributive over it.

Notice that, except that the use is a sentential one, $\vee$ exhibits almost the kind of orderliness that seemed to suggest the *undistributive 'and'/conjunctively distributive 'or'* correlation earlier.

$$(\alpha \vee \beta) \rightarrow \gamma$$

is logically equivalent to

$$(\alpha \rightarrow \gamma) \wedge (\beta \rightarrow \gamma),$$

which is not implied by

$$(\alpha \wedge \beta) \rightarrow \gamma.$$

Then again,

$$\alpha \rightarrow (\beta \wedge \gamma)$$

is equivalent to

$$(\alpha \rightarrow \beta) \wedge (\alpha \rightarrow \gamma),$$

and (one may be tempted to say 'and so')

$$\alpha \rightarrow (\beta \vee \gamma)$$

is equivalent to

$$(\alpha \rightarrow \beta) \vee (\alpha \rightarrow \gamma).$$

There is, however, one dissimilarity, attributable to the truth-functional character of $\rightarrow$ and $\wedge$. This is that material implication distributes disjunctively over a conjunctive antecedent, and negation over conjunction. So while it is true that

$$(\alpha \wedge \beta) \rightarrow \gamma$$

is not equivalent to a conjunction of conditionals, it is equivalent to a disjunction, and this represents a disanalogy with the central cases of the list correlation. This in itself does not count against the analogical account, since disjunctive distribution over antecedent disjunction is not a property attributed by any but a few angry philosophers to the ordinary language 'if . . . then . . .', but we do take negative contexts to distribute disjunctively over 'and'. Again on the debit side, few take disjunctive distribution over consequent disjunction to be a property of 'if . . . then . . .' Consideration of these cases (*conjunctively distributive 'and'/ undistributive 'or'*) is deferred to a later chapter. Consider for the moment just those cases of 'or' in antecedents of conditionals. Here are cases where the correlation could gain a truth-functionally reliable purchase in a way describable along grammaticological lines. Back to Claudia, Monica, and Sophia (with parentheses marking the transformations):

(19) If (Claudia or Monica) accepts, then Sophia will refuse.

Here the ellipsis view works, and no hidden negative elements are required to obtain the desired result. Successively we obtain

(19′) If (Claudia accepts or Monica accepts), then Sophia will refuse

by the grammatically required distribution, and finally

(19″) (If Claudia accepts, then Sophia will refuse) and (if Monica accepts, then Sophia will refuse)

by the logically required distribution. And apart from the fact that negatives tend to distribute disjunctively over 'and', the case for negation fits tidily into the grammaticological framework:

It will not be accepted by (Claudia or Monica)

becomes

Not [(It will be accepted by Claudia) or (it will be accepted by Monica)]

and so

(It will not be accepted by Claudia) and (it will not be accepted by Monica).

It is just this sort of case, after all, that has suggested the grammaticological account.

The analogical account would assume that an unproblematic explanation can be given for these, and presumably for some other cases and that such cases represent the well-founded and paradigmatic core of the distributive idiom. However, the explanation of *these* equivalences, as distinct from the account of the logical equivalences of formulae, can depend only partly upon doctrines of truth conditions of conjunction and disjunction, and must depend for the rest upon the assumed properties of conditionals. Few suppose that the conditional of English is exactly the → of propositional logic. Falsity conditions of disjunction will explain the distribution of negation, but truth conditions alone will not explain the distribution of the conditional over antecedent disjunction. Consider how the argument would go.

(21) If Claudia accepts, then Claudia accepts or Monica accepts

and

(22) If Monica accepts, then Claudia accepts or Monica accepts

both by the truth conditions for disjunction. But now we must get from (21) and (19) to

(23) If Claudia accepts, then Sophia will refuse

and from (22) and (19) to

(24) If Monica accepts, then Sophia will refuse

and then from (23) and (24) to their conjunction (19″). How are the inference to (23) from (19) and (21) and the inference from (19) and (22) to (24) to be justified?[4] There are two natural answers: (a) by the transitivity of the conditional and (b) by left-downward monotonicity.

The property of being left-downward monotonic (LDM) may be defined for a binary function > as follows: > is LDM if and only if, from $\alpha > \beta$ and the provability of α from γ, we may infer $\gamma > \beta$. If we think of an LDM function more generally as one that is monotonic downward along some relation or other (in this case provability), we may think of transitivity as the property of being monotonic downward along itself ('along its own graph' to be more correct). Now there is not much to be said about either of these properties here, except that neither of them finds a secure place among the properties of conditionals that philosophers have recently tried to model. And whether there is some standard use of 'if . . . then . . .' constructions for which one or both of those properties is required is not an issue that can be definitively thrashed out here. Suffice it to say that the tense and mood of the *if*-clause and the *then*-clause make no relevant difference to the reading of such conditionals. 'If Claudia or Monica were to accept (had accepted), then Sophia would (would have) refuse (refused)' is read as equivalent to a conjunction. The relevance of these properties here is that they cannot be taken for granted as part of a justification for conjunctive distribution over a disjunctive antecedent. By contrast, conditional theorists regard *that* property, under the heading 'disjunctivity' or 'left-disjunctivity' as a separate issue. A conditional might be left-disjunctive; that is, it might satisfy

$$(\alpha \vee \beta > \gamma) \leftrightarrow ((\alpha > \gamma) \wedge (\beta > \gamma))$$

without more generally being LDM. Now the reason why *this* is of interest to us is that it prompts the question: when left-disjunctivity is adopted as the extent of the left-downward monotonicity of a conditional, what justification is there for its assumption? The answer might take two forms. The first is that the conditional satisfies some selection of other properties that taken together make it left-disjunctive as well. For example, suppose that > transposes, that is, satisfies:

$$(\alpha > \beta) \rightarrow (\neg\beta > \neg\alpha).$$

Suppose as well that '>' is right-upward monotonic (RUM), that is, satisfies the condition that if $\alpha > \beta$ and γ is provable from β, then $\alpha > \gamma$. Then it will also be left-disjunctive. We could argue as follows:

$\beta \vee \gamma > \delta$	[Assumption]
$\neg\delta > \neg(\beta \vee \gamma)$	[Transposition]
$\neg\delta > \neg\beta \wedge \neg\gamma$	[De Morgan]
$\neg\delta > \neg\beta$	[RUM]
$\beta > \delta$	[Transposition]
$\neg\delta > \neg\gamma$	[RUM]
$\gamma > \delta$	[Transposition]
$\beta > \delta \wedge \gamma > \delta$	[PL].

---

4. Or for that matter (21) and (22) themselves; we cannot take for granted that the conditional logic will have the principles required.

But transposition is another property disputed among conditional theorists who nevertheless accept left-disjunctivity. And in the face of the rejection of the principles of LDM and transposition, all that remains to suggest itself as an answer to the question is that the English conditional happens to have that property. If this is so, then there may be some point in thinking of the antecedent 'Claudia or Monica accepts' as elliptical for 'Claudia accepts or Monica accepts' since it is more conveniently represented propositionally, but the warrant for claiming that they are equivalent here is only the suspect one provided by the equivalence of the two conditionals distinguished by those antecedents; no explanation is facilitated by the ellipsis assumption for the equivalence of both conditionals to conjunction. In fact, apart from the evident fact that we sometimes want an *if*-clause to take a sentential filling, a conditional logic that rejects transitivity, left-downward monotonicity and transposition is in approximately the same position with respect to left-disjunctivity as the logic of preference is to the distribution principle. The justification for each property lies just in the analogy with the natural language case.

One final point about the 'or' of the antecedent 'Claudia or Monica accepts'. We have noted that the disjunctive distribution of '( ) accepts' takes us no forrader in explaining the equivalence of the conditional with conjunction, but a stronger point can be made. Recall the assumption that underlies both the grammaticological and the analogical accounts, that there is this important difference between *or*-lists and *or*-sentences: there can be no classification of lists as disjunctive independently of an understanding of what distribution is required, while for an *or*-sentence (that is, for a sentence consisting of two indicative sentences joined by 'or') the classification is a matter of its truth value, independently of how functions distribute over it. If this is accepted, then we can have no basis for taking the *if*-clause occurrence of 'Claudia or Monica' as a disjunctive list rather than as a conjunctive one or vice versa independently of having a basis for attributing a scope. (See Chapter 7.) The sense of the conditional requires that it be disjunctive with respect to '( ) accepts', and that it be conjunctive with respect to 'If ( ) accepts, then Sophia will refuse'. Of course none of this speaks with finality against an analogical account of the conjunctively distributive *or*-list; it merely shrinks the core of paradigmatic and independently explicable cases of the phenomenon. In particular, distribution of *if . . . then*-contexts over *if*-clause *or*-lists is not proved to be one of the cases upon which the analogical uses depend, but may itself be one to be explained by the analogy.

4.2.7 The quantificational account

Distinctions drawn by reference to lists of one sort or another have long been used to mark quantificational distinctions. Thus Geulincx:

> . . . *Omnis homo est doctus*; sensus enim est: *Et Petrus est doctus et Paulus est doctus etc.*
> . . . *Aliquis homo est doctus*; sensus enim est: *Vel Petrus est doctus vel Paulus est doctus etc.* (Land 1891, 216)

So it is a plausible tactic to try to dissolve the puzzle of conjunctively distributive *or*-lists by showing that the sentences containing them can be rewritten quantificationally with embedded disjunctions. So, as an example we rewrite

(0) I prefer shiitakes or truffles to morels or oysters

as:

(0′) I prefer anything which is a shiitake or a truffle to anything which is a morel or an oyster

and represent it as:

$$(x)(y)(Sx \lor Tx \rightarrow (My \lor Oy \rightarrow Pxy)),$$

which gives us, by standard first order derivation, the desired result:

$$(x)(y)(Sx \rightarrow (My \rightarrow Pxy))$$
$$\land (x)(y)(Sx \rightarrow (Oy \rightarrow Pxy))$$
$$\land (x)(y)(Tx \rightarrow (My \rightarrow Pxy))$$
$$\land (x)(y)(Tx \rightarrow (Oy \rightarrow Pxy)).$$

By a similar rewriting we may represent

(5) You may have tea *or* coffee

as

$$(x)(Tx \lor Cx \rightarrow Px)$$

which, again without mystery, gives

$$(x)(Tx \rightarrow Px) \land (x)(Cx \rightarrow Px),$$

understanding 'Tx' to mean 'x is an act of having tea' (perhaps 'having tea at this sitting') and so on. On the other hand, we may represent 'You had tea or coffee' by an existentially quantified formulation:

$$(\exists x)((Tx \lor Cx) \land Dx)$$

with 'Tx' understood as before, and 'Dx' as 'You did x'. Thus, the 'or' that behaves as we think logic tells us to expect is representable by ordinary disjunction, but so is the 'or' that seemed to behave conjunctively. In the event, each was behaving disjunctively after all; we had merely failed to notice the implicit universal quantifier.

I postpone discussion of the quantificational connection to chapter 6, where we shall see a close kinship between the central claim of the quantificational account and a principle first enunciated by Augustus De Morgan. For the moment I offer only an observation. The tactic, if it has removed the distributive puzzle, has put a quantificational puzzle in its place: why should some contexts–say comparisons–bear implicit universal quantification, while others bear only existential?

4.2.8 Lists of sentences

There are points of contact between sentential and list-forming uses of 'or' that further complicate the relationship between the logic of sentences and what we may perhaps by now call the logic of lists. The person who wants to classify the first ∨ of

$$(\alpha \lor \beta) \to (\gamma \lor \delta)$$

as conjunctive and the second ∨ as disjunctive may be made to seem not altogether mistaken, or at least the mistake may be made to seem not altogether unpardonable, by the reflection that → is sometimes spoken of as material implication rather than as the material conditional. Understanding it as implication, we expect the corresponding transitive verb to have noun-phrases in both subject and object places. Reading it as implication, one might fail to distinguish between the role of 'or' in " 'Either α or β' " understood as the name of a disjunction, and the role of 'or' in "Either 'α' or 'β' " understood as a list of (names of) sentences. The schema which when spoken sounds

Either α or β implies either γ or δ

(with α, β, γ and δ replaced by declarative sentences) can be understood either as

'Either α or β' implies 'either γ or δ'

or as

Either 'α' or 'β' implies either 'γ' or 'δ'

or as a combination of them. The one interprets 'or' as a sentential connective, and 'either α or β' as a disjunction; the latter interprets 'or' as a list punctuation and 'either "α" or "β"' as a list that is conjunctive or disjunctive depending upon how the rest of the sentence is to be distributed over it. The point can be made in terms of *that*-clauses. The first may be thought of as:

That α or β implies that γ or δ;

the second as

That α or that β implies that γ or that δ.

If the second is read cumbrously as equivalent to the conjunction of 'that α implies that γ or that δ' and 'that β implies that γ or that δ', then 'that α or that β' is understood as a conjunctive construction. But if the distributive idiom is as we have suggested previously, then in view of the fact that the sentence

Both 'α' and 'β' imply 'η'

would certainly be interpreted as being equivalent to

'α' implies 'η' and 'β' implies 'η',

the sentence

That α or that β implies that γ or that δ

could reasonably be read as equivalent to

(that α implies that γ or that δ) or (that β implies that γ or that δ).

In fact it requires little to nudge the interpretation in the disjunctive direction and a little emphasis on the subordinate occurrences of 'or' to obtain a conjunctive reading for each of the disjuncts, just as it takes little intonational effort to draw a conjunctive reading for the passive form

Either β or γ is implied by α

where 'β or γ' is read as the list ' "β" or "γ" '.

Some contemporary philosophers may bear the use/mention distinction next to their hearts so that, cilice-like, it is always in mind. But it is unlikely that it has played much of a role in shaping the idiomatic automatisms of ordinary discourse. And it is likely that at least much of the time in language, non-philosophers operate with conjunctive or disjunctive lists of sentences and not with conjunctions or disjunctions. In writing we can mark the difference between disjunctive proposition and *or*-list of propositions by the use of inverted commas or *that*-clauses. In speech, there is often no indication in what we are uttering whether they are to be taken as conjunctions or disjunctions rather than lists, and often no factual answer to the question as to which is intended. But since sentences understood as predications of listed things often stand in different equivalence relations from sentences understood as truth-functional constructions, we can sometimes find a reliable marker of the prevalence of operations with lists in the equivalences that we tend to accept, although not, by any means, in all cases. As we have seen, we might accept the equivalence of the sentence that when sounded (again with sentences for α, β and γ)

α or β implies γ

and the sentence that, when spoken, sounds

α implies γ and β implies γ,

does not indicate whether we are treating the expression

α or β

as a disjunctive propositional expression or as a conjunctively distributive *or*-list. The equivalence holds in either case. Furthermore, our acceptance of the equivalence between

α or β implies γ

and

$$\alpha \text{ implies } \gamma \text{ or } \beta \text{ implies } \gamma$$

does not indicate whether we are making the acceptable move of distributing 'implies γ' over a disjunctively distributive *or*-list or making the unacceptable claim that

$$\text{`}\alpha \text{ or } \beta\text{' implies `}\gamma\text{'}$$

is equivalent to

$$\text{`}\alpha\text{' implies `}\gamma\text{' or `}\beta\text{' implies `}\gamma\text{'.}$$

Usually, however, when we make a move ambiguously either unacceptable in the logic of propositions or acceptable in the logic of lists, there is a prima facie case that we are operating with lists of propositions rather than with junctive propositions. The insistence of some teachers of elementary logic that one sort of move is the correct one and the other mistaken results from a failure to recognize the possibility of non-propositional transformations of sentences containing propositional expressions. For example, the schema

$$((\alpha \vee \beta) \rightarrow \gamma)$$

is equivalent to the schema

$$(\alpha \rightarrow \gamma) \wedge (\beta \rightarrow \gamma).$$

But the natural reading for a sentence that, when spoken, sounds

$$\gamma \text{ is not implied by either } \alpha \text{ or } \beta$$

is

$$\gamma \text{ is not implied by } \alpha \text{ and } \gamma \text{ is not implied by } \beta.$$

This is because the spoken sentence is, in the absence of clues precluding this interpretation, naturally taken as meaning

$$\text{`}\gamma\text{' is not implied by either `}\alpha\text{' or `}\beta\text{',}$$

not as meaning

$$\text{`}\gamma\text{' is not implied by `either } \alpha \text{ or } \beta\text{'.}$$

On the one reading, this sentence has the form

$$\varphi \text{ is not true of } a_1 \text{ or } a_2,$$

which means

$$\varphi \text{ is not true of } a_1 \text{ and is not true of } a_2.$$

It is not essentially different from

What I said is not implied by what you said or what the chairman said.

The transformation here may well be partly a propositional one. It may be that an intermediate step resulting in the sentence

It is not the case that 'γ' is implied by 'α' or 'γ' is implied by 'β'

intervenes between the initial

'γ' is not implied by 'α' or 'β'

and the final

'γ' is not implied by 'α' and 'γ' is not implied by 'β'.

But the intermediate step depends upon taking 'α or β' as a list rather than as a disjunction. Similar considerations apply to the sentence that, when spoken, sounds

Either α or β is false.

It is at least equally natural to interpret it as equivalent to

Either 'α' is false or 'β' is false

as to interpret it as equivalent to

'α' is false and 'β' is false.

Fortunately for social concord, there is sufficient give in the fabric of speech for the use/mention distinction to be disregarded much of the time, and we may be confident that it has not preyed much upon the minds of our forebears, whether logicians or other. The purposes of post-Fregean logic probably were not theirs, and while we imagine that there was some orderliness in their speech we do not expect it to have that of *PL*. As it concerns the use of 'or' we have only begun to say what the character of that orderliness might have been.

All of the accounts that we have explicitly considered in this chapter have had two characteristics in common. First, they are all truth-conditional accounts; that is, they seek to explain conjunctive distribution over *or*-lists by giving an account of the truth conditions for the sentences in which the *or*-list occurs. Second, they all draw their explanatory resources from the syntax-cum-semantics paradigm of propositional and first-order logic, for they all require that we rewrite the sentence containing the *or*-list as a putatively equivalent sentence embedding propositional disjunction. On the assumption that the propositional idiom that they adopt is the classical one, it follows that whatever semantic treatment they prescribe will be one that preserves the representability of 'or' ultimately as a union of classes of semantic indices. We shall see neither of these characteristics survive the considerations of the following chapter.

4.3 The Larger Picture

4.3.1 Comparison and negation

The question of the involvement of negation in comparison has a long history in philology and was discussed at least as long ago as 1859 (in Pott 1859, cited by Small 1924). The origins of the connection are ancient. Thus Small:

> The adversative element in comparison is plainly recognized through an examination of the language of savage and primitive peoples, and by a study of the comparative syntax of the I-E. languages. Thus, in languages without a comparative form, *A is skilful, B not skilful* is equivalent to *A is more skilful than B*. This view of the idea of opposition in comparison is supported by the use of negation to express comparison in the I-E. languages and by the adversative nature of comparative particles. (1924, 15–16)

(Compare Crocodile Dundee's 'Call that a knife? *This* is a knife.') Suggestively, Small cites as representative of the early development of comparative constructions a sequence of examples from Greek, the first of which uses οὐκ, and the last of which uses ἤ:

> βέλτιον τοῦτο, οὐκ ἐκεῖνο (parataxis with adversative relation) = "*better this, not that*"
>
> βέλτιον τοῦτο, καὶ οὐκ ἐκεῖνο (copulative particle) = "*better this, and not that*"
>
> βέλτιον τοῦτο, ἀλλ' οὐκ ἐκεῖνο (adversative particle) = "*better this, but not that*"
>
> βέλτιον τοῦτο, ἤ ἐκεῖνο (disjunctive particle) = "*better this than that*" (17–18)

In English, some temporal comparatives have retained related uses and some have reverted to related uses in retirement. So we have

> Do it before I lose my temper,

which promotes doing it as an alternative to my eventual loss of temper, and does not imply that I will lose my temper after you do it, as does

> He did it before I lost my temper

and

> I did this rather than that,

which implies that I did this but did not do that. In the case of temporal comparatives particularly, there is a temptation to suppose that the explanation for conjunctive distribution over 'or' lies in an equivalent sentence-embedding form. Certainly we take from

> Do it before I lose my temper or call my brother

the promotion of doing something or other as an alternative to eventual outburst, and as alternative to eventual summoning of the bro. And in the genuinely temporal uses, the recasting is vindicated. If we model the sentence:

Morris crawled before he stood or walked

on its most likely reading, the model will locate some of the temporal indices of 'Morris crawls' in the portion of the model earlier than any of those of 'Morris stands or Morris walks', and thus before any of those of 'Morris stands' and before any of those of 'Morris walks'. So this reading takes that sentence to entail that Morris crawled before he stood and crawled before he walked. Except tacitly, the model does not invoke negation. It does locate some of one set of indices in the complement of the other, but it would do this even were the *before*-construction located in a negation-free language. Moreover, the corresponding model for

Morris crawled until he stood or walked

will also locate some of the temporal indices of 'Morris crawls' in the portion of the model earlier than any of those of 'Morris stands or Morris walks', and thus before any of those of 'Morris stands' and before any of those of 'Morris walks'. So the model for this sentence also tacitly invokes negation, but that fact grounds no conjunctive construal. Accordingly if we wish to argue that in the former, preclusive use of 'before' a conjunctive construal is invited by association with the temporal case, we need not construe ourselves as thereby finding a hidden negation. Again, thoroughly mixed and fanciful comparisons such as

Mary is cleverer than Sally is obtuse or Sandra is funny

defeat statement without whole sentences except by elliptical omission of the third occurrence of 'is', and we are not debarred from treating the *or*-compound as a propositional disjunction. We can indeed contrive a means of giving the disjunction a scalar value as a function of the scalar values of its disjuncts. We can rate Mary's cleverness, Sally's obtuseness, and Sandra's funniness all on a scale of 1 to 10. If we take the quoted sentence as claiming that Mary's cleverness is greater than either Sally's obtuseness or Sandra's funniness, we might model this as Mary's cleverness rating's exceeding the maximum of the other two. Clearly, if we merely transfer the ratings to the corresponding sentences, we can obtain the rating of the disjunction by a calculation compellingly analogous to the way in which we classically calculate truth values. The whole sentence can take the value of the excess of the lefthand sentence over the righthand, or the truth value 1 if the excess is greater than 0. Every such model generates an equivalent paratactic model: translate the scalar values to truth values, by mapping the maximum value to 1 and all others to 0, giving the comparison a truth value as a function of the classical values. That is, any such model making the comparison true generates a bivalent model for the corresponding paratactic version of the comparison (Mary is clever; Sally is not obtuse; Sandra is not funny). Such an approach cannot consistently calculate truth values for comparisons of opposite sense. It will yield the wrong value for

Mary is less clever than Sally is obtuse or Sandra is funny

unless the value of disjunctions is calculated differently, since this comparison, understood as claiming that Mary's cleverness is less than either Sally's obtuseness or Sandra's funniness, will require the lefthand sentence to have a value less than the minimum, not the maximum of the righthand members.

Gilles Fauconnier (1979) goes beyond the explanation of the conjunctively distributive 'or' in comparisons, 'a is φ-er than b or c', which locates the semantic representative of a φ's in the semantic representation of the negation of 'b is φ or c is φ'. He formulates a rule that abstracts from these cases the general negation-like property of implication-reversal, which he locates in the scalar semantic representation itself. Thus any comparative 'a is φ-er than b or c' implies the conjunction 'a is φ-er than b and a is φ-er than c' because 'b φ's' implies 'b φ's or c φ's'. Notably, so long as the semantics of the comparison is such that the *or*-construction is plausibly represented by a union of indices, the implication-reversal rule will work. Thus not only does the sentence 'Fred is up and about earlier than Jim or Harry' entail the sentence 'Fred is up and about earlier than Jim' on such a semantic account, but as well this last entails the sentence 'Fred is up and about earlier than Jim and Harry', and that essentially because the conjunction entails its conjuncts. But the consequence is an odd one in the general case. We do not want a semantic account according to which 'Fred *rises* earlier than Jim' entails 'Fred *rises* earlier than Jim and Harry' because this compares occasions, not intervals, and suggests that there is an occasion of Jim's and Harry's rising. That occasion may, to be sure, be represented as an intersection. But the semantics will have the sentence true if that intersection is empty. For comparison scales on which *or*-constructions are not plausibly represented by unions of positions on the scale, the implication-reversal rule will give incorrect implications. 'Fred is heavier than Jim and Harry', on this rule, should imply 'Fred is heavier than Jim and Harry and Milicent'. Moreover, even if the application of the rule is somehow restricted to comparisons with *or*-lists, the rule does not explain the *equivalence* of the comparison with conjunction.

It seems that, even in comparisons in which 'or' joins whole sentences and does not seem to form a list, the function of 'or' is to attract a conjunctively distributive reading rather than to form a disjunction. And, paralleling the case of *if*-clauses, a paraphrase listing *than*-clauses is always available that will attract a conjunctively distributive reading with the slightest nudge at the 'or':

> Mary is less clever than Sally is obtuse or than Sandra is funny.

So while we can devise ad hoc representations of such sentences as embedding disjunction, it is more natural to construe the 'or' other than as forming a disjunction.

4.3.2 Polarity construals: A preliminary mention

Linguists interested in formulating more far-reaching generalizations than any we shall have occasion to moot have, for good and ill, seen the conjunctive 'or' in a correspondingly broader context of similar linguistic phenomena. Polarity items are those expressions that are acceptable within the scope of negation-like elements, but in some measure suspect without, or vice versa. This simplicity of that formulation is deceptive. It suggests that there is a simple descriptive delineation of the class of negative polarity items and a correspondingly simple descriptive characterization of the class of positive polarity items. In fact, the tags reflect only an initial overly simple intuition, and happen to have survived its gradual refinement. The fundamental observation is that such items as 'ever' 'any' 'yet' seem to occur in clearly negative sentences that have no straightforwardly corresponding affirmative. Thus, for example, we do not form an acceptable affirmative from

George has not read any of the pamphlets

simply by dropping the 'not', and we do not form a satisfactory negation from

George has pretty well finished the pamphlets

by adding one. Other items, such as 'some', are acceptable inside or outside the scope of negations (though the former perhaps because of the influence of logical theory), but do not form contradictories straightforwardly by the addition of 'not'. Thus

George has not read some of the books,

formed by adding a 'not' to

George has read some of the books,

accedes more readily to a subcontrariety reading than to a contradiction reading. Others, notably intensifying adverbs such as 'very' and 'especially', behave variously depending upon whether they modify 'positive' or 'negative' adjectives. Thus

He is not very (especially) ill

means approximately

It's not true that he's very (especially) ill

and would not be said of someone who is known by speaker and hearer to be well, but

He isn't very well

suggests that the referent isn't well, and, said of someone known to be sick, would suggest that he is very unwell. But the items, which under this description would be called negative polarity items, can also occur in sentences without explicit negation as

George has read hardly any of the pamphlets

or

George has hardly read any of the pamphlets.

So the search for an adequate account is in part an attempt to formulate what counts, for this family of purposes, as being negation-like, that is, to formulate what it is about negation that it shares with other elements of language that it and they should trigger the use of 'any' 'ever' or conjunctively distributive 'or' or other negative polarity items. Fauconnier's implication-reversal has been one such mooted negation-like property. Even when an account has been given of 'negation-like' that accounts satisfactorily for the occurrences of negative-polarity items, in the presence of these negation-like elements, it remains to sort out which of these items are, like conjunctively distributive 'or', 'yet' and 'any', acceptable within the scope of modals (You may have any biscuit), and which, like 'ever', do not, and why.

Since our interest lies primarily in understanding how natural language 'or' gives rise to propositional disjunction, we shall not deal with the question of negative polarity in the sort of generality that linguists have attempted. An account that unified all such phenomena might be the more convincing for its very generality, but several observations suggest themselves. First, whether all of the phenomena that linguists have studied under this heading *should* be unified is something we might expect a theory to tell us. However, an account that *plausibly* unified the phenomena as they relate only to conjunctively distributive 'or' and 'any', but explained both those that have been considered under the heading of negative polarity items and those that have been labelled 'free choice' occurrences would be attractive. And if it did not apply to other items in the larger catalogue, that fact would in itself be suggestive. It might suggest a family of regularities, themselves unified by some higher-order account governing the nature of linguistic regularities themselves. Again, an account would gain explanatory power from being diachronically plausible even if not–and perhaps especially if not–synchronically completely general. Languages evolve, but they do not evolve by the simultaneous subversion of every instance of any regularity, but more likely by false analogies and by expanding the domain of local realizations of earlier larger-scale regularities in ways that then piecemeal subvert the original. Backformations are a simple example: 'pea', formed as the singular of the supposed plural 'peas' and 'pea' pluralized to give 'peas' as a now genuinely plural form (Jespersen 1949, ii, 144), 'escalate' from 'escalator', and so on. Finally, the insistence upon an explanation of conjunctively distributive 'or' which makes essential reference to negation-like triggers may still suggest to us that the correct explanation lies in the truth and falsity conditions of disjunction or in the semantic representation of 'or' as unions. An account that finds the origins of disjunction in part in these conjunctive uses of 'or' would be consonant with what we also know of the etymology of the word.

4.3.3 The place of negation

The inclination to find the explanation of conjunctively distributive 'or' in the distribution of propositional negation over propositional disjunction must be diminished by the observation that propositional negation is itself an invention and not primordial in natural language. The logical device of external negation taking whole propositions within its scope was a technical innovation of the Stoics or possibly the later Peripatetics. Like the Stoic notion of disjunction, it was foreign to normal Greek usage, as it was to the logic of Aristotle. Some philosophers may wish to argue that the introduction of propositional negation marked the discovery or recognition of a deep feature of human thought, but they will have to press this claim against the contrary claims of the facts of human language. Chief among these is one empirically demonstrable fact remarked by Horn (1989, 446), 'the extreme typological rarity of syntactic external negation':

> In natural language, negation is not a mechanism for forming compound propositions. Logicians treat negation as a propositional connective even though it does not connect propositions, but in constructing artificial languages one is free to do what one wants, and furthermore, in the kind of artificial languages acceptable within the orthodox conception of logic there is no choice. (Katz 1977, 238; cited by Horn 1989, 468)

I shall not rehearse the detailed arguments here, but rather refer the reader to the work of Dahl (1979) and Horn. It is sufficient for present purposes to add a parallel observation about 'or'. Disjunctive occurrences of 'or' as a sentential connective are, if not quite rare, at least not among the commonest uses of 'or' in spoken or written English.[5] When these facts are faced, the hope that some understanding of conjunctively distributive 'or' can be derived from a truth-conditionally based distribution of negation over propositional disjunction must seem forlorn.

---

5. As an example, in (Trollope 1864), there are over eight hundred occurrences of the word 'or'; of these only four are disjunctive occurrences between whole sentences.

Logic and Punctuation

... He goes on about the wailing and gnashing of teeth ... it is quite manifest to the reader that there is a certain pleasure in contemplating wailing and gnashing of teeth, or else it would not occur so often.　　　　　　　　BERTRAND RUSSELL

5.1　Natural logics

5.1.1　Introduction

I must say what is meant by 'logic' and by 'natural'. It is usual to make some or other distinction between a *formal axiomatic system* and the *logic* that it generates. A formal axiomatic system typically has three elements: a language, a set of axioms, and a set of rules. The language of the system is itself a triple consisting of a set of atomic sentences, a set of constants, and a recursively defined set of well-formed formulae (wffs). A formal axiomatic *propositional* system might have, as elements of its language, all p_i (i a natural number) for atomic sentences, the (primitive) constants $\neg$ (negation) and $\rightarrow$ (conditionalization) for constants, and for well-formed formulae, the smallest set that includes the set of atomic sentences (as primitive wffs) and is closed under negation and conditionalization. The axioms for a formal axiomatic propositional system would typically be a small set of wffs that will be primitive elements of the *logic*, and the rules, some closure conditions on the *logic* the system generates. Finally, the logic generated by the formal system would be the smallest set of wffs that includes the set of axioms and is closed under the rules. The elements of the logic are its theorems. Axioms are primitive theorems. This is what is meant here by 'logic', and in particular a propositional logic is one that can be specified in the way sketched. Strictly, I have been writing as though propositional logic could be assumed to be *classical* propositional logic. Nothing that I want to say actually requires this. Theorists disaffected with the classical account may well want to add $\land$ and $\lor$ as additional primitive constants. But I am assuming that, though they might not wish to do so, logicians of nonclassical persuasions could if they wished augment the vocabulary of classical propositional logic with connectives of their choosing. Their interest in doing so would be to produce a logic that in the sense intended here would be more natural than classical propositional logic. We must say what is intended by this usage.

Nothing in the presentation of a formal axiomatic system tells us explicitly what its connectives mean, though some authors may help along the presentation by suggesting informal readings for them. But to label $\neg$ as negation and $\rightarrow$ as conditionalization is already to give some hint of their intended interpretation and, if there is one, of the philosophical purpose of defining the formal system. The labels create an expectation that the connection $\neg$ has some connection with the standardized philosophical negator 'It is not the case that . . .' or with the various negating devices of real English, and that $\rightarrow$ can be rendered familiar by an association with English conditional forms, such as 'if . . . then . . .' or, had we instead labelled it 'implication', with the English verb 'implies'. A formal axiomatic system does, however, impose some or other notion of *proof* and gives, via that notion, some account of the inferential role that its constants can play. Generally speaking, an axiomatic system of classical propositional logic of the sort envisaged here will have a notion of proof according to which a proof of a wff α from an ensemble Σ of wffs is a finite sequence of wffs, the last of which is α and every member of which is either an element of Σ (i.e., a premiss), a substitution instance of an axiom, or justified by an application of *Modus Ponens* to two previous lines). The question must then arise whether the application of the labels can be justified by a comparison of the inferential role of the connectives in proofs on the one hand with the inferential character of the English vocabulary suggested by the labels, as revealed in the practices of intelligent speakers of English on the other. This question asked in relation to a particular connective of the logic is the question about the naturalness of the logic with respect to that connective. Thus we may ask of classical propositional logic whether it is a natural logic of the conditional or of implication or of negation. Some, at least, would answer no.

Our interest is then directed toward logics considered as codifications of classes of inferences, inferences the licence for which derives from the principles (axioms and rules) of the logic concerning particular of its constants, not necessarily considered in isolation from one another. What logics in particular?

A particular axiomatic system is typically obtained by enriching a propositional formal system and is labelled with this or that Hellenic tag according to the natural language vocabulary that its proper constants are intended to, or happen to suggest. Thus, for example, a modal system augments the set of propositional constants by the addition of the unary constant $\Box$ (necessitation). It is called 'alethic' or 'deontic' or 'epistemic' or 'doxastic' depending upon whether the axioms and rules that it also adds yield inferential characteristics suggestive of 'Necessarily . . .' or 'It ought to be that . . .' or 'So-and-so knows that . . .' or 'So-and-so believes that . . .' or some other English prefixable expression. In the case of von Wright's study of preference already cited, an axiomatic presentation would add the binary connective P. Von Wright has proposed the tag 'prohairetic' (from προαίρεσις = a choosing of one thing before another).

Thus we can ask, for example, of a particular alethic modal logic or deontic (modal) logic whether it is a natural modal or deontic logic, meaning by this whether the inferential properties of its $\Box$ as revealed in the proofs that it licenses are in accord with those of the English counterpart ('Necessarily . . .' or 'It ought to be that . . .' or 'It is obligatory that . . .') as revealed in ordinary inferential practice.

5.2 Natural Deontic Logic

5.2.1 Deontic systems

Deontic logicians are by no means unanimous about their point of formal departure: whether it is the language of 'ought' and 'may' or the language of 'obligation' and 'permissibility'. Many deontic logicians cheerfully treat the two kinds of language as one. Others, while avowedly representing *It ought to be the case that* . . . , seize upon the ready-made nominalizations of *obligations* and *permissions* rather than speak of *oughts*. Since the language of 'may' and 'ought' is the language in which we give permission and moral advice, while the language of 'obligation' and 'permission' is the language in which we allege moral facts, the distinction is a significant one for the study of discourse. But we will not dwell upon that distinction here, merely step over and around it. Again, deontic logic for some is just the study of modal logics lacking the principle [T]: $\Box p \to p$, and they expect none but suggestive or fanciful associations with ordinary normative discourse. Our interest here lies with the conception of deontic logic that admits as a constraint upon a formal system that it be guided by the appropriate usages of everyday discourse. But, although the distinction lies close to the bosom of this study, we need not much bother with the question whether deontic logic should merely formalize moral reasoning or, what is different, attempt to make explicit the inferential relationships inherent in natural normative discourse, or experimentally attempt constructions of deontic logics with semantics based upon historical ethical theories.

However the role of deontic logic is construed by its practitioners, there are two aspects of the enterprise about which questions of naturalness naturally arise: we may ask whether a formal deontic system in the theorems that it generates accurately reflects the central relationships among items of English deontic vocabulary, and we may ask of the same system whether its theses accurately reflect the behaviour of the same deontic vocabulary in relation to other logical vocabulary, 'and', 'or', 'if . . . then . . .' which we take the non-deontic constants of the system intuitively to represent. In the first of these interrogations, questions arise about the representation of relationships within the same deontic category. For example, we may ask whether the system is an attempt to illumine the inferential character of permissions construed as the grantings of permission, or among action-types within the category of the permissible. Are we, as we contemplate the wffs of the system, to have in mind typical instances of sentences such as 'a may do such-and-such' or of 'It is permissible for a to do such-and-such'? Does the system assume that these need not be distinguished? Does it merely ignore the distinctions? Of these questions we shall have something to say, since they are questions that distinguish kinds of deontic discourse. Second, and on this score we shall have less to say, it asks about the relationships among distinct deontic categories. Which deontic categories of obligation, permissibility, or prohibition are regarded as primitive? Which pairs are interdefinable? Here mainly the second genus of question will occupy our attention: questions about the relationship between the properly deontic and other logical vocabulary.

Concerning the first kind of question, it must be remarked that syntactically the relationship between the constants of deontic systems and the ordinary deontic vocabulary of English is not even as straightforward as that between $\rightarrow$ and 'if . . . then . . .' constructions, or between $\neg$ and the philosophers' 'It is not the case that . . .'. We do sometimes overhear, in philosophical exchanges, such sentences of the form 'It is not the case that a φ's, but it is the case that a ψ's', doubtless uttered in moments of fatigue or inattention, instead of 'a φ's but doesn't ψ, poor thing.' But we do not often find ourselves, or even our colleagues, muttering, 'It ought to be that this student is passed,' or 'It is obligatory that this student be passed', but more naturally, 'This student ought to be passed' or 'We are under an obligation to pass this student'. There is no very direct translation of the deontic $\square$ (or sometimes O) and English constructions involving 'ought' or 'obligatory'. The slightly weaker, but syntactically more manageable expressions such as 'It is fit that . . .' or 'It is proper that . . .' have not been considered. There is so far no *Cathecontic*[1] logic.

Then again, one of the insights that has lent deontic logic some of its appeal is its capacity to make explicit the supposed duality of deontic categories. Corresponding to the notion of deontic 'necessity' as represented by $\square$ is the notion of deontic 'possibility' represented by $\Diamond$ (or sometimes P), read 'It is permitted that . . .' or 'It is permissible that . . .'. Typically $\Diamond$ (P) is introduced as an abbreviation by the definition:

$$\Diamond\alpha =_{\text{df.}} \neg\square\neg\alpha \text{ (or } P\alpha =_{\text{df.}} \neg O\neg\alpha).$$

Or in a system in which $\Diamond$ (P) is the primitive modal connective, the connective $\square$ is introduced by the corresponding definition:

$$\square\alpha =_{\text{df.}} \neg\Diamond\neg\alpha \text{ (or } O\alpha =_{\text{df.}} \neg P\neg\alpha).$$

In either case, the equivalences $\Diamond\alpha \leftrightarrow \neg\square\neg\alpha$ and $\square\alpha \leftrightarrow \neg\Diamond\neg\alpha$ are important features of the standard systems. In what follows we will refer to them indifferently as the Duality Principle.

Reading '$\square\neg\alpha$' as 'It is forbidden that α', we obtain the not entirely implausible account of permissibility according to which what is permissible is what is not forbidden. The readings neglect the evident facts that permissions are sometimes occurrences and sometimes mere non-interferences, as forbiddings are sometimes occurrences and sometimes restrainings, and that 'permissible' means something more like 'worthy of being permitted', than like 'permitted'. As in the case of deontic necessities, deontic possibilities are more naturally expressed using infinitive phrases than using *that*-clauses. We tend even when merely formally asserting the permissibleness of some course (as distinct from giving permission) to use a construction such as:

It is permissible for Veronica to invite her family to the shearing

1. From τὰ καθήκοντα (that which is meet, fit, or proper).

or

Veronica is permitted to invite her family to the shearing

rather than one such as

It is permissible (or permitted that) Veronica invite her family to the shearing.

But we are more likely to say more simply (whether merely asserting permissibleness or actually granting permission):

Veronica may invite her family to the shearing.

The reading of the deontic wffs, requiring as it does the introduction of noun clauses where English prefers an infinitive phrase, makes detailing the demands of naturalness initially a little awkward, but it would seem a plausible requirement that a deontic logic that deserves to be called 'natural' must preserve in its proof theory usual features of the inferential practices of normal deontic vocabulary, whatever syntactic distortions the formal propositional idiom may dictate. On this score, the standard deontic logics are more or less natural in at least two respects: the distributivity of *obligatoriness* over *and*, and the duality of *obligatoriness* and *permissibleness*. In the main, to say that it is obligatory to do two things is to convey what we would convey by saying of each of them that is obligatory. This is reflected in the principle

$$[\text{K+}] \, \Box\alpha \wedge \Box\beta \leftrightarrow \Box(\alpha \wedge \beta).$$

Deontic logicians have denied one or the other or both halves of that equivalence.[2] The aggregation half (left to right) is troublesome to those who do not assume that obligations come from one source, and therefore wish to deny that when they are in conflict they yield a single impossible obligation. But it is not troublesome to those who accept what von Wright calls Bentham's Law, which precludes conflicting obligations, and when obligations are not in conflict there is little in ordinary moral discourse to distinguish one half of the equivalence from the other. It would be odd as an instance of moral direction to enjoin α and enjoin β but to deny having thereby enjoined $\alpha \wedge \beta$.

Again, we help ourselves to a variety of forms for the communication of permissions and prohibitions. To invite someone to feel under no obligation to refrain from doing something is to invite that person to feel free to do it, and thus to give someone leave to do it. Moreover, it is a liberal principle that what is not forbidden is permitted, where we understand what is forbidden to be just that which we are obligated not to do. This is the duality principle consequent upon one or the other of the definitions mentioned previously:

$$[\text{DP}] \, \Diamond\alpha \leftrightarrow \neg\Box\neg\alpha.$$

Taken together, [K+] and [DP] yield as a theorem of standard systems that $\Diamond$ distributes disjunctively over disjunction:

---

2. Schotch and Jennings (1981) discuss deontic logics with weakened aggregation. Van Fraassen (1972) restricts monotonicity more generally.

$$\Box\neg\alpha \wedge \Box\neg\beta \leftrightarrow \Box(\neg\alpha \wedge \neg\beta) \qquad \text{[K+]}$$
$$\neg\Diamond\neg\neg\alpha \wedge \neg\Diamond\neg\neg\beta \leftrightarrow \neg\Diamond\neg(\neg\alpha \wedge \neg\beta) \qquad \text{[DP]}$$
$$\Diamond\neg(\neg\alpha \wedge \neg\beta) \leftrightarrow \neg(\neg\Diamond\neg\neg\alpha \wedge \neg\Diamond\neg\neg\beta) \qquad \text{[PL]}$$
$$\Diamond(\alpha \vee \beta) \leftrightarrow \Diamond\alpha \vee \Diamond\beta \qquad \text{[PL]}$$

5.2.2 The first myth as a deontic puzzle

At this point, the claims of the logic textbooks should be recalled to mind. If it is right that the sentence

You may have tea or coffee

should be construed as an exclusive disjunction of assertions of permissibility, then a natural deontic logic whose propositional idiom dictates that that form be represented by

$$\Diamond(\alpha \vee \beta)$$

must have as a theorem the equivalence

$$\Diamond(\alpha \vee \beta) \leftrightarrow \Diamond\alpha \underline{\vee} \Diamond\beta.$$

But by the duality principle and propositional logic it will then also have the equivalence

$$\neg\Box\neg(\alpha \vee \beta) \leftrightarrow \neg(\Diamond\alpha \leftrightarrow \Diamond\beta)$$

and therefore the equivalence

$$\Box\neg(\alpha \vee \beta) \leftrightarrow (\Diamond\alpha \leftrightarrow \Diamond\beta)$$

which, by De Morgan's Principle, yields

$$\Box(\neg\alpha \wedge \neg\beta) \leftrightarrow (\Diamond\alpha \leftrightarrow \Diamond\beta)$$

which, by the Distribution Principle yields the equivalence

$$\Box\neg\alpha \wedge \Box\neg\beta \leftrightarrow (\Diamond\alpha \leftrightarrow \Diamond\beta).$$

But by propositional logic,

$$(\Diamond\alpha \wedge \Diamond\beta) \rightarrow (\Diamond\alpha \leftrightarrow \Diamond\beta).$$

Thus, we arrive at the implausible principle

$$\Diamond\alpha \wedge \Diamond\beta \rightarrow \Box\neg\alpha \wedge \Box\neg\beta,$$

which, by substituting α for β, and applying the Duality Principle, yields

$$\Diamond\alpha \rightarrow \neg\Diamond\alpha.$$

What is permitted is forbidden! The consequences are no less dramatic if we take the textbook claim to entail only the equivalence

$$\Diamond(\alpha \veebar \beta) \leftrightarrow \Diamond\alpha \veebar \Diamond\beta.$$

In this case we can argue:

$\Diamond\neg(\alpha \leftrightarrow \beta) \leftrightarrow \neg(\Diamond\alpha \leftrightarrow \Diamond\beta)$	[PL]
$\neg\Box(\alpha \leftrightarrow \beta) \leftrightarrow \neg(\Diamond\alpha \leftrightarrow \Diamond\beta)$	[DP]
$\Box(\alpha \leftrightarrow \beta) \leftrightarrow (\Diamond\alpha \leftrightarrow \Diamond\beta)$	[PL]
$(\Diamond\alpha \wedge \Diamond\beta) \rightarrow (\Diamond\alpha \leftrightarrow \Diamond\beta)$	[PL]
$(\Diamond\alpha \wedge \Diamond\beta) \rightarrow \Box(\alpha \leftrightarrow \beta)$	[PL]
$(\Diamond\alpha \wedge \Diamond\neg\alpha) \rightarrow \Box(\alpha \leftrightarrow \neg\alpha)$	($\neg\alpha$ for β)
$(\Diamond\alpha \wedge \Diamond\neg\alpha) \rightarrow \Box(\alpha \wedge \neg\alpha)$	[PL].

If any action is indifferent, then a contradiction is obligatory! We may, of course, now infer

$$(\Diamond\alpha \wedge \Diamond\neg\alpha) \rightarrow \Box\alpha \qquad\qquad \text{[DP] \& [PL]}.$$

What is indifferent is obligatory! In fact the textbook authors, in regarding such cases as

You may have tea or coffee

as unproblematically cases of exclusive disjunction, are at odds not only with plausible desiderata of standard deontic systems, but with those deontic logicians who have fixed upon the same class of examples as anomalously conjunctive (since at odds with [K+] and [DP]) and requiring to be represented in non-standard deontic systems. Von Wright summarizes the state of play:

> On a normal understanding of the word "or" in normative language, disjunctive permissions are *conjunctively*, and not *disjunctively* distributable. If someone is told that he may work *or* relax this would normally be understood to mean that he is permitted to work but also permitted to relax: it is up to him to *choose* between the two alternatives. Disjunctive permissions of this character I have called Free Choice Permissions. Opinions on their logical status differ considerably. Some logicians think that they only apparently conflict with the distribution law $P(p \vee q) \leftrightarrow Pp \vee Pq$. Another attitude is to reject, at this point, the analogy with modal logic and build a deontic logic which incorporates a distribution principle $P(p \vee q) \leftrightarrow Pp \& Pq$. (1981, 8–9)

Adopting the principle corresponding to the conjunctive interpretation

$$\text{[CD]} \quad \Diamond(\alpha \vee \beta) \leftrightarrow \Diamond\alpha \wedge \Diamond\beta$$

in the presence of [DP] and [K+] leads to the odd result that if anything is obligatory then everything is

(1) $\Diamond(\neg\alpha \vee \neg\beta) \leftrightarrow \Diamond\neg\alpha \& \Diamond\neg\beta$	[CD]
(2) $\neg\Box\neg(\neg\alpha \vee \neg\beta) \leftrightarrow \neg\Box\neg\neg\alpha \& \neg\Box\neg\neg\beta$	[DP]
(3) $\neg\Box(\alpha \wedge \beta) \leftrightarrow \neg\Box\alpha \wedge \neg\Box\beta$	[PL]
(4) $\Box(\alpha \wedge \beta) \leftrightarrow \neg(\neg\Box\alpha \wedge \neg\Box\beta)$	[PL]

(5) $\Box(\alpha \wedge \beta) \leftrightarrow \Box\alpha \vee \Box\beta$ [PL]
(6) $\Box\alpha \rightarrow \Box\alpha \vee \Box\beta$ [PL]
(7) $\Box\alpha \rightarrow \Box(\alpha \wedge \beta)$ [PL]
(8) $\Box(\alpha \wedge \beta) \rightarrow \Box\beta$ [K+]
(9) $\Box\alpha \rightarrow \Box\beta$ [PL].

It would seem that one or the other of the two points of contact with natural language must be relinquished. Either the *natural* equivalence of the two forms

A may φ x or y

and

A may φ x and A may φ y

or, as we see at step (5), the *natural* inequivalence of the forms

A ought to φ x and y

and

A ought to φ x or A ought to φ y

will not survive the formalization.

Faced with the choice, most deontic logicians have sensibly abandoned the natural equivalence in favour of the duality of 'ought' and 'may', a course which in the usual treatments gives the equivalence of

$$\Diamond(\alpha \vee \beta)$$

and

$$\Diamond\alpha \vee \Diamond\beta,$$

and the dual equivalence of

$$\Box(\alpha \wedge \beta)$$

and

$$\Box\alpha \wedge \Box\beta$$

that we have already noted. About these equivalences one may have doubts of another sort. They obliterate distinctions that we may well need to preserve. But that problem can be solved without resort to the radical alternative that rejects duality or makes everything obligatory if anything is. Nevertheless, here is a respect in which deontic logics are not natural. For none of our worries about [K+] or [DP] concerns cases where inconsistent obligations do not arise. Yet it seems that even for those unproblematic cases, either not all the equivalences or not all the inequivalences in the natural language of 'may' and 'ought' can be preserved into a reasonable formal deontic system.

Since von Wright's first introduction of the term, the phenomenon of the conjunctively distributive *or*-list has come in for a certain amount of discussion among deontic logicians under the heading of 'free choice permission'. Of the treatments on the subject of the behaviour of 'or' specifically in that context, that of Hans Kamp's 1973 Aristotelian Society presentation remains the most insightful and, perforce, radical. Kamp takes the subject one stage beyond approaches adhering to the syntax-cum-semantics paradigm of logical analysis, in that he rejects the notion that formulae for granting permission should be regarded as assertions: 'the very attempt to grasp the logical properties of permission statements by reducing them to assertions is misguided' (1974, 62). As we shall eventually see, in that sentiment, this account will agree with Kamp's. But possibly because he does not consider a broad enough range of similarly puzzling cases, his own proposed solution to the paradox of free choice permission preserves a conservative, essentially logical point of view.

> . . . As logicians have realized with regard to assertions for at least a century, 'or' stands essentially for set theoretic union: The set of possible situations in which a disjunctive assertion is true is the union of the sets of possible situations which realize its disjuncts.
>
> 'Or', I maintain, *always* stands for set theoretic union. Previously we could not see that it does have this function also in permission statements because we lacked the appropriate understanding of what permission statements *do*. And so we saw ourselves forced into the implausible and totally *ad hoc* doctrine, that in such statements 'or'—usually at least—plays the same role that 'and' plays in assertions. (1974, 65)[3]

We shall be in a better position at the end of this book to judge what relation the doctrine which Kamp rejects as 'implausible and totally *ad hoc*' bears to the general account of 'or' that I set out. But we shall see before that, that the general claim that 'or' always stands for set-theoretic union is not tenable even outside the realm of comparatives, where such a view can hardly stand. And we may observe immediately that Kamp's view that free choice permissions raise from prohibition the union of classes of not-otherwise-prohibited worlds, neglects the very feature of such formulae that misleads the textbook authors, namely that such formulae do not grant permission to do both the things that they severally permit. To be sure, Kamp admits that his account does not say enough to manage all the further complications ('You may do A or B, but I would prefer that you do A' and so on), but that feature is sufficiently general among the examples for it to be incredible that it has no role to play in the explanation of this use of 'or'.[4]

From our point of view, the discussions of free choice permission treat the deontic case too much in isolation from similar distributive phenomena in other deontic and non-deontic contexts. Even within the realm of deontic examples involving permission, the heading 'free choice permission' suggests an unduly narrow view of the puzzle. Conjunctive distribution occurs not only over *or*-

3. McCawley (1981) accepts Kamp's as the correct account of free choice permission, though his remarks about the Ambrose and Lazerowitz example suggest that he might wish to see 'set theoretic union' replaced by 'union minus intersections' in some cases.

4. See Makinson (1983) for a discussion at an oblique angle to Kamp's and a partial bibliography of earlier essays. Makinson considers the puzzle in quantificational terms.

compounds of actions, but over *or*-compounds of subjects as well. Thus the sentence

Fred or Bill may come

on its deontic reading would ordinarily be taken to mean

Fred may come and Bill may come,

and in this case as in the others, it is possible to inflect the sentence in such a way that permission is not given for both of them to come, and in any case, permission for both to come is not implied. It seems curious to call this a case of free choice permission, but the distribution nevertheless requires explanation.

5.2.3 'Or' in forbiddance

In any catalogue of divergences between the natural inferential characteristics of deontic language and the principles of deontic logic, others must appear that arise from the apparent inconsistencies within natural usage. Just as we naturally understand the permission formula

You may have tea or coffee

to mean

You may have tea and you may have coffee,

we naturally understand the forbiddance formula

You may not have tea or coffee

to mean

You may not have tea and you may not have coffee.

Obviously, we cannot have both of these facts of deontic usage reflected in equivalences in a well-behaved deontic propositional logic. The former would require

$$\Diamond(\alpha \vee \beta) \leftrightarrow \Diamond\alpha \wedge \Diamond\beta$$

and the latter:

$$\neg\Diamond(\alpha \vee \beta) \leftrightarrow \neg\Diamond\alpha \wedge \neg\Diamond\beta,$$

which, taken together, would give:

$$\neg(\Diamond\alpha \wedge \Diamond\beta) \leftrightarrow \neg\Diamond\alpha \wedge \neg\Diamond\beta$$

contrary to De Morgan's Theorem, but also contrary to another fact of deontic discourse, the one that the textbook writers have got right, the one that seems to have given rise to the exclusive disjunction story, namely, that actions jointly forbidden may be severally permissible. This is what the last equivalence would deny.

5.2.4 Preprocessing and compositionality

Deontic systems, whose authors almost invariably adopt a propositional idiom to replace the more natural infinitive phrase of deontic discourse, in effect preprocess deontic sentences of English by distributing a portion of the context of an *or*-list across the 'or'. Thus the representation of

a may φ or ψ

replaces the auxiliary 'may' by the deontic sentence-forming prefix 'It is permitted that . . .', and the noun phrase a is distributed across the *or*-list of verbs 'φ or ψ' to give the disjunction 'a φ's or a ψ's'. The resulting form:

It is permitted that a φ's or a ψ's

is then in a standard form corresponding to the form

$$\Diamond(\alpha \lor \beta).$$

This substitution of clause for infinitive phrase, sentence-forming prefix for auxiliary, and so on, is what is meant here by the term 'preprocessing'. No logician actually performs such a translation, but insofar as the formal system is supposed to inform us about the inferential behaviour of sentences of a natural language, some such preprocessing must be assumed and tolerated if the claim is to be properly assessed. Implicit in any such claims, however, there may lurk additional assumptions or conclusions that require separate treatment. These assumptions I shall call assumptions of logical compositionality. This is the assumption that the conversational understanding of the whole is a function of some conscious or unconscious understanding of the logical behaviour of the parts. Consider a simple example:

I haven't read either your latest novel or Geraldine's.

We understand this as an admission not to have read the addressee's latest novel and an admission not to have read Geraldine's (latest or only or somehow otherwise picked out by context) novel. To see this as an instance of one of De Morgan's laws at work, we have to be prepared to represent it as:

It is not the case that either I have read your latest novel or I have read Geraldine's (latest or only, etc.) novel

and that as equivalent to

It is not the case that I have read your latest novel and it is not the case that I have read Geraldine's (latest or only, etc.) novel.

But more is required by the hypothesis than that. It is required that the understanding of the original remark be a function of the understanding of the behaviour of 'n't' or other negating device as applied to sentences joined by 'or'. This is an assumption of logical compositionality. I shall not to try to engender an illusion of exactness about the definition. The question is a question about *logical* aspects of understanding, those pertaining to *logical* words of natural language, and apart from the bruises earned by some as topical mascots of logicians, no mark separates the logical words from the rest. Nevertheless, as applied here, the notion of compositionality will be applied almost exclusively to phenomena of distribution, where by it is meant the claim that the manner of distribution of a context $\lambda(\,)$ over some expression formed with 'or', 'and', 'but', and the like is a function of the manner of distribution of subcontexts. We shall speak in these cases of distributive compositionality. We shall be occupied mainly in denying it.

For the deontic logician, the question about the correct treatment of the natural language counterpart is answered after the preprocessing into standard form has been carried out. It is the residual question about the proper distribution of the sentence-forming prefix over disjunction, and is to be answered with due regard to the effects this decision will have elsewhere in the system.

5.2.5 The order of preprocessing

When the sentence contains more than one element for which there is a corresponding constant in the language of the system, the question arises about the correct placing of the constants in standard form. For example, in the formula

(0) You may not have tea or coffee,

at least three candidates are *syntactic* possibilities:

(1) It is permitted that either it is not the case that you have tea or it is not the case that you have coffee;
(2) It is permitted that it is not the case that either you have tea or you have coffee;
(3) It is not the case that it is permitted that either you have tea or you have coffee,

which seem to correspond to the wffs

(1') $\Diamond(\neg\alpha \vee \neg\beta)$
(2') $\Diamond\neg(\alpha \vee \beta)$
(3') $\neg\Diamond(\alpha \vee \beta)$,

respectively.

Now one might be tempted to say that the matter of correct preprocessing of the original sentence can be settled by sorting out, for each relevant piece of vocabulary—'may' 'not', and 'or'—what is its scope in the original sentence. We will not put the matter in those terms here. The scope of a connective in a formal setting can be given unproblematically as the shortest wff in which the connective occurs. It cannot in general be stated precisely for elements of sentences of natural language, and when it is, the determination is usually implicitly dependent upon some or other preprocessing. In particular, for the kinds of problems we are considering, determinate scope is also dependent upon determinate distributivity, and that is what we seem in these cases not to have. Nevertheless, the grammatical notion of the scope of a sentence element, meaning roughly the range of other sentence elements to which it stands severally in some single grammatical relationship, may be a useful expository tool.[5]

A cue that helps to narrow the range of candidates, in this case precluding reading (1), is provided by the expectation of parallel structure. This is the expectation that if a single sentence element is to be understood to stand in the same grammatical relationship severally to more than one other sentence element, then those other elements will be presented in parallel grammatical structure.[6] Thus we cite a failure of parallel structure in

> You can either do the dishes or the cups

since it presents to 'either' the verb phrase 'do the dishes' on the one hand and to 'or' the noun phrase 'the cups' on the other. We want either

> You can either do the dishes or do the cups,

which presents two verb phrases, or

> You can do either the dishes or the cups,

which presents two noun phrases. In (0), if we supply the adverbial 'either' to make the grammatical scope of the 'not' and of the 'have' explicit, we must offer

> (0′) You may not have either tea or coffee

and may not offer

> (0″) You may either not have tea or coffee.

Thus

> (4) It is permitted that either it is not the case that you have tea or you have coffee

is precluded as a reading of (0). Similarly, we may not offer

> (0‴) You may not either have tea or coffee.

Thus (1) is precluded. But as between the remaining pair, (2) and (3), the question, in ordinary discourse, is a matter of idiom. (0) means

> (5) You may not have tea and you may not have coffee,

and the choice of (3) over (2), given the principles of the formal system, happens to be in accord with that fact. We have seen the accord disappear or become obscured in other cases. In yet others, the final distributive understanding of the

5. We shall see in Chapter 10 that although the notion of scope can play an informal role in an explanation of how particular natural language occurrences of 'or' prompt particular readings of the sentences in which they occur, it cannot always help in a way which serviceably justifies, explains, or underwrites preprocessing as a preliminary to formal representation.

6. The expectation is not always met, even by respectable writers. Consider the following from De Morgan: 'First, a geometrical proposition may either be a purely *formal* consequence of those which precede, or it may require (as most do) a further infusion of geometrical matter' in Heath (1966), p. 240.

whole sentence is influenced decisively by the particularities of its sentential components. This is especially noticeable when *or*-list permissions occur in *if*-clauses. Compare the sentences

If I may have either tea or coffee, I'll be content

and

If I may have either tea or coffee, I'll have coffee.

On their most plausible readings, only the former receives a reading in accord with the preprocessing required by the standard deontic system. On its most likely reading it is equivalent to

If I may have tea, I'll be content and if I may have coffee, I'll be content,

which accords with a representation as

$$P(\alpha \vee \beta) \rightarrow \gamma$$

which permits:

$P(\alpha \vee \beta) \rightarrow \gamma$
$P\alpha \vee P\beta \rightarrow \gamma$ [Distribution]
$(P\alpha \rightarrow \gamma) \wedge (P\beta \rightarrow \gamma)$ [PL].

The second sentence by contrast could not, on its most natural reading, be represented by

$$P(\alpha \vee \beta) \rightarrow \alpha$$

where $P(\alpha \vee \beta)$ is treated as in the standard system; for it will not be taken to imply that if I may have coffee, I'll have tea, but only that if I am given the opportunity to choose, that is, if I may have tea and I may have coffee, then that is the choice I will make. What is to be made of these two examples? Is the former a vindication after all of the standard deontic systems, an instance where the formalism has got it right, and the latter a recalcitrant aberration? This is the question of distributive compositionality. Considering only the evidence of conversational understanding, there is no reason to suppose that the coincidence of use and formalism is any more than an accident. The English sentence is understood as abbreviating a conjunction of conditionals in the one case and as a conditional with conjunctive antecedent in the other. If we suppose that a listener, hearing such a sentence as one of these, must referee a competition between distributive competitors, then in the one competition the *if*-construction wins, and in the other the *may*-construction does. Against this we must weigh the possibility of replacing the *may*-construction by some nearly synonymous construction using 'obliged' or 'forbidden' and obtaining a conversationally equivalent result together with the distributive characteristics of the alternative deontic vocabulary. We would get about the same results more longwindedly, though with varying clarity, from

If I'm not obliged not to have tea or coffee, I'll be content

and

If I'm not obliged not to have tea or coffee, then I'll take tea.

Again, however, the second requires a good intonational thump on the 'or', and even so, the listener is extricated from puzzlement principally by the *then*-clause. In the clearer version that follows, the repeated verb phrase makes the intended sense easier to discern.

If I'm not obliged not to have tea or to have coffee, then I'll take tea.

But as far as the conversational evidence takes us, these two examples, like the previous, are instances of the same general abbreviative phenomenon.

5.3 Unnaturalness Elsewhere

5.3.1 The deontic unnaturalness of propositional logic

Even if distributivity in truth-functional cases finds its correct explanation in an intermediate translation into disjunction plus operator, truth conditions of disjunctions provide no clue as to how things should go where that transformation is a preliminary to formalization in a system with non-truth-functional connectives. Here there is precious little to go on, beyond the requirement of consistency and the distributive idiom of the raw natural language case. In the formalization of deontic logic there are other desiderata. The frame-theoretic apparatus already worked up for the study of modal logics lies available, provided that we are prepared to think of obligatoriness as a kind of deontic necessity, and this in itself satisfies a somewhat deeply felt unificationist urge. It is furthermore in accord from a distributivity point of view with generally held conceptions of how *ought* constructions behave. The result is that the conjunctive distribution of permissibility over disjunction goes by the board. This is not an objection; if we want a deontic logic at all, we want a consistent deontic logic, and the distributive conventions of deontic vocabulary of ordinary language are, in the required respects, inconsistent.

It would seem then that no well-behaved formal deontic system could be natural at every point of contact with ordinary uses of deontic. But we can go further. Judged by similar standards, not even a well-behaved propositional logic can be natural at every point of contact with ordinary deontic usage. For normally we would understand the formula

You may have tea or you may have coffee[7]

addressed to a, as giving permission to have tea and giving permission to have coffee, that is, as yielding, in the right conditions as to authority, the truth of the conjunction

---

7. Legrand (1975) discusses similar examples. The importance of these uses of 'or' was urged upon me by Souren Teghrarian.

a may have tea and a may have coffee.

So that formula is, on this reading, conversationally equivalent to the formula

You may have tea, and you may have coffee

on its *as-of-now* reading, according to which it is non-committal on the question whether permission to have one beverage lapses if the other one is taken up. With similar qualifications, we would ordinarily take the formula

You may go or you may stay

as giving permission to go and permission to stay, as yielding the truth of the conjunction

a may go and a may stay

and so as conversationally equivalent to the formula

You may go, and you may stay.

In such examples the terminologies of distribution and ellipsis seem to diverge; that is to say, the sentence:

You may go or stay

may be elliptical for

You may go or you may stay,

but this claim does not amount to the claim that the *or*-list is disjunctively distributive. Any account that seeks to marry the two forms as ellipsis and expansion must account for the fact that the *or*-list of verbs can be introduced by 'either' without losing its conjunctive reading, while generally speaking, an *or*-compound of sentences cannot be introduced by 'either' without inviting at least a doubt as to a conjunctive reading, though a conjunctive reading is if anything strengthened in either case by a terminal 'either'.[8]

Such examples also point up a weakness in the assumption of the formalisers, namely, that their representations that involve preprocessings of *or*-lists to yield embedded *or*-compounds of whole sentences can be justified by a rule that *or*-compounds of whole sentences are always disjunctive. Of course, if we want a representation of these sentences in a language in which meaning is given truth-conditionally, one is available to us. But they must be represented by propositional conjunction, and not by theorematically equivalent forms embedding disjunction. If there is a generalization about the kinds of cases in which *or*-lists are conjunctive, it is not one that will reliably tell us about the distributive properties of unary logical connectives. What makes propositional logic deontically unnatural in our sense is that the *or*-compound of deontic sentences takes a conjunctive reading which the corresponding wff formulated with $\vee$ cannot have. Such examples must also cast further doubt upon one of Kamp's larger principles, that 'or' *always* stands for set-theoretic union. But it must also

---

8. The worry need not be serious one; conjunctive 'either . . . or . . .' after 'may' is the rule. Conjunctive *or*-compounds of whole sentences are not by any means the rule.

seem to reprieve some such view, that there are statements in which 'or'—usually, at least—plays the same role that 'and' plays in assertions. We shall eventually give reasons for supposing that a close kin to this claim is true even for what we think of as genuinely disjunctive assertions. For the moment the matter must hang from its cliff.

5.3.2 A natural logic of preference

Recall that von Wright's essay *The Logic of Preference* introduces a binary connective *P* to be understood as a propositional relation of intrinsic preference. This, he explains, is the relation which obtains between two things in virtue of someone's liking one of them more than the other. A wff

$$\alpha \, P \, \beta$$

is read 'A state of affairs in which α is true is intrinsically preferred (by some fixed agent) to a state of affairs in which β is true'. There is a difficulty with the very notion of *intrinsic* preference that von Wright has not taken into account and is worth considering briefly. It arises in the conflation, throughout his essay, of two sorts of preference, the first being the sort of preference that we express by saying that *we like one thing more than another*, and the second the sort we express by saying that *we would rather the one thing than the other*. The two are not the same and are frequently in conflict. It might be true of me that I like eggs, bacon, sausage, and black pudding more than oat bran porridge, but nevertheless true of me that I would rather eat bowls of porridge than breakfasts of eggs, bacon, sausage, and black pudding, because I find them less worrisome. However, even if we restrict our attention to the cases in which our likes and our 'druthers' are in agreement, there is, for the programme that von Wright outlines in his essay, a significant reason for distinguishing them. It is that the restriction to intrinsic preferences really belongs to the former sort and not to the second. Just as we may have extrinsically inexplicable likes and dislikes, so we may have extrinsically inexplicable orderings of these. But just as we cannot merely want an object X, but must want to φ X (for some verb φ) in order for the satisfaction conditions of our wants to be specifiable, so for our druthers to be understood, we must be able to supply verbs φ and ψ, since it cannot be that I would simply rather some object a than b. There must be some φ and ψ such that I would rather φ a than ψ b. Some intrinsicality restriction may yet be salvaged when this is done; that is, it may be that I would rather φ a than ψ b just for the sake of φ-ing a, but it will not be of the sort that von Wright has in mind. At the same time, it is this implicit verb that permits intermediate distribution as part of preprocessing, and thereby the representation of the preference relation *P* as a sentential connective, and so preferences by the form $\alpha \, P \, \beta$. Genuinely intrinsic preferences that were merely ordered likings could not be represented in this way except those that are the liking of one kind of state of affairs better than another.

From the point of view of natural distribution over 'or', the distinction is not so important. The sentence

I like a better than b or c

means

I like a better than b and I like a better than c,

just as

I would rather φ a or ψ b than χ c

means

I would rather φ a than χ c and I would rather ψ b than χ c.

Again, the context distributes conjunctively whether the *or*-list of objects (verb phrases) is in the righthand or lefthand position. Here, it seems, naturalness provides grounds for having as a principle the equivalence of

$$((\alpha \vee \beta) \, P \, (\gamma \vee \delta))$$

and

$$((\alpha \, P \, \gamma) \wedge (\alpha \, P \, \delta) \wedge (\beta \, P \, \gamma) \wedge (\beta \, P \, \delta)).$$

And there seems to be no independent natural language dual making contrary demands. But the case is not so simple, for consider what the natural dual of '$\alpha \, P \, \beta$' would be: presumably '$\neg(\neg\alpha \, P \, \neg\beta)$' and the outer negation will compete for conjunctive distribution with the rest of the context. Setting aside the complication of inner negations, which play no role, consider the English sentence:

I don't like riding or shooting any better than skiing

as an answer to the remark, 'Well, if you don't like skiing why not go riding or shooting?' Since the answer is naturally taken conjunctively, it cannot be represented in the formal system as the negation of a preference having a disjunctive lefthand member, as the following shows:

$\neg((\alpha \vee \beta) \, P \, \gamma)$
$\neg((\alpha \, P \, \gamma) \wedge (\beta \, P \, \gamma))$ [Distribution]
$\neg(\alpha \, P \, \gamma) \vee \neg(\beta \, P \, \gamma)$ [De Morgan].

The case of negative preferences expressed using the 'rather than' construction is less clear. 'Rather' is a comparative adverb[9] in affirmatives conventionally placed before the verb, but is as likely as not to be placed after the verb in negatives, as

I wouldn't go riding or shooting rather than skiing,

expressing the negative preference by a negated conditional choice (the same conditional choice interpretation that is also available but idiomatically dormant in the positive). Here again, the negation competes and, in the natural interpretation of the sentence, wins for conjunctive distribution over the *or*-list of par-

9. The positive form 'raþe'(= early) is defunct.

ticiples. By contrast, if the negative preference is expressed by the more difficult form,

> I wouldn't rather go riding or shooting than skiing,

which awkwardly keeps the idiom intact, or by the formal

> It is not the case that I would rather go riding or shooting than skiing,

the positive context naturally wins the competition for conjunctive distribution over the *or*-list, and the result is a disjunction in agreement with the principle of distribution; in the former case, a slight stress on the 'or' will reverse the order of the distributions, and in the latter, it is the costive formality that does the work.

Again, the ease with which the positive context wins first distribution can vary between the case in which the *or*-list is in the first place and in the second, and even that can vary between the two forms of preference. Thus

> I don't like Parmenides' thesis any more than that of Zeno or Melissus

will naturally let the negation distribute in preference to the positive context, contrary to the distributive principle, but

> I would not go skiing rather than riding or shooting

will more naturally let the positive context distribute first, in contradistinction to the earlier example with the *or*-list in the lefthand member. Sheer distance from the 'not' seems decisive.

Yet again, *or*-lists in preference sentences embedded in *if*-clauses present problems of unnaturalness, and depend upon extra-logical considerations for their distributive sense. Consider

> If you would prefer eggs or fish to cereal, it can be arranged.

There are two competing renditions:

> (1) If you would prefer eggs to cereal or fish to cereal, it can be arranged

and

> (2) If you would prefer eggs to cereal and fish to cereal, it can be arranged.

Now neither of these is quite right, since they both seem to leave the anaphoric 'it' high and dry. We set that problem aside for the moment and take the main clause to mean something like 'things can be arranged accordingly'. The question is, Accordingly to what? In (1), the understanding is that

> (1') If you would prefer eggs to cereal, it can be arranged that you have eggs rather than cereal and if you would prefer fish to cereal, it can be arranged that you have fish.

In (2), the understanding is rather that

(2′) If you would prefer eggs to cereal and fish to cereal, it can be arranged that you have eggs or fish.

Now the way that (2′) is to be understood is complicated by the modal 'can' in the main clause in a way that we will sort out finally later. For the moment, let us note that that clause on one understanding means

it can be arranged that you have eggs and it can be arranged that you have fish.

Whether that understanding is to be given a role depends upon other matters, as whether the decision to be taken is to be taken on one occasion or many or on one occasion for many, and also upon what the decision is. This last point deserves remark.

To say that I would rather a or b than c may suggest a willingness to leave to the host the choice as to which to serve up, and the context may be such that the matter is left to chance. Consider the form

I would rather a or b

as a formula for committing oneself to a choice and not for expressing a general disposition to choose one or the other of the two rather than the implicit further alternative. We must distinguish between what may be called 'closed' choices and 'open' choices. To illustrate, imagine breakfasts being brought around on a two-tiered cart. On the lower tier are breakfasts consisting of (once) hot cereal, and on the upper a mixture of breakfasts, some of which feature fish and some of which eggs. Each breakfast wears a cover to mitigate the effects of a draughty passage from the kitchen, and the waiter wears a look that seems to forbid closer investigation. The choice that faces us is a closed one. If we prefer eggs to cereal and fish to cereal we will choose a breakfast from the upper tier. But we may prefer one from the upper tier though we are indifferent as between eggs and cereal and between fish and cereal. We may just prefer surprises within a narrow range to particular certainties. If the choice is being made for several occasions, the formula may reflect a tolerance for variety. The conditional undertaking (if undertaking it be) of (2′) may be to supply the animal protein of the guest's choosing on each occasion or merely an undertaking that something from the preferred range of alternatives will be presented, an undertaking that, on a fundamentalist logical construal, the host can live up to by serving fish on every occasion or always serving eggs. This is the ambiguity of the anaphoric 'it' in (2) and residually of the 'it can be arranged that you have eggs or fish' of (2′).

What ought to be the distributive properties of the P of a natural prohairetic logic depends upon whether the preferences are those associated with dispositions to make closed choices in certain ways or with dispositions to make open choices in certain ways. If open choices, then it may be that conjunctive distribution is a suitable or natural feature of P. If closed, then whether P should distribute conjunctively, disjunctively, or not at all may not be a *logical* matter. There may be no way of deciding independently of the adoption of the strategy that lies at the heart of a proposed semantic for the system. If, semantically, a preference is represented by an advantage lying in one set of states and a disadvantage lying in another, distribution may depend upon whether novelty or surprise is to be treated as conveying an advantage or upon whether the strategy in choosing is that of minimizing possible loss or that of maximizing possible gain. We might always choose the closed disjunctive package provided that we preferred at least one of the possible contents to the alternative if our strategy were to maximize possible gain. We might require that we preferred both of the possible contents if our strategy were to minimize possible loss. In the first of the three (where surprise is advantageous), we would expect no distribution. In the second, we would expect disjunctive distribution and only in the third would we expect P to distribute conjunctively over disjunction.

In all of these examples as in those of the previous section, the information conveyed may well be sensitive to the way adopted for conveying it. Negation and preference will always be well-behaved (in the sense that it will do what the logician wants it to do), even if the semantics is derivative from normal discourse, provided that the discourse fixes the distributive order discretely, as in

It is false to say of x, 'x likes a better than b or c',

but replace the direct quotation with indirect, and alter the case by placing the *or*-list in the lefthand member, and the whole context competes for distribution:

It is false to say of x that he likes a or b better than c

and wins with the slightest nudging stress on the 'or'. A similar remark might be made of preferences in *if*-clauses.

A final observation: although the positive form of 'rather' has passed from use, the positive of 'sooner' has not, and both forms are used in a preference-related sense. Thus we can express the denial of

I would sooner (or 'rather') φ than ψ

as

I would as soon ψ as φ.

But if we introduce S into a propositional prohairetic system as the propositional counterpart of the positive form, it will prove a false, or at least unnatural friend. Once *or*-lists are introduced, 'soon' behaves unreliably from the formalizer's point of view. The reason is that although we imply it, we do not express the exact denial of

I would sooner (or 'rather') φ than ψ or χ

by

I would as soon ψ or χ as φ.

Since the former is equivalent to a conjunction, its denial ought to be equivalent to a disjunction. But the latter is also equivalent to a conjunction.

5.3.3 Prohairetic deontic logic

Various authors (for example, van Fraassen 1972 and Jennings 1974) have proposed semantical accounts of obligation which are in one way or another *axiological* in character. Such a semantics treats obligation as derivative from the comparative goodness of states of affairs, in particular taking an action, say that of bringing about α, to be obligatory iff α-states are better than $\neg\alpha$-states. Clearly this simple statement covers many important questions, since typically there would be many of each kind of state represented in an arbitrary model of such a semantics. How the comparison between particular states is to ground a comparison between sets of states is a central problem.[10] However that is done, and there are numerous competing intuitions, it seems clear that whatever class of models is adopted for unary deontic logic will at the same time provide a class of models for a binary connective that compares arbitrary pairs of wffs, and not just wffs and their negations. Such a connective would be properly regarded as a preference connective. No attempt to say what principles of preference are plausibly included in a formal prohairetic system could afford to ignore the evidence of such investigations. While this is not the place to examine the details of such work, we can consider briefly its consequences for the problem at hand. If some such semantic account is adopted, then the prohairetic language can be taken as primitive and the unary deontic connectives defined. For certain proposed prohairetic principles, the deontic consequences of their adoption can be remarked.

Let us consider a unary deontic operator $\Box$ defined in a logic of preference by

$$\Box\alpha =_{\text{df.}} \alpha \, P \, \neg\alpha$$

with the dual, permissibility, consequently to be understood by the equivalence

$$\Diamond\alpha \leftrightarrow \neg(\neg\alpha \, P \, \alpha).$$

If we try in the preference logic to reflect the natural distributive properties as von Wright advocates, the defined deontic operators will have some unusual features. The deontic necessity will, for example, be non-monotonic. That is, it will lack the rule

$$[\text{RM}] \vdash \alpha \to \beta \Rightarrow \vdash \Box\alpha \to \Box\beta$$

and thus (though this will not in itself be thought by all to detract from it as a representative of obligation), the $\Box$ will not be the $\Box$ of the standard deontic systems. Suppose that $\Box$ preserves logical implications. Then if one ought to repay the neighbours' ten dollars, then one ought either to pay them their ten dollars, or poison their dog. By the definition, we infer that poisoning the next-door dog is preferable to keeping the ten dollars and the poison.

Second, certain apparently innocent circumstances will render the deontic logic liable to the full indignity of all-if-any obligation (p. 121). Merely introduce into the language of the preference logic a propositional constant μ, and into the prohairetic system, the 'minimum standards' principle:

$$[\mu] \vdash \neg(\neg p \, P \, p) \leftrightarrow p \, P \, \mu.$$

10. Dubbed the type-lowering problem by P.K. Schotch.

By the prohairetic distributive principle, we will now have the deontic distributive principle

$$\vdash \Diamond(p \lor q) \leftrightarrow (\Diamond p \land \Diamond q)$$

and all the havoc that that principle wreaks. Now the constant, μ, must be understood as something like an arbitrary minimally disliked kind of state of affairs, since any permitted kind of state of affairs is preferred to it and every forbidden kind of state of affairs is thought at least as bad. A pessimist may argue that there is no such kind of state of affairs. But it is a curious feature of the system that the mere hypothesis of such a kind of state of affairs should have the consequence that if anything is obligatory, then everything is.

5.3.4 Unnatural alethic modal logic and propositional logic

Such failures of naturalness are not restricted to deontic or prohairetic systems. The examples cited earlier involving permission have their parallels in our ordinary use of alethic modal vocabulary. So, for example, the sentence

Possibly she's unconscious or dead

would be taken to moot two possibilities: that she is unconscious and that she is dead, and, as in the case of permissions, even possibilities that are explicitly distinguished as such can be joined with 'or' while expecting a conjunctive reading. Such constructions are common in all types of literature as well as in ordinary speech. A modal logic that failed to represent this equivalence would therefore be, by that measure, modally unnatural.

More extreme, but equally common cases are those in which two occurrences of the modal auxiliary verb lie within the scope of the 'or', but that nevertheless require a conjunctive reading. These must make us doubt the legitimacy of the demand for natural logics. A few random samples will make the point:

To use the name 'Mycenaean' for the last phase of the Bronze Age, or to call the dominant people 'Mycenaean Greeks', may be misleading or may not, but it is convenient, and by now unavoidable. (Andrews 1971, 21)

. . . textiles may or may not have played the same part in the economy of the mainland. (30)

The necessity concerned might be construed rather as some sort of physical necessity, without modifying the form of the system. Or it might be construed as conditional necessity, relative to some unspecified set of premises as parameter. (Quine 1960, 196–197)

The coin may or may not be here. (Chandler 1942, 393)

They might or might not have heard the shots. (Chandler 1939, 43)

Clouds may obscure the stars much of the time, or the glow of the lights of civilization may reflect from low-hanging mist and smog.... (Neely 1989, xiii)

Our understanding of such sentences is such that on a truth-conditional construal, they must be understood as conjunctions. And in each the conversational effect is all but indistinguishable from the corresponding *and*-construction with a verb phrase repeated or a parallel adverbial phrase introduced:

The coin may be there and it may not.

They might have heard the shots and they might not.

Clouds may obscure the stars much of the time, and sometimes the glow of the lights of civilization may reflect from low-hanging mist and smog....

So we find

Well it might be something and it might not. (Neely 1989, 112)

We have already seen examples (p. 70) of the *if . . . or if . . .* construction, which must be anomolous for a pure grammaticological account of the conjunctive 'or'. It is pervasive and acceptable both in spoken English and in literature and technical writing

I think that I could have stood it if he had just said no, or if he had explained that he was committed to the Buffalo firm, or if he had just bothered to be polite. (Lathen 1961, 172)

If a problem says: 'There is either a T or a Q,' that means that at least one of T and Q on the board, maybe both; that is, the sentence, 'There is either a T or a Q' is true if there is a T but not a Q or if there is a Q but not a T, or if there is both a T and a Q. (Osherson 1975, 67)

Such constructions also give rise, by a displacement of the 'or if . . .' clause to the end of the sentence, to another anomolously conjunctive use of 'or' joining whole sentences as from

If you ate less fat, or if you took more exercise, you would feel better

to

If you ate less fat, you would feel better. Or if you were to take more exercise, say . . .

to some such as

If you ate less fat, you would feel better. Or if you took more exercise, that would improve things a little.

But we are also likely to give a conjunctive reading to:

> If you were to hold the accelerator pedal to the floor while running the starter motor, it would blow out the carburetor, or if you were to take off the air cleaner for a while it would let some of the excess fuel evaporate.

The reason for the persistence of some of these uses of 'or' may well be a felt need to emphasize the distinctness rather than the cumulativeness of the possibilities mooted, 'and' being sufficient separation when they are clearly not compossible. In others, the conditional case, say, it may be that each alternand is seen as a conditional representation of a possible course, a representation that gives for each, the reason why one might follow it. Nevertheless, insofar as the inference from 'Possibly α or β' to 'Possibly α' is not allowed for in any standard alethic modal logic, they all fail of naturalness in their representation of 'or'. Similarly, propositional logic, which does not license an inference construable as representing the form 'Possibly α or possibly β; therefore, possibly α' or an inference of the form 'If α then β or if γ, then δ; therefore if α then β' must be accounted propositionally unnatural in its failure to do so.

5.3.5 Natural logic humanely construed

We may yet raise the question as to whether there is, in the non-technical sense, a natural logic to these uses. After all, the plain person understands what is meant when permission is given and manages to reason in some fashion or other without giving up that distributive equivalence that propositional deontic logic must reject. The same is true for dealing with their own and others' preferences. The same is true of our reasoning about possibilities. Are there codifiable principles that govern the natural use of these terms and that yield those equivalences as theorems of sorts? We conclude with a sketch of an entirely different kind of account, one according to which the natural principles that dictate these equivalences are neither deontic nor prohairetic nor modal nor propositional nor, in the ordinary sense of the word, logical at all.

5.4 The Punctuationist Account

Consider once again the various confectionary examples of the textbooks. What ought to catch the mind's eye about such a sentence as

> You may have pie or cake

is not the implicit denial of permission to have both pie and cake, which, of course, it need not have,[11] but that the most natural reading of the sentence takes it to have the force of the conjunction:

> You may have pie, and you may have cake

on its *as-of-now* reading, which may also be lent the sense of denying permission to have both, though again it need not. That is the significant fact for

---

11. In fact we could, without oddity, add 'Come to that, why not have a little of both?'

the punctuationist account of conjunctive 'or', not that it is conjunctive but that it is *non-combinatively* conjunctive, that it conjoins *dispersively*. The puzzle, hitherto expressed, Why does 'You may have . . .' distribute conjunctively over 'pie or cake'? which suggests that the meaning of 'or' is already fixed, gives way to the question, Why should 'or' have this use in this context? The punctuationist account takes 'or' as providing punctuation for lists and asks why we should punctuate a list with 'or' in certain contexts when we want it to receive a conjunctive reading. As we have seen, the underlying puzzle has been widely discussed in deontic logical contexts under the heading of *free choice permission*. But it has been discussed always in the form of the earlier question, always against an understanding that fixes the meaning of 'or' according to the syntax-cum-semantics paradigm of recent logical practice. We have already observed that the label *free choice permission* suggests too narrow a construal of the problem even within the purview of deontic logic since it seems to neglect such cases as

Jules or Jim may have pie,

in which also 'or' seems to conjoin dispersively. What is more, the distribution principle notwithstanding, it seems that in English there need be no difference in respect of distribution over 'or' between formulae of permission and statements of permissibility. Even when 'or' joins whole permission-granting clauses, as in

Jules may have pie or Jim may have pie

the result may require a conjunctive reading, or rather may be taken either as a granting of permission to Jules, and a granting of permission to Jim, or as an assertion of two permissibilities. And as we have seen, the puzzle is not a puzzle peculiar to deontic discourse, but seems to arise in other kinds of modal and conditional contexts, and in some cases thence to infect assertoric uses when the modal or conditional portions are within its scope. We may assemble groups of examples to illustrate the shift from

$$\text{Possibly } \alpha \text{ or } \beta$$

to

$$\text{Possibly } \alpha \text{ or possibly } \beta,$$

from

$$\text{If } \alpha \text{ or } \beta, \text{ then } \gamma$$

to

$$\text{If } \alpha \text{ or if } \beta, \text{ then } \gamma$$

to

$$\text{If } \alpha, \text{ then } \gamma \text{ or if } \beta, \text{ then } \gamma,$$

where all of each group can receive a conjunctive reading. It would seem impossible to say why the language did not retain some other connective for this use, or why in its development no other connective sprang up or was borrowed from elsewhere for the job. But we can say why, for all but the last of each group, we do not use the only other connective that comes readily to hand, namely, 'and'. The reason is that to use 'and' in those cases would invite a combinative reading, and that is what, in those cases, we want not to do.

So the question becomes two questions, both of them non-logical ones. The first is, Why do we abbreviate the conjunctive sentence

You may have pie and you may have cake

by an ellipsis that uses 'or'? The second, How does this conjunctive use of 'or' joining whole sentences square with our understanding of 'or' as a disjunctive connective? The answer in the one case must be that the corresponding sentence with 'and' is not an ellipsis and means something else. The second will require a more profound change in our understanding of the disjunctive 'or'. The puzzle, properly understood, is not one of logic alone, but of logic in relation to discourse.

We will set aside for detailed discussion later the cases in which 'or' joins whole sentences. For the present we need only bear in mind that whatever we say about the other cases must not become a liability for our final account, since that must also illuminate those uses. But these apparently conjunctive uses of 'or' joining whole sentences must cast doubt upon the ultimate usefulness of the language of distribution and cast a new light upon what we have called the ellipsis view of non-sentential uses of 'or'. Certainly our understanding of ellipsis must shift slightly from the place given it from some earlier writers, as say, Reichenbach:

> In conversational language some of these words are sometimes used to combine, not sentences, but words, such as in 'Peter or William will go with you'. We consider this sentence form an abbreviation standing for 'Peter will go with you or William will go with you.' (1947, 23)

Doubtless Reichenbach took the significance of this thesis to be that non-sentential uses represent abbreviations of structures properly regarded as disjunctions. Again, such examples make apparent that the question of autonomous coordinative uses of 'or' as raised by Dik (1968) has a purely grammatical dimension, which may be considered independently of any logical assumptions about how whole sentences joined by 'or' are to be interpreted. Our own explanation must also take into account the place of 'or' in comparisons, where the logically tinged language of conjunctive distribution seems unavoidable. With regard to them we may note that, although they present a similar distributive idiom,

Jules is heavier than Jim or John

being taken to mean

Jules is heavier than Jim and Jules is heavier than John,

unlike the earlier cases, the sentence

Jules is heavier than Jim or Jules is heavier than John

can hardly be given a conjunctive reading. The punctuationist account asks, Why 'or' as the punctuation of the list 'John, Jim'? and that question must be construed as, Why 'or' rather than 'and'? Its answer is that it is because 'and' has an undistributive or combinative sense here that 'or' takes on the task of conjoining separatively. I suspect that, although the approach is the correct one, and the combinative-separative distinction is the and-or distinction in such cases, that distinction cannot explain entirely or universally the phenomenon of conjunctive distribution over 'or'. For in other comparatives that are also conjunctively distributive, as

Jules is politer than Jim or John,

'and' could not make undistributive sense and is not even idiomatic. It may be that the idiom exists generally because it is needed in some contexts, and has come analogically to be applied to others, two sentences being more strikingly similar in their both being comparatives than they are dissimilar in respect of the interpretability of 'and'. It may be that we can say no more than that idiom demands an 'or' in such contexts, that no deeper explanation is possible. Alternatively, we may try the thesis, as eventually we shall, that 'or' can *always* be understood that way, even in its disjunctive ones. We are not yet in a position to do so.

In the absence of any more comprehensive account, the punctuationist explanation that we have sketched requires that we postulate generalization from critical cases. The formal theorist, intent upon some sort of logical explanation, may wish to be given a say in the matter, for we seem to be postulating an analogical explanation once more, though this time with a different analogy and therefore a different core of directly explainable cases. Once again we must weigh the alternative analogical account. We have ample truth-functionally explicable cases of conjunctive distribution of connectives over propositional disjunction. The biconditionals

$$\neg(p \vee q) \leftrightarrow \neg p \wedge \neg q$$

and

$$((p \vee q) \to r) \leftrightarrow ((p \to r) \wedge (q \to r))$$

provide two obvious central examples. Why not hypothesize a generalization from the truth-functionally explicable cases to the non-truth-functional ones? It is time to lay the earlier analogical account to rest.

5.4.1 Punctuation and analogy

Recall that the analogy expects an intermediate distribution across the *or*-list to yield a propositional disjunction within the scope of a propositional operator. It follows that such an approach does not hold much promise for the cases in which 'or' joins whole sentences conjunctively, for here the disanalogy with truth-functionally explainable cases seems indissoluble. Again in the comparative cases, which seem in any case irreducibly non-propositional, it has even a last-ditch character when subjected to careful scrutiny, and only the more so when a hidden negation is taken to be a part of the story. For it is partly the unreliable behaviour of negation in such contexts that makes one suppose that the explanation is not to be had in *any* translation into a propositional idiom. How negation distributes seems to depend upon how the negating adverb is worked into the sentence.

You may not have pie or cake

will be taken to mean

You may not have pie and you may not have cake

(but, notice, not to mean

You may have either both or neither).

However,

It is false that you may have pie or cake

could, in many contexts, naturally be taken to be the denial of the permission formula in its primary conjunctive sense, so

It is false that you may have pie or it is false that you may have cake.

Both sorts of comparatives behave analogously

Jules is no heavier than Jim or John

and

Jules is no politer than Jim or John

will be taken as conjunctions of negations, as is

Jim or John is at least as polite (heavy) as Jules

or

Jules is at least as polite (heavy) as Jim or John.

Again, even the cases where we might suppose that the logic of truth-functions would always impose an unambiguous and truth-functionally correct reading are capable of upset by wording and intonation. Consider the sentence

If either Jules *or* James is telling the truth, then John is a liar.

As a logician, one feels a nagging professional obligation to say that that sentence is equivalent to the conjunction

If Jules is telling the truth, then John is a liar and if James is telling the truth, then John is a liar *because* it is equivalent to:

> If either Jules is telling the truth or James is telling the truth, then John is a
> liar,

that is, because of the intermediate distribution. But there is no truth-functional
explanation for the ease with which we can intonationally force a conjunctive
reading of:

> If it is false that *either* Jules or James is telling the truth, then John is a
> liar.

Nor can there be a truth-functional explanation of the equivalence of 'if . . . or if
. . .' conditionals with conjunction. As we noted earlier, the sentence

> If Jules is telling the truth or if James is merely exaggerating, then John is
> in trouble

is naturally understood equivalently to the corresponding conjunction of conditionals, yet contains no disjunctive clause. In fact we can, in general, translate
conditional sentences with disjunctive *if*-clauses into sentences with *or*-lists of
if-clauses without change of meaning, producing thereby, for any such case
where a truth-functional explanation of distribution is in the offing, an
equivalent sentence for which it will not work.

We may go further. Even in simple cases where distributivity coincides with
what truth conditions would impose, the *explanation* of distribution in terms of
truth conditions has no greater claim to our acceptance than the punctuationist
explanation. And this is true *precisely because* similar distributivity is found
where truth conditions do not dictate them, as, say, in comparative constructions. Indeed, when we consider that the earlier evolution of human languages
was an evolution of habits of discourse, a hypothesis that finds in that evolution
an unconscious recognition of—or even a slow awakening to—the theory of
truth-functions must surely be required to bring forward some very strong
positive evidence before it can claim our serious attention. To assume without
question and in the absence of persuasive evidence that truth-functional compounds came about as, say, reflections of a developing logicality in human apprehension looks to be reviving in the historical order precisely those features of
Wittgenstein's Tractarian viewpoint rejected so resolutely in the metaphysical
sphere in the *Philosophical Investigations*. This is not an argument from
authority. There was no evidence for the Tractarian vision of a Boolean
algebraic world, only the spell cast by recent developments; Wittgenstein was
right to reject the vision. Those discoveries were not discoveries of physical or
metaphysical fact; they were discoveries of possible things for logicians to do.
They were not the only possible things for logicians to do, so they need not be
assumed to have been the things that earlier logicians had been trying to do, still
less what speakers of natural languages had been trying to do. That assumption
of evolving logicality imposes this consummation not only upon ourselves and
our own language, but even upon defunct speakers of defunct languages.

Let us return to a simple example. Once one accepts that the sentence form

If *a* or *b* had φ'd, then Q

is an *abbreviation* of the sentence form

If *a* had φ'd, then Q and if *b* had φ'd, then Q,

the natural question to ask is: *Why is it abbreviated with 'or'?* An explanation that hypothesizes that ordinary English embodies an implicit understanding of truth-functions must ring false—even farfetched—when other facts about such conditionals are borne in mind. It is as if someone sought to offer us a Jungian explanation of why the French think that wood is masculine or why the Romans thought that water was feminine. It might not seem mere romance if we had not already realized that the labelling of the French articles *la* and *le* as feminine and masculine and the corresponding labelling of first and second declension Latin nouns as feminine and masculine came *after* their use with key gender-specific nouns, and not before.[12] On a thoroughgoing punctuationist view of the matter, the introduction of the notion of disjunction into our view of things came after and not before the abbreviation of

It is false that *p* and it is false that *q*

by

It is false that *p* or *q*.

Again the question is, Why abbreviate using 'or'? This is not the question as to why a particular speaker on a particular occasion chooses 'or'; it is rather the question, Why is our language like that? Part of the punctuationist answer, not by any means the most important part, is: Consider the alternatives. The more important part of the punctuationist thesis would have us resist the temptation to find disjunctivity at the core of the meaning of 'or'. On the punctuationist account, the core meaning of 'or' is the one that its etymological root in 'other' has given it: that of a separative, more or less adversative conjunction. Its use in lists we want to classify as conjunctive is, as it were, the use nature gave it. How then do its disjunctive uses arise? The kernel of that answer is this: Among the environments that require the services of an explicitly separative conjunction are those featuring negation. The disjunctive uses of 'or' are derivative from this particular separative use. The use of 'or' as a reading for a connective having the falsity condition of disjunction, a punctuationist view would claim, arises precisely because negating adverbs are among those parts of speech that require some non-combinative or separative punctuation in their abbreviated forms. This is by no means a complete answer; part of the explanation must await a proper understanding of the use of 'or' as it occurs between whole sentences, especially those we correctly regard as disjunctive.

With the punctuationist explanation in hand, we can look once more at Boole's observation that 'and' in subject terms is used to designate unions while in predicate terms, 'or' seems generally to be used in this sense. The punctuationist view tells us why this explanation, though generally correct, is

---

12. There was in fact just such a controversy in fifth century B.C. Athens when the gender classification was first proposed.

less than we can say by way of explanation. In the first place, verbs agree in number with subject terms, not with predicate terms. So

The scholar and the man of the world desire happiness

with its plural verb makes it clear that the claim is made about scholars and about men of the world; that interpretation is reinforced by the repeated article. Take away the second 'the' and supply a conditional auxiliary, as in

A scholar and gentleman would acknowledge sources

and an intersection reading is more natural. Here we would get a union reading by replacing 'and' by 'or'.

Now as it can be given to the behaviour of 'or' in negative contexts, so the punctuationist story can be told about the antecedent 'or' in conditional sentences.

If α or β, then γ

abbreviates

If α, then γ and if β, then γ

which is distinct in meaning from

If α and β, then γ.

If we accept that conditionals are left downward monotonic, or that the conditional is transitive and that all conditionals of the form

If α and β, then α or β

are true, then we will insist that the conditional with 'or' in the antecedent implies the same conditional with antecedent 'and' replacing antecedent 'or'. But suppose that we do not accept that the conditional of ordinary discourse is transitive or left downward monotonic, but rather count ourselves among the many philosophical logicians who are at pains to give an analysis that does not impose those properties. When we give up those assumptions, the position is analogous to that of permission sentences. If we say

If Fred or George goes, I stay

we imply that

If Fred goes, I stay and if George goes, I stay.

But we do not commit ourselves to

If Fred and George go, I stay.

The last is not incompatible with the initial assertion, and like permission to our infants to glut on various confectionary combinations, it may be denied by context or intonation, as

I for one will not gladly force conversation from either of them; so if Fred or George goes, I will stay, but neither will I stay here and tidy up without help.

This, then, is a punctuationist account of the conjunctively distributive 'or'. Since it offers as well a punctuationist view of the discourse roots of truth-functions, it comes closer than the grammaticological, analogical, or quantificational accounts canvassed to providing a unified account of 'or' in English. It has implications that touch upon the nature of logic vis-à-vis natural language. According to this view, what we have thought of as the avatar in discourse of the falsity condition for disjunction, namely, the conjunctive distribution of negation over 'or', itself is just an instance of a more general *separative* use of 'or'. The distributive fact derives from the use of 'or' to abbreviate conjunctions of negations. This use of 'or' is idiomatic, not only in this case but also in other cases where *and*-junctions cannot be abbreviated with 'and' because 'and' can have, in such contexts, distinct undistributed sense. It is, incidentally, an account that the Wittgenstein of the *Investigations* would find congenial, for it is an account that begins properly to 'turn the whole investigation around'.

The punctuationist explanation of the conjunctively distributive 'or' is at the heart of our account of the origins of disjunction. And although it cannot in its present form be quite the complete story, it is the key to the answer to our initial question, Where does disjunction come from? But there remain deficiencies and gaps. In the first place, the language of distribution, though well enough suited to a discussion of equivalences of written forms, seems an unsuitable idiom for an account of spoken discourse. In the second place, distribution, particularly over lists, will sometimes yield whole sentences joined by 'or'; while the punctuationist story may give an account of the behaviour of such sentences inside the scope of negation, it does not have much to say about unnegated sentences joined by 'or'—either those that are naturally taken to be conjunctive or those that are paradigmatically disjunctive. In the third place, though it may seem at first perverse as a criticism, the account is too tidy, even for the non-sentential occurrences of 'or'. There are sometimes subtle differences between a sentence containing an *and*-list and the same sentence with 'or' replacing 'and', even though in both cases the list is conjunctively distributive. For example, 'Mary is different from ( )' distributes conjunctively over either an *and*- or an *or*-list, but the form 'Mary is different from Laurie or Alison' seems to refrain from suggesting that she differs from them in the same respect. 'Mary is different from Laurie and Alison' does not.[13] The overall account of 'or' in discourse has to be such as to suggest that the manner of our marking these subtler distinctions is suggested and nurtured by our manner of marking those more fundamental. All this is to say that our final account must be one that suggests how uses of 'or' evolve, what it is in the uses of 'or' at one stage that makes an innovative use an acceptable one. It must accommodate the dynamical aspect of linguistic change. Nevertheless, we shall see in later chapters evidence for an account of 'or' founded primarily in its punctuational duties rather than the logical properties of contexts and the truth conditions of propositional disjunction.

13. We may wish to ask whether the behaviour of 'is different from' with respect to *or*-lists is part of the explanation of the attempts in common usage to assimilate assertions of difference to comparisons in the increasingly common 'different than'.

The punctuationist account has it that the *separative* function of 'or' is more fundamental than its *logical* function, that its logical role is an artefact, in part, of our selection of negation as a focus of theoretical interest and representation. It requires a difficult adjustment of viewpoint so long as we restrict ourselves to indicative sentences where the more customary logic-dominated view competes. But if the punctuationist account is correct, then we ought to see the separative function of 'or' in those non-indicative sentences where the customary view cannot so easily outshout the rival. Consider the pair of questions

What has this to do with you or me?

and

What has this to do with you and me?

of which the former embodies two queries or the same query about Laurie and Richard severally, and the latter, in the absence of separation by pause or other cues, one query about them jointly. Or if that distinction seems to arise from the erotetic use of those sentences as forms of denial, consider the pair

How does that decision affect Laurie or Richard?

and

How does that decision affect Laurie and Richard?

To be sure, the former question may query a disjunctive claim and receive only some such answer as 'By requiring that at least one of them receive fewer benefits'. But there is a use of the question to ask about the effect on Laurie and about the effect on Richard that does not, except at several removes of incidentalness, inquire about the solution of the disjunction

That decision affects Laurie or that decision affects Richard.

Again, *or*-lists of vocatives are merely separative lists, not disjunctive. Consider

Laurie or Richard, I need a finger on this knot

which addresses the prompt to the addressees severally, as contrasted with

Laurie and Richard, I need help lifting this crate.

5.4.2 Punctuation and polarity

The punctuationist thesis can be restated in the language of polarity and triggering environments, but diachronically, not synchronically understood. Expressed in these terms, the characteristic of those environments that have given rise to conjunctive 'or' is that, like negative polarity environments, they either do not distribute over 'and' or have autonomous undistributive sense. That feature is shared by downward entailing environments and modal environments. We might indeed be tempted to abstract this feature as the defining character of negative polarity. It is a temptation that we ought to resist, at least for purposes of understanding how 'or' works. Terminology that makes explicit mention of negation will serve only to reinforce a wrong habit of thought, that disjunctivity or something truth-conditionally like it is at the heart of the role of 'or'. It would be better to cultivate an otherwise-angled point of view. If we must think of 'or' as having been assigned or having otherwise acquired some job in language, it would be better to think of its function as more essentially lying in a spectrum of uses that are at one extreme merely separative and at the other both separative and adversative, leaving the question of its disjunctive uses for the moment no more fully answered. We might begin by noting the inadequacy of a truth-conditionally conjunctive representation of conjunctive sentential 'or'. Noting this amounts to nothing more than seeing that 'but' more closely captures the flavour of 'or' in some cases where we want to make its conjunctive character plain. So, in

> She may have walked over to the college, or she may be in the gatehouse. (MacDonald 1964a, 19)

truth-conditionally we may wish to represent the 'or' by ∧, but we would better understand this instance as intermediate in the spectrum of adversativity between 'and' and 'but'.[14] Where in this scale a particular instance should be placed may be governed materially by the nature of the alternatives or by stress. So we may contrast the last example, where the alternatives are comparably insipid, with the next:

> She may have left him on account of a girlish whim. Or she may have had deep dark reasons. (MacDonald 1964a, 20)

And we may test the effect of placing stress upon the initial 'may' as though to contrast the odds, as the material contents seem to contrast the stakes. At the same time we should note the loss of separation when the 'or' is actually replaced by 'but'. It becomes unclear whether the second hypothesis is offered as an alternative or as an additional possibility.

Second, we can note that in its distribution of employment opportunities, the language seems sometimes to have paid more attention to adversativity-contrasts than to those implicit in our conventional truth-conditional representations. Just as we find adversative 'or' sharing some of the conjunctive work with adversative 'but', we find 'but' sharing some of the disjunctive load with 'or' as in:

> It never rains but it pours.

5.5 Arrogative 'Or'

Having said that the use of 'or' provides an explicitly distributive (conjunctive) construction in contexts in which the use of 'and' has undistributed sense, and having offered that as the solution of the puzzle of conjunctive 'or', I must try to say why it should have been 'or' that has found its way into this office. Historically, it has acquired the job through influence, in particular through its early association with 'other' (hence with *alius*), and later through its adverbial as-

14. In fact, we may wonder whether these uses represent a lingering influence of the homophonous French 'or'.

sociations with 'otherwise' and 'else'. Since these last are relative adverbs, we may conclude that where 'or' can be replaced by 'else' or 'otherwise', 'or' is a relative adverb as well.

5.5.1 Parallel structure and 'else'

Justifications for the claim that 'or' can have an exclusive sense sometimes take the form of remarks that 'or' in certain instances means 'or else' or 'or if not'. Thus, for example,

> To make it clear that p and q are exclusive alternatives, people sometimes say "p or *else q*." (Kelly 1988, 222–223)

The same is to be found in attempted explanations of the use of *aut* where it joins mutually exclusive alternatives. Thus Smith:

> . . . *truncis arborum aut admodum firmis ramis abscisis, trunks of trees, or (*if they were not to be had*) very stout branches, . . .* (Smith 1855, 116)

As we have already seen, neither device cues an exclusive 'or' or indicates exclusivity of disjuncts. 'α or else β' and 'α or, if not α, then β' are from the point of view of logical representation, merely equivalent to 'α or β'; nothing is added by either supplementation. But the examples serve to remind us of the quasi-comparative etymological roots of 'or' in the word 'other' and those of 'else' in *alius*. They also remind us that other adverbs, such as 'alternatively' and 'rather', are also sometimes introduced. Moreover, we can distinguish two classes of cases: those where 'or' can be replaced by one or another of 'else', 'otherwise', 'alternatively', or 'if not', and those where it can not. The more notable are those where it can:

> She was already engaged, or she might have accepted him[15]

because in such cases, the first clause is independently asserted. But whether we replace 'or' by 'else' or by 'or else', by 'otherwise' or by 'or otherwise', by 'if not' or by 'or, if not', we will invite a useful question in each case: 'Else than what?' 'Otherwise than what?' 'Alternatively to what?' 'If not what?' In the first two pairs of cases, these may be seen as questions of the scope of an implicit *than*-clause, in the third of an implicit *to*-phrase, and so on. For simplicity, I shall, in all such cases, call this the *than*-scope of the occurrence of 'or'.

Questions about *than*-scope are questions whose existence is obscured by our ordinary stylistic preoccupations with parallel structure. Consider one of our central kinds of examples, free choice permission:

> You may have either ice cream or cake.

The requirement of parallel structure is that what occurs between the 'either' and the 'or' be of the same grammatical category as what follows the 'or'. Thus if

---

15. Zandvoort (1957), 227. He also gives an example with an independent imperative clause: 'Hurry up, or we shall be late.'

we want to pass the 'have' into the *or*-construction, we must place it in both the *either*-phrase and in the *or*-phrase as:

You may either have ice cream or have cake,

putting a verb phrase in each place. The requirement of parallel structure therefore gives to such a transformation the appearance of a distribution of other sentence elements across the *or*-construction. We cannot quite get away with passing the subject term into the *or*-construction, but with judicious paraphrasing we get the form

It is (hereby) permitted that either you have cake or you have ice cream,

still preserving parallel structure in the ordinary grammatical sense, this time by having a whole clause in each place. The final question—whether that form is equivalent to propositional conjunction or propositional disjunction—is then seen as the question whether the deontic prefix distributes conjunctively or disjunctively over propositional disjunction.

5.5.2 *Than*-scope and conjunctive distribution

However, consider the sentence in its penultimate form with the 'either' omitted and 'else' or 'if not' inserted, and ask the obvious question, 'Else than what?' The answer reveals parallel construction, but of a more complex variety. The sentence

You may have ice cream or if not, have cake,

when the *if*-clause is made explicit may become

You may have ice cream or (if you do not have ice cream) have cake,

or it may become

You may have ice cream or (if you do not want ice cream) have cake

or

You may have ice cream, or (if you do not like ice cream) have cake

or

You may have ice cream, or (alternatively to having ice cream) have cake

and so on. If we think of the 'or' as separating indifferent alternatives, we may think of two symmetric clauses: a clause with an implicit 'else' or 'if not', contemplating the exclusion of the first alternative, and a second clause contemplating the corresponding exclusion of the other. The nature and terms of the contemplated exclusions may vary from case to case and may, in any particular case, be indeterminate; the force of the 'if' may be different (as it is between the first of the previous paraphrases and the second and third); nevertheless, we can mark the scope by asking, for the reading of the sentence, *Else than what?* or *Al-*

ternatively to what? or *If not what?* and note the answer that the reading requires. The force of the whole, at least as regards the *than*-scope of 'or', may be expressed in these terms in a succession of two sentences:

> If you do not have (want, etc.) ice cream, you may have cake. If you do not have (want, etc.) cake, you may have ice cream.

or by an *and*-construction.

> If you do not have (want, etc.) ice cream, you may have cake. and if you do not have (want, etc.) cake, you may have ice cream.

The distinction between a conjunctive and a disjunctive construal of 'You may do A or B' emerges as a difference in the *than*-scope of the occurrence of 'or'. On the former, its *than*-scope excludes the modal 'may'

> You may (else than you do B) do A or (else than you do A) do B.

On the other it includes it:

> You may (else than you may do B) do A or (else than you may do A) do B.

Let us adopt the device of marking the left *than*-scope of 'or' using square brackets, so that, setting aside the question of whether the order is preferential, the two readings of the sentence 'You may have ice cream or cake' are marked by:

> You may [have ice cream] or cake (conjunctive reading)

and

> [You may have ice cream] or cake (disjunctive reading).

I shall call the former instance of 'or' *arrogative* to mark its characteristic feature: that it arrogates, as its *than*-scope, a portion of the sentence that remains properly regarded as being within the scope of another grammatical element of the sentence.

5.5.3 *Than*-scope of arrogative 'or'

We have applied the notion of *than*-scope to the case that we earlier described as conjunctively distributive, but it can also be invoked to illuminate cases where 'or' anomalously joins whole sentences but with conjunctive force. In the case of permissions conjoined with 'or', the *than*-scope would be marked as

> You may [have ice cream] or you may have cake.

If we apply the notion to the displaced *or if* clauses of some earlier examples (p. 137) we obtain:

> If [you ate less fat], you would feel better. Or if you took more exercise, that would improve things a little,

which we can distinguish from the *than*-scope in the disjunctive reading:

[If you ate less fat, you would feel better.] Or if you took more exercise, that would improve things a little.

and

If [you were to hold the accelerator pedal to the floor while running the starter motor], it would blow out the carburetor, or if you were to take off the air cleaner for a while it would let some of the excess fuel evaporate

to be distinguished from:

[If you were to hold the accelerator pedal to the floor while running the starter motor, it would blow out the carburetor], or if you were to take off the air cleaner for a while it would let some of the excess fuel evaporate.

We shall have more to say about these examples a little later.

5.5.4 Non-commutative cases

Symmetric scope arrogation would seem to be a feature of some commutative conjunctively distributive uses of 'or' , as well as some cases where 'or' conjunctively joins whole sentences, but not all conjunctive occurrences of 'or' are symmetrically arrogative. Consider

I must go or I'll be late,

which is not to be represented as of the form

$\Box$(I go $\lor$ I'll be late)

nor yet as of the form

$\Box$(I go) $\lor$ I'll be late,

but rather must be understood as

[I] must [go] or I'll be late;

that is, as

I must go; if I don't go, I'll be late.

Since we may take the speaker to be saying unconditionally that he must go, the whole sentence cannot be represented as a disjunction. Compare

He has five days to make some progress, or the government will take action,

which means

He has five days to make some progress. If he does not make progress in five days, the government will take action.

Or Tennyson's

She must weep or she will die[16]

which, again, must be understood as

She must weep. If she does not weep, she will die.

Strawson has noted related examples:

> At a bus-stop, someone might say: 'Either we catch this bus or we shall
> have to walk all the way home'. He might equally have said 'If we don't
> catch this bus, we shall have to walk all the way home'. It will be seen that
> the antecedent of the hypothetical statement he might have made is the
> negation of the first alternate of the alternative statement he did make.
> Obviously, we should not regard our catching the bus as a sufficient con-
> dition of the 'truth' of either statement; if it turns out that the bus we
> caught was not the last one, we should say that the man who had made the
> statement had been wrong. The truth of one of the alternates is no more a
> sufficient condition of the truth of the alternative statement than the falsity
> of the antecedent is a sufficient condition of the truth of the hypothetical
> statement. And since '$p \supset p \vee q$' (and equally, '$q \supset p \vee q$') is a law of the
> truth-functional system, this fact sufficiently shows the difference between
> at least one standard use of 'or' and the meaning given to $\vee$. (1952, 90)

The explanation lies in the presence of the modal element 'will have to,' the
force of which is that when the bus in question has departed, no further non-
pedestrian conveyance remains to us. In fact, a philosophically fundamentalist
parsing of the sentence might take the effective scope of the necessity to extend,
grammatical form notwithstanding, to the whole alternation of catching the bus
and walking home. What is being claimed to be inescapable, such an account
might insist, is the disjunction 'we catch this bus or we walk home'. Any logic
whose language had a representative for the modal element of the sentence
would not permit the inference of the modalized disjunction from the mere truth
of one of the disjuncts.

A fundamental fact about 'or', which in these examples happens to be particularly apparent but which is obviously a feature universal over its uses in
spoken discourse and common in particular written uses, is that 'or' is not
always used as a device for making a particular connection between two items
of speech, but does always provide a device for a particular range of ways of
adding an item of speech to one already uttered. This feature is preserved in
written form in the examples we have just noted and as well in those we
consider next. But it clearly must be given a central place in any detailed
explanation of the workings of 'or' in English as well as in any account of the
natural language origins of disjunction.

---

16. 'Home they brought her warrior dead' from *The Princess*

5.5.5 Paraphrasing conditionals

I leave the topic of *than*-scope with a class of examples that at once provide an illustration of the idea and suggest that a new approach, pragmatic in character rather than syntactic, is required. These are *or*-constructions conversationally interchangeable with so-called counterfactual conditionals. Consider the sentence

If I had known you were coming to this thing, I'd have offered you a lift.

It has been remarked often enough in the literature that although such sentences suggest conversationally that the *if*-clause mentions a circumstance that did not obtain, this is by no means essential to our accession to the truth of the conditional claim. Our example might well draw some such reply as

But you did know that I was coming to it, because I mentioned it at the meeting. And as a matter of fact you did offer me a lift, and I told you I was going with Charles. You had the Parkins mess on your mind at the time and you immediately forgot. So not to mention it.

which would not be taken to refute the claim. In fact, the conversationally suggested claim is not part of the analysis of the conditional, and if it is to be made explicit, this is done by conjoining it to the conditional itself:

I didn't know you were coming; if I had, I'd have offered you a lift.

Now in propositional logic, the material conditional

$$\alpha \to \beta$$

is equivalent to the disjunction of its negated lefthand member and its righthand member:

$$\neg\alpha \lor \beta$$

and something like a corresponding conversational alternative is available in natural discourse. One may hear:

If you don't hand over the money, I'll shoot you,

and a little later, for the sake of variation,

Look, either you hand over the money or I shoot.

But we respect, in our account of the conversation, that two different kinds of linguistic event have taken place: in the one case a threat, and in the other an ultimatum. The same is true in the case of approximate *or*-paraphrases of *if*-sentences having, as the initial example has, a pluperfect *if*-clause and perfect conditional *then*-clause. We would say:

I didn't know you were coming, or I would have offered you a lift.

But this cannot be treated as a standard *disjunctive* translation, since on its most natural interpretation we must take it as in part an assertion of its lefthand member. And it is a conversational alternative, but not in the truth-conditional sense equivalent to its *if-then* counterpart.

Strawson seems to have overlooked these conversational alternatives to what he would have called 'subjunctive conditionals'.

> It is a . . . difference between 'if' sentences and 'or' sentences that whereas, whenever we use one of the latter, we should also be prepared to use one of the former, the converse does not hold. The cases in which it does not generally hold are those of subjunctive conditionals. There is no 'or' sentence which would serve as a paraphrase of 'If the Germans had invaded England in 1940, they would have won the war', as this sentence would most commonly be used. (1952, 92)

The sentence

> The Germans didn't invade England in 1940, or they would have won the war

or its near relative

> It's a good job the Germans didn't invade England in 1940, or they would have won the war

are not strictly paraphrases of the conditional, in that I might be thought imprecise if I offered either as a philosophically or formally correct restatement, and this because we do not take subjunctive conditionals *formally* to imply the falsity of their antecedents. But either is a *conversational* equivalent in the sense that either could have been uttered instead of the conditional to much the same conversational effect. Strawson may have missed the point through a preoccupation with *or*-sentences that had equivalent *either... or...* forms. His own diagnosis of the difficulty, though its relevance is otherwise doubtful, is clear at least on this point:

> . . . this is connected with the fact that 'either . . . or . . .' is associated with situations involving choice or decision. 'Either of these roads leads to Oxford' does not mean the same as 'Either this road leads to Oxford or that road does'; but both confront us with the necessity of making a choice. (92)

Of course no *or*-introduction inferences would involve such *or*-sentences as conclusions. Their assertion involves the assertion of their first clause, but the notion of truth conditions does not straightforwardly apply to the whole construction. Again, such *or*-sentences are non-commutative in the sense that what we say by uttering them could not be said by uttering their component clauses separated by 'or' but in the opposite order.

5.5.6 The parallel with 'but'

Jespersen remarks on a contrastive use of negation that in some respects parallels these arrogative uses of 'or':

In the case of a contrast we have a special negation; hence the separation of *is* (with comparatively strong stress) and *not* in Macaulay E. 1. 41
the remedy is, not to remand him into his dungeon, but to accustom him to
the rays of the sun.—*Do* is not used in such sentences as AV.Matt. 10. 34 I
came not to send peace but a sword I Wilde P. 135 my ruin came not from
too great individualism in life, but from too little I Dickinson S. 14 We
meet not in drawing-rooms, but in the hunting-field.
Even in such contrasted statements, however, the negative is very often
attracted to the verb, which then takes *do*; we do not meet in drawing-
rooms, but in the hunting-field — the latter part being then equivalent to:
but we meet in the hunting-field I I do not complain of your words, but of
the tone in which they were uttered I I do not admire her face but (I
admire) her voice I He didn't say that it was a shame, but that it was a pity
I Tennyson 464 I did not come to curse thee, Guinevere (contrast not
expressed). (1917, 45)

Jespersen's interest here is in the form of negation. But we may see 'but' at the
centre of the phenomenon, where it may be regarded as occurring arrogatively.
Supplement it with 'rather' or 'instead' and the question arises, Rather than
what? Instead of what? and the answer indicates its arrogated scope. In 'they did
not content themselves with whispers, but shouted to each other of their new
playground beneath our dear ex-warden's well-loved elms. . .' (Trollope 1857,
435), the *than*-scope of this 'rather' would be 'content themselves with
whispers'. Contrast this with 'It was true that he could not himself intone the
service, but he could procure the co-operation of any number of gentlemanlike
curates well trained in the mystery of doing so' (54), where we may read the
(non-arrogative) 'but' as though supplemented by a 'nevertheless', the *than*-
scope of which is 'It is true that he could not himself intone the service'.

5.5.7 Final examples

There is a corresponding but slightly altered difference in the case of approximate *or*-paraphrases of *if*-sentences having a perfect *if*-clause and present
conditional *then*-clause. Consider:

If there were pure oxygen present, we would see a more rapid discolora-
tion,

which might serve to deny the presence of pure oxygen or to indicate how that
would alter the case. (Imagine, alternately, circumstances drawing the responses:
'I didn't say *pure* oxygen!' and 'What about pure nitrogen?') We may imagine
the *or*-paraphrase:

There is no pure oxygen present, or we would see a more rapid discolora-
tion

in either setting. Imagine for the second

There is no pure oxygen present, or we would see a more rapid discolora-
tion. There is no pure nitrogen present, or we would see a decrease in size.

What is to be made of this and the symmetrically arrogative ', or' of the previous examples? Both require omission of the auxiliary 'either' and if we wish to paraphrase it we will most naturally do so by replacing ', or' by 'alternatively' in the earlier examples, and in the latter examples by '; else' or '; otherwise' or by making the conditional of the righthand component explicit (by '; if I had', in the one case, by '; if there were', in the other). This is to make of the sentence a kind of conjunction. Theorists who wish to make heavy semantic weather of *if*-constructions like those cited here may wish to find in their *or*-counterparts, as well as in the earlier, symmetrically arrogative cases, a new and especially noteworthy kind of disjunction, requiring special semantic treatment. Certainly their syntactic properties seen in this light will be impressively exotic, since the earlier sort implies both of its 'disjuncts', and is implied by neither; and this last implies but is not implied by its lefthand 'disjunct' and is not commutative. The simplest account, however, is otherwise. Like 'alternatively' and like 'otherwise' and 'else', 'or' in such contexts is a relative adverb.[17] On a severely fundamentalist parsing, it modifies the auxiliary 'may' in the earlier example, and 'would' in the latter. In all the cases cited we could, more illuminatingly, regard 'or' as modifying whole sentences. Those observations having been made, it is obvious that the subject of adverbiality must figure importantly in our final account. But other topics must be introduced before that notion can be refined and its place in the scheme of things made clear.

---

17. Like 'instead' or 'rather', 'but' in its occurrences in Jespersen's citations can also be construed as adverbial.

P A R T

2

Orphan 'Any'

6

General Noun Phrases

6.1 'Or' and Quantification

6.1.1 De Morgan's Rule

The equivalences named for De Morgan are so closely associated in twentieth-century logic with the truth and falsity conditions for disjunction and conjunction that it may be difficult to imagine other than that the falsity conditions of *or*-sentences and *and*-sentences suggested the equivalences to their namesake. It is instructive, therefore, to consider the text surrounding his introduction of the principles in 1847. (*P* and *Q* are terms; *p* is *not-P* and so on.)

> The contrary of PQ is p,q; that of P,Q is pq. *Not both* is either not one or not the other, or not either. *Not either P nor Q* (which we might denote by: P,Q or .P,Q) is logically '*not P and not Q*' or pq and this is then the contrary of P,Q.
> The disjunctive name is of two very different characters, according as it appears in the universal or particular form: so very different that it has really different names in the two cases, *copulative* and *disjunctive*. This distinction I here throw away: opposing *disjunctive* (having one or more of the names) to *conjunctive* (having all the names). The disjunctive particle *or* has the same meaning with the distributive copulative *and*, when used in a universal. Thus, 'Every thing which is P or Q is R or S' means 'Every P *and* every Q is R *or* S.' But PQ is always 'both P and Q in one'. Accordingly
> Conjunctive PQR uses *and* collectively.
> Disjunctive P,Q,R in a universal uses *and* distributively. P,Q,R in a particular uses *or* disjunctively, in the common sense of that word.
> 'Either P or Q is true,' is an ambiguous phrase which is P,Q)T or T)P,Q according to the context. (De Morgan 1847, 118–9)

In De Morgan's notation, 'X)Y' means 'All X are Y', and he treats propositional argument syllogistically by treating the propositional uses of 'P', 'Q', and so on as proper names of propositions with 'T' and 'F' introduced as predicates. So we may take his remarks as applying directly to the logic of lists, and only derivatively to the logic of propositions.

> . . . a proposition entering as part of a proposition, enters merely as a name, the predicates being usually only *true* or *false*, or some equivalent terms. . . . Thus, 'It is true that he was fired at' is 'the assertion (that he was fired at) is a true assertion.' (117)

His point here is then that the two readings of 'Either P or Q is true', namely, 'P is true *and* Q is true', and 'P is true *or* Q is true' arise through our taking the sentence to mean 'All P or Q cases are true cases' and our taking it to mean 'All true cases are P or Q cases', respectively. In the former the 'or' occurs in a universal and is, as we would say, conjunctively distributive; in the latter the 'or' occurs in a particular and is therefore disjunctively distributive. As for the corresponding *and*-formations, far from imagining them dual in some structurally significant way, he treats the distributive case with 'and' in the particular term as a simple abbreviation (+ should be understood as conjunction).

> Whatever has right to the name P, and also to the name Q, has right to the compound name PQ. This is an absolute identity, for by the name PQ we signify nothing but what has the right to both names. Accordingly X)P + X)Q = X)PQ is not a syllogism, nor even an inference, but only the assertion of our right to use at our pleasure either one of two ways of saying the same thing instead of the other.

We may remark as well that De Morgan's explanation of the two readings of 'Either P or Q is true' ought to suggest a parallel explanation for the two readings of 'Either P or Q is false', according to which, on the disjunctive reading 'P or Q', is in the predicate, and on the conjunctive reading it is in the subject. But when the explanation is applied to explaining the unambiguous cases, as 'The assertion that P or Q is true (false)', we require a predicate understanding for the one and a subject understanding for the other and some complicated negotiations as well, since in this case neither P nor Q is asserted.

De Morgan's Rule has implications for individual predications involving 'or', 'and', or general terms. De Morgan explains:

> If 'this X be a Y' it is one Y only: it is 'this X is *either* the first Y, *or* the second Y, *or* the third Y, &c.' If there be 100 Y's, there is, to those who can know it, 99 times as much negation as affirmation in the proposition: and yet most assuredly it is properly called *affirmative*. But if it be 'this X is not a Y,' we have 'this X is not the first Y, *and* it is not the second Y, *and* it is not the third Y &c.' The affirmation is what is commonly called disjunctive, the negation conjunctive. A disjunctive negation would be no proposition at all, except that one and the same thing cannot be two different things: any X is either not the first Y *or* not the second Y. And in like manner a conjunctive affirmation would be an impossibility: it would state that one thing is two or more different things. (59)

Recall the rule that we attributed to George Boole (p. 72):

Boole's Rule
And-lists of general terms represent unions in the subject place; *or*-lists of
general terms represent unions in the predicate place.

As a parallel, we may extract from De Morgan's comments a version we name
for him:

De Morgan's Rule
Or has the same sense as the distributive *and* in a universal term. *Or* is
disjunctive in particular terms

A quarter of a century later, Venn, properly regarded as a successor of Boole
rather than of De Morgan, would express the puzzle of the relationship between
the English uses of 'and' and 'or' and their supposed logical roles more
explicitly.

> Thus 'Lawyers are either barristers *or* solicitors', 'Lawyers consist of
> barristers *and* solicitors', must be taken as being equivalent statements.
> They both alike say what the class of Lawyers is made up of, or co-
> extensive with, the two classes of 'barristers' and 'solicitors'. Whether a
> barrister can be a solicitor they do not give the slightest hint. Nor if such
> be the case do they unequivocally inform us whether these common
> members are to be included or not; though as inclusion is the far more
> usual case this would be very strongly assumed in the absence of any
> statement to the contrary. (1894, 45)

Venn also offers an explanation (akin to De Morgan's justification for regarding
singular propositions as affirmative) for the discrepancy between the *and*- and
or-constructions in individual predications. The word 'lawyers', he says, is
'taken somewhat more collectively' when identified with 'barristers *and*
solicitors', 'somewhat more distributively' when identified with the term
'barristers *or* solicitors'.

> Hence when our subject is an individual a real distinction will be
> introduced by the use of one term rather than the other. Thus to say of any
> person that 'he is deceiver or deceived', is by no means the same thing as
> to say that 'he is deceiver and deceived'. But the distinction here seems
> merely forced upon us by the necessity of the case and not by the nature of
> the grouping of the two classes. The individual cannot, like a class, be
> split up into two parts. (1894, 45)

After an attempted explanation of Boole's working restriction to disjoint
classes[1] Venn considers how natural language makes the corresponding distinctions.

> We must now take some notice of the attempts of popular language to
> express the above meanings. That it can do this, by using words enough
> for the purpose, is obvious; but there is something almost bewildering in

---

1. Venn's explanation for Boole's using (A not-B) + (B not-A) as the representation of 'or' is the
not-implausible one that Boole wished to avoid any numerical complications that would arise
through his counting the elements of the intersection twice. The explanation is in keeping with
Boole's actuarial interest in probability theory.

the laxity, in the combined redundancy and deficiency, of our common vocabulary in this respect. Broadly speaking we employ two conjunctions, 'and' and 'or' for thus aggregating classes; these terms being practically synonymous in this reference, and both alike leaving it to be decided by the context whether or not they exclude the common part. Often there *is* no such part, the terms being known to be exclusive of one another; but if there be such, and the context does not make our meaning plain, we often add a clause 'including both', or 'excluding both', or something to that effect, in order to remove all doubt. (1894, 45)

There is a hint that he is not perfectly satisfied with the explanations that he has been able to give, for he concludes,

This must rank among the many perplexities and intricacies of popular speech, but it does not seem at variance with the statement that regarded as mere class groupings, independent of particular applications, '*A* and *B*', '*A* or *B*', must as a rule be considered as equivalent.

The puzzlement about 'and' and 'or' could be felt by logical theorists as long as they were still encouraged by their adopted formal idiom to pay attention to the behaviour of lists in natural language. With the adoption of a propositional idiom, the puzzle receded from view. But propositional logic cannot dissipate the cloud of puzzlement from the logic of lists; it can only ignore it as it ignores much else that puzzled nineteenth-century theorists. And as we have already seen, even in the propositional case we can sometimes interchange 'and' and 'or' without upset to the likely readings of the results. Again we find unnoticed examples even among the sentences of De Morgan's own discussions:

A proposition may [enter only] for its matter, *or* it may enter in such a way that its truth is the matter . . . [2]

as we have found unregarded examples of conjunctively distributive 'or', even propositional ones, deposited here and there in the prose of modern textbook authors.

One kind of explanation of the conjunctively distributive *or*-list might almost have been inspired by De Morgan's Rule that 'or' has the same sense as the distributive 'and' in universal terms and disjunctive in particular terms. On this 'morganic' account, those sentences in which *or*-lists are conjunctively distributive should be construed categorically as sentences in which the 'or' occurs in a universal term; those sentences in which *or*-lists are disjunctively distributive should be construed categorically as sentences in which the 'or' occurs in a particular term. Thus we can morganically explain that the standard reading of '*A* is heavier than B or C' as '*A* is heavier than B and A is heavier than C' reflects an understanding of it as meaning that every B or C item is an item than which A is heavier. By contrast, we explain the equivalence of 'Mary is related to Sheila or Patricia' to 'Mary is related to Sheila or Mary is related to Patricia' by giving its categorical translation as 'All Mary (or 'all items identical to Mary') is an item (are items) related to Sheila or Patricia'. The scheme, which invites us to treat these examples as A-propositions (i.e. as of the form 'S_aP',

---

2. (1847, 117). The italics are mine. I have reversed the bracketed words for clarity.

'All S are P'), would require that we treat a sentence such as 'A or B is heavier than C or D' as an E-proposition ('S_eP', 'No S are P') to account for the conjunctive distributivity of both lists. It would be rendered in some such way as 'No A or B item is a not-heavier-than-a-C item or a not-heavier-than-a-D item.' As it stands, though in keeping with what we have called 'De Morgan's Rule', it goes rather against a later more general and more vigorously maintained precept of De Morgan's. It is argued at length in his famous 1860 Cambridge lecture, where it is embodied in the complaint against syllogistic that there all relation

> other than that signified by *is* and denied by *is not* . . . is avoided by the dictum that it shall be of the form of thought to consider the relation and the related predicate as *the* predicate, and the judgment as a declaration or denial of identity between this and the related subject (Heath 1966, 213).

On the basis of his observation that it is the relational properties of the relation signified by the copula rather than anything unique to that relation that validates syllogisms, De Morgan argues vigorously for an expanded conceptions of form and of logic to encompass the study of relations in general, their properties and those of their compositions. It is reasonable to suppose that the De Morgan of the 1860 address, faced with a choice between alternative explanations of these distributional equivalences, would have repudiated the remarks of 1847 in favour of a more suggestive hypothesis, one that would assign the equivalences to the properties of the *heavier than* relation, rather than to those of universal and particular terms.

The explanation that, overall, I would wish to urge accords better with the views of the later than with those of the earlier De Morgan. Nevertheless, let us persist in calling this a morganic approach, and consider its benefits. If we translate the S_aP and S_eP forms into the more explicit terms of sets and quantifiers, they become respectively:

$$\forall x \in S, \exists y \in P: x = y$$

and

$$\forall x \in S, \forall y \in P, x \neq y.$$

The work done by the distributed character of the universal term is done by the universal quantifier, that of the undistributed particular term by the existential quantifier. Taking into account the presence of 'or' in the first two cited examples by unions of classes, we would obtain for the former

$$\forall x \in B \cup C, \exists y \in A^*: x = y$$

understanding A^* as the class of things than which A is heavier. For the second, we would have

$$\forall x \in M, \exists y \in S^\wedge \cup P^\wedge: x = y$$

understanding $S^\wedge$ ($P^\wedge$) as the class of things related to Sheila (Patricia). The third example (with two *or*-lists) becomes

$$\forall x \in A \cup B, \forall y \in C' \cup D', x \neq y$$

understanding C′ (D′) as the class of things not heavier than a C (D). Now this in itself would be a cumbrous approach to the matter, requiring that we hypothesize implicit negations where the English shows only one more *or*-list. No one has actually offered this account and we may be sure that the more mature De Morgan would not have done so. But it may prompt us to bear in mind, in the less strikingly graceless attempts as well, that there is a distinction between having available a *representation* of a linguistic phenomenon within a formalism and having an *explanation* of it. When the sentences of the morganic account are replaced by their typical first-order translations, much of the paraphernalia, including the extra negations, are dropped, yielding a more seductively simple representation. The three become:

$$(\forall x)(\forall y)(Ax \wedge (By \vee Cy) \rightarrow Hxy)$$

$$(\forall x)(Mx \rightarrow (\exists y)((Sy \vee Py) \,\&\, Rxy))$$

$$(\forall x)(\forall y)(Ax \vee Bx \rightarrow (Cy \vee Dy \rightarrow Hxy))$$

The distributive behaviour of 'or' is thus explained by reference to one or the other of two understood facts about disjunction: when 'or' invites conjunctive distribution, by reference to the behaviour of $\vee$ in antecedents; when it invites disjunctive distribution, by reference to the behaviour of $\vee$ in consequents. By similar measures we get a representation for permissions. 'It is permissible to do a or b' is represented by some such form as

$$(\forall x)(x = a \vee x = b \rightarrow Px).$$

And preferences: 'a or b is preferred to c or d' is represented by some such form as:

$$(\forall x)(\forall y)(x = a \vee x = b \rightarrow (y = c \vee y = d \rightarrow Pxy)).$$

These would indeed be the translations of the more cumbrous sentences of the morganic story, but they would not in all cases be the most direct representations of the English sentences whose categorical forms the morganic story introduces. In particular, the more likely representation of 'Mary is related to Sheila or Patricia' would introduce individual constants for 'Mary', 'Sheila', and 'Patricia' and represent the original as a disjunction of atoms:

$$Rab \vee Rac.$$

In fact, even in the conjunctively distributive cases, if the lists are of individuals rather than of kinds, the more direct representation in first-order language is as conjunctions of atoms. Thus 'Mary is taller than Sheila or Patricia' can be represented as

$$Tab \wedge Tac.$$

It is only in order to have the 'or' of the list matched by a '$\vee$' in the representative as

$$(\forall x)(\forall y)(x = a \rightarrow (y = b \lor y = c \rightarrow Txy))$$

that we require quantifiers at all. So the translation into first-order logic gives the conjunctively distributive case a representation in which disjunction figures, and that perhaps relieves us of any necessity to hypothesize a non-disjunctive 'or', but it replaces one puzzle with another. Now we must ask why some instances of 'or' should *require* a representation with universal quantification and others require only existential quantification, or none at all.

0.1.2 The real quantificational puzzle

The real quantificational puzzle is one that none of the nineteenth-century logicians so far cited has noticed or at least has thought worth dwelling upon. This is the relationship between the uses of 'either' and 'both', between those of 'any' and 'every', and, one might as well mention though it concerns us less, among those of 'ever', 'anytime', and 'always'.

Among the kinds of environments in which conjunctively distributive *or*-lists typically occur are those in which for some of their instances an *and*-list has an undistributive use, and for which therefore a conjunctively distributive mode of listing is required. But this admits the fact that an *or*-list is usually conjunctively distributive in comparative adjectival or adverbial expressions regardless of whether an *and*-list could conceivably have an undistributive use in the particular environment. In fact, in comparative environments conjunctively distributive *or*-lists are idiomatic whereas *and*-lists are not. But even with the exceptions, we can in general predict the classes of environments in which conjunctively distributive *or*-lists normally occur. By contrast, we can note about a general noun phrase of the sort 'either A' that although in positive environments its natural reading is generally speaking like that of a restricted universal quantifier, it is not always idiomatic in environments where we want a universal quantifier over an independently identified pair of items. Thus in contexts in which we know that a particular pair of days is intended, we do not say 'I studied on either day', but rather, 'I studied on both days'. A corresponding point can be made about 'any'. We do not say, 'I studied on any day last week' but 'I studied on every day last week'. There may be a barely detectable difference in the degree of conviction with which we reject the two forms, the 'either' form being less unacceptable than the 'any'. Consider, for example, 'There was a ditch on either side of the hedge', which is quite acceptable. And in some instances, the numerical definiteness of 'either' may make for an analogical use prescinding a shared property as a basis for choice. But the form is often at least questionable, and one would be justified in asking, for example, whether 'both days' was meant.

In habitual present-tense environments, either is admitted (and, since this sentence is of that sort, we might have said 'both are admitted'). In the future, the use of 'either' suggests assent and does not imply 'both', but 'both' suggests prediction, though differences arise when quantification is over types as opposed to particular individuals. Thus, 'We will accept either offer' is distinct in meaning from and does not imply 'We will accept both offers', but 'We will accept either sex' spoken of military recruitment, say, rather than a planned adoption suggests that the offer does not lapse after the first recruit. The difference between the last two is, of course, between 'We will accept *a child* of either sex' and 'We will accept *recruits* of either sex'. The use of 'both' with the singular noun suggests, for reasons mentioned by Venn, assent to adopt a hermaphrodite, or simply mistaken usage; used with the plural noun, while it does not rule out hermaphrodite recruits, it readily acquiesces in the alternative distributive reading.

In some modal environments, *either* form may be used, but again, it is only in particular cases where they receive different readings. Thus in the previous sentence the '*either*' could be replaced by *both*, but 'You may have either dessert' will receive a different reading from 'You may have both desserts'. Why the difference? Presumably in the general case, it is clear that the 'both' implies only that on some occasions one will be used and on others the other, and that partly because it is understood that both cannot or will not be used on any single occasion.

In *if*-clauses 'either' may occur and is distinguished from 'both' as 'If you eat either dessert, you will be sick; if you eat both desserts, you will appear greedy'. In *then*-clauses, 'either' is questionable but demands the same reading as 'both', or else some additional legitimizing element is present that makes 'either' acceptable, but with a different reading from that of 'both'. So 'If you press the button both bells ring' where 'either bell rings' is questionable, but 'either bell might ring' means that it could be one or the other. Similarly 'If you were to ask her, either A would accept' means that a_1 would accept if you were to ask her, and so would a_2.

In statements of preference, 'either' sometimes invites a distinct reading from 'both', but 'both' in the absence of a verb can receive the same reading, as 'Which of these do I prefer to that one?' I prefer both (or 'either') of these to that one. In the presence of a verb as in 'I would rather have either of these than have that one', 'either' is acceptable and expects a reading distinct from the one expected when 'both' is used.

In negatives, 'either' is acceptable and will invite a reading different from that invited by 'both'. So 'I don't know either A' means 'I don't know a_1 and I don't know a_2'. 'I don't know both A's' implies only that at least one of them is unknown to me.

Parallel remarks could be made about 'any' and 'every' for cases where quantification is not restricted to two-member classes.[3]

The question has been raised both by philosophers and by linguists whether 'any' ought to be regarded as a universal or as an existential quantifier, or as sometimes one and sometimes the other. Quine (1960) and other philosophers writing on the subject three decades ago tended toward the universal rather than the existential thesis. Later authors have entered evidence that has seemed to suggest that in some settings 'any' can receive *only* an existential reading, so that if there is to be a single unified account, the existential account must be it.[4] I now think this is a misstatement of the case. To ask the question whether 'any' *is* existential or universal seems to presuppose that 'any' is a quantifier, whereas

3. Lexicographers report occasional uses by respectable writers of 'either' and 'both' for classes of more than two; the distinction of size is not material here.

4. The main examples given below are from Jennings (1967). Others may be found in Carlson (1980).

such evidence as is typically considered in such attempts is evidence only that some sentences in which 'any' occurs can be *represented* by sentences in which one or the other sort of quantifier occurs, or else must be represented by an existentially quantified sentence if represented quantificationally at all. And if, on a quantificational representation, 'any' sometimes requires an existential representation and sometimes not, this fact might be taken to show that a unified account of how 'any' functions will not be an essentially quantificational account at all. Our interest in any case is not so much to give a complete account of 'any' as to consider such evidence as its connections with 'or' can provide that 'or' is not essentially disjunctive.

'Any', like 'either', is unidiomatic in some simple environments in which the use of 'every' is readily understood universally, and in other environments in which 'any' is admissible; the features of the environments that seem to license its use also seem to obscure the answer to the question whether it is existential or universal in that setting. If we modify some of our *either* examples, assuming an extra member so as to make them conform to standard uses of 'any', we may see that certain *any*-phrases given a short-scope existential representation will yield the same result achieved by giving the *any*-phrase a long-scope universal representation. The equivalence of the two can be appreciated by reflecting that the following pairs of first-order formulae are equivalent:

$$\neg(\exists x)Fx$$

and

$$(\forall x)\neg Fx;$$

$$(\forall x)(Fx \rightarrow p)$$

and

$$(\exists x)Fx \rightarrow p.$$

There is, however, a rule of thumb in baby logic, that in English conditionals with pronominal reference from the *then*-clause to the noun phrase of the quantifier, the sentence should be represented with a long-scope universal quantifier. The last of our previous conditional examples is a case in point. The 'she' of 'she will accept', the story goes, refers grammatically to 'either A' ('any A' in our adaptation) and therefore must be represented by an occurrence of the individual variable of the quantifier; that is, the sentence must be read

$$(\forall x)(Fx \rightarrow Gx)$$

and cannot be read as

$$(\exists x)Fx \rightarrow Gx,$$

which is not well formed. Now, since no one wants to let the sense of 'any' depend upon whether there is pronominal reference in the *then*-clause to the quantified noun phrase of the *if*-clause, it seems better to say that whether there is such reference or not, *any*-phrases should be treated as universal. There can, however, be pronominal reference to an antecedent *some*-phrase, as in 'If some animal were to walk through here, it would be injured', which also, in the even-handed manner of baby logic, we ask our students to represent by:

$$(\forall x)(Ax \wedge Wx \rightarrow Ix).$$

So the question about the status of 'any' has sometimes been asked in the form 'Does "any" sometimes mean "some"?'

Now the behaviour of 'any' and 'some' in *if*-clauses is sometimes explained by reference to the disjunctive character of existential quantification and the conjunctive character of the universal quantifier. Thus, if we imagine ourselves restricted to a small domain of, say, three individuals, a_1, a_2, and a_3, to which the common noun A is being applied, then to say that every A φ's is to say that a_1 φ's and a_2 φ's and a_3 φ's. To say that some A φ's is to say that a_1 φ's or a_2 φ's or a_3 φ's. So the equivalence of the forms

If a_1 φ's or a_2 φ's or a_3 φ's, then α

and

If a_1 φ's, then α and if a_2 φ's, then α and if a_3 φ's, then α

explains the equivalence of the forms

If some A φ's, then α

and

If any A φ's, then α

since the latter predicates of every A, (call it a_i), that

If a_i φ's, then α.

Thus the puzzle about the meaning of 'any' comes round to the puzzle about 'or', for the form

If any A φ's, then α

can be expressed by the *or*-list containing

If a_1 or a_2 or a_3 φ's, then α.

And in general, the constructions in which 'any' rather than 'every' is acceptable are the constructions in which 'or' naturally receives a conjunctively distributive reading. This is not to say that an *any* noun phrase can always be replaced by an *or*-list; that is obviously false. Consider 'any' with mass nouns: 'If there is any water . . .' and infinite sets: 'If any natural number . . .' Nor is it claimed that the general rule holds without exception. Neither the bounds of permissible usage in the case of 'any', nor the bounds within which an *or*-list naturally draws a conjunctively distributive reading are fixed or can be precisely drawn; it is therefore unlikely that every new use for the one will represent a plausible corresponding use for the other. Nevertheless, there is a sufficient overlap of the two classes of environments, and indeed sufficient instances in which the one may be replaced by the other, that there is a tension between the conventionally felt need to find, if possible, a universal quantificational reading for 'any' and the equally conventional urge to understand 'or' disjunctively. We have seen that in the case of 'or' the force of this requirement was not urgently felt by nineteenth-century logicians and we may conjecture that the inclination to regard the matter as settled, and, what is more, settled in the conventionally comfortable way is an unexamined habit of optimism inherited from more recent logical forebears. The same may well be true of 'any'. Though it is not yet time to dwell upon the relevance of etymologies, it must be clear in the case of 'any' that sufficient of its Latin ancestor *unulus*, a diminutive of *unus* (one), and of its Old High German ancestor *einag* comes to us through it that it has at least a whiff of the meaning 'even one' still about it, even if we can always represent it by truth-conditionally equivalent forms in 'all'. It speaks eloquently of our capacity to be beguiled by an ideal that the two needs, so evidently at odds, should urge themselves upon us at once: on the one hand, to read 'or' disjunctively even in conjunctively distributive occurrences, but on the other, to read 'any' as a universal quantifier even when 'any A' can be replaced by a conjunctively distributive *or*-list. The same inclinations would be felt presumably in the case of 'either', except that its restricted application to two-item cases lessens its interest.

6.1.3 A rehearsal of the facts

In the following, the facts about 'either' and 'or' are set out schematically with some examples. They are stated in terms of what we may call conversationally interchangeable constructions. In the case of list-containing sentences and the results of distribution over the list, it means no more than that the use of one of the sentences would have no material conversational effect that would be absent from the other. In the case of lists and general noun phrases, conversational interchangeability amounts to this: when there is a general noun phrase that will pick out, for conversational purposes, just the items of some list, we can with equal propriety say what we want using the noun phrase instead of the list or vice versa. The mention of propriety is intended to remind us that we will not call two sentences conversationally interchangeable in virtue of the fact that we can *get away with* using one rather than the other, where, in the case of assertions, we get away with an assertion if our interlocutor knows how to go about assigning it a truth value. So it is not intended just as a weak or quasi-logical relationship between sentences in which the assignment of a particular truth value to one sentence is significant for the assignment of a particular truth value to the other.   The propriety is idiomatic propriety. Finally, to say that two sentences are conversationally interchangeable is not to say that they are conversationally indistinguishable. The point of this is, of course, not to say the obvious, that one need not be a copy of the other. It is rather that, since the vocabulary and syntax are different, opportunities for significant intonational and stress variation may be available for the one form that are not available for the other. To say that 'You may have a or b' is conversationally interchangeable with 'You may have a and you may have b' is not to deny that the 'or' provides a point upon which a great thumping stress will give the recipient of the permission a clear hint that she is not to help herself to both a and b.

Suppose that 'a_1' and 'a_2' are proper names and 'A' is a common noun, and it is understood that a_1 is an A and a_2 is an A. Then

1. In an environment in which the list 'a_1 or a_2' is conjunctively distributive, we can substitute 'either A' for the list.

If the environment '$\underline{\lambda}(\ )$' is such that $\underline{\lambda}(a_1$ or $a_2)$ is conversationally interchangeable with $\underline{\lambda}(a_1) \wedge \underline{\lambda}(a_2)$, then,

   (a) $\underline{\lambda}(a_1$ or $a_2)$ is conversationally interchangeable with $\underline{\lambda}$(either A)

and

   (b) '$\underline{\lambda}(\ )$' is an environment in which 'either A' is acceptable.

For example, the sentence 'Mary is taller than Hilda or Jane' is conversationally interchangeable with 'Mary is taller than Hilda and Mary is taller than Jane', which is conversationally interchangeable with 'Mary is taller than either girl'. This claim implies that 'either' is acceptable here. For *any* true sentence consisting of *any* conjunctively distributive two-membered list of A's occurring in the environment '$\underline{\lambda}(\ )$' whether an *and*-list or an *or*-list, a true sentence would be produced by substituting the expression 'either A' for the list, but not every such resulting sentence would be acceptable English and therefore not every such pair of sentences would be conversationally interchangeable. For example, the sentence 'Maureen and April were present' is conversationally interchangeable with 'Maureen was present and April was present'. But whereas we might get away with 'Either girl was present' since it would be understood to mean the same as the two previous, the use of 'either' here is questionable. We would more naturally say 'Both girls were present'.

2. When the list 'a_1 or a_2' is substituted for any acceptable occurrence of 'either A', the original sentence and the resulting sentence are conversationally interchangeable.

3. It is false that for every environment in which 'either A' is acceptable, a substituted *or*-list would be conjunctively distributive.

A corresponding list of facts can be given for the expression 'both A's' and two-termed *and*-lists, but because, as it appears, distributive *and*-lists are always conjunctively distributive the correlation is more straightforward.

4. Sentences differing only in that one has a two-termed *and*-list 'a_1 and a_2' where the other has 'both A's' are conversationally interchangeable.

What do these 'or/either' and 'and/both' correlations together with the distributive correlation between *and*-lists and conjunctively distributive *or*-lists tell us about the relation between the conversational roles of 'both' and 'either'? If the distributive correlation were universal, then first, in any environment in which an *or*-list would receive a conjunctively distributive reading, it would be unacceptable to intersubstitute between 'either A' and 'both A's', and counterinstances to the distributive correlation would also be counterinstances to this restriction on intersubstitution. Second, in any environment in which an *or*-list would receive a disjunctively distributive reading, intersubstitution between 'either A' and 'both A's' would produce either a change of sense or an unacceptable or questionable usage. For example, in the environment 'You may have ( )', the list 'a_1 or a_2' would be conjunctively distributive. The sentence 'You may have a_1 or a_2' is conversationally interchangeable with the sentence 'You may have a_1 and you may have a_2', which is conversationally interchangeable with 'You may have either A'. The inference to the sentence in which 'either A' is replaced by 'both A's' is unwarranted, just as it is logically objectionable to infer from the sentence 'You may have a_1 or a_2' the sentence 'You may have a_1 and a_2'. In the environment '( ) is sick', an *or*-list would receive a disjunctively distributive reading. Accordingly, although it is not *logically* objectionable to pass from the sentence 'Either A is sick' to the sentence 'Both A's are sick' or vice versa, the form 'Either A is sick' is questionable.

6.2 Some Modern Sources

6.2.1 Geach's account

It would be wrong to generalize from these data to an account of the difference between 'either' and 'both' that simply asserts baldly that for any environment '$\underline{\lambda}( )$',

'$\underline{\lambda}$(either A)' is true iff '$\underline{\lambda}(a_1) \wedge \underline{\lambda}(a_2)$' is true

and

'$\underline{\lambda}$(both A's)' is true iff '$\underline{\lambda}(a_1$ and $a_2)$' is true.

For such an account would ignore four significant facts, three of which we have already remarked:

(a)   that for some environments $\underline{\lambda}$, '$\underline{\lambda}$(both A's)' is true iff '$\underline{\lambda}(a_1) \wedge \underline{\lambda}(a_2)$' is true, since for some environments '$\underline{\lambda}(a_1$ and $a_2)$' is true iff '$\underline{\lambda}(a_1) \wedge \underline{\lambda}(a_2)$' is true.

(b)   that for some environments $\underline{\lambda}$, '$\underline{\lambda}$(either A)' is odd;[5]

(c)   that it is usually in those environments in which 'a_1 and a_2' is distributive;

and, finally, a fact that remains to be discussed,

(d)   'either' and 'both' occur in non-indicative environments for which the question of truth and falsity does not straightforwardly arise.

Nevertheless, let us suppose for the moment that this sort of account can be given, even if only for declarative occurrences. If these equivalences hold, and if

5. Exceptions are such constructions as 'at either end' or 'on either side'.

these equivalences account for the difference between 'either' and 'both', then there is a precise analogy between the 'either/both' distinction and the 'any/every' distinction as Geach (1962) has expressed this latter distinction. According to Geach, the distinction between 'any' and 'every' is accounted for by the following pair of equivalences:

'f(any A)' is true iff 'f(a$_1$) $\wedge$ f(a$_2$) $\wedge$ f(a$_3$) $\wedge$ . . .' is true

'f(every A) is true iff 'f(a$_1$ and a$_2$ and a$_3$ and . . .)' is true.

If this and the previous pair of equivalences hold, then the expressions 'either A' and 'both A's' differ from the expressions 'any A' and 'every A' just in that while the latter pair of expressions are typically used in speaking about the whole set of A's, the previous ones are usually restricted to two-item subgroups or two-item classes. If the 'either/both | every/any' analogy is thoroughgoing, then the expression 'any A' ought to be related to an exhaustive, conjunctively distributive *or*-list of A's in precisely the way that 'either A' is related to a two-termed conjunctively distributive *or*-list of A's. And 'every A' ought to be related to an exhaustive *and*-list of A's in the same way that 'both A's' is related to a two-termed *and*-list of A's. We will find a correlation between the naturalness of 'any A' in a particular environment and the undistributiveness of an *and*-list in that environment. Consequently, we shall find a correlation between the acceptability of 'any A' in a particular environment and the conjunctive distributiveness of an *or*-list in that environment.

As might be expected, when Geach sets out to show the correctness of his account of the 'any'/'every' distinction, he does so by putting the distinction to work in a pair of sentences for which the alleged correlation seems to hold:

Tom can lawfully marry any sister of Bill's,

Tom can lawfully marry every sister of Bill's.

The former sentence, he claims, is true, assuming the names of the sisters, iff the sentence

(Tom can lawfully marry Mary) and (Tom can lawfully marry Jane) and (Tom can lawfully marry Kate)

is true. The second sentence, he claims, is true iff

Tom can lawfully marry Mary and Jane and Kate

is true. The same equivalences hold for the corresponding 'either/both' pair of sentences. If Bill has only two sisters, Mary and Jane, then

Tom can lawfully marry either sister of Bill's

is true iff

(Tom can lawfully marry Mary) and (Tom can lawfully marry Jane) is true. The sentence

Tom can lawfully marry both sisters of Bill's

is true iff the sentence

Tom can lawfully marry Mary and Jane

is true. But although this truth-conditional account is undoubtedly correct, we could, as we know, construct another pair of sentences, one containing 'every' or 'both' and the other 'any' or 'either', for which this distinction cannot be made. Where '$\underline{\lambda}(\ )$' is the environment 'Tom has just married ( )' rather than 'Tom can lawfully marry ( )', then

'$\underline{\lambda}($any A$)$' is true iff '$\underline{\lambda}(a_1) \wedge \underline{\lambda}(a_2) \wedge \underline{\lambda}(a_3) \wedge \ldots$'

is true, and

'$\underline{\lambda}($every A$)$' is true iff '$\underline{\lambda}(a_1) \wedge \underline{\lambda}(a_2) \wedge \underline{\lambda}(a_3) \wedge \ldots$'

is true.

There is, however, one difference. Whereas the sentence 'Tom has just married every sister of Bill's' simply means '(Tom has just married Mary) and (Tom has just married Jane) and (Tom has just married Kate)', the sentence 'Tom has just married any sister of Bill's' does not *simply* mean this. In this case, *we have to give this truth-conditional account of this sentence if we are to give any account of it at all.* The sentence 'Tom has just married any sister of Bill's' is an unidiomatic form. This could have been predicted, since the environment 'Tom has just married ( )' is an environment in which an *or*-list would be only disjunctively distributive, and therefore we would expect that the expression 'any A' or 'either A' is unacceptable. However, the environment 'Tom can lawfully marry ( )' is an environment in which an *or*-list would be conjunctively distributive, and in this environment, we expect either 'either A' or 'any A' to be acceptable, and to require an account different from the one required by 'both A's' or 'every A' in that environment.

As we saw above, if '$\underline{\lambda}(\ )$' is the environment 'Tom can lawfully marry ( )', then the account we give of '$\underline{\lambda}($every A$)$' is different from the account that we give of '$\underline{\lambda}($any A$)$'. If '$\underline{\lambda}(\ )$' is the environment 'Tom has just married ( )', then '$\underline{\lambda}($any A$)$' and '$\underline{\lambda}($every A$)$' demand the same account. With whatever justice, the distinction is often drawn by recomposing the sentence as one embedding a subordinated *that*-clause and distinguishing possible scopes for universal quantification. Thus we re-write 'Tom can lawfully marry . . .' as 'It is permitted that Tom marries . . .' and introduce the symbol 'P' to represent 'It is permitted that' and 't' to represent 'Tom marries'. Then we write 'P(t(every A))' for 'Tom can marry every sister' and 'P(t(any A))' for 'Tom can marry any sister'. The following equivalences then hold:

'P(t(every A)' is true iff 'P(t($a_1) \wedge$ t($a_2) \wedge$ t($a_3) \wedge \ldots$)'

is true, and

'P(t(any A))' is true iff 'P(t(a_1)) $\wedge$ P(t(a_2)) $\wedge$ P(t(a_3)) $\wedge$ ...'

is true. This is not quite Geach's account. Geach collapses 'P' and 't' into a single 'f' which is undistributive over 'a_1 and a_2 and a_3 and. ...' On the more detailed recomposition, we explain this non-distribution by the fact that 'P' is not distributive over 't(a_1) $\wedge$ t(a_2) $\wedge$ t(a_3) $\wedge$...' On Geach's account, the difference between 'f(any A)' and 'f(every A)' is that the former is equivalent to the conjunction of predications of the A's severally, and the latter is equivalent to the predication of 'f' of the conjunction of the A's. We have seen, however, that although it may be true that 'f(every A)' is always equivalent to the predication of 'f' of the conjunction of the A's, sometimes the sentence 'f(a_1 and a_2 and a_3 and ...)' is equivalent to the conjunction of the results of predicating 'f' of the A's severally. An account that makes the difference out to be no more than the difference between 'f(a_1 and a_2 and a_3 and ...)' and 'f(a_1) $\wedge$ f(a_2) $\wedge$ f(a_3) $\wedge$ ...' is therefore clearly inadequate.

6.2.2 Stoothoff's account

In an essay written when the puzzle was still only a philosophers' conversation piece, Robert Stoothoff (1964) suggests that 'any' and 'every' statements be distinguished by reference to the scope of proposition-forming operators. The difference between 'g(any F)' and 'g(every F)', he claims, is the difference between

$$(x)(Fx \rightarrow dGx)$$

and

$$d(x)(Fx \rightarrow Gx)$$

where 'dG(a)' is equivalent to 'g(a)'. Accordingly, he exhibits the difference between 'Tom won't come any day next week' and 'Tom won't come every day next week' as a difference in scope of $\neg$ in

$$(x)(Dx \rightarrow \neg Ctx)$$

and

$$\neg(x)(Dx \rightarrow Ctx),$$

which are read respectively as 'For every x, if x is a day next week, then Tom won't come on x' and 'It is false that for every x, if x is a day next week, then Tom will come on x'. Similarly, he claims, the difference between 'Tom is willing to come any day next week' and 'Tom is willing to come every day next week' can be represented as the difference between

$$(x)(Dx \rightarrow WtCtx)$$

and

$$Wt(x)(Dx \rightarrow Ctx).$$

He goes on to argue that this account is viable for any pair of 'any' and 'every' statements, no matter how complicated. One of his conclusions is that

> In particular, the logical fallacy contained in arguments of the pattern 'Any F may be G/∴Every F may be G' should be regarded as the result of ignoring the scope of the modal word 'may', not merely as a result of confusing 'any' and 'every'. (157)

Disregarding any difficulty that may attach to the notion of 'the scope of the modal word' Stoothoff's conclusion comes closer to the truth than Geach's account permits. He has noticed that it is the presence of certain proposition-forming operators that makes the confusion of 'any' and 'every' logically objectionable. As a general explanation of the difference between 'any' and 'every', however, it misses the important datum that within his narrow range of examples, it is only in the presence of certain proposition-forming operators that 'any' comes into use at all.

6.2.3 A first approximation

The most generally correct account we can give of the distinction between 'any' in its acceptable instances and 'every' seems to be the one given in the equivalences:

'$\underline{\lambda}$(any A)' is true iff '$\underline{\lambda}$(a_1 or a_2 or a_3 or ...)' is true,

'$\underline{\lambda}$(every A)' is true iff '$\underline{\lambda}$(a_1 and a_2 and a_3 and ...)' is true.

The necessity of the restriction to acceptable instances should be obvious from earlier remarks. Note that the first of the equivalences does not claim that every environment in which 'any' is acceptable is an environment in which a substituted *or*-list would be conjunctively distributive. That is not so, even for declarative cases. Indeed, the conversational interchangeability of sentences having 'any A' and sentences having 'a_1 or a_2 or a_3 or ...' depends upon such a list's having different distributive properties in different environments, in other words, upon its being sometimes conjunctively and sometimes disjunctively distributive. This need not alarm us; it certainly ought not to alarm anyone who would want to claim that '$\underline{\lambda}$(every A)' is equivalent to '$\underline{\lambda}$(a_1 and a_2 and a_3 and ...)' since even this translation depends upon the *and*-list's having different distributive properties in different environments. The distributive properties of the *or*-list differ apparently more vividly than those of the *and*-list.

The situation would seem to be this: we can translate the sentence 'You may have any A' into 'You may have a_1 or a_2 or a_3 or ...' because in the environment 'You may have ( )', the list 'a_1 or a_2 or a_3 or ...' is conjunctively distributive. But if we translate the sentence 'If any person wishes to go, then he may do so' into the sentence 'If p_1 or p_2 or p_3 or ... wishes to go, he may do so', the equivalence of this sentence to a propositional conjunction of conditionals to which the original sentence is equivalent would appear to depend upon the *or*-list's being disjunctively distributive in respect of the environment '( ) wishes to go'. If the *or*-list were conjunctively distributive *in respect of that environment*, the whole conditional would not be equivalent to a propositional conjunction and so would not be equivalent to the original sentence. If our account depends upon translation into *or*-lists, and translation into *or*-lists depends upon the list's permitting distribution differently in different environments, then this account is tantamount to one that claims that the meaning of 'any' changes from environment to environment. But then this account is less uniform than the account in terms of a correlation with propositional conjunction. For that account, by invoking the notion of scope, takes conditional sentences in its stride. According to such an account, in the conditional sentence 'If any person wishes to go, he may do so', what is predicated of p_1, p_2, p_3, and so on, is that if he wishes to go, he may do so. As Geach says, in this sentence the scope of 'any person' is 'If _____ wishes to go, he may do so', not merely '_____ wishes to go'. The dilemma is this: the conditional sentence

If f(any A), then g

is equivalent both to

If $f(a_1) \vee f(a_2) \vee f(a_3) \vee \ldots$, then g

and to

If $f(a_1)$, then g $\wedge$ if $f(a_2)$, then g $\wedge$ if $f(a_3)$, then g $\wedge$ ....

If we accept the correlation with propositional conjunction as the correct account of 'any', we will say something like 'The first is equivalent to the second because it is equivalent to the third'. If we accept the account of 'any' according to which its logic is that of an *or*-list, we will say something like 'The first is equivalent to the third because it is equivalent to second'. Accepting the first account preserves continuity of correlation with propositional conjunction at the expense of having to introduce the notion of scope. Accepting the second preserves the substitutability of an *or*-list at the expense of having to accept an apparent change in logical meaning. The conditional sentences so far examined provide in themselves no means of deciding between the two accounts. They are compatible with either account of 'any'. We shall have to devise an experiment to decide the case.

In *The Principles of Mathematics*, Bertrand Russell has hinted at an account of 'any' rather like the one I am suggesting. Russell's example is the conditional 'If you met Brown or Jones, you met a very ardent lover'. About it, Russell says, adopting an expository style reminiscent of Venn's or De Morgan's:

> The combination of Brown and Jones here indicated is the same as that indicated by *either* of them. It differs from a disjunction by the fact that it implies and is implied by a statement concerning both; but in some more complicated instances, this mutual implication fails. (1937, 57)

Since the sentence 'If you met any suitor of Miss Smith, you met a very ardent lover' is equivalent both to 'If you met Brown or Jones, you met a very ardent lover' and to the conjunction of 'If you met Brown, you met a very ardent lover' and 'If you met Jones, you met a very ardent lover', Russell concludes that the kind of conjunction by which *any* is defined 'seems half-way between a conjunction and a disjunction'. It is tempting to hear in the contrasting style of Geach's reaction to this the confident response of one century to the previous:

> If this difficulty arose at all, it would have arisen in the propositional calculus, independently of any referring phrase's being used. "If p or q, then r" is equivalent to "(If p, then r) and (if q, then r)"; but this gives no warrant for the idea that the "or" in "if p or q" is a peculiar connective 'half way between a conjunction and a disjunction'. (1962, 78)

It ought to be clear from previous chapters that the one place where it is certain that this difficulty would *not* arise is in the propositional calculus. This is so because the sort of conjunction by which Russell is claiming 'any' is understood is not a sort of propositional conjunction. The 'or' Russell labels 'peculiar' is an 'or' by which lists of proper names are constructed, not the 'or' of propositional disjunction. There is, however, no warrant for supposing that this 'or' is peculiar, or for supposing that it is half-way between conjunction and disjunction. Geach continues:

> For the rest, Russell's perplexity depends upon his ignoring the *scope* of referring phrases . . . the scope of the referring phrase in ['If you met any suitor of Miss Smith, you met a very ardent lover'] is "If you met _____, you met a very ardent lover."

Thus the sentence 'If you met any suitor of Miss Smith, you met a very ardent lover' conforms to the propositional conjunction pattern of less complicated 'any' sentences. It is curious feature of Geach's explanation that it should refer in just the manner it does to the fact that 'If p or q, then r' is equivalent to '(If p, then r) and (if q, then r)'. He says:

> . . . precisely because the 'any' phrase has a long scope, and because "If p or q, then r" is equivalent to "(If p, then r) and (if q, then r)", ['If you met any suitor of Miss Smith, you met a very ardent lover'] corresponds to a conjunction of the results of inserting "Brown" and "Jones" instead of the "any" phrase.

One would have expected, in Geach's account, to find the opposite claim: it is not because 'If p or q, then r' is equivalent to '(If p, then r) and (if q, then r)' that 'If you met any suitor of Miss Smith, then you met a very ardent lover' is equivalent to propositional conjunction. Rather it is because this sentence is equivalent to propositional conjunction that it is equivalent to a conditional sentence having a disjunctive *if*-clause. This latter equivalence is, so far as the account of 'any' is concerned, an irrelevant by-product of the equivalence with propositional conjunction.

The scope account does seem to capture the feel of the conditional with 'any' in its *if*-clause. When emphasis is placed on the word 'any', the sentence has the feel of the predication of a property of any A, and falls without noticeable inferential *sudor* into a propositional conjunction. It must be said, however, that much the same is true of the conditional sentence 'If you met Brown *or* Jones, you met a very ardent lover' when the principal emphasis is placed on the word 'or'. But this is not taken to preclude the equivalence of 'you met Brown or Jones' to 'you met Brown or you met Jones', despite the fact that, read this way, the sentence seems a mere abbreviation, much as does 'You may do A or B' with the principal emphasis placed upon 'or'. Geach's final conclusion is that:

> there seems as little warrant for Russell's saying that in 'complicated cases' there is no longer an equivalence between a predication about *any* so-and-so and the conjunction of corresponding predications about the several so-and-so's. (79)

Put this way, Geach's view seems unquestionable. Any acceptable sentence of the form 'f(any A)' is equivalent to 'f(a_1) ∧ f(a_2) ∧ f(a_3) ∧ . . .'. A fortiori, any conditional sentence that can be represented as having the form 'f(any A)' can be shown to be equivalent to a conjunction of the predications of 'f' of the A's severally. What is questionable is that conditional sentences can be regarded as predications about any A *whenever* the expression 'any A' occurs in the *if*-clause. An effective refutation of the position would seem to require a counterexample in the form of a conditional sentence with 'any' in its *if*-clause, that does not conform straightforwardly to the propositional conjunction pattern.

6.2.4 Quine's view

In *Word and Object*, Quine gives a view rather like Geach's: '"If any member contributes, I'll be surprised" [(1)] . . . asserts of every member that if he contributes, I'll be surprised' (1960, 139). We shall see that there is a reading on which this equivalence is less straightforward than the equivalence of the similar (2) 'If any member contributes, I'll shake his hand' to the assertion of every member that if he contributes I'll shake his hand. We see that there is a difference between them, without necessarily seeing what it is, when we consider what will make them false. If there is any circumstance in which I will not shake the hand of m_2 even if he contributes, then (2) is simply not true. But (1) is compatible with the qualification 'Of course, if m_1 contributes, I shan't be surprised if m_2 contributes'. To put this another way, if I have said, 'If any member contributes, I'll shake his hand', then the fact that m_3 has contributed provides a reason for predicting that I will shake his hand. If it does not, then what I have said is incorrect. But even if I have said, 'If any member contributes I'll be surprised', the fact that m_3 contributes does not in itself provide grounds for predicting that I will be surprised. Of course, *as things now stand*, (1) being the case, if m_3 contributes, then I'll be surprised, just as, as things now stand, if m_1 contributes, then I'll be surprised, and so on, exhausting the list of members. But this gives us no grounds for saying that m_1 having contributed, I'll be surprised if m_2 contributes; it is only if, *things being as they are*, m_2 contributes, that there are grounds for predicting that I shall be surprised. Thus the statement 'If any member contributes, I'll be surprised' does not quite assert of every member that if he contributes, I'll be surprised. At most, it asserts of every member that, *as things now stand*, if he contributes, I'll be surprised. On the most likely reading, (2) is conversationally interchangeable with 'I'll shake the hand of every member who contributes'. But on its most likely reading, (1) is not interchangeable with 'Every contribution from a member will surprise me'.

In the sentence 'If any member contributes, I'll be surprised', we can see the relevance to the sense of the sentence, of the substitutability of an *or*-list for 'any A'. Suppose that there are four members: m_1, m_2, m_3, m_4. For 'm_i contributes' I write '$C(m_i)$', and for 'I'll be surprised', 'S'. Substituting an *or*-list of members for the expression 'any member', the sentence 'If any member contributes, I'll be surprised' can be written

If $C(m_1$ or m_2 or m_3 or $m_4)$, then S,

which we may take to be interchangeable with

If $C(m_1) \lor C(m_2) \lor C(m_3) \lor C(m_4)$, then S.

Writing 'H' for 'I'll shake his hand', (2) can be written

If $C(m_1) \lor C(m_2) \lor C(m_3) \lor C(m_4)$, then H.

Now propositional logic would seem to dictate that since 'If p or q, then r' is equivalent to 'If p, then r and if q, then r', these sentences share a logical form, each being equivalent to a conjunction of conditional sentences. But for reasons we have already noted, the conjunctions that result from distribution are different in character for those two sentences, and we should say why this is so. Of course, if we do not distribute 'If _____, then H' over the *if*-clause, then, as Quine points out, we leave the word 'his' in 'I'll shake his hand' high and dry. By contrast, consider the result of replacing the conditional form by some such as 'I would be surprised to learn that ( )', formulated with an *or*-list of members. The sentence

If $C(m_1) \lor C(m_2) \lor C(m_3) \lor C(m_4)$, then I'll be surprised

becomes

I would be surprised to learn that $C(m_1$ or m_2 or m_3 or $m_4)$.

On one reading, this suggests that, as things now stand, $C(m_1)$ would surprise me; that, as things now stand, $C(m_2)$ would surprise me; and so forth. This is the reading on which it is interchangeable with the result of distributing 'that C' over the *or*-list of members to produce an *or*-list of *that*-clauses:

I would be surprised to learn that $C(m_1)$ or that $C(m_2)$ or that $C(m_3)$ or that $C(m_4)$.

But another reading is available, that in which the 'C', but not 'that C' distributes over the list to give a single disjunctive *that*-clause:

I would be surprised to learn that $C(m_1)$ or $C(m_2)$ or $C(m_3)$ or $C(m_4)$.

Asserted, this sentence would provide grounds for predicting that if first word of contributions reached me in the form of a report that $C(m_1)$, I would show surprise. But this is so only because that $C(m_1)$ implies that $C(m_1)$ or $C(m_2)$ or $C(m_3)$ or $C(m_4)$. Just in order to make, in Anscombe's phrase, an honest proposition of what I have said, I need not express surprise on every subsequent occasion on which a new contribution is reported to me. A snowballing of contributions might even have been expected if only the initial hurdle of pressing one member to give could be cleared. My surprise is at the truth of the disjunction, not at the slow unfolding of its solution. Herein lies the difference between these two sentences. $C(m_1)$ makes a difference to what will subsequently surprise me; $C(m_1)$ makes no difference to subsequent handshakings. Without adding the qualification 'as things now stand', the most that can be predicted on the basis of the former conditional together with $C(m_2)$ is that either I will be surprised or I will have been surprised at a previous contribution. Thus, if we are to distribute 'If _____ , then S' over '$C(m_1) \lor C(m_2) \lor C(m_3) \lor C(m_4)$', either we must strengthen the *if*-clause of each resulting conjunction by the addition of ' . . . and no one else has contributed', or we must weaken the *then*-clause of each resulting conjunct by the addition of ' . . . or I will have been surprised by a previous contribution.' Or again, if I have said 'If any member contributes, I'll be surprised', then I can be expected to show surprise even if all I learn is that $C(m_1) \lor C(m_2) \lor C(m_3) \lor C(m_4)$, but having said, 'If any member contributes, I'll shake his hand', I cannot be expected to shake anyone's hand, having learned only this much.

Part of the explanation why 'If _____ , then S' is not straightforwardly distributive over '$C(m_1) \lor C(m_2) \lor C(m_3) \lor C(m_4)$' is that disjunctive surprises are, in some respect, like disjunctive beliefs and assertions. Just as one could assert or believe that p or q without asserting or believing that p or that q, one can be surprised that p or q without being surprised that p or that q. In fact, when the disjunction in question is uniformly predicative, as in our example '$C(m_1) \lor C(m_2) \lor C(m_3) \lor C(m_4)$', the likely sentence for expressing the surprise is 'I am surprised that any member has contributed', which is conversationally interchangeable in our case with 'I am surprised that $C(m_1) \lor C(m_2) \lor C(m_3) \lor C(m_4)$, but not with the conjunction of the results of attaching 'I'm surprised that . . .' to each of the disjuncts. If we are forced to put the point in terms of conjunctions and disjunctions, universal and existential quantification, then in this environment, 'any' is without doubt disjunctive rather than conjunctive, existential rather than universal in force. Furthermore, the fact that in the conditional sentence the truth of S could be guaranteed by the truth of the *if*-clause shows that, on a truth-conditional account, the antecedent has a truth value; its truth conditions are those of the corresponding propositional disjunction.

It is tempting to suppose that a truth-functional understanding of the conditional would be sufficient to lay the matter to rest. If the conditional is true, then, for each i, if m_i contributes, the consequent of the conditional 'If $C(m_i)$, then S' is true, so each of the conjoined conditionals is true, and therefore the conjunction of conditionals is true as well. However, this would be an oversimple understanding of the conditional, which is not simply truth-functional. What the conditional claims is that a certain state of affairs would occasion surprise. What each of the conjoined conditionals got by distribution asserts is, therefore, that its antecedent condition would occasion surprise. Even if the surprise predicted in each conjunct is surprise at the same thing, the truth of this common *then*-clause does not warrant any more than a truth-functional conditional claim. It does not warrant the claim that the truth of each antecedent *would occasion* surprise.

So this sort of conditional environment is importantly similar to certain environments in which the correctness of 'any' is correlated with conjunctive distributivity of *or*-lists, although the similarities are masked by their superficially dissimilar grammatical structures. But rid the conditional sentence of its conditional appearance, and the similarities become apparent. Represent the environment 'If ( ), then S' schematically by 'D( )'. We can now express the conditional sentence 'If any member contributes, I'll be surprised' as 'D(C(any M))', which is true iff it is true that $D(C(m_1$ or m_2 or m_3 or $m_4))$, which is true iff it is true that $D(C(m_1) \vee C(m_2) \vee C(m_3) \vee C(m_4))$ is true. If 'D' were straightforwardly distributive, then this last formula would be equivalent to

$$D(C(m_1)) \wedge D(C(m_2)) \wedge D(C(m_3)) \wedge D(C(m_4)).$$

But the nature of D is such that this conjunction must be qualified by the statement to the effect that it is compatible with

(if $C(m_1)$, then $\neg(D(C(m_2))) \wedge \neg(D(C(m_3))) \wedge \ldots$) $\wedge$ (if $C(m_2)$, then $\neg(D(C(m_1))) \wedge \neg(D(C(m_3))) \wedge \ldots$) $\wedge \ldots$.

Compare this with the schematic representation of 'Tom can lawfully marry any sister of Bill's'. We represented this sentence as 'P(t(any A))', which is true iff it is true that $P(t(a_1$ or a_2 or $a_3))$, which is true iff it is true that $P(t(a_1)) \wedge P(t(a_2)) \wedge P(t(a_3))$. This conjunction is compatible with the qualification

(if $t(a_1)$, then $\neg P(t(a_2)) \wedge \neg P(t(a_3)))$ $\wedge$ (if $t(a_2)$, then $\neg P(t(a_1)) \wedge \neg P(t(a_3)))$ $\wedge$ (if $t(a_3)$, then $\neg P(t(a_1)) \wedge \neg P(t(a_2)))$.

Note the dissimilarity in the refinement that the qualification brings about. Whereas the sense of the qualification to the second sentence is such as to exclude the simultaneous performance of any two of $t(a_1)$, $t(a_2)$, and $t(a_3)$, the sense of the qualification to the conditional sentence is not such as to preclude the prediction of surprise upon the simultaneous contribution of several members. The qualification merely removes the certainty of surprise at each contribution.

The question as to whether in a sentence of the form 'If f(any A), then g', the expression 'any A' is disjunctive in sense, involves the question whether the *if*-clause of such a sentence is itself propositional. If such a sentence can be regarded as merely a predication of 'If f___, then g' of any A, then what is grammatically the *if*-clause is not really a *clause* at all, and has no truth value. If, however, the expression 'f(any A)' is a propositional expression, then the truth conditions of the entire sentence are such that the truth conditions of 'f(any A)' must be those of propositional disjunction. Whether there are such sentences in which 'f(any A)' has a truth value and is therefore disjunctive in sense should be discoverable by considering what relations hold between *if*- and *then*-clauses of uncomplicated conditional sentences and seeing whether there are sentences of the form 'If f(any A), then g' in which these relations hold between 'g' and 'f(any A)'. One such relation is that of relative tense.

6.3 Experiments

6.3.1 Tense differences in conditionals

The subject of tense differences in conditionals has recently come in for more serious and detailed study in its own right.[6] My discussion here touches upon the subject only as it provides useful laboratory specimens.

Consider first that only some conditional sentences state the logical consequences of propositions; that is, only some conditionals are like

(1) If Robinson is a bachelor, then Robinson is a male.

Other conditionals state the outcomes—actual, predicted, or contemplated—of actions, events, policies, and occurrences; that is, some conditional sentences are like

(2) If it rains, the track will be treacherous

and

(3) If you persist in your complacency, you will cause resentment.

In some non-logical conditional sentences, there is a difference in tense between the *if*-clause and the *then*-clause. But even in conditionals in which there is no difference in grammatical tense, such as

(4) If it rains, then we usually postpone the race

it is clear that the event introduced in the *then*-clause (i.e., the postponement) is understood to be later in time than the event introduced in the *if*-clause (i.e., the rain). Conditional sentences of logical or semantic connection such as (1) can undergo tautological transformations such as transposition straightforwardly. (1) is taken to be equivalent to

(1′) If Robinson is not a male, then Robinson is not a bachelor.

Non-logical conditional sentences with tense differences usually require some adjustment of tense in undergoing this sort of transformation. For example, (2) becomes

(2′) If the track is not slippery, then it will not have rained.

In (2), the present tense of the *if*-clause carries with it the implication of a determinate time reference having as one limit, the time of the occurrence of the event mentioned in the *then*-clause. This is an indication that the futurity of the *then*-clause relative to the *if*-clause is a built-in feature of this sort of conditional construction.

---

6. See in particular Dudman (1983, 1984, 1985, 1986 and 1989). The points made in this section are essentially those of Jennings (1967).

The fact that for some conditional sentences the *then*-clause is future relative to the *if*-clause affects the possibility for these sentences of undergoing certain transformations. Sometimes compensatory adjustments of tense must be made. But in some cases, such adjustments would be insufficient to save the sense of the original sentence. This is the case for a certain set of non-logical conditional sentences having disjunctive *if*-clauses.

In propositional logic, the formula

$$(p \vee q) \rightarrow r$$

is equivalent to the formula

$$(p \rightarrow r) \wedge (q \rightarrow r)$$

and the ordinary language counterpart of this equivalence also holds. 'If p or q, then r' is normally equivalent to 'If p, then r and if q, then r'. But when there is a difference in tense between the *if*-clause and the *then*-clause, special difficulties are introduced for this transformation. This question arises:

Is it always the case that if the tense of the *then*-clause is future relatively to that of the disjunctive *if*-clause, then in the propositional conjunction resulting from distribution, the *then*-clause of each conjunct will be future relatively to the *if*-clause of each conjunct in addition to remaining future relatively to the *if*-clause of the original sentence?

It is clear that sometimes this is the case. It is clearly so, for example, in the sentence

(5) If m_1 contributes or m_2 contributes or m_3 contributes, then he will be warmly congratulated,

which is equivalent to

(5′) If m_1 contributes, then he will be warmly congratulated and if m_2 contributes, then he will be warmly congratulated and if m_3 contributes, then he will be warmly congratulated.

The *then*-clause 'he will be warmly congratulated' is clearly future relatively to each of 'm_1 contributes', 'm_2 contributes', and 'm_3 contributes', even if these events do not occur simultaneously. But it is not so clear that the futurity of the *then*-clause is preserved throughout the same transformation for the sentence

(6) If m_1 contributes or m_2 contributes or m_3 contributes, then I'll be surprised.

If in its distributed form

(6′) If m_1 contributes, I'll be surprised and if m_2 contributes, I'll be surprised and if m_3 contributes, I'll be surprised

the *then*-clause of each conjunct is future relatively to the *if*-clause, then (6′) is not equivalent to (6). For on the basis of (6′) one can predict, under certain conditions, three occurrences of the event in the *then*-clause. As we have seen, on the basis of (6), one can predict only one such occurrence. If we accept Geach's view that in a sentence of the form 'If f(any A), then g' the scope of 'any A' is always 'If f____, then g', then we must accept that if there is any tense difference at all between antecedent and consequent, it will be between antecedent and *then*-clauses of the members of the resulting conjunction of conditionals. On this view, 'g' cannot be future relatively to 'f(any A)', because, as we have remarked, on this view, 'f(any A)' cannot be regarded as propositional. Geach's account provides an implicit proof that this is so. On Geach's view, any occurrence of the form 'f(any A)' is equivalent to propositional conjunction. So if an antecedent occurrence of 'f(any A)' is a proposition, it is equivalent to a propositional conjunction. But if it is a propositional conjunction, the sentence as a whole is not equivalent to propositional conjunction. But it is. So the antecedent occurrence of 'f(any A)' is not equivalent to a propositional conjunction; so it is not propositional. It follows that the grammatical tense of the verb contained in 'f' of 'f(any A)' must merely represent the tense of the verb in 'f' of 'f(a_1)', 'f(a_2)', and so on of the resulting propositional conjunction. But the sentence 'If any member contributes, I'll be surprised' provides an example of the form 'If f(any A), then g' in which the tense of 'g' is future relatively to 'f(any A)', and so provides a sentence of this form in which the *if*-clause has propositional sense independently of the translation of the sentence into propositional conjunction. Moreover, the sense of the sentence as a whole is such that the *if*-clause 'f(any A)' must be disjunctive.

6.3.2 Anaphora in the *then*-clause

There is another sort of conditional sentence for which an *if*-clause containing 'any' can be propositional and disjunctive in sense. In the course of arguing for the equivalence of the sentence 'If any member contributes, he gets a poppy' to propositional conjunction, Quine provides a clue to their construction. His argument is that if there were not this equivalence, then the pronoun 'he' would be left high and dry. It is partly the need to take into account references from the *then*-clause to constituents of the *if*-clause that determines the account that we give of the *if*-clause. There are two ways in which reference to the *if*-clause can be made. They can be illustrated by some examples:

(1) If Fred tells me a story, I'll believe it;

(2) If Fred touches my Laphroaig, I'll know it.

In (1), the referent of 'it' is 'story'; in (2), the referent of 'it' is the whole of the *if*-clause. If the reference of 'it' were unclear, we could discover what it was by asking 'What will you believe?' or 'What will you know?' and the answer to this question will make the reference explicit: 'I'll believe the story' or 'I'll know that Fred has touched my Laphroaig'. But when the reference of 'it' is to the entire content of the *if*-clause, the answer to this question can give us more than the reference of 'it'; it can give us an indication of the sense of the *if*-clause. If the *if*-clause happens to contain an occurrence of 'any', an anaphoric whole-clause reference will introduce possible readings not immediately evident when such reference is absent. Consider the following sentence:

If any of your guests touches my Laphroaig, I'll know it.

A possible (and the most plausible) answer to the question 'What will you know?' is 'I'll know that some guest has touched my Laphroaig'. In saying, 'I'll know it if any voter votes for me', a candidate would not be claiming that he will know the identity of his supporters, but that he will know it if he has some. Suppose that there are three guests: g_1, g_2, g_3. The sentence 'If any of your guests touches my Laphroaig, I'll know it' is then equivalent to a three-termed conjunction of sentences predicating something-or-other of g_1, g_2, and g_3, but it is not equivalent to the three-termed conjunction,

If g_1 touches my Laphroaig, I'll know it and if g_2 touches my Laphroaig, I'll know it and if g_3 touches my Laphroaig I'll know it.

In each of the conjuncts of this sentence, the reference of 'it' is to the *if*-clause, and the effect of this is to imply that I will know the identity of the poacher, which goes beyond the sense of the original sentence. To get a three-termed conjunction equivalent to the original, we must substitute for 'it' in such a way that what we substitute can occur in the *then*-clause of each of the three conjuncts. Assuming that there are only the three guests, such a conjunction would be the following:

If $T(g_1)$, I'll know that $T(g_1) \vee T(g_2) \vee T(g_3) \wedge$
if $T(g_2)$, then I'll know that $T(g_1) \vee T(g_2) \vee T(g_3) \wedge$
if $T(g_3)$, then I'll know that $T(g_1) \vee T(g_2) \vee T(g_3)$.

The fact that the disjunction '$T(g_1) \vee T(g_2) \vee T(g_3)$' is the proper substitution for 'it' indicates that the *if*-clause of the conditional is propositional and disjunctive.

6.3.3 Non-conjunctive 'any' in other environments

The phenomenon of the conditional is an intriguing one, and doubly so for purposes of a study of 'any' and 'or'. But if we want only to show that 'any' is sometimes non-conjunctive, there are easier examples than conditional sentences ready to hand. I list some sentences in which an expression of the form 'any A' stands in the place of disjunctively distributive lists where there is no equivalence of the sentence as a whole to propositional conjunction:

(1) I asked whether any voter had supported me,

in some settings (such as when we know the names of the voters), has the same force as the sentence 'I asked whether v_1 or v_2 or v_3 or ... had supported me', but never has the same force as the propositional conjunction 'I asked whether v_1 had supported me and I asked whether v_2 had supported me and I asked whether v_3 had supported me and ...'

(2) Did any member contribute?

which is equivalent to 'Is it the case that m_1 or m_2 or m_3 or ... contributed?' but not to a conjunction of questions. This sort of interrogative has special problems of its own, sometimes receiving a 'yes' or 'no' answer, but sometimes an answer specifying, in this case, which M contributed. The questions are equivalent in the sense that whatever state of affairs made the answer to one of them 'yes' or 'no' would make the answer to the other the same.

(3) I'm surprised that any member has contributed,

which means 'I'm surprised that m_1 or m_2 or m_3 or ... has contributed'.

The behaviour of 'any' in (3) merits closer attention. There proposition-forming prefixes that, like 'I am surprised that ...', can take 'any' constructions and where the construction is disjunctive in import. Some of these are 'I was thrilled (delighted) that ...' and 'I was shocked that. ...' Other prefixes such as 'I was informed that ...', 'I knew that ...', and 'I was aware that ...' do not take 'any' constructions in the absence of an independent legitimizing element.[7] We would naturally say, 'I was shocked that any member had opposed that measure', but we would not say 'I knew that any member had opposed the measure'. It is not at once obvious why one construction should be natural and disjunctive and the other unidiomatic, since both prefixes express awareness — the one reactive awareness and the other not. The question can be restated: Why is it permissible to say

I was surprised that any member had contributed,

while to express mere awareness of the same fact we would say,

I was aware that some member(s) had contributed

where the corresponding 'any' construction would be unacceptable?

The answer to this question seems to lie in the fact that the former sort of sentence has a reactive aspect and the latter does not. Both express awareness of the fact that m_1 or m_2 or ... had contributed, but one expresses a reaction or an attitude toward the fact. The force of 'any' in such sentences seems to be that one aspect of the particular solution of the disjunction is irrelevant to the reaction, — sometimes how many members contributed, sometimes who they are. (Contrast 'I'm surprised that any member has contributed' as a response to 'Three members have contributed' with the same sentence as a response to 'Jones has contributed'.)

The inappropriateness of 'any' with 'know' corresponds to the inappropriateness of the emphatic particle 'even' in

I knew that even one member had contributed.

Contrast

I was surprised that even one member had contributed.

7. Compare 'I knew that any member contributed' and 'I knew that any member would contribute'.

But we might note that in the presence of negative elements, 'know' and 'any' do not behave quite as the universal quantificational-cum-conjunctive account would suggest.

I do not officially know that anyone has contributed

implies a denial, for each item of the collection, that I officially know that that item has contributed, but it also implies that I do not officially know even that some item has contributed, and ceases to be true when I am officially told that someone has contributed.

By contrast, in negative environments, 'surprised' and 'any' lose contact.

I am not surprised that anyone has contributed

is less natural than

I am not surprised that someone has contributed

unless, in the first sentence, the 'anyone' is stressed, forcing a distributive reading, namely, that there is no one whose contribution surprises me.

6.4 Is 'Any' a Quantifier?

For the restricted purposes of this essay, the question whether *any* quantificational reading for 'any' is *required* is not an important one. I have argued only for the limited position that if 'any' is to be given a quantificational representation, there seems no choice but to represent it sometimes with a universal quantifier and sometimes with an existential. But one need only consider such sentences as 'I'm surprised that any dog is left alive' and 'Any fool knows that' to see the truth of that claim. More particularly, I have argued that even where a representation with a universal quantifier is available, an existential representation is sometimes dictated, especially in some *if*-clause occurrences. The more difficult because more confused issue is the significance for its occurrences in English of its representation as either quantifier. For although it is relevant to questions of the usefulness of first-order logic, the question remains whether differences of required quantificational representation are the significant determinants of its uses, and not merely artefacts of the quantificational language we choose to represent them. Furthermore, as we have seen in the case of conjunctive 'or', our language of representation may impose artificial requirements of consistency that do not arise in natural language uses. The uses of 'any' more plausibly have to do with the distinctions it preserves (with 'every' on the one hand, and with 'some' on the other) and these more to do with the available alternatives than with some truth-conditionally specifiable core meaning. So we might come plausibly to the partial rule that

'any' occurs *inter alia* in environments where 'every' has short scope,

a rule that (in its mention of scope) draws upon the quantificational representation, but does not depend upon or predict that that representation will always be universal or always existential.

For the rest, we have to explain why 'any' should be selected rather than 'some' in those cases where no universal quantificational representation is available. Why does one say on a particular occasion, 'I'm surprised that any member of the family attended' rather than 'I'm surprised that some member of the family has attended' but not 'I know that any member of the family attended' rather than 'I know that some member of the family attended'? Again, in cases where a universal quantificational representation is available, and where 'any' and 'every' and 'all' would have to receive the same representation, we want to know what determines the use of 'any' rather than 'every' or 'all'. Why on a particular occasion would one say '*Any* fool knows that' rather than 'Every fool knows that' or 'All fools know that'? The answer, it would seem, must be given in extra-quantificational terms. Zeno Vendler's early attempt at distinguishing among 'all', 'any', 'each' and 'every' tries to do just that. The distinction between 'every' and 'any' in Vendler's (1962) account is akin to the distinction between a sorted universally quantified proposition and its instantiation to an arbitrary individual of the appropriate sort:

To say

Any doctor will tell you . . .

is to issue a *blank* warranty for conditional predictions: you fill in the names. You choose Dr. Jones; well, then *he* will tell you if you ask him. You pick twenty-five others; then, I say, *they* will tell you if you consult them . . . If you do not ask any? In this case you do not use the blank; but it may still be good. (Vendler 1967, 85)

As the arbitrary individual of first-order logic is a fiction, so the representative may be only an imagined selection. The feature that the use of 'any' makes explicit is the *non-specificity* of the claim within the class of objects it is about, rather than its *universality* over the explicitly mentioned class. The element of selection in Vendler's account may be understood more generally to cover other ways in which the representative might come to one's attention. And the absence of explicit universality makes possible the implicit restriction of the manner of selection in certain uses. Thus in a particular instance,

Stay a little distance behind the main column to protect our rear. Send any stragglers on ahead.

Watch the street from your window. Report any enemy movements,

'any stragglers' may here mean 'any stragglers that you encounter in the course of your principal duties'; 'any enemy movements' may mean 'any enemy movements that come within sight of your position'.

From a philosophical point of view, it makes sense to distinguish at least three classes of use to which 'any' is applied: those where an *or*-list would be conjunctively distributive (as 'You may have any A'./'You may have a_1 or a_2'.), those in which an *or*-list would be disjunctively distributive (as 'Any member knows the handshake.'/'Syl or Sal knows the handshake. (Ask Syl first.)'), and those in which an *or*-list would be undistributive (as 'I'm delighted that any club member has participated'/'I'm delighted that Syl or Sal has participated.' ($\neq$

'I'm delighted that Syl has participated or I'm delighted that Sal has participated.')) In the last, especially, do we see the positive contribution of non-specificity which the use of 'any' makes, even when it is given an 'existential' reading. Consider for a moment just sentences (or readings of sentences) of this sort, that is, sentences where 'any' receives an existential if any quantificational representation and *or*-lists are undistributive in the sense given. We can distinguish three subclasses of this class: (a) those in which an *any*-noun phrase can appear, (b) those in which it cannot (as 'I know that Syl or Sal has participated') and (c) those in which it can appear only dubiously by itself or needs propping up in its 'existential' reading, but where it can appear as a supplement to an indefinite or even general noun phrase:[8]

I think she went to Lake Chapala deliberately to find a man. Any man. (MacDonald 1962, 3)

Suddenly she hoped that someone, anyone—man or woman—would see her through the rain and white oak trees and Canary Island pines. (Wambaugh 1978, 19)

They showed Jay Smith's picture to **every** doctor, nurse, patient, technician, secretary, janitor, security guard, gift shop worker, cafeteria employee, *anyone* who could feasibly have seen him during the weekend of June 22nd on any of the three shifts at Bryn Mawr Hospital. (Wambaugh 1987, 212. My bold; author's italics.)

I want a train, *any* train, that leaves soon.

I am looking for a bicycle, *any* bicycle, that works.

I am standing here only until a policeman, *any* policeman, turns up.

What this use illustrates with particular clarity is a general feature of 'any', not brought out in Vendler's account, that to use it is to warrant an expectation that a certain sort of challenge will receive the reply 'even that one'. Consider whatever scale you please (some scale may have been situationally suggested) on which to place policemen: slovenliness, fastidiousness, brutality, ineffectualness, dishonesty, scrupulousness. Consider the policeman that you would place at the extreme of the chosen scale. That one will do to send me about my business. A train to howsoever undistinguished a destination? What about the train to Burnaby? That will do. A bicycle howsoever rickety? What about this penny farthing that I'm taking to the museum? That will do. To reject an item within the class, however far along whatever scale, is to have changed one's mind or to have climbed down from the earlier claim. The universality of 'any', as must be evident from the last three examples, does not always entail representation as a universal quantifier and is derivative in character, deriving by monotonicity along all chosen scales. If even the oldest (least comfortable, most

---

8. Supplementary 'any' can occur in other settings where 'any' by itself is questionable, as for example, imperatives: 'Someone, anyone, please help me', and requests: 'Will someone, anyone, please take charge of this hamster?'

perilous, etc.) bicycle will do, then a bicycle in less extreme position (newer, more comfortable, safer) will also do.

The idea is a particular instance of the more ambitious theory mooted by Fauconnier (1979), which we have already considered in its application to conjunctive 'or' (p. 110). Fauconnier's idea is that certain particular comparisons (as 'Max works harder than even Hercules does') have the effect of universal quantification in virtue of the place of the exemplar on a scale. Thus, in the example, Max is said, indirectly, to work harder than anyone else. Fauconnier characterizes the comparative environment as one that reverses the scale (in this case, the scale of effort, making Hercules a minimum). Clearly it is not essential to describe the case in these terms, since transitivity (or self-monotonicity) of the 'works harder than' relation will give us the desired inferences about Max in relation to other workers. In any case, his argument is given in these terms:

> Let U____V be an environment which reverses implication (and therefore scales, and polarity):
>
> if $P \Rightarrow Q$
> then $U \, Q \, V \Rightarrow U \, P \, V$
>
> Consider the schema $R(x)$ and the complex schema $T(x)$ obtained by embedding $R(x)$ in U____V:
>
> $T(x) \Rightarrow U \, R(x) \, V$
>
> For any constant a, Existential Generalization allows us to write:
>
> (23) $R(a) \Rightarrow \exists x R x$
>
> Since U____V reverses implication, (23) yields:
>
> (24) $U \, \exists x R x \, V \Rightarrow U \, R(a) \, V$
>
> Since (24) is valid for any arbitrary constant a, we obtain, through Universal Generalization:
>
> (25) $\boxed{U \, \exists x R x \, V \Rightarrow \forall x \, U \, R(x) \, V.}$
>
> We shall call this property the *Existential Extraction Law*. (296)

Fauconnier wants to subsume some of the standard troublesome examples under this general principle, in particular the familiar:

> (29)   If anyone calls, I will answer the door.
> (30) $\forall x$ (if x calls, I will answer the door).
> (31)   If $\exists x$ (x calls), I will answer the door.
>
> In our presentation, this type of problem disappears since *any* is not a quantifier but rather indicates the extremity of a scale: the equivalence of (30) and (31) is only a special case of *Existential Extraction*. (297)

We have already seen examples, namely, those in which there is anaphoric reference to the whole of an *if*-clause, in which the problem will not disappear without quantificational remainder. But an infusion of the spirit of this idea into the treatment of earlier cases is equally clear. If I say that I am surprised that any member participated, it may be offered as against this that it was after all Syl that participated, good old Syl, who of all members has always been the most generous with his time and energies. But if I do not retreat, and if my surprise is not dissipated by the revelation, I might be expected to reply that in this instance participation had seemed onerous even beyond the endurance of Syl's pathologically generous nature. Even if in a particular instance, 'any' and 'every' are practically interchangeable and suitably represented by universal quantification, the question remains how the effect of universality is achieved, or by what usual means of achieving the effect, the use of 'any' in the one case, of 'every' in the other comes to be warranted. The case, in this respect, parallels that of conjunctive 'or'. Even if in a particular instance, 'or' and 'but' are practically interchangeable, as in

> . . . because in the former case we expect an indication of a maximum, and in the latter of a minimum.
>
> *Or*, perhaps, the explanation is rather this, that . . . (Jespersen 1934, 82. my italic)

> She may have met with foul play. *Or* she may have decided she didn't want to be married . . .(MacDonald 1964a, 2),

we may ask how the conjunctive effect is obtained by the use of 'or' and how it would be achieved by 'but', not expecting the same answer in each case. Similarly, the practical interchangeability of

> Any fool knows that

and

> Every fool knows that

may prompt us to ask how in each case the effect of universality is achieved, our answer in the one case mentioning the extremity of a scale and in the other not.

6.4.1 Implication reversal and polarity

We have already alluded to Fauconnier's applications of scale to the understanding of the behaviour of 'or' in comparisons. The intuition has found various employment in the work of other linguists, some of them adopting implication reversal, or more generally downward monotonicity, as the favoured generalization of negation for the purpose of picking out negative-polarity environments. William Ladusaw calls expressions which provide such environments 'downward entailing' (1980, 112). It is the familiar algebraic notion: δ is downward entailing (or downward monotonic) iff, if x is below y, then δy is below δx, where *belowness* is logical implication or inclusion or the like, depending upon the case. Such a δ generalizes negation or complementation, both of which are downward entailing. And, usefully, some weaker adverbs such as 'hardly' and 'rarely' are also downward entailing on this account. But it is worth repeating a difficulty we alluded to earlier: for some of the environments that occasion conjunctive distribution over 'or', that distribution over 'or' is the extent of their reliable downward monotonicity. *If*-clauses are a case in point. *Or*-lists in *if*-clauses are conjunctively distributive with respect to *if f( ),then* α, but conditionals, outside classical logic, are not in general downward entailing on the left. Nevertheless, conditional sentences are, as we have already observed, like modal environments in the way that they treat their *if*-clauses. By this I mean that the realization of an *if*-clause, as when a member contributes, may suspend the guarantees of the conditional as it applies to later contributors. The undertaking expressed in 'If any member disagrees, I'll resign' is to resign at the first sign of disagreement from the membership, but it cannot be taken to guarantee a resignation after each disagreement. Similarly, it cannot be taken for granted that the undertaking of 'You may have any beverage' will survive your first drink. In each case, though the sentence is undoubtedly conjunctive rather than disjunctive in character, it is conjunctive *as-of-now* (*ut nunc* to enlist an ancient tag) and does not imply that the activation of one conjunct, or that the taking up of one option, does not suspend the rest. Now linguists have wanted to distinguish 'polarity "any" ' from 'free-choice "any" ', the former category comprehending both negations and *if*-clauses, and the latter, modal environments. The correlation with 'or' suggests quite another taxonomy in which both *if*-clauses and modal environments, in allowing *ut nunc* conjunctions, are extreme examples of environments requiring separate conjunctive and general noun phrase constructions.

6.4.2 Conclusion

The main conclusion is a guarded form of one that many linguists have happily enough accepted: If noun phrases with 'any' are to be construed quantificationally, they must sometimes be represented by a universal quantifier, and sometimes by an existential. Earlier philosophers (notably Quine and Geach), considering only a narrow range of instances, have hoped that the existentially representable cases might, when considerations of scope were taken into account, prove to be universal after all. But, as we have seen, there are ineluctably 'existential' uses. And if there are cases that *must* be represented existentially, then it is useless to insist that all those cases that *can* be represented universally *must* be, even those for which a short-scope existential representation is available. But the larger conclusion is that we should question the view that 'any' is *essentially* a quantifier in anything like the first-order logical understanding of that notion.

Form and Meaning

A jar or a piece of cloth cannot be produced by a combination of a jar and a piece of cloth.   SWAMI NIKHILANANDA

7.1 Scope and Form

The notion of the scope of an occurrence of a logical constant is familiar and precise. Though the details may vary slightly from presentation to presentation, in general the propositional account takes the scope of an occurrence of a connective to be the least well-formed formula in which it occurs. Thus the scope of the occurrence of ∨ in

$$(p \lor q) \land r$$

is the (occurrence of the) wff '$(p \lor q)$' while the scope of the occurrence of ∧ is the whole wff '$(p \lor q) \land r$'. In first-order logic, the definition is complicated slightly by the presence of quantifiers and free and bound variables, but, allowing for propositional functions in zero variables, it need be no more complicated to state: the scope of an occurrence of a connective is the least propositional function in which it occurs. Thus the scope of the occurrence of ∨ in

$$(x)(\exists y)(\varphi x \lor \psi x \rightarrow \zeta y)$$

is the propositional function (in one variable): '$\varphi x \lor \psi x$'; the scope of the occurrence of → is the propositional function (in two variables):

$$(\varphi x \lor \psi x \rightarrow \zeta y);$$

the scope of the occurrence of the existential quantifier, $(\exists y)$ is the propositional function (in the single variable, x):

$$(\exists y)(\varphi x \lor \psi x \rightarrow \zeta y);$$

the scope of the universal quantifier, (x) is the propositional function (in no variables):

$$(x)(\exists y)(\varphi x \lor \psi x \rightarrow \zeta y),$$

that is, the wff itself.

The notion of scope as applied to occurrences of fragments of sentences of natural language is, not unexpectedly, a little less exact in its definition and a little more complicated in its application. For occurrences of vocabulary that roughly corresponds in its use to the constants of first-order and propositional logic, the account can, for many cases, draw upon the greater precision of its mathematical counterpart, even without a translation into more strictly parallel form. So we can disambiguate the sentence

> I shall change and play tennis or swim

by distinguishing between the interpretation in which the scope of the 'or' is 'play tennis or swim' and the scope of the 'and' is 'change and play tennis or swim' and the interpretation in which the scope of the 'or' is 'change and play tennis or swim' and the scope of 'and' is 'change and play tennis'. Roughly, we might say, the distinction is between the distributed form of the sentence bracketed thus:

> I shall change and (I shall play tennis or I shall swim)

and the distributed form bracketed so:

> (I shall change and I shall play tennis) or I shall swim,

and we might mark it in written or spoken form by punctuation, as the distinction between

> I shall change, and play tennis or swim

and

> I shall change and play tennis, or swim.

The problems become more noticeable when they arise for words that draw no benefit of analogy from the logical examples. So we might distinguish between an occurrence of the noun phrase 'large animal compound' meaning a compound for large animals, and another occurrence of the same noun phrase meaning a large compound for animals, by thus making explicit the particular prepositional character of the attribution, and marking the scope of the preposition involved. In the case of, say, 'heavy animal fat', the preposition might be 'from'. But in Quine's example 'large European butterfly', the idea of scope is introduced as a way of distinguishing one relativization of 'large' from another: 'large for a butterfly' from 'large for a European butterfly'. In the two previous examples, the two kinds of distinctions may be overlaid: a compound for large animals, an animal compound that is large for an animal compound, an animal compound that is large for a compound; fat from heavy animals, fat that is heavy for animal fat, animal fat that is heavy for fat, and, again, animals that are large as things go, animals that are large as animals go, and so on. One characteristic of this sort of example not noticeable in the previous one is that in some of them we can describe the difference as a difference in the grammatical construal of some of the words. The difference between these cases and those of propositional and first-order wffs is that in the latter cases the roles that the constants can play and the relationships that they can enter into are given explicitly and unambiguously in the formation rules. For modifiers of ordinary English, this is not so.

Unfortunately, not every case that looks on the surface as though its logical analogue might be a guide is free from such complications and worse. In particular, difficulties arise when a notion of scope is introduced to account for apparently existential or disjunctive occurrences of 'any'. With this and related examples in mind, Geach introduces a restricted notion of scope in the following way:

> Let us suppose that a complicated proposition abbreviated as "f(*A)" contains a clause "g(*A)" as part of itself: then we shall in general have to distinguish between taking a referring phrase "*A" as the quasi-subject of the whole of (the context abbreviated to) "f( )" and taking it as merely the quasi-subject of "g( )"; in the latter case we must treat only "g( )" not the whole of "f( )" as the scope of "*A". For example in (1) [If Jemima can lick any dog, then Jemima can lick any dog] the scope of the first "any dog" is "if Jemima can lick ____, then Jemima can lick any dog"; (1) expresses the supposition that this complex predicable is true of any dog. In (2) on the other hand [If Jemima can lick some dog, then Jemima can lick any dog] the proposition "Jemima can lick some dog" occurs as the antecedent, and the scope of "some dog" is merely the context "Jemima can lick ____". This difference in scope neutralizes the difference between them, so that (1) and (2) become practically the same. (1962, 66–67)

Now for complicated sentences such as Geach introduces, we may distinguish two kinds of cases: for a certain 'F', say, 'F_1' as applied to three A's, we may have

$$F_1(g(any\ A))$$

conversationally interchangeable with

$$F_1(g(a_1)) \wedge F_1(g(a_2)) \wedge F_1(g(a_3))\ (KF_1),$$

which is conversationally interchangeable with

$$F_1(g(a_1) \vee g(a_2) \vee g(a_3))\ (F_1A)$$

but not with

$$F_1(g(a_1) \wedge g(a_2) \wedge g(a_3))\ (F_1K).$$

For another, say, F_2, we may have

$$F_2(g(any\ A))$$

conversationally interchangeable with

$$F_2(g(a_1)) \wedge F_2(g(a_2)) \wedge F_2(g(a_3))\ (KF_2)$$

which is conversationally interchangeable with

$$F_2(g(a_1) \wedge g(a_2) \wedge g(a_3)) \ (F_2K)$$

but not with

$$F_2(g(a_1) \vee g(a_2) \vee g(a_3)) \ (F_2A).$$

'If ( ) votes, then α' is like $F_1( )$; 'If α, then ( ) may vote' is like $F_2( )$. In the second case, KF_2 is conversationally interchangeable with F_2K, so there is no distinction between taking the scope of 'any A' as being '$F_2( )$' and taking it as being '( ) may vote'. In the first case, KF_1 and F_1K are inequivalent, and since $F_1((\text{any A}))$ is conversationally interchangeable with KF_1 and not with F_1K, we must take the scope of 'any A' as being '$F_1( )$' and not as '$g( )$'. But since the scope of 'any A' is determined, on Geach's account, by which conjunctive or conjunction-containing sentence the sentence containing 'any' is equivalent to, reference to the scope of 'any' cannot be used *to prove* the correlation between 'any' and propositional conjunction. Indeed, this is not Geach's reason for the introduction of scope. Scope merely makes other explanations, including the disjunctive explanation of the role of 'any' in conditionals, unnecessary. Scope makes the propositional conjunction explanation available for these cases; it does not make it inescapable. On the contrary, it is the insistence upon a correlation with conjunction that makes the introduction of scope necessary. Scope makes this account possible here, but does it make it reasonable?

'Any' occurs in sentences of the form

$$F(g(\text{any A}))$$

even when '$g( )$' is not an environment in which it would normally occur. But even if '$g( )$' were an environment in which 'any' might normally occur so that '$g(\text{any A})$' were equivalent to

$$g(a_1) \wedge g(a_2) \wedge g(a_3) \wedge \ldots$$

for some F's, '$F(g(\text{any A}))$' would be equivalent to

$$F(g(a_1)) \wedge F(g(a_2)) \wedge F(g(a_3)) \wedge \ldots$$

and not to

$$F(g(a_1) \wedge g(a_2) \wedge g(a_3) \wedge \ldots).$$

For some F's for which this is true,

$$F(g(\text{any A}))$$

is equivalent to

$$F(g(a_1) \vee g(a_2) \vee g(a_3) \vee \ldots).$$

We might be tempted to say that in such a case, the meaning of 'any' has changed between '$g(\text{any A})$' and '$F(g(\text{any A}))$'. The notion of scope makes this explanation unnecessary. On a Geachian account, it is just the scope that has changed; the meaning remains the same.

7.1.1 Plural noun phrases

A final wrinkle for which the scope account would seem an unlikely smoothing iron concerns plural and mass noun phrases containing 'any'. First-order quantificational language deals only awkwardly with such phrases anyway, and the understanding sought for them in English would seem to be variable. Indeed, the existence of them in English seems to suggest that 'any', which, being a derivative of *unulus*, ought to have only singular use, has gone the way that 'none' seems to be heading: toward indifference as to numerical agreement. As we object to 'None of the passengers *were* injured', so perhaps *fastidiosi* of the past recoiled from the form 'If any of the passengers were injured, then α'. Nevertheless, the use is acceptable and even dictated where mutuality is to be understood, as in 'I'm surprised that any of them banded together' or 'If any of them should exchange salacious grins, that would indicate a merely prurient or frivolous interest'. Again, plural noun phrases are acceptable in negative constructions, as, for example 'He hadn't got any marbles' as opposed to (and here a mass noun example) 'He hadn't got any marble'. Even were there a representation, howsoever longwinded, of the sentence in universal quantificational form, it would require either that the plural be treated as a singular or that the quantification be over some set of items different from those introduced in the original: groups, pairs, amounts and the like. And again, in many such environments, the retention of 'any' in the scope-explicit version is unnatural, 'every' being expected.

Of course, no extra simplicity is gained for the account of 'any' by excluding a change of meaning when a change of scope can be postulated instead if there are environments in which a clause having an *any* noun-phrase as its subject can be replaced by a disjunction but where no translation into a conjunctive or a conjunction-containing sentence is available. Since in such cases the notion of scope is of no help, it may be questioned whether the scope account of 'any' in conditional sentences ever contributes to the explanation of the behaviour of 'any'. Attractive as it may seem, the notion of scope may be of only illusory relevance.

7.1.2 The scope of 'or'

Corresponding problems present themselves when we try to account for distribution over *or*-lists in certain sentences. There are, as we have noted, environments in which an *or*-list is conjunctively distributive. Although a sentence

$$g(a_1 \text{ or } a_2 \text{ or } a_3 \text{ or } \ldots)$$

is equivalent to

$$g(a_1) \wedge g(a_2) \wedge g(a_3) \wedge \ldots,$$

nevertheless, a conditional sentence having

$$g(a_1 \text{ or } a_2 \text{ or } a_3 \text{ or } \ldots)$$

as its antecedent clause would normally be taken to be equivalent to a conjunction of conditional sentences and not to a conditional having a conjunctive antecedent clause. That is, for some g's, a declarative occurrence of

$$g(a_1 \text{ or } a_2 \text{ or } a_3)$$

will be read as

$$g(a_1) \wedge g(a_2) \wedge g(a_3);$$

nevertheless, for some F's

$$F(g(a_1 \text{ or } a_2 \text{ or } a_3))$$

is equivalent to

$$F(g(a_1)) \wedge F(g(a_2)) \wedge F(g(a_3)),$$

which is equivalent to

$$F(g(a_1) \vee g(a_2) \vee g(a_3)),$$

but which is not equivalent to

$$F(g(a_1)) \wedge F(g(a_2)) \wedge F(g(a_3)).$$

The parallel with 'any' becomes clear as two possible explanations for the apparent inconsistency present themselves. First, we can say that although in the environment 'g( )', the list 'a_1 or a_2 or a_3 or . . .' is conjunctively distributive, in an environment such as 'F(g( ))' (for example, 'If g( ), then p'), the same list is disjunctively distributive. Alternatively, we can say that the list is conjunctively distributive in both cases, but in the conditional sentence it is conjunctively distributive in respect of 'If g( ), then p', not in respect of 'g( )'. We can, that is to say, give an account of the discrepancy by introducing the notion of scope. Like the scope account of 'any' in these environments, the second account avoids the necessity of postulating a change in meaning of 'or' between the environments 'g( )' and 'F(g( ))'. But like the scope account of 'any', it affords us no additional simplicity, but only *seems* to do so since it seems to offer us what our logical predilections prompt us to expect, namely a disjunctive reading for 'or'. We know that there are conjunctively distributive *or*-lists with no intermediate disjunctive reading. Nor ought we to dwell upon the fact that a conjunctive interpretation of 'or' preserves the correlation between 'any' and 'or' alongside the correlation with propositional conjunction. For on some occasions, an 'any' phrase is replaceable by a disjunctively distributive *or*-list where there is no equivalent propositional conjunction.

7.1.3 *Or*-lists with negations

The question of distributive stability that arises for conjunctively distributive *or*-lists likewise arises when negating elements are introduced, as in

(1) You may have shiitakes or oysters,

which is truth-conditionally equivalent to

(2) You may have shiitakes and you may have oysters.

As we have seen, an *or*-list may be read as conjunctively distributive in autonomous occurrences of the sentence, but the same sentence need not receive a reading as propositional conjunction when it is embedded in other environments. If we add a negative particle, the entire sentence is likely to receive a conjunctive reading

(3) You may not have shiitakes or oysters

would normally be taken to forbid both shiitakes and oysters. So the environment 'You may have ( )' cannot be taken to distribute conjunctively in this setting. By analogy with the claim for *any*-constructions, we could merely claim that the correlation with propositional conjunction is constant. That is, we could claim that the distributive properties of the list between (1) and (2) remain unchanged, that the list permits conjunctive distribution of the whole environment (whatever that may be) in both cases. This would be analogous to saying that 'any' takes the longest possible scope, as a means of maintaining the correlation between 'any' and propositional conjunction. But the desire to see 'any' retain a universal quantificational reading across all environments is essentially an expression of logical conservatism. The same conservative attitude presses us to regard the original conjunctive distribution as the anomaly to be explained away, and the conjunctive distribution of the negation as a triumph of traditional moral values. Those values do not permit us to explain our reading of the sentence

(4) You did not have shiitakes or oysters

as equivalent to propositional conjunction by a general rule of 'whole environment' conjunctive distribution of *or*-lists. Even if we accept the claim that the character of the *or*-list remains unchanged between (1) and (3), because the *or*-list is distributive with respect to its entire environment, then we must claim that the distributive properties of the list change between (4) and

(5) You had shiitakes or oysters,

which is equivalent to propositional disjunction. The 'whole environment' account, like the scope account, does not remove the necessity to postulate a change of sense; it merely postpones it to other cases.

Similar remarks hold for 'or' in conditional environments. If we say that 'or' is disjunctive in

$$\text{If } g(a_1 \text{ or } a_2 \text{ or } a_3 \text{ or } \ldots), \text{ then } p$$

just because this sentence is equivalent to

$$\text{If } g(a_1), \text{ then } p \wedge \text{ if } g(a_2), \text{ then } p \wedge \text{ if } g(a_3), \text{ then } p \wedge \ldots,$$

then we are bound to explain why we should regard the same list as anything but conjunctive in

$$\text{If } h(a_1 \text{ or } a_2 \text{ or } a_3), \text{ then p,}$$

where 'h' is such that

$$h(a_1 \text{ or } a_2 \text{ or } a_3 \ \ldots)$$

is equivalent to

$$h(a_1) \vee h(a_2) \vee h(a_3) \vee \ \ldots \,.$$

We are then in the following dilemma: either we must say that there is a change of meaning of 'or' between

$$g(a_1 \text{ or } a_2 \text{ or } a_3 \text{ or } \ \ldots)$$

and

$$\text{If } g(a_1 \text{ or } a_2 \text{ or } a_3 \text{ or } \ \ldots), \text{ then p,}$$

or we must say that there is a change of meaning between

$$h(a_1 \text{ or } a_2 \text{ or } a_3 \text{ or } \ \ldots)$$

and

$$\text{If } h(a_1 \text{ or } a_2 \text{ or } a_3 \text{ or } \ \ldots), \text{ then p.}$$

If, by contrast, we claim that there is no change of meaning in the second case, it is difficult to justify saying that there is no change of meaning in the first.

It may seem a gratuitous complication to say that the *or*-list in a conditional sentence

$$\text{If } g(a_1 \text{ or } a_2 \text{ or } a_3 \text{ or } \ \ldots), \text{ then p}$$

represents a special conjunctive use of 'or', especially since, at least under the assumption of monotonicity, a propositional conjunction results even if the *or*-list is disjunctive. Similarly, since usually a sentence containing 'any' is e-quivalent to a propositional conjunction, we seem to purchase greater unity in saying that in the conditional sentence 'If g(any A) then p', 'any A' has its normal sense, and that this sentence is equivalent to propositional conjunction because of the scope of 'any A'. It seems unnecessary to suppose that there has been a change of sense here, because propositional conjunction results even on the assumption that no change has taken place. However, the situation is compli-cated by the fact that in other environments 'or' clearly distributes conjunctively and in some environments 'any' constructions are clearly equivalent to disjunc-tion. Furthermore, acceptable *any*-sentences equivalent to propositional conjunc-tion will permit substitution of an *or*-list for the *any* noun phrase without violence to idiom or a change of truth conditions. In these cases, no plausible disjunctive reading of 'or' seems possible. On this substitutability rule, we face a dilemma that requires us to choose between postulating a change of meaning of 'any' and a change of meaning of 'or': if we say that the meaning of 'any' has not changed between 'g(any A)' and 'If g(any A), then α', then we must say that 'or' has not changed its meaning between

$$g(a_1 \text{ or } a_2 \text{ or } a_3 \text{ or } \ldots)$$

and

$$\text{If } g(a_1 \text{ or } a_2 \text{ or } a_3 \text{ or } \ldots), \text{ then } \alpha.$$

So we must say that 'or' has changed its meaning between

$$h(a_1 \text{ or } a_2 \text{ or } a_3 \text{ or } \ldots),$$

where it permits disjunctive distribution, and

$$\text{If } h(a_1 \text{ or } a_2 \text{ or } a_3 \text{ or } \ldots), \text{ then } \alpha,$$

which is equivalent to propositional conjunction. If, by contrast, we do say that 'any' has changed its meaning between 'g(any A)' and 'If g(any A), then p', then we must say that 'or' has changed its meaning between 'g( )' and 'if g( ), then α'.

But even if in spite of the general correlation between *or*-lists and *any* noun phrases, we want to claim that the possibility of substitution in conditional sentences is merely coincidental, the scope account imposes one change of meaning upon us. Even if it enables us to avoid postulating that the meaning of 'any' has changed between 'g(any A)' and 'If g(any A), then p', it nevertheless forces us to postulate that the meaning of 'g(any A)' has changed. This is so because in the first case a propositional conjunction could be substituted for 'g(any A)', and in the second case it could not. The scope account does not avoid change of meaning; it merely exchanges one change of meaning for another.

One final remark on this already laboured subject: Anyone tempted still by the modified general rule that 'any', where it *can be* construed as a universal quantifier, always takes the longest possible scope has not in the first place noticed that the positioning of negating elements plays a role, and in the second place has not embedded sufficiently many *any*-permitting environments. In the first place, depending upon stress and the way in which the negation is introduced, the scope of 'any' may remain constant between 'Any member may vote' and 'It's not true that any member may vote'; and though it may change between 'Any member may vote' and 'Not any member may vote', it may remain constant between the last and 'If not any member may vote, then α'.

Now this account may seem to invest both 'any' and 'or' with multiple personalities, but it should be remembered that if we consider interrogative environments, something like this is forced upon us. And if it seems to help to recognize that we need to apply some such label to a larger class of cases, then we might consider the adverbs 'ever' and 'always', which seem to make a distinction that in some respects parallels that of 'any' and 'every', and that of 'either' and 'both'. The main features that we noted as peculiarly characterizing 'either' and 'any' are (a) that they can occur acceptably only in certain kinds of environment; (b) that whereas sentences containing them are sometimes equivalent to propositional conjunction, sometimes they seem to have a disjunctive sense, notably in interrogatives and conditionals; and (c) that there is a general correlation between (1) an environment accepting 'any A' or 'either A' and one producing propositional conjunction when one of them is supplied to it and (2) this environment's being one in which an 'and' list would be undistributive or have undistributed sense; all of these apply to 'ever'. First, outside of poetic effort and sermons, 'ever' seldom occurs in affirmative sentences. We say 'There is always a policeman on that corner', not 'There is ever a policeman on that corner'. The major difference is that 'ever' can be used in any environment in which 'always' can be used, but its use in these environments is for a special literary or poetic effect, not for a logically significant distinction.

There are, however, situations in which intersubstitution between 'ever' and 'always' produces a logically significant change of sense. This can be seen from the following 'ever/always' pairs:

(a)   It is not always the case that α

(a')   It is not ever the case that α

(b)   Is it always the case that α?

(b')   Is it ever the case that α?

(c)   If it is ever the case that α, then β

(c')   If it is always the case that α, then β

The difference between (a) and (a') and between (c) and (c') can be expressed by paraphrases in which only 'always' is used, but in which its scope is varied. The difference between (a) and (a') is the difference between

(d) It is not the case that it is always the case that p

and

(d') It is always the case that it is not the case that p.

The difference between (c) and (c') is the difference between

(e) It is always the case that if p, then q

and

(e') If it is always the case that p, then q.

However, for each of these pairs of sentences we could approximate the distinction which it marks by substituting for 'always' an *and*-list of occasions and for 'ever' an *or*-list of occasions. In all of (a'), (b') and (c), an *or*-list would be disjunctively distributive with respect to at least part of its environment. Moreover, since the use of 'ever' in affirmative environments is archaic and largely displaced by 'anytime', we can say that for any normal use of 'ever', it can be replaced by a disjunctively distributive list of occasions.

If the word 'ever' can be regarded as subject to a historical process of specialization in which its use in simple affirmative sentences has passed to the poets because it does not enable us to say anything that 'always', 'forever', and 'anytime' do not permit us to say, then 'any' can be regarded as subject to similar historical processes. In spite of other shifts, its indicative use has been retained for those environments in which it enables us conveniently to make a distinction. The question of the scope of an occurrence of a 'logical' word of English, far from settling questions about the local meaning of such words, cannot itself be settled before semantical questions have been dealt with; the formulation of those questions of representation and interpretation may require a subtlety of discrimination beyond any that the language of 'meaning' can support.

7.2 Form and Meaning

7.2.1 Synonymy and variable meaning

Ultimately, we want to offer a unified story of the natural 'or', one that will account for the distributive properties of *or*-lists, whatever those distributive properties may be. We may hold out some hope that such an account will illuminate for us the place of 'any' in English discourse as well. It does not seem necessary to recast that avowal in terms of meaning. Unclear as the aim may be as to what will satisfy it, no part of it is to find a common *meaning* for 'or' for all occasions of its use. The language of meaning, apart from our vague notion of conversationally interchangeable expressions as ones that mean roughly the same thing, has no very clear place in the plan of this book. Yet to say that in some environments *or*-lists permit conjunctive distribution, even in some environments in which an *and*-list would do so as well, may suggest to some that it is part of our claim that 'or' sometimes means 'and'. Again, to say that in some environments a noun phrase 'any A' will have the same effect as the corresponding 'some A' noun phrase may suggest to some that this amounts to claiming that 'any' sometimes means the same as 'some'. Even if those claims are explicitly disavowed, the very claim that the distributive properties of *or*-lists vary from environment to environment may amount, for some at least, to a claim that the meaning of 'or' is different in different environments and, if our claim that the sense of *any* noun phrases is always that of an *or*-list depends upon the variable distributive properties of *or*-lists, then this may seem tantamount to saying at least that 'any' has different meanings in different environments. So the significance of these apparent differences in the ways that 'or' and 'any' go about their affairs deserves a brief discussion.

Peter Geach particularly has advised against explanations requiring the postulation of change of sense or meaning:

> There is, to be sure, a strong temptation to say: In the context "If Jemima can lick ____, then Jemima can lick any dog", "any dog" means the same

as "some dog", even though they mean different things from one another in other environments. I think we should resist this temptation. (1962, 61)

and again

The expression "In the context of the propositions P_1, P_2, the meaning of E_1, E_2 is the same" is a muddling one: it may mean no more than that P_1 which contains E_1, means the same as P_2 which contains E_2 and is otherwise verbally the same as P_1; or it may seek to explain this by the supposition that here E_1 and E_2 mean the same, though perhaps not elsewhere . . .

The question whether a pair of expressions can be synonymous only sometimes has obvious connections with the question whether a word can mean one thing on one occasion and something else on another, since in environments in which E_1 is not synonymous with the expression E_2, the meaning of E_1 must be different from what it is in those environments in which E_1 and E_2 are synonymous. If the meaning of a word is always the same, there will be no pair of expressions that are synonymous in some environments but not in others. Now it has been no part of the present account of 'or' and 'any' that the meaning is different in different environments; at least we have not claimed that this is a precise or even suitable characterization, certainly not that it is essential to a correct characterization of their story that it be given in those terms. Nevertheless, if it is fallacious to infer from the available information that in this environment 'any' means the same as 'some', it may equally be fallacious to infer that here the sense of 'any dog' is the logic of a disjunctively distributive list of dogs. It is, accordingly, worthwhile to examine Geach's arguments against this sort of inference. His statement of the fallacy is as follows:

We just cannot infer that if two propositions verbally differ precisely in that one contains the expression E_1 and the other the expression E_2, then, if the total force of the two propositions is the same, we may cancel out the identical parts and say that E_1 here means the same as E_2.
I shall call this sort of inference *the cancelling-out fallacy*. . . .

Geach offers as a simple example of the cancelling-out fallacy, the argument that the predicable '____ killed Socrates' must mean the same as the predicable '____ was killed by Socrates' because 'Socrates killed Socrates' means the same as 'Socrates was killed by Socrates'. This example seems conclusively to preclude the possibility of inference of this sort, for if there is one instance of the relevant '$\alpha \wedge \neg\beta$', then the falsity of the corresponding 'If α, then β' is guaranteed. It seems clear that Geach considers this counterinstance sufficient to establish its fallaciousness, since apart from it, no argument is offered.

7.2.2 The forms of arguments

In general, if an argument is valid, then a more specific argument of comparable form is also valid, and if an argument is invalid, then an argument of greater generality but of comparable form is also invalid. For example, if the argument 'Jones is a man; therefore, Jones is mortal' is a valid argument, then 'Jones is a thirty-nine-year-old invalid Asian gentleman; therefore Jones is mortal' is also valid. Similarly, if 'Jones asserted "p" loudly and with great conviction; therefore, "p" is true' is invalid, then so is the argument 'Jones asserted "p"; therefore, "p" is true'. The terms 'specific', 'generality', and 'comparable form' are not perfectly transparent. But we can find precise paradigms within the propositional calculus, from which the extension to ordinary English arguments will be clear enough.

In the simple language of the propositional calculus, the relation of relative specificity can be cashed out in terms of the relation of substitution instantiation. A wff α is a substitution instance of a wff β if and only if α is obtained by uniformly substituting an occurrence of some well-formed formula γ for every occurrence of some propositional variable p_i in β. Two facts about the propositional calculus will secure the analogy. First, the set of theorems of propositional logic is closed under uniform substitution. Second, an argument has a proof in the propositional calculus if and only if its conditionalization is a theorem. That is, there is a proof of β from the ensemble of wffs $\{\alpha_1, \alpha_2, \ldots \alpha_n\}$ if and only if the conditional

$$\alpha_1 \rightarrow (\alpha_2 \rightarrow (\ldots \rightarrow (\alpha_n \rightarrow \beta)) \ldots)$$

is a theorem. Thus what corresponds to our informal notion of a more specific argument form can be given in the following way: Let A be an argument and C(A) its conditionalization. Then B is a more specific form than A if and only if C(B) is a substitution instance of C(A), but C(A) is not a substitution instance of C(B). Indeed, we can identify *the form of an argument A* in the propositional calculus with the set of all arguments B whose conditionalization is obtained from the conditionalization of A by uniform substitution. An argument of greater specificity (less generality) of form than that of A is one whose form is a proper subset of the form of A. Thus if an argument has a proof in the propositional calculus, then so has any argument of greater specificity of form. Now the provable arguments of the propositional calculus are exactly those arguments valid in the ordinary truth-tabular sense. So we may add that if an argument is valid in the truth-tabular sense, then so is any argument of greater specificity (less generality) of form. Conversely, if an argument is invalid in the truth-tabular sense, then so is any argument of greater generality of form. Finally, the notion of validity can be applied to forms as well as arguments. We can say that a form is valid if and only if every argument of that form is valid. So validity is preserved under relative specificity; a form is valid only if every more specific form is valid. Conversely, if a form is invalid, so is every more general form.

What is the connection between relative specificity of form as characterizable in the setting of the propositional calculus and the corresponding relation in the natural setting? The most obvious difference between the two is that, in an argument of the propositional calculus there are always propositional variables for which to make uniform substitutions. In the ordinary language case, there are not. So the notion of the set of all possible substitution instances has no direct application in the ordinary language case, and neither therefore does the uniform substitutional notion of form, except trivially in the sense that the set of substitution instances of the conditionalization of the argument is the unit set of the conditionalization itself, so that there is exactly one argument of the same form and none more specific. To apply the notion of form usefully to arguments of ordinary language, we must first substitute appropriate variables for some elements of the arguments — either propositional variables for whole declarative sentences, predicate variables for predicates, and so on. Having done that, we have available to us something closely analogous to argument form in the uniform substitutional sense. And we can apply a notion of formal validity that is a close kin of the truth-tabular notion; that is, it will have the property at least that the form is valid only if every less general form is valid. And the form will be invalid only if every more general form is invalid. But two observations may be made. There are in general more ways than one of substituting variables for elements of an argument. Second, only some of the ways of doing so will yield valid forms. Consider as an example the simple argument:

> A: All animals are mortals; all prophets are animals; therefore all prophets are mortals.

We would obtain a form of which the given argument is an instance by replacing the common nouns by variables. We might, for example, produce:

> A′: All A's are M's; all P's are A's; therefore, all P's are M's,

thereby showing that the argument has the form of a first figure syllogism in Barbara, a valid form. But we might have used a different variable for each distinct occurrence of a common noun, producing

> A″: All A's are M's; all P's are B's; therefore, all Q's are N's,

from which also the original argument can be got by 'uniform substitution', but the form this schema represents is not valid since it has invalid as well as valid substitution instances. More vividly, we might have introduced propositional variables, ignoring the internal structure of the component sentences, producing the schema

> A‴: p; q; therefore, r,

from which also A can be got by 'uniform substitution'. This form, which of course is invalid, is shared by all two-premiss arguments valid or invalid.

7.2.3 The fallacy fallacy

Those philosophers are not far off who regard the notion of fallacy as one of the more fatuous products of the philosophical cottage industry, as the whoopee cushion of intellectual exchange. It is at least fair to say that the imputation of fallacy must itself always be a kind of ad hominem. For fallaciousness is a property of *reasoning* and not of the form of argument. There is no such thing as *the* form of an argument, but there is such a thing as the mistaken belief that a particular argument form is valid. Nevertheless, it is evidently possible to present a valid argument in the mistaken belief in the validity of some form that it happens to have. Thus someone could present a valid argument of the form:

$$p \vee q \rightarrow p \wedge q; \ p \wedge q; \ \text{therefore}, \ p \vee q$$

in the belief that the form

$$p \rightarrow q; \; q; \text{ therefore, } p$$

was valid. Such a person would no doubt be committing the fallacy of affirming the consequent. But there would be no grounds for accusing him of committing the fallacy in his having affirmed the consequent that he did. The mistake is important enough and sufficiently widespread to be given a label. I suggest *The Fallacy Fallacy*. A person commits one form of the fallacy fallacy when he infers the invalidity of an argument from its having an invalid form. Of course, in this form it can be represented as a simple error in the manipulation of quantifiers. To say that an argument is valid is to say that it has a valid form; thus to say that it is not valid is to say that it has *no valid form*, not that it has some invalid one. There is a related, more objectionable form of the fallacy fallacy that a person commits by inferring faulty reasoning from the invalidity of an argument form. In this guise the fallacy is a kind of ad hominem.

Now none of this is intended to impute to Geach a commission of the fallacy fallacy; to infer this from the form of his argument would be to commit the fallacy fallacy ourselves. But it ought to alert us to a distinction that the inflammatory language of fallacy tends to muddy. It is the distinction between being able to give a general account of the role that a word plays that applies to more than one kind of environment, and having a representation of the environment types in which some single element does the work of that word. The cancelling-out fallacy cautions us against inferring of words (in particular, 'any' and 'some') that usually have distinct meanings, that they have the same meaning in sentences equivalent and otherwise identical. But just to point to the inadequacy of the argument supporting a difference of meaning of two occurrences of a 'logical' word — say, 'any' — does not in itself establish that no difference of meaning need be postulated. For a positive argument we need more than a representation of the two *any*-containing sentences in an artificial language where the quantificational role can be taken up by some single piece of quantificational vocabulary. Merely to note the possibility of translating the sentence form 'If any a φ's, then α' into 'It is true as regards any a that if it φ's, then α' is not to show what the 'meaning' of 'any' was in the original sentence, and the artificiality of the translation is such that we cannot properly judge whether it is the sort of English environment in which 'any' rather than 'every' would be acceptable.

Now sometimes we must have recourse to the language of meaning, and where we have no alternative the language is harmless enough. No problems attend the explanation that within the environment of a particular dialect of English, in the sentence 'Are you going the no?' the word 'the' means 'or', although in other environments, even within the dialect, the two words have different meanings. We legitimately draw this conclusion from the way the sentence as a whole is used, from the sorts of answers that it seems to invite, and so on. If we must use the language of 'meaning' here, then we may say that we infer that 'the' means 'or' precisely because two sentences differing only in one's having the one and the other's having the other mean the same. But there are more interesting and fruitful questions to ask, such as how the use has come about, and how the two sentences, alike as they may be in meaning, nevertheless differ in their conversational effect or fit. And the same may be said of occurrences of 'any' and 'some', even those in which someone who is set upon talking about meaning would want to say that they meant the same, and even those in which additionally no artificial quantificational paraphrase is available to distinguish them.

What is wrong with the conclusion that 'any' means 'some' in certain environments is not that it implies that 'any' sometimes has 'disjunctive' or 'existential' rather than 'conjunctive' or 'universal' sense; roughly speaking, both the conclusion and the implication are true. But the loose notions of 'meaning' and 'sense' do not let us say what of interest there is to be said. It is not so much incorrect as unhelpful to say that in some environment 'any' means 'some'. Similarly, it seems unnecessary to resist the thesis that in such a sentence 'any' has a disjunctive sense. But to understand the role of 'any' in such environments, we must look, not at those environments in which it is plausible to say that 'any' has the same role as 'some', but at those in which, although 'any' is disjunctive in sense, nevertheless its role is different from that of 'some'; for it is likely these environments for which the disjunctive use of 'any' has survived.

7.2.4 Where the distinction matters

Consider interrogatives. Generally, a sentence of the form 'Is any A f?' is equivalent to a sentence of the form 'Is it the case that a_1 or a_2 or a_3 or ... is f?' So is a sentence of the form 'Is some A f?' But the conversational fit of the two sentences need not be the same. Contrast the sentences 'Did any member vote against the proposal?' and 'Did some member vote against the proposal?' Each, we may presume, is equivalent to the interrogative having a disjunctive list of members where 'any member' or 'some member' is. But contrast the following conversations:

A: We had to scrap the proposal.
B: Why? Did some member vote against it?

and

A: We had to scrap the proposal.
B: Why? Did any member vote against it?

Why is the 'some' form of the question more natural than the 'any' form? Possibly because the question 'Did some member vote against it?' frames in interrogative form a ventured affirmative answer to the preceding 'Why?' 'Did any member vote against it?' does not. Interrogratives with 'some' can play this complementing role because expressions of the form 'some A' are disjunctive in affirmative as well as in interrogative sentences. But it is precluded for interrogatives with 'any', because in the corresponding affirmative sentences, an *any*-construction is acceptable only if legitimized by some modal or other 'any'-admitting element, as in

A: Voting isn't much of a privilege these days.
B: Why? Can any member vote?

In interrogatives in which the 'any' noun phrase occurs as the subject of a *that*-clause governed by an intensional verb, the distinction between the interrogative with 'any' and the same interrogative with a substituted 'some' parallels the distinction between truth value and solution of a disjunction. Again the distinction between the interrogatives seems to require reference to a corresponding distinction in affirmative forms. Just as to know that $\alpha \vee \beta$ is not necessarily to know that α or to know that q; to know that some A φ's is not necessarily to know of some that it φ's. Now in descriptions that we give of what we see or hear or smell or taste, the description that we give is frequently determined in part by what we know to be the case; when we describe (though, of course, not when we identify) what someone else sees, hears, and so on, we frequently tailor our description to what we suppose him to know to be the case. So usually the description that we would give of what someone else sees corresponds at least roughly to the description that we suppose that he would give himself. For example, even if we know that the cellist whose playing Mary hears is Stephanie, if we know that Mary does not know that it is Stephanie playing, we might not want to describe *what Mary hears* as Stephanie playing. We might want to say that Mary hears someone playing the cello; moreover, we might say this on some occasions only if we believed that it was a cello being played and not, say, a bass viol. So although the sentence 'S hears some A φ-ing' may be thought, roughly speaking, to imply and to be implied by the sentence 'There is some A that S hears φ-ing', the force of these sentences is different because the second, by its convolving suggests an insistence that S knows the identity of the φ-er; the simpler version does not. It is the fact that 'some' has this use in these affirmative sentences that accounts for its use in the corresponding interrogative sentences, and for the noticeable divergence of conversational fit between these interrogatives and those with substituted 'any'. Consider, for example, the sort of situation in which we might ask a question of the general sort 'Did you hear some A φ-ing?' and the sort where we might ask rather 'Did you hear any A φ-ing?' The force of the second of these is something like that of 'Is there some A whom you heard φ-ing?' The force of the first question is more like 'Did you hear something that you would describe as some A φ-ing?' Similarly, the question 'Did I hear any A φ-ing?' unless I have forgotten and want reminding, seems designed to test someone else's knowledge of me; but the force of 'Did I hear some A φ-ing?' is closer to 'Was that some A that I heard φ-ing?' The reason why the first question is odd as a request for an identification of what I heard is that if there had been some A, say, a_m, such that it would have been suitable to say that I heard a_m φ-ing, then I would have known it, so if my asking the question suggests that I do not know it, then the answer to the question is obviously 'No', and I should have known *that*. So the force of the question 'Did I hear any A φ-ing?' when it is not a request for a reminder, is such as to suggest that I understand myself to be in a better position than anyone else to answer it. But the force of the question 'Did I hear some A φ-ing?' is such as to suggest that I am not in the best position to answer it. This difference would be reflected in the sorts of affirmative answers that we would give to them. We would answer the question 'Did I hear any A φ-ing?' with 'Yes, you heard a_m. (Don't you remember?)' We would answer the question 'Did I hear some A φ-ing?' with 'Yes, it was a_m φ-ing. (Couldn't you tell?)'

The examples illustrate why it is unhelpful to dwell upon environments in which 'any' and 'some' look as though they mean the same and argue on the basis of some general rule that they cannot. If we want to discover the role of 'any' in a particular kind of environment, we should look, not at the role of 'any' in other kinds of environment as given in a general rule, but at the role of syntactically acceptable alternatives to 'any' in environments of the same kind. Where intersubstitution between syntactically acceptable alternatives is logically unobjectionable, we discover why this apparent redundancy exists by finding environments of the same kind in which these syntactical alternatives are *not* also logical or not also conversational alternatives, that is, where intersubstitution between them is logically or conversationally objectionable.

One final observation: it remains unclear what role the notion of logical form can play in a study of natural language inference. Although it seems clearly to have some place, there seem to be questions in which it cannot provide the final verdict. Among these are questions of meaning of 'logical' vocabulary. The case is otherwise than in propositional logic, where implicit notational conventions enable us to say of two occurrences of, say, $\vee$ that they are both occurrences of the same piece of vocabulary, though perhaps slightly differently formed. For any two wffs having $\vee$ as their principal connective, we may say they are both of the form of disjunction, that they share the form '$P \vee Q$', however disjunction is interpreted in particular models for particular formal systems. But in English and other natural languages, there can be no such certainty. It seems plain enough that we will not want to say that the sentences

It happened or it didn't

and

It might have happened or it might not

both have the logical form of a disjunction if we understand the second one to imply

It might have happened

but the first one not to imply

It happened.

There is room here for the distinction between sharing a grammatical form and sharing a logical form, in this instance the former applying and the latter not. The question of the logical form of a natural language is a question regarding the representation of the sentence in the language of the logic in question; it is therefore a question about the *meanings* of the words of the sentence that we regard, for that occasion, as its 'logical' vocabulary. If we are to give a unified account of 'or' in English, the account will have to explain both of these uses of 'or', and it seems therefore unlikely that such an account will be got by finding some common logical form into which may be translated every sentence containing an occurrence of 'or'. Having ceased to strive against that ineluctable fact, there seems little point in glutinously clinging, against the evidence, to the hope for a unified *quantificational* account of 'any'.

7.3 Heteronomy and Discontinuous Syntax

I have claimed that some non-indicative uses of 'some', as, for example, in certain interrogative constructions and in certain *if*-clauses, are borrowed from related indicative uses. In such cases the form of the interrogative is made to fit the form of an answer to it, or, to put the matter another way, the question is formed as it is as though to ask about the truth or falsity of the corresponding indicative. It is therefore the use of 'some' in the corresponding indicative that gives rise to the use of 'some' in the interrogative. Similarly the *if* clause introducing some conditionals may take up the form of the corresponding direct assertion. It should not be assumed that sentences are perfectly autonomous. In some instances the choice of noun phrase is dictated, not by internal quantificational requirements, but by the role of the same noun clause in related sentences. If this claim of *heteronomy* is true for some examples, then this points up the inadequacy of a mere quantificational translation of sentences introducing 'some' as an account of its use for those examples. We shall encounter the same phenomenon again here.

I hope by now to have shown that, notwithstanding the fact that it has seemed natural to many authors to regard 'any' and 'some' as simply the English counterparts of the universal and existential quantifiers of first-order logic, it is a simplehearted view. If we do so, we must account for the differences between 'every' and 'any' in some other way, since in many environments they seem both to correspond to the universal quantifier if to any, yet only in certain environments is 'any' acceptable. We must entertain another possibility, namely, that even where they are interchangeable, they achieve their effects in discourse in markedly different ways.

7.3.1 Some preliminary illustrations

I. Formatting characters:

In the programming language C, printf() is a function belonging to a library of standard input/output functions. It prints its argument to the standard output, typically the monitor. Thus, if in the course of running a C programme, the system were to come to a line

```
printf("So far so good!\n");
```

it would print to the monitor screen the message "So far so good!" followed by a carriage return.

Printf() can also be used to print to the CRT screen the calculated value of a variable. So if a programmer wanted the C programme to tell its user at some stage, say the integer representing the size of an insect population according to an implemented computer model, the programmer might include in his programme the line:

```
printf("The population is now %d.\n", popsize);
```

The '%d', which is called a formatting character, indicates that the value is to be printed to the screen in decimal format. 'Popsize', we are supposing, is an integer variable declared earlier in the programme, which has the value representing the calculated size of the insect population. So if the value of popsize is 9 when the system reaches the quoted line, then it will print to the CRT screen the following message:

The population is now 9.

followed by a carriage return. Had the programmer declared another variable, say a floating point variable, 'fpopsize', then had the programmer included the line

fpopsize = popsize

assigning the floating point variable whatever value popsize has, then the line

printf("The population is now %f.\n", fpopsize);

with '%f' instead of '%d', the message

The population is now 9.000000.

would have been called forth to the screen, the value having been formatted as a floating decimal.

The point of the illustration is that if we try to parse the quoted sentence within the scope of the printf() functor as an English sentence, we will come to grief over the syntactic relationship of the formatting instruction '%d' or '%f' to the rest of the sentence. Superficially the grammar of the quoted sentence suggests that '%d' is a predicate noun; in fact, it is an indication of how the space in the sentence is to be filled before the sentence is expressed. In reality, the entry 'popsize', a variable, provides the system a memory address from which it retrieves the value, but there is nothing wrong with our describing popsize in more familiar terms as a variable magnitude and the programme line as a command to print that magnitude to the screen in a particular way. So while grammatically a sentence, followed by a noun, the expression is pragmatically a quoted partial sentence with a space, together with a two-part instruction for how the space is to be filled.

II. Pious Practice

In Leviticus 24:11 we read of an 'Israelitish' woman's son who blasphemed 'the name'. A little later we learn his grisly fate and that of anyone who does likewise: 'as well the stranger, as he that is born in the land, when he blasphemeth the name, shall be put to death'. King James's translators helpfully supply the phrase '*of the Lord*' but it is more likely that it was not the name that was reviled, but its bearer, *hashem* ('the name') being a scribal substitution in the text at a time when the name itself was coming to be considered ineffable. Some similar explanation is offered by lexicographers for the curious wording of God's warning to the Israelites not to cross an angel that he has it in mind to send them as a guide, 'for he will not pardon your transgressions: for my name *is* in him' (Exodus 23:21; Brown et al. 1907, 1029).   This pious practice of scribes is probably the origin of the related Jewish practice of substituting *hashem* for *Adonai*. The earlier understanding of the substitute as an indication of what occurs at that point in the real text seems to have given way to a fictional understanding of the substitute as reverential indirection by which reference to God is made without utterance of his name. The words 'the name' thus come to act as much as a name as the original did, the fiction trading upon the generic character of the substitute. The feature of this usage that interests us is shared with the English colloquial and sometimes slighting usage 'what's-his-name' (or 'what's-her-name') as in 'What's-his-name was just here looking for you' where the actual reference is to the bearer of the elusive name, but the form is interrogatory of the name, and not of its bearer, so that the underlying explanation of the usage is that it fills the place in the sentence with a gender-specific indication of what ought to be there. That is, it makes reference to a known extralinguistic object by reference to an unrecollected but presumably recognizable linguistic one. The interlocutor ventures plausible callers (as 'Was it Rob? . . . Henry? . . . Dennis? . . .') *incidentally, and only incidentally,* providing plausible replacements for the placeholder in the names of the candidates referred to.

III. Filling up forms

The distinction so far is between two modes of guidance to understanding of a text or an utterance, the one by reference to the object spoken of, the other to the linguistic object by which that speaking of is done.   We find both kinds of guidance in instructions for filling up forms, receiving sometimes such help as:

I,_____ do hereby . . .
(vendor's name)

and sometimes such help as

I, _____ do hereby . . .
(vendor)

the one indicating to us what to insert and the other indicating to us what the document will eventually say.

7.3.2 The indirection of 'any'

The hypothesis that these examples are intended to illustrate is that, in their primary use, noun phrases involving 'any' are placeholders that indicate a range of possible substitutions and indifference as to which substitutions within that range are made for it. Thus, when a lecturer asks a question such as 'So, given the values entered earlier, what value must I place in the main column? A philosophy student this time. . . . No takers? Anyone?' the 'anyone' is in a place to which a name, 'Mr. Jones', were there a Mr. Jones in the class, might have been supplied instead. In that case Mr. Jones would have treated the question as directed to him and answered or declined. In the present case, each student, residually, is invited to hear the question, if he cares to, as directed to him. The force of 'any' in *if*-clauses is to be similarly accounted for. Our understanding of 'If any A φ's, then α', according to this hypothesis, can be brought out by a paraphrase using something closer to the French *n'importe quel*: if an (and it doesn't matter which) A φ's, then α.

The puzzling features of the behaviour of 'any' arise in part from its combining this instructional parenthesis, the indication of indifference as to selection, with the ordinary force of the indefinite article 'a' or 'an' (extended, as we have seen, to plural uses), so that the question of scope cannot be made comfortably to apply. To try to make the alleged scope of 'any' explicit is to rewrite the sentence in a form in which the use of 'any' is usually unidiomatic, and the indifference only implicit. Thus, for example, though one might say, 'If you had come any day last week, you might have found him at his desk', only the utter artificiality of the form distracts us from the unsuitableness of 'any' in such a construction as 'Any day last week was such that. . . .' Even should we permit the form as a way of making our meaning entirely explicit, all available analogies of normal use suggest 'every' as the better choice.

So there is some connection, at least between some declarative *any*-constructions and quantification, a connection that is brought out by observations as to what quantified sentence would, in the right circumstances, be conversationally interchangeable with a given *any*-containing sentence. It is by no means clear that the introduced quantifier could, in all cases, be a universal quantifier. And it is important to see how tenuous such a connection is. The claim is that, in discourse, approximately the same information could be conveyed by a quantificational construction as is conveyed by the *any*-construction. (One is tempted to say, 'the same *quantificational* information'.) Thus to offer the sentence 'Had you come any day last week, you would have found him working' is incidentally to offer information about every day last week. It may be claimed that that information is what would have been expressed by the philosopher's sentence, 'It is true as regards every day last week, that had you come on that day, you would have found him working'. But the representation — and the analysis that it represents — while available straightforwardly only for a limited range of cases, manages to import a weight of theoretical assumption disproportionate to its explanatory candlepower. Notions of truth value, information content, and so on applicable to whole sentences go nowhere toward telling us how *any*-constructions achieve the effect that they do in discourse. So while it is true that what was said in 'Had you come . . . working' is true if and only if what would have been said in 'It is true as regards . . . working' is, this observation does not tell us *how* the former manages to tell us what we would have been told by the latter.

The conclusion is then that although sentences containing 'any' can be roughly *represented* by a quantified sentence, 'any A' should not, on that account, be regarded as a quantifier, since it achieves its conversational effect otherwise. The alternative view with which we leave this discussion is that in its primary use it should be thought of as akin to a labelled space as: 'Had you come_____, you would have found him in the study' with the space labeled, as it were, below the discourse line, with the instruction indicating the range from within which fillings are invited.

This use inevitably gives rise to a secondary use through anaphora and other reference. Thus, if a speaker says, 'Any member can use the club canoe' with 'any' in its primary use, another may counter 'If that's true, then canoeing has just lost its charm for me', which, when made explicit is 'If (just) any (old) member can use the club canoe, then canoeing has just lost its charm for me'. This heteronomous use of 'any', either indirectly in 'that's true' or in the repeated sentence, though it puts paid to the long-scope, universal-quantifier account of 'any', does make 'any' in such cases look more like a quantifier than like a labelled space. But the translation is not required for an understanding of the repetition; that is just a feature of discourse practice. Moreover, the claim that 'any' in its primary use marks a labelled space is not intended to deny that, at least in some indicative instances, there could be a rough quantificational paraphrase of what is said. It claims only that what is said is said otherwise than by quantification. It will become apparent later what relevance this labelled-space account of *any*-constructions has for our account of *or*-lists.

8

'Or' in Opaque Contexts

> . . . Moses said unto his people, Verily God commandeth you to sacrifice a
> cow . . . They said, Pray for us unto thy Lord, that he would show us what cow it
> is. Moses answered, He saith, She is neither an old cow, nor a young heifer, but a
> middle age between both: do ye therefore that which ye are commanded. They
> said, Pray for us unto thy Lord, that he would show us what colour she is of.
> Moses answered, He saith, She is a red cow, intensely red, her colour rejoiceth the
> beholders. They said, Pray for us unto thy Lord, that he would further show us
> what cow it is, for several cows with us are like one another, and we, if God
> please, will be directed. Moses answered, He saith, She is a cow not broken to
> plough the earth, or water the field, a sound one, there is no blemish in her. They
> said, Now hast thou brought the truth. Then they sacrificed her . . .   KORAN

8.1 Undistributive *Or*-Lists

In truth-conditional terms, an *or*-list 'a or b' is undistributive in an environment
$\underline{\lambda}$ when $\underline{\lambda}$(a or b) does not imply either '$\underline{\lambda}$(a) or $\underline{\lambda}$(b)' or '$\underline{\lambda}$(a) and $\underline{\lambda}$(b)'. If we
restrict our attention, as the notation prompts us, to lists of noun phrases, the
abstract notion of such a sentence has about it an air of paradox, since in the
abstract the items of the list seem likely to represent in some way what the
sentence says something about. What could it mean to say something about a or
b independently of saying something about one or both of a, b severally? The
case with *or*-lists is in this regard fundamentally different from the case for
and-lists. Conceptually a may be pasted to b in a multiplicity of ways,
permitting a corresponding multiplicity of correct attributions to the *pasticcio*
that would be false of its constituents: a weight, a mass, a volume, a social status
and so on. But there seems no such variety of conceptual orbitings of individuals
corresponding to lists of noun phrases formed with 'or'.

There are several reasons why, prima facie, we should resist seeking an
account that tries to preserve the parallel between undistributive *or*-lists and undistributive *and*-lists beneath the grammatical level. The first is the one already
mentioned, that to treat an *or*-list as standing for some mental diaeretic combination of the items of the list does not accord with any familiar conceptualization.
A second is that such an account seems genetically unlikely, or at least unil-
luminating as to genesis; that is to say, it offers no plausible suggestion as to
how such a construction should have evolved. A third is that undistributive *or*-

lists of verbs or of other parts of speech can occur, not just of noun phrases, so that our account must not, by its choice of idiom, suggest an unwarranted narrowness of application. The puzzle of distribution arises for any of the following:

(0) I want a yawl or a ketch.

(0′) I want to buy or hire a yawl.

(0″) I want to buy a yawl sooner or later.

(0‴) I want to buy up or into a yawl.

(0‴′) I want to buy a fibreglass or ferro-cement yawl.

Philosophers especially may be tempted to consider undistributive *or*-lists of noun phrases as part of a theory of reference and to neglect the phenomenon elsewhere. Even if undistributive lists of prepositions are not of direct philosophical interest, they are obliquely relevant to the philosophically more central cases, since an account must be less plausible if it suggests a discontinuity where none is. The most influential philosophical discussion of environments in which *or*-lists have undistributive readings has been Quine's exploration in *Word and Object* (1960) of a phenomenon he calls 'opacity'. It is clear enough that the term 'opacity' and its cognates were introduced as an illuminating and suggestive metaphor. As such it has attracted many hoping to see by its light. But it is fair to say that although the metaphor has been suggestive to many, its light has been diffuse, and the precise terms of its intended application remain unclear. In particular, when one takes opacity of a property of such a environment as 'Mary wants ( )', it is unclear whether the intended suggestion of the metaphor is that the environment is one into which we cannot look to find the object (in this case, the object of Mary's want) or whether, having supplied a nominal to the environment, say, in the form of an indefinite noun phrase, we cannot see through that nominal to a worldly item for which it stands. Again, the characteristic marks of such environments are variously given. On the one hand, an opaque environment is said to be one into which one may not quantify; that is, to say that Mary wants a yawl is not to say that there is a yawl that Mary wants. On the other hand, an opaque environment is said to be intensional in the sense that substitution of extensionally equivalent terms is not in general truth-preserving. To these we may as well add a feature that accounts for our interest, that with respect to such environments, *or*-lists are in general undistributive; that is, distribution of such an environment over *or*-lists does not in general preserve truth.

Now our interests here are not Quine's and do not contact except incidentally the bumper literature that the subject has spawned. In particular, it should be noted that the significance for us of the restriction on 'quantifying in' should not be understood only as the conversational unavailability of a certain kind of paraphrase. In its opaque occurrences, the sentence 'Mary wants a yawl' is not conversationally interchangeable with 'There's a yawl that Mary wants', but in remarking this, we do not intend anything about the representation of 'Mary wants a yawl' in first-order logic or anything about implications or non-implications of existence or non-existence of worldly items. In general, let us own to a merely descriptive use of the notion of opacity, as picking out a class of occurrences of certain environments that must by now be generally familiar. Our interest in them has entirely to do with explaining the undistributiveness of *or*-lists in such occurrences of such environments.

8.1.1 Opacity

We may conveniently take up our discussion of the behaviour of 'or' in intensional environments where Quine left the subject of the opacity of certain verbs:

> What we have been remarking of 'hunt' or 'look for' and 'endeavor' applies *mutatis mutandis* to 'want' and 'wish'; for to want is to wish to have. 'I want a sloop' in the opaque sense is parallel to
>
> [Earnest is endeavoring (-to-cause) himself to shoot a lion]
>
> 'I wish myself to have a sloop (to be a sloop owner)'; 'I want a sloop' in the transparent sense, 'There is a sloop I want', comes out parallel to
>
> [Earnest is endeavoring (-to-cause) himself and a (certain) lion to be related as shooter and shot.]
>
> Only in the latter sense is 'want' a relative term, relating people to sloops. In the other or opaque sense it is not a relative term relating people to anything at all, concrete or abstract, real or ideal. It is a shortcut verb whose use is set forth by 'I wish myself to have a sloop', wherein 'have' and 'sloop' continue to rate as general terms as usual but merely happen to have an opaque construction 'wish to' overlying them. This point needs to be noticed by philosophers worried over the nature of objects of desire. (Quine 1960, 155–156)

It is notable that the restatement of a transparent λ(an A) as 'There is an A that $\underline{\lambda}$' remains ambiguous as between making *existence* and merely *particularity* explicit. Thus, 'I want a sloop' has transparent sense even if the sloop wanted is the first sloop off an expected but as yet nonexistent assembly line, and still warrants the restatement as 'There is a sloop that I want'. Similarly, 'I have a mental image of a sloop' requires to be restatable as 'There is a sloop of which I have a mental image, namely, this one', even though that cannot be taken to imply the existence of any non-imaginary yacht. (We may say, if inclined, 'There is a yacht before my mind'.)

With the same proviso, remarks parallel to Quine's apply to *or*-lists in opaque environments, and this whether it is a list of proper names or of general terms, but distinctions may be made as to degrees of translucence, correlating in the first instance with distributivity. Thus, the claim

(1) I want a yawl or a ketch

may be transparent to the degree that it is to be understood as equivalent to

(2) I want a yawl or I want a ketch

but opaque to the extent that the resulting disjuncts are to be understood in opaque sense. Or it may be thoroughly opaque. In this latter case, it would be natural to say that the occurrence of 'or' forms a single general term from two general terms. Mary's claim

(3) I want Cicero or Gellius

(supposing these to be shorthand references to particular volumes) in transparent sense may mean

(4) Mary wants Cicero or Mary wants Gellius

but may still, in easily imaginable circumstances, not admit, *salve veritate*, substitution of alternative ways of naming the volumes in question. Again, if (3) is perfectly opaque and not to be understood as equivalent to (4), it would seem natural to think of the occurrence of 'or' as forming a general term of two referring terms. There is, however, a possible case for which the classification is not straightforwardly provided in the language of opacity and transparency. We may imagine Mary sitting just out of reach of the two volumes, clearly marked 'Cicero' in the one case and 'Gellius' in the other, and (being a person of some precision and more patience) insistent when asked whether she wants 'Cicero' or she wants 'Gellius' answering 'No'. We take it that the uses of 'Cicero' and 'Gellius' are referentially transparent both in her denial that she wants them severally, and in her claim to want Cicero or Gellius. Thus an opaque occurrence of an indefinite general term can consist of transparent occurrences of singular terms joined by 'or'. The same point can be put in another way: By analogy with what has been said of opaque occurrences of indefinite general terms of the form 'an A' it is false that there is *some thing* that Mary wants. Call these two volumes 'antemary' volumes and suppose them the only antemary volumes, then we may paraphrase Mary's claim as

(5) Mary wants an antemary volume

and the denial that Mary wants either of the antemary volumes is just the denial of

There is an antemary volume such that Mary wants it.

But since the occurrences of 'Cicero' and 'Gellius' are transparent in (3) we may nevertheless quantify into the opaque environment at each position. Thus it follows from (3) that

(6) There is an antemary volume such that Mary wants it or Gellius (namely Cicero)

and

(7) There is an antemary volume such that Mary wants it or Cicero (namely Gellius).

The examples suggest that the metaphor of opacity is not quite what is wanted, and some of Quine's own examples suggest as well that the *referential/non-*

referential distinction distinguishes cases along misleading lines. His example of a two-role subject that combines referential and non-referential use is a further case in point

> An example in which this same phenomenon of two-role subject comes out more vividly is:

> (4) Giorgione was so-called because of his size,

> which anyone is ready enough to paraphrase into:

> Giorgione was called 'Giorgione' because of his size. (Quine 1960, 153)

This is not to deny that one of the functions that the name 'Giorgione' plays in Quine's (4) is non-referential, and he is right in claiming that a substituted 'someone' at least does not produce a justifiable existential generalization. Nevertheless, the generalization

> Someone was called what he was called because of his size

is a justifiable generalization from his (4). It is rather that the anaphoric 'so-' is bound to the name supplied to the place of 'Giorgione', and 'someone' does not supply a name to that place. If we introduce a convention to make the binding clear, the resulting generalization

> Some x is |x|-called because of his size

is justified. However, the interest is not in the occurrence of 'Giorgione' and its role vis-à-vis reference or non-reference that captures our interest, but the special character of the anaphora. We will consider that special feature in a later section; for the present, it is sufficient to consider an example in which anaphora has the effect of making an *or*-list undistributive and for which no such unusual duality of role need be invoked. The conditional

> (8) If Jules or Jim calls, it will surprise me

has a reading according to which it is equivalent to

> (8′) If Jules calls, it will surprise me and if Jim calls, it will surprise me.

On this reading the claim of (8) is that a call from Jules would occasion the surprise that Jules calls and a call from Jim would occasion the surprise that Jim calls. On this reading the reference of the anaphora, 'it', is fixed after distribution. There is, however, a second reading on which the reference of the anaphoric 'it' is fixed before distribution, to the disjunction, and the expected surprise consequent upon Jules' calling is the same as the anticipated surprise of Jim's calling, namely the surprise that Jules or Jim calls. Imagine that their voices, when heard over the telephone, are indistinguishable. Of course, when the sense of the anaphoric 'it' is made explicit, as in

> (8″) If Jules or Jim calls, that Jules or Jim has called will surprise me

the 'and' expansion is unproblematic. One might wish to account for this as a case in which the *if*-clause has a double role,[1] but it is more natural to explain the difference between the two as a matter of whether the anaphoric reference is fixed before or after distribution.

In this example, it is more evident than in (1) (I want a yawl or a ketch) that some intermediate distribution over the *or*-list is available, but in (8) the resulting sentential 'or' remains undistributive even when the intermediate distribution has been performed to produce

(8‴) If Jules calls or Jim calls, it will surprise me

if the reference of 'it' is to the whole *if*-clause. And again, we can combine the two kinds of examples to produce more grades of what on Quine's metaphor remain degrees of translucency:

(9) If Mary wants a yawl or a ketch, it will surprise me.

In other examples an *or*-list in an *if*-clause might have an undistributive reading, for reasons having solely to do with the use to which the 'or' is put, rather than anaphoric technicalities. Consider

If it's her neck or yours, she'll spill. (Chandler 1942, 511)

Here, on the intended reading, the predicate noun phrase 'her neck or yours' is not distributive either with respect to 'It's ( )' or with respect to 'If it's ( ), she'll spill'.

Finally, if we take the propriety of 'quantifying in' as an indicator of referential transparency, then we must recognize that partial transparency can result from partial indeterminacy, even when the verb phrase is one that would, when given an *or*-list as object, be taken to distribute disjunctively over it. If Mary says that she bought Franklyn the red car or the blue car, we may only assume that she bought him the red one or she bought him the blue one, but has forgotten which. It would be a misleading way of saying that she had put down sufficient money to secure either of them, and that he was to choose between them. If, however, Mary reports that she bought Franklyn a car, it may be that there is no car such that Mary bought it for Franklyn, simply because her having bought it may amount only to her having given over an amount of money with the understanding that a car of the agreed sort would be delivered. But there is as well a middle case. It may be that there is a particular car that Mary bought, but no particular car that Mary bought for Franklyn, as, for example, if Mary bought two cars: one for herself, and one for Franklyn, but remains indifferent as to who receives which. 'I bought one for each of us' does not, on this reading, mean 'For each of us there is one that I bought for him', but only 'I bought them for us, and in sufficient quantity for us each to have one'. The degree of particularity of her intentions is reflected in the particularity with which the dative pronoun will permit existential generalization. 'I bought one car for each of us' may mean just 'There are two cars that I bought for us.'

---

1. It would have to be the *if*-clause and not the noun phrase that was doing double duty, although precisely the replacement severally of proper nouns by the noun phrase can make the difference.

8.1.2 Undistributive exclusive 'or'

Recall that if there were a genuine example of exclusive disjunctive 'or' in English, then neither the negation of such a sentence nor a conditional sentence having such a sentence as its *if*-clause would be equivalent to conjunction. If we introduce 'xor' and permit uses between non-sentential parts of speech analogous to those of 'or', we will have examples of *xor*-lists that are undistributive when embedded in conditionals and negations. So, for example,

> (9) If Jules xor Jim contributes, the number of contributors will equal last year's

does not imply

> (10) If Jules contributes, the number of contributors will equal last year's
> |*| if Jim contributes, the number of contributors will equal last year's

where |*| is replaced by any of 'and', 'or', or 'xor', at least on the truth-functional understanding of the conditional, since the conditional would be true if both Jules and Jim contribute, even if the numbers do not match (its *if*-clause being false), but in this case both the constituent conditionals of (10) would be false. But considering the various ways of expressing 'xor' with available vocabulary, we find some *or*-lists that distribute and some *or*-lists that do not:

> (11) If Jules or Jim is the next contributor, the number of contributors will equal last year's

distributes, but

> (12) If Jules or Jim contributes, but not both, the number of contributors will equal last year's

does not distribute because distribution leaves the clause 'but not both' without a reference for the anaphora. However, when the anaphoric reference is replaced by its explication, the resulting sentence,

> (13) If Jules or Jim contributes, but not both Jules and Jim contribute, the number of contributors will equal last year's,

is equivalent to the conjunction

> (14) If Jules contributes, but not both Jules and Jim contribute, the number of contributors will equal last year's and if Jim contributes, but not both Jules and Jim contribute, the number of contributors will equal last year's.

The anomalies of (9) and (12) parallel those of Quine's 'I want a sloop' and 'Giorgione was so-called because of his size' (disregarding the special character of the anaphora in the last). It is true that (9) does not imply that there is something such that if it contributes, the numbers will coincide; and (12) does not imply that if someone contributes but not both, then the numbers will tally. The reason for the failure of distribution in (9) also parallels the reason for the failure of quantifying into 'I want a sloop'. In the one case, the unexplicated general noun phrase *masks* the points at which existential generalization can occur. In the other case, the introduction of 'xor' *entangles* the distribution by incorporating both a part of what is to be distributed and what it would distribute over. In the one case, the replacement of the indefinite noun phrase by an *or*-list of referential noun phrases lays bare the points at which the sentence is susceptible to generalization. In the other case, the replacement of 'xor' by standard vocabulary separates the matter to be distributed on the one hand from the junctor over which distribution is to take place on the other. It would therefore be preferable to say that the indefinite noun phrase 'a sloop' is quantificationally opaque in 'I want a sloop' and to say that the noun phrase 'Jules xor Jim' is distributionally opaque in (9).

8.1.3 Undistributive 'or' in questions

The subject of distribution in questions is made problematic by the difficulty of saying when two questions are equivalent, and upon what grounds. However, there is no difficulty in recognizing distributed and undistributed forms, and in distinguishing ways in which questions are typically understood. When one's philosopher-colleague on the lift answers 'Yes' to the question whether the lift is going up or down, we recognize, and not just from the environment, that the asker expects an answer drawn from 'Up', 'Down', not from 'Yes', 'No'. In the undistributed form,

(15) Is the lift going up or down?

a rising terminal inflection (with perhaps a stop after 'up') invites a 'yes/no' response, and a falling terminal inflection, with no stop after 'up', invites an 'up/down' response. To the second voicing of the question, there corresponds what may be called a distributed form of the question:

(16) Is the lift going up or is it going down?

also, unless to express exasperation, given a falling terminal inflection. The question asks in which of two directions the lift is travelling by asking of each direction in turn whether the lift is going in that direction. The answer expected is one that indicates the question to which 'Yes' is the answer or, more directly, in which direction it is tending. The answer 'Neither', though equally tiresome, would at least not depend for its point upon a perverse refusal to acknowledge the conventional markers of the *kind* of question being asked.

To give a question a distributed reading may be to treat the question as representing more than one question, but in particular cases it may be difficult to sort out the linguistic from the non-linguistic social practice that determines how it is taken, particularly when the reading treats the question as distributive with respect to the people addressed. For example, the question

(17) Is anyone going my way?

addressed to a group may, depending upon a variety of circumstances, be treated as a request for information satisfiable by a 'yes' that does not indicate which of the group addressed makes the answer correct, or a 'no' that means simply that no one is. But it may also be treated distributively by each member of the group as a question addressed to him or her, so that a 'yes' is a personal admission and a 'no' means only 'Not I'. Similarly, the question

Who's going my way?

asked of a group may be treated simply as a request for information, so that anyone addressed may volunteer anyone's name, but it may be treated as the same question distributively addressed, so that the only answers forthcoming are to the effect: 'I am' or 'I am not'. But whether, in such circumstances, the reception of the question is being shaped by linguistic or by other social under-standing may vary with the social weather, as may the atmosphere that surrounds the response.

As in indicative, so in interrogative sentences, anaphora may preclude a dis-tributive reading. Contrast

(18) Why get a job or go to college, when you can travel?

with

(19) Why get a job or go to college, when you can do both?[2]

The former asks two questions that might occur in distributive form joined with 'and' or joined with 'or' as:

(18') Why get a job, when you can travel, and why go to college, when you can travel?

or

(18'') Why get a job, when you can travel, or why go to college, when you can travel?[3]

But (19) could not, syntactically, be two questions because of the 'both' in the *when*-clause, and even if the anaphora is replaced by its explication

---

2. The advertising slogan of an East Sussex youth training scheme.

3. Particularly in rhetorical questions, to which no answer is expected, English is practically indif-ferent as between the use of 'and' and the use of 'or'. Rhetorical questions might as well be merely *mentioned* as questions that could be asked. The effect of 'or' then is consonant with an understand-ing of the succession of questions as a recital of questions that could be asked, that is, of alternative questions. We may compare Old Testament Hebrew or Jacobean practice as revealed in the Standard Version of the Bible:

Shall vain words have an end? Or [Hebrew: אוֹ] what emboldeneth thee that thou answerest? (Job 16:3)

Again, compare the three verses:

What is man that thou art mindful of him? and [Hebrew: וּ] the son of man that thou visitest him? (Psalms 8:4)

Lord, what is man that thou takest knowledge of him! *or* [Hebrew: no word] the son of man that thou makest account of him? (Psalms 144:3)

What is man that thou art mindful of him? or [Greek: 'ἤ'] the son of man that thou visitest him? (Hebrews 2:6) (Paul purports to quote Psalms 8:4.)

(19') Why get a job, when you can get a job and go to college and why go to college, when you can get a job and go to college?

the restatement as two questions loses the point of the original form, since getting a job and going to college is not an exclusive alternative either to getting a job or to going to college. The point of the question depends upon the fact that the *when*-clause forces us to read the *why*-clause exclusively: 'do only one of the two'. Of course the slogan is a play on words whose catch depends upon our being made to revise a first reading of the *why*-clause as 'do at least one of the two'.

The last example (19') has perhaps sufficiently illustrated a point made earlier, that undistributive *or*-lists occur between parts of speech other than noun phrases, but it cannot quite convince us of the further remark that, for that reason, we ought not to resist accounts that rely upon postulating indefinite proper names for objects of intentional attitudes. However we need not labour the point. Parallel to 'I want a yawl or ketch' we may notice such cases as 'I want to buy or hire a yacht', 'I want to hire a yacht fifty or sixty feet in length for two hundred dollars a day or less', and so on.

8.1.4 Disjunctive proper names

The suggestion that *or*-lists be thought of as a kind of proper name has been considered by other authors, notably Peter Geach, in connection with occurrences in distributive environments:

> We must not . . . too readily assume that we understand a disjunction of proper names. A child could no doubt be taught the use of a common, shared name "tripodortowzer" in simple acts of naming—taught to use that name precisely for each of the two dogs Tripod and Towzer. But what would then be meant by the question "Is tripodortowzer eating that bone?"? It looks as though the answer ought to be "Yes" or "No" according as the predicable "eating that bone" (suitably understood from the environment of utterance) did or did not apply to what is named by "tripodortowzer"; but since this name would name either of two dogs, this situation is incurably ambiguous. Thus "Tripod or Towzer is eating that bone", which is not ambiguous if the predicable can be understood from the environment of utterance, cannot be taken as an answer to our supposed question; nor, therefore can its grammatical subject "Tripod or Towzer" be equated with the supposed common name "tripodortowzer". And no other possible way immediately suggests itself of construing a list formed with "or" as a genuine complex subject or quasi subject. (1962, 67)

The argument is a persuasive one. If we treat 'tripodortowzer' as a proper name, then (a) the only way of construing this proper name is as a proper name common to the two dogs, and (b) on this construal there are occasions of use[4]

---

4. It would sometimes unambiguously just pick out the dog eating the bone. For some purposes it would give insufficient information, as to which human to send the bill for the bone, but the giving of insufficient information for reidentification for some purpose does not constitute ambiguity. The *or*-list of names would be similarly deficient.

and there are φ's such that 'Tripodortowzer is φ-ing' is ambiguous on those occasions, whereas 'Tripod or Towzer is φ-ing' is not. Therefore 'Tripod or Towzer' does not stand for something for which a name can be introduced. The case is illuminated if we consider the infantile use of unarticled common nouns. In some circumstances, the occurrence of 'dog' in 'Dog is φ-ing', construed as a proper name would be ambiguous. But that occurrence of 'dog' is neither proper name nor indefinite noun phrase by any plausibly attributed intention. And even if, construed as a proper name, it would be ambiguous in such circumstances, it would not be ambiguous if construed as a general term; the same holds of 'tripodortowzer'.

There is, as Geach remarks elsewhere (1962, 66), a difference between mathematically available construals of *or*-lists of nouns and mathematically available construals of *or*-lists of verbs. In the latter case it is open to us to think of them as representing sums of relations; in the former it 'does not so readily fit into a logical scheme'. But the difference can at least be mathematically marked. Think of 'or' as a function that takes an ensemble of n-place predicate terms to an n-place predicate term; semantically it will be represented by a function from the representatives of those terms to their join. But we may also think of 'or' as a function that takes an ensemble of individual constants to a general term, whose semantic representation will be a function taking the representatives of those constants to the least set containing them. Geach's device of *or*-concatenation might likewise be deployed grammatically as a function that takes an ensemble of proper nouns to a common noun. On this application, what would be needed to rescue 'Tripodortowzer is φ-ing' from ambiguity is an indefinite article.

The idea that *or*-lists of verbs more easily than *or*-lists of nouns can be given set-theoretic semantic construals, namely, as unions of relations, should not lull us into the assumption that apparent lists of verbs are not really lists, but some form of combination. The mere possibility of such a representation does not establish its correctness as a report of how lists of verbs work, and consideration of a few examples will not in any case suffice to establish that the representation is always available. Moreover, cases arise that, like *or*-lists of *if*-clauses, cast doubt upon that semantic representation as the most illuminating account. Consider, for example, how infinitives will be formed. The union representation would have us treat 'sits or runs' in 'Socrates sits or runs' as a compound verb that semantically picks out the union of the set of activities picked out by 'sits' and the set of activities picked out by 'runs'. We could refer to that activity by a compound gerund 'sitting or running' or by a compound infinitive 'to sit or run'. So we could give instructions on sitting or running from various initial postures, which might begin 'To sit or run, you first. . . .' But then we must say how to construe *or*-lists of infinitives.

> Most gracious queen, we thee implore
> To go away and sin no more;
> Or, if that effort be too great,
> To go away at any rate.[5]

---

5. Anonymous response to Thomas Denman's peroration in defence of Queen Caroline at her trial before the House of Lords in 1820, reported by Priestley (1969, 277). 'If no accuser can come forward to condemn thee, neither do I condemn thee: go and sin no more.' Priestley remarks ' . . . as he had been arguing for two days that no sin had been committed, this was anything but apt . . .'

To change this order—or to make any of the disk drives on this computer inaccessible from the lead—move the cursor over drive #, where # is the number of the lead you want to change. (LapLink 1989, 157)

We should resist the precept that a set-theoretic union must be contrived for every occurrence of 'or' in favour of some discourse-theoretical account that codifies the work that 'or' does in the punctuation of speech.

8.2 The Propositional Gloss on Opacity

A number of points emerge from our admittedly brief discussion of opaque environments. First, it must be clear from what we have said that the oddities of opaque environments should not be regarded exclusively as a cluster of referential phenomena or of phenomena surrounding the use of normally referential vocabulary. In its quantificational form it results from the masking of generalization points, while in its distributional form it results from entanglement of what is to be distributed with what it is to be distributed over. This last suggests that the pure notion of distribution should be reserved for use in connection with proper lists, that is, those formulated with 'and', 'or', or ','; that 'a_1 xor a_2' is not such a list; and that the inequivalence of $\lambda(a_1 \text{ xor } a_2)$ to $\lambda(a_1)$ or $\lambda(a_2)$, to $\lambda(a_1)$ and $\lambda(a_2)$ and to $\lambda(a_1)$ xor $\lambda(a_2)$ is not in itself a failure of distribution over 'xor', but a disguised failure of distribution over 'or'. But it may also seem to suggest even more persuasively than Quine's more constricted account that a proper understanding of opacity requires the recognition of a propositional element where there seemed grammatically to have been only a noun or verb or prepositional or adjectival or adverbial phrase. That in turn suggests that there is an explanation to be had for a wide range of undistributive *or*-lists, which once more seems to make propositional disjunction rather than *or*-lists the fundamental linguistic phenomenon involving 'or'. In what follows we consider that proposal.

8.2.1 Refining the idea of distributivity

The first upshot of the proposal is the obvious inadequacy of the definitions of distribution with which we began. There we proposed the notation of '$\lambda(\ )$' as a representation of the rest of the sentence surrounding an occurrence of a list. On this proposal, in the case in which an *or*-list is undistributive, the environment may or may not mask the division between what is to be distributed and what is not, but there is always such a division. For an example in which the division is not masked, consider

(20) Jack knows that Mary or Helen picked up the spaghetti

the inequivalence of which to

(20′) Jack knows that Mary picked up the spaghetti or Jack knows that Helen picked up the spaghetti

should not, it is claimed, persuade us that its occurrence of 'Mary or Helen' is an undistributive *or*-list on any reasonable construal of the notion. Rather, its equivalence to

> (20″) Jack knows that Mary picked up the spaghetti or Helen picked up the spaghetti

should count as showing the disjunctive distributivity of the list with respect to the environment '( ) picked up the spaghetti'. One accommodation of the intuition would define distributivity of a list 'a_1 or a_2' in $\underline{\lambda}(\ )$ by the biconditional

> a_1 or . . . or a_n is *-junctively distributive in the sentence '$\lambda(a_1$ or . . . or $a_n)$' iff that sentence is equivalent to a sentence containing a sentence '$\mu(a_1$ or . . . or $a_n)$' which is equivalent to the *-junction of '$\mu(a_1)$', . . . and $\mu('a_n)$'.

The accommodation does not straightforwardly solve the terminological problem in all cases, and there are sentences such as 'If it's her neck or yours, she'll spill' in which an *or*-list will remain undistributive even under this more liberal regime. Its unstraightforwardness is evident in such examples as (0) (I want a yawl or a ketch), where the most natural analysis recognizes an infinitive phrase rather than a *that*-clause as implicit in the original, even if accepting, as A. J. Kenny has claimed, that

> for "I want X" to be intelligible at all as the expression of a desire, the speaker must be able to answer the question "What counts as *getting* X?" (1963, 115)

Kenny's condition for the intelligibility of sentences of the form 'I want X' can be expressed as the condition that a person who has a want must be able to specify what state of affairs would have to obtain in order for his want to have been satisfied. The want must always be expressible by means of an infinitive phrase, in such a way that it is clear what state of affairs this is. So we can supply a verb,[6] in this case perhaps 'own' and rewrite (0) as

> (00) I want to own a yawl or a ketch

and this as

> (00′) I want to own a yawl or to own a ketch.[7]

But this falls short of showing distributivity of the *or*-list on the more liberal understanding. We must have recourse to some such more artificial and therefore more dubious construction as

> (000) I want that I own a yawl or a ketch

and thence

---

6. Possibly distinct verbs for distinct items of the list. Consider 'I want tea or death.'

7. This of course assumes that the sentence is transparent with respect to the implicit verb phrase. For any generic transitive verb 'to φ' that English might have, covering a range of possible relationships between people and yachts wider than the range covered by ownership, the want merely to φ a yawl or a ketch would be possible.

(000′) I want that I own a yawl or I own a ketch.

But we should not reject the analysis just on account of the dubious syntactic credentials of this expression of it. Quine's linguistic point and Kenny's pragmatic one can be accommodated within the general restriction that 'want' should take a noun or an infinitive phrase. Simply let it be hypothesized, as it plausibly might be, that all desires are desires for states of affairs, and rewrite 'a wants b or c' as 'a wants a state of affairs in which φ(b or c)' supplying a 'φ' as Kenny's pragmatic point requires. It is true that this noun phrase rewriting must in turn be capable of rewriting with an infinitive phrase, but the range of verb phrases   available ('realize', 'see realized', 'bring about', 'see brought about', and so on) for such a noun phrase is so narrow as to make iteration otiose. As a matter of idiom, if the understood verb were 'avoid', for example, the desire would not be expressed as a desire for the state of affairs. Thus we retain a suitable syntax while providing the propositional component within which the *or*-list is distributive.

8.2.2 Quine vs. Quran: heteronomous requirements

Having accepted that a propositional representation of the content of a comprehensible desire is always available, we must nevertheless ask whether that representation constitutes an *explanation* of the workings of apparently undistributive *or*-lists in expressions of desire and more generally in constructions taking infinitive phrases and infinitively expansible noun phrases. Other examples of such constructions are

(21) Chains or snow tires are obligatory (or 'required');

(22) You ought to notify Alison or Laurie;

(23) I need alcohol or boiling water;

(24) Members must be logicians or linguists;

(25) You owe the library ten dollars or an hour's shelving.

The requirement that there be conditions of fulfilment must indeed apply to a wider class of conditions than just desires. But if that requirement is satisfied by the specification of a verb phrase, the availability as well of a propositional translation may be not merely an irrelevant by-product, but even a misleading one if we dwell exclusively upon it. For we may be tempted to think of the environment as *essentially* a unary sentential connective: 'It is required (or 'obligatory') that . . .' and, neglecting the reason for insisting upon an implicit verb phrase, think now in terms of truth conditions rather than consider what the original sentence accomplished in discourse and how.

Questions of monotonicity in particular are an unnatural artefact of this truth-conditional approach. We may ask whether a sentential operation is monotonic along logical implication, but there is no similar relation between verb phrases to ask the question of. Thus it will be claimed that if you ought to notify Alison, then you ought to notify Laurie or Alison, because 'You notify Alison' implies 'You notify Laurie or Alison'. But if the purpose of the verb phrase was only to specify the condition of fulfilment, then there may be no obligation whose condition of fulfilment is specified by 'to notify Laurie or Alison'; only one whose condition of fulfilment is specified by 'to notify Alison'.

To put the matter another way, we may say that α specifies the condition of fulfilment of a requirement when

the requirement is fulfilled if and only if α is true,

not when

α is true if the requirement is fulfilled.

On this construal, the requirement that a vehicle wear snow tires or chains does not follow from the requirement that it wear snow tires. On the rejected construal it does. The recognition that the function of a statement of a requirement is to specify the conditions of its fulfilment explains the oddity, which the 'essentially propositional' approach requires us to ignore, in supposing that we can infer 'Members must be logicians or nuns' from 'Members must be logicians', 'He needs alcohol or arsenic' from 'He needs alcohol', or 'Hale wants liberty or death' from 'Hale wants death'.

Assumptions of such strong logical properties as monotonicity, though they make the lives of formal semanticists convenient, are at odds with the pragmatic considerations that make expressions of wants work by specifying the conditions of their fulfilment. To draw an analogy from chemistry, the working of language may sometimes require the strong forces of entailments and of necessary and sufficient conditions. But throughout much of its workings, it is rather the weaker conversational forces that, like hydrogen bonds and van der Waal forces, make its parts hang together and address one another as they should, not the stronger inferential forces based upon alleged truth conditions. To be sure, some of those weaker forces are inferential, but they are rather the inferences that shape or guide our responses, than the inferences that enable us to replace one sentence with a cloud of others that are jointly equivalent to it. For example, if expressions of wants are to work as we require them to, then if Mary says 'I want a', I must be able to infer that if I give Mary a, that will satisfy her want; that is, 'a' must be portable from her expression of want to other environments, and it must behave properly when thus transplanted. This properness may require some quite distinct feature absent in the original occurrence. So, for example, when 'a' is an *or*-list, its conjunctive distributivity in some environments is an essential element of the successful functioning of environments where, on the surface, it is undistributive. Others of these weak conversational forces permit resolutions of general requirements into the specific courses of actions that lead to their particular fulfilment, as if Mary, having gone into a shop, says to the shopkeeper, 'I would like a teapot'. It is proper for the shopkeeper to say, 'We have just these three in stock—as it happens, one of each size. Which would you like?' and for Mary to respond, 'I'd like the middle one, please'. The shopkeeper need not be represented as inquiring about Mary's propositional attitudes; he is inviting her to choose. And Mary need not be represented as replacing a non-specific propositional attitude by a more specific one of the same sort, rather than as following up a less specific enquiry with a particular request. Equally, however Moses' constituency frame their request for elucidation ('Pray for us unto thy Lord, that he would show us what cow it is'), we cannot tell from the text whether God had already settled upon a cow or subsequently drew up his successive short lists in view of the particular cows on offer.

8.2.3 Opaque 'any'

In witness of those general observations, we may notice that an account of 'or' in opaque environments must take into account the fact that in such environments an or-list can sometimes be replaced by an *any*-construction rather than by an indefinite noun phrase and that the effect of the *any*-replacement will in general be different from the indefinite noun phrase. Thus one may say without perplexing, 'I want a horse, but I don't want that one', but not 'I want any horse, but I don't want that one', rather than 'I want any horse but that one.' The first of these two points has nothing to do with the opacity of 'I want ( )' or with the expression of a negative want. It is true 'I want a horse' does not imply that there is a horse that I want, and it is true that 'I don't want that horse' might sometimes have the force of a claim that I want to avoid or cease having that horse. But the force of 'I don't want that one' here is not to deny that a want for that horse is being expressed, to deny the particular want, nor yet to insist that I want not to have that horse, but to deny that with regard to the want in question, that that horse will satisfy it, however much I might welcome the ownership or the use of it. The force of 'any horse' here is that of a description 'below the discourse line'. Its effect is to say, 'If you fill in with a reference to whatsoever horse, treat my want as though it were the want of that horse and act accordingly, I shall be satisfied'. In the event it may be false, but that will only be a reason to wish retrospectively that one had couched the request less permissively.

8.2.4 *Than*-scope of undistributive 'or'

Finally, we can apply the idea of *than*-scope to undistributive cases of 'or'. We have already noted that the pragmatic requirement for an understood verb phrase in expressions of want is not essentially a distributive requirement, since a distinct (finite or infinitive) verb phrase might be required for each item in a list. (Consider 'Charlie wants egg and sausages or a Mozart quintet'.) So we may consider undistributive lists with verb phrases in place. As before, our account of *than*-scope must recognize the variability of the nature and terms of the contemplated exclusion of whatever lies within it. An analogue is retained in modal logics, and will serve to illustrate the property. Consider, for the sake of specificity the modal system K axiomatized by

[RN] $\vdash\alpha \Rightarrow \vdash\Box\alpha$ (The Rule of Normality)
[RM] $\vdash\alpha \to \beta \Rightarrow \vdash\Box\alpha \to \Box\beta$ (The Rule of Monotonicity)
[K] $\vdash\Box p \wedge \Box q \to \Box(p \wedge q)$ (The Aggregation Principle).

Now K does not have as a theorem the distribution principle

$$\Box(\alpha \vee \beta) \to \Box\alpha \vee \Box\beta,$$

but it does have the principle

$$\Box(\alpha \vee \beta) \rightarrow (\Box\neg\alpha \rightarrow \Box\beta) \wedge (\Box\neg\beta \rightarrow \Box\alpha).$$

So although, extending the bracketing convention, we might mark the *than*-scope of $\vee$ in $\Box(\alpha \vee \beta)$ by $\Box([\alpha] \vee \beta)$, the terms of the contemplated exclusion are those of $\Box\neg\alpha \rightarrow \Box\beta$.

Analogously, we may infer from the information that

Necessarily you either register before the deadline or lose your citizenship

together with the information that registration is impossible, that *necessarily* you lose your citizenship, whereas from the quoted information together with the information that you merely have not yet registered we may infer that you will in fact lose your citizenship if you do not. At least before the deadline, we want to say, it is only the disjunction that is necessary. We may observe a similar phenomenon in expressed wants. If Hilda says that she wants a yawl or a ketch, we treat this as her wanting a ketch only if her having a yawl is in some way ruled out and not merely false, but unless we take the order of the list to be significant, we do in fact treat the expression of the want as the expression of a pair of conditional wants with that proviso. So we take the sentence

Hilda wants a yawl or a ketch

as telling us at least

Hilda wants [a yawl] or a ketch.

The nature of the ruling out will vary from case to case, but in each the environment itself applied to the exclusion of an alternative is sufficient. If Hilda tells us that she wants to have a yawl or a ketch and wants badly not to be the owner of a ketch, we may take her to have been telling us in her pedantically dramatic way that she wants a yawl. If her distaste for ketches is a later development we take this as a refinement of her want. But so long as the presumption of indifference is in force, we take Hilda's desire for a yawl or a ketch to be a pair of conditional wants: the want of a yawl if no ketch can be provided *and* the want of a ketch if no yawl can be provided.

Parallel remarks apply to deontic environments. From the suggestion that one ought to do one or the other of two things, we normally take two pieces of conditional advice, that if the first course is precluded, one ought to do the second: that if the second is precluded, one ought to do the first. The nature of the preclusion is unspecified, but typically it would comprehend physical impossibility and conflicting requirements; that is, we would typically take the advice to apply to one course if, for some reason unknown to the adviser, one ought not to follow the other. We have spoken here of deontic environments in discourse. In monadic deontic systems, where the fiction is indulged that artificial deontic sentences of the form 'It ought to be the case that α' have truth values, and usually that the deontic connective is monotonic, there is likely to be no means of expressing this conditionality, though the deontic form of the modal principle

$$\Box(\alpha \vee \beta) \rightarrow (\Box\neg\alpha \rightarrow \Box\beta) \wedge (\Box\neg\beta \rightarrow \Box\alpha)$$

may be a theorem. And the models for such systems will make

$$\Box(\alpha \vee \beta)$$

true if

$$\Box\alpha$$

is, whatever the truth value of

$$\Box\beta.$$

However, in natural discourse, both in the case of certain conjunctively distributive *or*-lists *and* in that of certain undistributive *or*-lists, we find something like a conjunctive sense, and in each we find what we may call weakened conjuncts. The weakening in question is the conditionality of each and differs in stringency from the first sort of environment to the second. 'You may do a or b' gives one permission to do a if one decides not to do b *and* gives one permission to do b if one decides not to do a. Advice that one ought to do a or b is conditional advice to do a if b is precluded *and* conditional advice to do b if a is precluded. Each formula is mute as to what is permitted or advised when the conditions fail, and each may or may not express a preference as to which course is followed.

What appears to emerge from these examples is a hint that in discourse the more primitive distinction between 'or' and 'and' is not a distinction of truth value, but a distinction rather of status of discourse elements connected by them. Without preliminary discussion, we cannot say in detail what this amounts to, but we can illustrate the general line of the account by noting the respect in which propositional logic preserves a truth-functional analogue of the distinction we shall claim to find in discourse. It lies in the equivalence of the form

$$p \vee q$$

to the form

$$(\neg q \rightarrow p) \wedge (\neg p \rightarrow q).$$

To see what is being illustrated, we must consider the second as the truth-functional analogue of a succession of conditional assertions: a conditional assertion of p and a conditional assertion of q. The illustration is, in the nature of the case, a coarse-grained one. It will be no more than a trivial emendation of the conventional view to cite that equivalence as an explanation of the sentential use of 'or' in discourse. All that the illustration amounts to is the substitution of $\wedge$ for $\vee$ and the compensating operations on p and on q. What is illustrated is just this: a succession of sentences composed with 'or' replaced by a succession of forms containing non-assertive occurrences of those sentences either composed with 'and' or as separate acts of speech.

8.2.5 *Than*-scope and non-commutative lists

The idea that expressions of wants that embed *or*-lists express separate conditional wants for the items listed has application where we suppose that the order of the items in the lists has no significance. Where the order counts, the reading must reflect the fact. Consider in particular the class of such examples that, even when expressed in apparently distributed form, resist a disjunctive reading

I want that money on my desk by two o'clock or your resignation.

The idea of *than*-scope enables us to see why in such a case we can use distributed form without inviting a disjunctive reading. Consider

I want that money on my desk by two o'clock or I want your resignation,

which we may take not merely to indicate an order of preference, but to express a want of the money. The *than*-scope is as for an undistributive reading:

I want [that money on my desk by two o'clock] or I want your resignation,

not as for a disjunctive reading:

[I want that money on my desk by two o'clock] or I want your resignation,

but we take from the utterance that the speaker unconditionally wants the money on his desk by two o'clock. Parallel remarks apply to the example that Lambert and van Fraassen give as of exclusive disjunction:

H. wanted liberty or he wanted death.

On the reading of this sentence that reflects H's sentiments as we understand them to have been, it would be marked

H. wanted [liberty] or he wanted death;

nevertheless, on the proposed reading we take it to be telling us that H. unconditionally wanted liberty. So on this reading it is not a disjunction.

Funny Velentine

The Second Myth of 'Or'

δύναται λέγειν καὶ περὶ τῶν Δυνατῶν, τοῦ τε, ὃ Διοδώρειον λέγεται, ὃ ἢ ἔστιν ἢ ἔσται·

Perhaps he is speaking about the possible, about Diodorus' account: that which is or will be.   ALEXANDER OF APHRODISIAS

Diodorus possibile esse determinat, quod aut est aut erit.
Diodorus defined the possible as what is or will be.   BOETHIUS

9.1 Modern Sources

The second myth is cheerful handmaiden to the first, and, perhaps because of its classical hearkenings, has an undeniable charm. Perhaps, as other legends do, those of spiders' nests in beehive hairdos or those of Ovid's *Metamorphoses*, it speaks to us usefully of atavistic fears or discreditable longings. But, like other myths, it will, of a certainty, continue to charm us even after we have convinced ourselves that it is factually false. Copi again:

> The Latin word "vel" expresses weak or inclusive disjunction, and the Latin word "aut" corresponds to the word "or" in its strong or exclusive sense. (1961, 241)

Jeffrey:

> Latin provides two words for the two senses of "or": *aut* for the exclusive sense ("but not both") and *vel* for the inclusive sense ("or maybe both"). (1967, 10)

Lemmon:

> (The symbol ∨ is intended to remind classicists of the Latin 'vel' as opposed to 'aut': For $P \lor Q$ is understood not to exclude the possibility that both P and Q might be the case.) (1965, 19)

Massey:

> The connective 'v' is called the *wedge* and derives from the Latin word 'vel', which means 'or' in the weak or inclusive sense. (1970, 9)

Suppes:

> The Latin word 'vel' has approximately the sense of 'or' in the non-exclusive sense, and consequently we use the sign 'v' for the disjunction of two sentences in this sense. (1957, 5)

Rescher:

> Thus we employ the letter "v" (*vee*)—from the Latin *vel* = *or* in its inclusive sense—to represent the inclusive "or." (1964, 179)

Richards:

> In Latin there are two words that do duty for our English 'or' and they are different in meaning. One, 'vel', joins two sentences in such a way that if one or both of them is true, so is the whole thing. . . . But Latin has a second word, different in meaning from 'vel', that also has to be translated as 'or'. That is 'aut' (pronounced *out*). It joins two sentences in such a way that if one of them is true, so is the whole thing; but if both flanking sentences are true, then the whole is false. We abbreviate 'aut' by '≢' (crossed tribar). . . . (1978, 83)

Hacking:

> The Romans actually had two different words for our single "or." They used the word "aut" for the exclusive sense. They used the word "vel" for the inclusive sense. (1972, 92)

W.V.O. Quine:

> We must decide whether v is to be construed in an exclusive sense corresponding to the Latin 'aut' or in an inclusive sense, corresponding to the Latin 'vel'. (1961, 12)

And so on. The allusion to Latin seems, since Vatican II, to have been dropped as a part of the canon of the logical text. As early as 1976, we find a mere vernacular echo of the practice:

> Some languages—though English is not one of them—have two different words for two different senses of "or."(Manicas 1976, 71)

9.2 *Aut*, Damned Myth!

9.2.1 Latin

The question about the way Latin is or is not is of course as irrelevant as the character of English to the truth-tabular interpretations we give for the connectives of propositional logic. It adds nothing to the logical understanding of logic students to understand the workings of Latin. Doubtless a large plurality of them find it a perplexing irrelevance. So we can be thankful that when such remarks disappear from the *genre*, no one need mind.

Now it is true that in Latin one sometimes finds *aut* used to join terms that are antithetical or in some way opposed, as,

> *Omne enuntiatum aut verum aut falsum est* (Cicero 1942, 222)
> Every statement is either true or false

> *Aut vivam aut moriar* (Terence 1965, 54)
> I shall either live or die.

So the intuition that *aut* is somehow cued by disjointness or exclusion is partly right. But it would be a better account of *vel*, a surviving imperative form of the verb *volo*, to say that it is used in contexts in which a choice is offered, as,

> *vel imperatore vel milite me utimini* (Sallust 1930, 36)
> Use me as your supreme commander or as a private soldier.

even when, as in this case, the antitheticality of the terms might otherwise indicate *aut*. As Lewis and Short put it,

> In general *aut* puts in the place of a previous assertion another, objectively and absolutely antithetical to it, while *vel* indicates that the contrast rests upon subjective opinion or choice; i.e. *aut* is objective, *vel* subjective, or *aut* excludes one term, *vel* makes the two indifferent. (1879, 210)

And Glare gives first in his list of uses for *aut*:

> (introducing two or more logically exclusive alternatives) Either . . . or . . . (or)

with the examples:

> *aut intra muros aut extra*

and the Ciceronian

> *quidquid enuntietur . . . aut uerum esse aut falsum.* (1982, 219)

Clearly the distinction as noted by the lexicographers does not fit well onto the distinction between 1110 and 0110 disjunctions. In the first place, a choice could be made between mutually exclusive alternatives, as between *imperator* and *miles*. Second, and more important, the antithesis or mutual exclusion of terms joined by *aut* does not always yield, after distribution, exclusive disjuncts. For example, in

> . . . *tribunos aut plebem*

the magistrates and the mob are contrasted, and certainly exclude one another, conditions sufficient, on the lexicographers' account, to warrant the use of *aut*. But once a verb is added, as in

> *... tribunos aut plebem timebat*
> ... feared the magistrates or the mob,

the resulting predicate is not exclusive at all; clearly fearing the magistrates does not exclude fearing the common people. We shall see presently that it is that non-exclusive reading that gives the intended meaning. Examples of this sort of exclusivity are readily found. Consider

> *aut adversa ... aut prospera*
> either adverse ... or agreeable.

The two terms are opposed and perhaps incompatible. But when a context is supplied as

> *Aut adversa eventura dicunt aut prospera* (Gellius 1977, 3: 18, 20)
> They predict adverse outcomes or agreeable ones

the resulting sentence is not to be understood as an exclusive disjunction.

Third, even the distinctions that are made — and are in some imperfect way suggestive of the 1110/0110 distinction — are not always made using *aut* and *vel*, and sometimes *aut* joins terms that are, in one way or another, related. Consider

> *equi icti aut vulnerati consternabantur* (Lane 1899, 265)
> the horses, being hit or wounded, were being made frantic

or

> *aut cum obsit ... aut cum nihil prosit ...* (Cicero 1949b, 60)
> When [the narrative] is a hindrance or in no way a help.

Fourth, Latin repeated conjunctions to indicate scope, as modern English uses 'either ... or ...', but in the Latin of the time of Galen, *vel* correlated with *aut* and *aut* with *vel* occur, though no doubt less commonly than *vel* with *vel* or *aut* with *aut*. Fifthly, Latin had numerous other words for various uses for which English uses 'or', among them *seu*, *sive*, *an* and the enclitic *ve*; the distinctions made are numerous and subtle, and there is a good deal of overlap between the occasions warranting the use of one of those words and those where one might plausibly wish to use *aut* or *vel*.

At least as important as any of these considerations for shedding the myth is this: even if *aut* always joined antithetical terms (which it did not), and even if after distribution this antithesis always yielded mutually exclusive alternands (which it did not), this would not imply that ... *aut* ... means '... or ... but not both'. Where it joined such terms, the hypothesis would not be required. Moreover, in its actual use it frequently joined terms that were not in themselves antithetical, and in these cases the resulting sentences are not uniformly, or even as a general rule, to be understood in such a way as to be representable by exclusive disjunction. The most that can be said of these cases is that the special force of *aut* was to alternation what the special force of *at* or *autem* was to conjunction. Just as we do not have a special truth-functional connective for the adversative 'but', we require no special connective for the representation of *aut* as used in ordinary Latin. The use of *aut* rather than *vel*, like the use of *at* rather than *et*, might reveal something of the frame of mind of the speaker, but it need play no special role in the determination of whether what the speaker said was true.[1]

9.2.2 Greek

One plausible source of the second myth may well lie in a particular potting of the history of logic itself. There involution of issues concerning the exclusiveness of disjunction is to be found on a scale that outmatches those of our own technically more advanced textbooks. The difference is that, historically, one does discern a bias in favour of a kind of exclusive disjunction, a preoccupation that may be traced ultimately to the Stoics or later Peripatetics, and intermediately through many generations of authors writing about logic in Latin. We will consider the Stoics' proper contribution to the story more fully later. At the moment we ask only whether they might have been indirectly the origin of the second myth of 'or'. The Roman commentators regularly used *aut . . . aut . . .* to translate the Stoics' ἤτοι . . . ἤ . . . . The Stoics adopted as one of their logical primitives a notion in certain superficial respects akin to modern notions of exclusive disjunction, and represented it in premisses in which ἤ (with auxiliary ἤτοι) was the connective. What is to the present purpose is that such constructions no more meant ' . . . or . . . but not both' in ordinary Hellenistic Greek than *aut . . . aut . . .* meant that in ordinary Latin. As in the case of *aut . . . aut . . .*, ἤτοι . . . ἤ . . ., when it was used, was used indifferently between antithetical and non-antithetical terms, between sentences mutually exclusive and otherwise. The role of ἤτοι . . . ἤ . . . in the Stoics' theoretical apparatus had therefore to be fundamentally different, at least initially, from that of καὶ . . . καὶ . . . ('both . . . and . . .') in one important respect.[2] Anything that they might infer from a sentence principally compounded with καὶ they could infer solely from the presence of καὶ given its ordinary meaning when joining whole sentences. By contrast, solely from the presence of ἤτοι . . . ἤ . . . with its ordinary meaning joining two whole sentences, they could not infer that only one alternand was false, only that at least one alternand was true. Unless ἤτοι . . . ἤ . . . was given a special technical (one might almost have said 'ceremonial') meaning, it could only have been from the additional information about the mutual exclusiveness of the disjuncts that the falsity of one of them could have been inferred as well. Indeed, only from the fact that the particular instance of ἤτοι . . . ἤ . . . occurred in a ceremonial logical setting, or from someone's inferring the falsity of one alternand after the assertion of the other, could one have guessed that ἤτοι . . . ἤ . . . was being given a technical sense, and that could be only one possible hypothesis among others. Commentators such as Cicero, Galen, Sextus Empiricus, and Diogenes Laertius seem to the careful modern reader to waver between representing Stoic disjunctive arguments as *formally* valid and representing them as valid in consequence of their

1. Pelletier (1978, 65) has made a related point about the use of *aut* and *vel*, but his claim that 'from the extant Latin literature it seems that *vel* and *aut* are used to mark the distinction' between the cases where the truth of exactly one alternand and where only at least one alternand is expected by the speaker gives the mythologizers more ground to stand upon than the truth of the matter would accord them.

2. In fact conjunction did not play an important role in Stoic logic, possibly because they found no physically puissant relationship in nature to which it corresponded.

content. This is put down by some historians as a Peripatetic influence, by others as a confusion between validity and soundness. But given the facts about ordinary Greek and Latin, the matter must have seemed ambiguous or at least unclear. In any case the Stoic notion of διεζευγμένον, which historians of logic translate as 'disjunction' was, on the nearest construal, a notion of items exactly one of which must hold, not of a compound   formed with ἤτοι . . . ἤ . . . . Moreover, the Stoic relationship of διεζευγμένον had no fixed arity, and that fact alone ought to be sufficient to contraceive any myth of ἤτοι . . . ἤ . . . as well as lay to rest at least the myth that *aut* meant v̲. Again, if we consider the few discussions of the related notion of παραδιεζευγμένον, which would bear a relation to non-exclusive disjunction roughly analogous to that borne by διεζευγμένον to exclusive disjunction, we find the same ἤτοι . . . ἤ . . . used in the examples offered ('Socrates walks or Socrates converses'; Mates 1953, 53).

Now it is obvious that in Latin translations and discussions of Stoic logical theory, *aut . . . aut . . .* should occur in the ceremonial position occupied by ἤτοι . . . ἤ . . . The use of *aut* in Latin suggested in ordinary use an objective separation of alternands, which is part of what the Stoics had in mind. Certainly no other Latin 'or' word would have been more suitable. But we can no more infer from this the meaning of *aut* in ordinary Latin than we can from this use of ἤτοι . . . ἤ . . . that it was exclusive in the formal sense in ordinary Greek. In fact, apart from the representation of the ceremonial uses of ἤτοι . . . ἤ . . . in logical contexts, lexicographers have not recognized any claim of *aut . . . aut . . .* as its only suitable translation. Thus we find, for example, in one historic lexicon (Schrevelius 1805), as the Latin translation of 'ἤτοι', '*sive, seu, vel, certe*' and for 'ἤ', '*vel, an*'. In another we find instead for the former, '*vel quidem, vel sane*' ('or even' 'or indeed'), and for the latter, '*aut, vel*' and for ἤ . . . ἤ . . ., 'aut-aut, vel-vel, sive-sive' (Hedericus 1832).

It is unclear as well (though this is to anticipate) to what extent the modern notion of logical form has application here. When in the *Topica*, Cicero gives as an example,

Aut hoc aut illud; hoc autem; non igitur illud (Cicero 1949a, 424)

it is a temptation for the modern reader to suppose that he intends to give what Stoic logicians regard as a valid form, but this interpretation finds less warrant than another: that it is merely a mode of argument construction by which a valid argument would result from the substitution of incompatible alternatives for *hoc* and *illud*. In fact, a charitable interpretation of the larger passage requires the latter. He offers as the seventh mode

Non et hoc et illud; non autem hoc; illud igitur. (424)

While this could not without stipulation represent a valid *form*, there could nevertheless be valid arguments of this form, provided that the right sentences were substituted, as for example

Not both Not-p and p; not not-p; therefore p.

This is usually reported as a gaffe, but even if we take this to be an account of a valid form in the modern sense, then having regard for the ordinary meanings of

Latin words, the second of Cicero's argument forms is no more strange than the first, even if it is inaccurate as a report of Stoic logical practice.

We find a similarly puzzling unclarity in Aulus Gellius' discussion of Bias' well known syllogism that begins 'You will marry a woman either beautiful or ugly'. Favorinus' reaction is said by Gellius to have been that this sentence is not a proper disjunction. But it is unclear on the face of it whether he thought that the argument was, on that account, invalid or merely not a proof that one ought not to marry.

> Favorinus . . . declared that this was not a fact, and that it was not a fair antithesis, since it was not inevitable that one of the two opposites be true, which must be the case in a disjunctive. (Gellius 1977, 1: 411)

We will return to questions of Stoic doctrine as a separate topic. There is no doubt that they bequeathed to the history of logic a preoccupation with a kind of exclusive disjunction, and that in the way in which logic tends to regiment natural language, *aut* gained prominence as a disjunctive connective. But among later Latin authors, the question as to the status of a disjunction was never the question whether *aut* or *vel* was used. Thus Priscian:

> *Disiunctivae sunt, quae, quamvis dictiones coniungunt, sensum tamen disiunctum et alteram quidem rem esse, alteram vero non esse significant, ut 've, vel, aut'*, (Keil 1961, 2: 97)

and among his examples:

> *vel dies est vel nox.*

And although the question as to whether an exclusive notion of disjunction or a non-exclusive sort was the more fundamental or natural or useful was a frequent topic of discussion for medieval logicians, nevertheless it is clear that for them the question was not whether some assumed sense of *aut* or *vel* dictated by facts about Latin was more desirable. In any case, Latin itself was undergoing changes, and as it gave way to local languages as the vehicle of ordinary expression, even such discriminations as might earlier have been made contextually possible by rules of thumb had lost their shape. Thus we find in the twelfth-century French of Marie de France that '*aut . . . aut*' in the form '*u . . . u*' had displaced '*sive . . . sive*' in contexts in which modern French would have '*soit . . . ou*':

> *U bel li seit u pas nel vueille*[3]
> Whether he wants it or not

In the same century, when Abelard advocated dropping the exclusivity requirement for disjunction inherited from Boethius, and did himself abandon it, he did not on that account discontinue his use of *aut* as the disjunctive connective. Nevertheless, he took genuine disjunction to hold between two propositions when the negation of either disjunct *necessarily* implies the other disjunct, and he used *vel* to represent the merely contingent counterpart of that intensional connection (Abelard 1956, 485ff, 530–532). That usage is certainly congruent

---

3. From 'Bisclavret', 276. Cited by Rohlfs (1960; 83 in the English translation. For a discussion see 159).

with one ordinary classical Latin usage reported by the lexicographers, and supports if only morally the intuition that *aut* represents a stronger connection than *vel*, if only in degree of adversativity. In the sixteenth century the Scottish logician Caubraith took disjunction to be non-exclusive (*Ad veritatem disiunctivae affirmativae requiritur et sufficit alteram eius partem principalem esse veram* . . .; Broadie 1985, 161n.) and used *vel* throughout, even in examples having incompatible disjuncts, as '*Sortes currit vel Sortes <non> currit*. In the seventeenth century, the *Logica Hamburgensis* is indifferent as to which of *aut*, *vel*, and other similar words occur:

> Disjuncta Enuntiatio, ἀξίωμα διεζευγμένον dicta Stoicis, est, cujus vinculum est Conjunctio disjunctiva *Aut, Vel*, et similes, ut *Aut dies est, aut nox est. Vel pugnandum, vel cedendum*. (Jungius 1957, 104)

He claims that every disjunction (grammatically construed) is ambiguous as between being a complete disjunction and a subdisjunction, that is, between satisfying, on the one hand, the condition that exactly one of its members is true, and on the other permitting either all of its members to be true, or all of them false:

> Ambigua est omnis Disjunctiva, quia per easdem particulas, et *completè-disjunctiva* et utraque *Sub-disjunctiva* effertur. (105)

For the sort of disjunction that Jungius had in mind, Latin, far from using its larger resources of *or*-words to disambiguate, is completely transparent to the ambiguities. The Port Royal Logic, published thirty years later, explicitly *defines* disjunction as a pair of sentences joined by *vel*: *Les disjonctives sont de grand usage, et ce sont celles où entre la conjonction disjonctive* vel, ou. But both of its affirmative Latin examples are sentences joined by *aut*:

> *Amicitia pares aut accipit, aut facit.*
> *Aut amat, aut odit mulier, nihil est tertium.*

The authors may have been relying upon the known etymological continuity between *aut* and *ou*, offering instances of the one as though instances of the other. However, their one negative example uses *vel* where, on two scores, classical Latin might have expected *aut*:

> *Non omnis actio est bona vel mala.* (Arnauld & Nicole 1662, Chapter 9)

Modern textbook writers evidently did not invent the chivalric expository style.

That is the second myth, that Latin not only possessed truth-functional vocabulary but also was possessed of a clearer, since more explicit notation for distinguishing exclusive from inclusive disjunction. The ultimate source of the myth remains a mystery.

9.3 Heredipety

A claim of the punctuational thesis is that the taxonomy imposed by the truth-functional view of natural language — the division of uses of 'or' into inclusive and exclusive cases — is at at right angles to the natural grammatical divisions of the uses of 'or'. What seem to be instances of naturally occurring truth-functionally grounded equivalences corresponding to De Morgan's laws and left disjunctivity in conditional constructions are merely instances of grammatical regularities that hold as well in areas in which truth-functional logic lays no heredipetous claim.

9.3.1 The second myth revisited

Now it remains a matter for counterfactual speculation what additional persuasive power would be gained for a truth-functional theory of the natural 'or', had it been fact rather than fancy that the inclusive/exclusive distinction corresponded to the *vel*/*aut* distinction in Latin. Perhaps one would be strengthened in the conviction that such a distinction would arise naturally in a language by the disclosure that the Latin language had evolved the means to make it explicit. But the converse presumably would also be a reasonable conjecture. If the distinction is a natural or an important one, one would expect a language with a fund of 'or'-like words to devote some of them to making the distinction. Let us apply this same test to the punctuational view. Let us ask, that is, whether the taxonomy that the punctuational thesis claims to be the more natural one fits any more closely the explicit grammatical ordering of Latin. Since philosophers are so seldom afforded the pleasures of making empirical hypotheses inspired by a theory and then finding them confirmed, the outcome of such an inquiry is particularly gratifying. For among the uses of *aut* in Latin are those corresponding to the central conjunctively distributive uses of 'or' in English. Lewis and Short (1879) list among the uses of *aut* (but not of *vel*):

I e: repeated after negatives,
Nihil est aut fragile aut flexibile quam . . .
Nothing is as fragile or as malleable as . . .

I g: in comparative clauses,
talis autem simulatio vanitati est conjunctior quam aut liberalitati aut honestati.
But such a pretense is more closely akin to vanity than to generosity or character.

Now if one were looking for a knock-down argument to dismiss the claim that in Latin *aut* stood for exclusive disjunction, the former of these classes of uses of *aut* would provide it. Negation does not distribute over exclusive disjunction. It hardly needs emphasizing that in neither of the particular examples given can *aut* be construed exclusively, nor that in both of these cases *aut* invites a conjunctively distributive construal. It is worth underlining the lexicographers' grammatical description of the first example. *Aut* is used to 'carry on a previous negation' to another term. This starkly non-truth-functional description is the one adopted by other grammarians who have noted the idiom. The same description could be given of the corresponding occurrences in English of 'or'. This is the use of *aut* in the previously (incompletely) cited example:

Nemo tribunos aut plebem timebat.

No one feared the magistrates or the common people.

It should be clear that this does not mean 'Everyone either feared neither of them or feared both' and that the earlier negative example does not mean 'Everything is either both as fragile and malleable as . . . or neither as fragile nor as malleable as. . . .'

It is easy to find as well the use of *aut* in antecedent clauses, in which it invites conjunctive distribution and therefore cannot be construed exclusively. A votary of the cult of the exclusive *aut* would add a little lustre to its claims by finding a single example of a Latin conditional sentence satisfying two conditions: first, having an *if*-clause consisting of two main clauses (say, α and β) separated by *aut* and second, requiring to be understood as inequivalent to the conjunction of the conditionals retaining the *then*-clause, but having α and β severally as their *if*-clauses. An alternative experiment to similar effect would search for a negative adverbial construction that did not distribute over *aut*. The following does not, of course, disprove the existence of such examples, but it is especially poignant since it is drawn from Aulus Gellius' discussion of διεζευγμένον and its truth conditions:

> *Ex omnibus quae disiuguntur unum esse verum debet, falsa cetera. Quod si aut nihil omnium verum aut omnia plurave quam unum vera erunt, aut quae disiuncta sunt non pugnabunt, aut quae opposita eorum sunt contraria inter sese non erunt, tunc id disiunctum mendacium est . . .*
> (*Noctes Atticae.* XVI. VIII. 13–14.)
>
> Of all statements which are contrasted, one ought to be true and the rest false. But if none at all of them is true or all or more than one of them are true, or the contrasted things are not at odds, or those which are opposed to one another are not contrary, then that is a false disjunction . . .[4]

Clearly the sense of this is that any of the four cases separated by *aut*[5] will make the disjunction false. And, again, it is obvious that more than one case could occur together to the same effect. We find as well in some antecedent uses of *aut* some latitude in the matter of grammatical agreement, a plural verb providing, as in Boole's example, a reinforcement for the intended distributive understanding:

> . . . *si quid Socrates* aut *Aristippus contra morem consuetudinemque civilem fecerint locutive*[6] *sint* . . .[7]
> . . . if Socrates or Aristippus did or said something contrary to the manners and usages of their city. . . .

Now the principal division that distinguished the use of *aut* from the use of *vel* in Latin was not the distinction between conjunctive and disjunctive distribution

---

4. At least one translator (John Rolfe in Gellius 1977) has found it natural to translate this passage into the 'if . . . or if . . .' construction.

5. Notice the use of the enclitic *ve* for the subsidiary division *plurave quam unum* ('or more than one'). There is no intended *logical* distinction between the *aut* and the *ve*, which is derivative from *vel*.

6. Notice again the use of the enclitic *ve* for the subsidiary division *fecerint locutive sint* ('did or said').

7. Cicero. *Off.* I, 148. See also Lane (1899) 127f.

any more than the distinction between exclusive and inclusive disjunction. It was, though this is to oversimplify, the distinction between the objective separation of terms and the separation that was a matter of choice. As we have seen, the two are not themselves exclusive. Whether *aut* or *vel* was the appropriate choice on an occasion was a matter of which kind of separation was to the fore. Distributive sense is not itself dependent upon the choice of 'or' word. We may find clear illustrations of contrary cases. One particularly good illustration that deserves to be quoted here is found in the *Ad C. Herennium*. There, in the space of a few paragraphs, notably parallel otherwise in construction, 'Cicero' (or Cornificius, or whoever wrote the work) uses successively *aut*, *an*, and *vel* accordingly as (i) the terms it connects refer to objectively alternative external circumstances, (ii) a question is to be resolved, or (iii) there is an element of human volition. Nevertheless, there can be no question that the sense of each example is that of a conjunction of 'when . . . then . . .' sentences abbreviated.

> *Ex contrariis legibus controversia constat cum alia lex iubet* aut *permittit, alia vetat quippiam fieri . . .* (*Auct. Her.* I. XI. 20.)
> Controversy results from conflicting laws when one law orders *or* permits a deed while another forbids it . . .

> *Iuridicalis constitutio est cum factum convenit, sed iure* an *iniuria factum sit quaeritur.* (I. XIII. 18)
> An issue is juridical when there is agreement on the act, but the rightness *or* wrongness of the act is in question.

> *Ex remotione criminis causa constat cum a nobis non crimen, sed culpam ipsam amovemus, et* vel *in hominem transferimus* vel *in rem quampiam conferimus.* (I XV. 25)
> A cause rests upon the rejection of the responsibility when we repudiate, not the act charged, but the responsibility, and either transfer it to another person *or* attribute it to some other circumstance.

Latin no more than any other natural language was entirely rigid about the uses to which its vocabulary could be put, and any generalization is valuable only as an indicator of preponderant usage. Moreover, the origins of the words that it happens to have will have shaped the ways in which distinctions are made. Given the origins of *vel*, it is natural to express permissions offering choice by such constructions as 'Do A *vel* do B', and to state permissibilities correspondingly by some such construction as '*Licet* to do A *aut* to do B'. And we find such constructions as:

> . . . *omnia posse inter se vel similia vel dissimilia demonstrari* (Cicero. *Inv.* II. L. 152.)
> . . . all things can be shown to be similar or dissimilar,

in which a *vel*-list is conjunctively distributive. The correspondence between Latin uses of *aut* and English conjunctively distributive uses of 'or' will not then be perfect. But that ordinary Latin so preponderantly uses *aut* in comparisons and in negated constructions suggests that cueing a conjunctive distribution represents a class of uses reserved mostly as its province, that province, not exclusivity in the propositional sense, which is *ipso facto* ruled out.

9.3.2 Etymology

This role as cue for conjunctive distribution is as much sanctioned by the etymology of *aut* as the role as cue for choice is sanctioned by the etymology of *vel*. Its Indo-European source is 'au', to which root there came to be attached various particles. In Greek the same root gives rise to αὖ (*again, further, moreover, besides*), which, as Liddell and Scott (1864) observe '(as *again* is connected with *against*, German *wieder* with *wider*) it takes on the sense of *on the other hand, on the contrary*'. With the addition of –τε, it yields αὖτε (*again, furthermore, next*). With the addition of –τις it yields αὖθις (*moreover, besides, in turn, on the other hand*). In Latin it yielded the early form *auti*, thence *aut*, but also *autem* (*on the other hand, but, yet, however, nevertheless*). The same Indo-European source gave birth to Gothic *auk* and ultimately to English 'eke'.

The temptation to think that *aut* had, any more than English 'or' has, some logical disjunctive meaning, rather than additiveness-cum-adversativeness at the core of its use should be further diminished when we reflect that the particle –τε that attached to it in Greek also had its Indo-European source in k^we, which found its way into Latin as the enclitic *que* (*and*). It is illuminating to consider the terms in which a syntactician (as opposed to a logician) describes the fates of these phonological resources:

> The particle *k^we, which eventually yielded the Greek τε, is, with the particle *we, the only conjunction whose Indo-European character can be attested to. Both were unaccented and enclitic, and both were vulnerable: *we could not survive phonetically in Greek without the support of ἤ to which in the end it was assimilated; *k^we, though phonetically robust, was completely displaced by καί, the most important of the particles with which it could combine. Just as nothing of –*que* or –*ve* survives in Romance languages, so Greek replaced ἤ by εἴτε and τε by καί. Lastly, as *we seems to have possessed, in addition to its disjunctive meaning, a comparative meaning which is archaic but which can scarcely be connected with a strictly disjunctive reading of the particle, so τε, at least early on, admits of an understanding quite different from that of a connective: this is the generalizing use of τε in which it would be equivalent to the familiar everyday expression 'sometimes'. Now the semantic connection between 'and' and 'sometimes' (*des fois*) is so far from being evident that some have questioned whether there were not two homonymous but distinct particles; other authors have contrariwise denied the existence of distinct τε's and sought to account for the 'generalizing' instances of τε using the same idea of jointure.[8] (Humbert 1960, 434–435)

8. La particule i.e. *k^we, qui donne en grec la forme attendue τε, est avec la particule *we, la seule conjonction dont le caractère indo-européen puisse être garanti. *Atones et enclitiques* l'une et l'autre, elles étaient fragiles toutes les deux: *we ne pouvait phonétiquement subsister en grec sans l'appui de ἤ (dans laquelle elle a fini par se perdre), *k^we, qui était phonétiquement viable, a été complètement évincée par la plus importante des particules auxquelles elle pouvait s'associer, c'est à dire καί; de même qu'il ne subsiste rien dans les langues romanes de –*que* ni de –*ue*, de même le grec a remplacé ἤ par εἴτε et τε par καί. Enfin, comme *we semble avoir possédé, outre sa valeur disjonctive, une valeur de *comparaison*, qui est ancienne, mais qu'on ne peut guère rattacher au sens proprement

It seems clear that, in the case of *aut* and, as we might by now suspect, in the case of 'or', that its more primitive uses lay in a kind of conjunction, and that only later did something like a disjunctive force emerge. The same author on *aut*'s etymological first cousin, the Greek particle αὖ:

> The particle αὖ, to which we must add αὖτε (limited to Epic Greek) and αὖτις (Ion. αὖθις), is evidently related to the Latin *aut, autem* (Oscan *aut, auti*); but unlike the Italic which makes a strong adversative of this particle, capable of expressing *alternation (aut , , , aut)*, αὖ must combine with δέ in order to express opposition. Its proper meaning, it seems, was 'from another side'. It was particularly useful for expressing a movement back, a repetition. Used infrequently to express weak opposition, it was mainly employed to form those pleonasms through which Greek likes to express return movement: αὖ πάλιν, αὖ πάλιν αὖθις etc.[9] (385)

As with the English 'or' the puzzle is not to understand how the conjunctive uses of *aut* are to be explained in the face of its disjunctive meaning, but how its disjunctive use arises out of a more primitive meaning that is adverbially conjunctive and more or less adversative. The second myth, like the first, gives way to the puzzle. Latin, like English, awaits its dissolution, and as we shall see, provides a useful clue.

---

disjonctif de la particule, τε comporte aussi, du moins à date ancienne, une toute autre valeur que celle d'un lien: on parle en ce cas de la valeur généralisante de τε, qui équivaudrait à l'expression vulgaire bien connue: «des fois». Or le lien sémantique entre *et* et *des fois* est si loin d'être évident qu'on a pu se demander s'il ne s'agissait pas de deux particules homonymes, mais différentes; au contraire, d'autres auteurs . . . ont nié l'existence de deux τε différents, et pensé pouvoir expliquer les exemples «généralisants» de τε par la notion même de jonction.

9. La particule αὖ, à laquelle il faut joindre αὖτε (limité à la langue épique) et αὖτις (ion. αὖθις), s'apparente évidemment à lat. *aut, autem* (osque *aut, auti*); mais, à la différence de l'italique, qui fait de cette particule une *adversative* forte, capable d'exprimer l'*alternative (aut . . . aut)*, il faut qu'elle s'associe à δέ pour avoir valeur *d'opposition*. Il semble que sa signification propre était: «d'un autre côté». Elle était particulièrement apte à exprimer un *mouvement en retour*, une *répétition*. Peu fréquente pour rendre une faible opposition, elle est surtout employée pour former ces «pléonasmes» par lesquels le grec aime à rendre le *mouvement en retour*: αὖ πάλιν, αὖ πάλιν αὖθις etc.

10

Stoic Disjunction

10.1 What Stoic Disjunction Was Not

10.1.1 The Undemonstrables

The discontinuity between nineteenth-century logic and its vestiges in twentieth-century logical theory will no doubt come more fully to light as the numerous seams of pre-Fregean logical theory are mined for future applications. In the case of Stoic logic, from which much pre-Fregean theory derives, there is already substantial philosophical interest; in consequence, the distinctness of their approach has already begun to become apparent as the comparatively meagre ore of early evidence yields to the refinement of sensitive and theoretically unencumbered scholarship. Certain aspects of Stoic doctrine will no doubt remain controversial. But it is evident that the earlier modern commentators on the Stoics, labouring under the overburden of twentieth-century conceptions, were misled by superficial similarities in two of the assumptions that they seem universally to have made: first, that the Stoics operated with essentially the modern notion of logical form and, second, that they operated, again essentially, with the modern notion of exclusive disjunction, whether extensional or intensional. The jewel that distracted early scholars and prompted these conclusions is that most startling of all the Stoics' theoretical achievements in logic: the set of five argument schemata called the Undemonstrables, whose formulation is most often attributed to Chrysippus (c. 280–206 B.C.). It was the manner of their presentation of the Undemonstrables, with ordinals as placeholders for sentences, that suggests the modern notion of form. It is the presence of disjunction (διεζευγμένον) in the major premises of the fourth and fifth that seems to suggest that the Stoics operated with the modern notion of exclusive 'or'. Those are

[IV]	Either the first or the second;
	the first;
	therefore, not the second.

and

[V]	Either the first or the second;
	not the first;
	therefore, the second.

The remaining three schemata are:

[I]   If the first, then the second;
        the first;
        therefore, the second.

[II]   If the first, then the second;
        not the second;
        therefore, not the first.

[III]   Not both the first and the second;
        the first;
        therefore, not the second.

10.1.2 Hasty conclusions

Consider first the accepted doctrine that undemonstrables IV and V rely upon exclusive disjunction.

I. M. Bocheński:

> ...out of the fourth and fifth undemonstrables which were fundamental in Stoic logic, we see that exclusive disjunction (matrix "0110") was meant. (1963, 91)

W. and M. Kneale (on Galen's remark that 'Either it is day or it is night' is equivalent to 'If it is not day it is night'):

> Possibly his expression is loose and he means to say that the disjunctive statement is equivalent to the bi-conditional 'It is not day, if and only if, it is night'. For the assertion of such an equivalence would indeed be in keeping with the Stoic doctrine of disjunction, provided always that the conditional is understood to convey necessary connection. (1962, 162)

Benson Mates:

> Two basic types of disjunction were recognized by the Stoics: exclusive and inclusive. Exclusive disjunction (διεζευγμένον) was most used, and is the only type of disjunction which occurs in the five fundamental inference-schemas of Stoic propositional logic. (1953, 51)

Łukasiewicz:

> It is evident from the fourth syllogism that disjunction is conceived of as an exclusive 'either-or' connective. (1967, 74)

Ian Mueller:

> 'The first or the second' is true if and only if exactly one of the first and the second is true.
> (In modern logic it is customary to use "or" inclusively, and hence to substitute "at least" for "exactly" in the truth conditions for disjunction.

The fourth undemonstrable argument shows that disjunction is exclusive in the Stoic system.) (1978, 16)

10.1.3 Some evidence

All of these authors cite ancient sources for this account, among them, Cicero, Gellius, Galen, Sextus Empiricus, and Diogenes Laertius. Their accounts are the following:

Cicero:

> There are several other methods used by the logicians, which consist of propositions disjunctively connected: Either this or that is true; but this *is* true, therefore that is not. Similarly either this or that is true; but this is not, therefore that *is* true. These conclusions are valid because in a disjunctive statement not more than one [disjunct] can be true.[1]

Gellius:

> There is another form which the Greeks call διεζευγμένον ἀξίωμα and we call *disiunctum*. For example: "Pleasure is good or evil or it is neither good nor evil." Now all statements which are contrasted ought to be opposed to each other, and their opposites, which the Greeks call ἀντικεί-μενα, ought also to be opposed. Of all statements which are contrasted, one ought to be true and the rest false.[2]

Galen:

> . . . the disjunctives have one member only true, whether they be composed of two simple propositions or of more than two.[3]

Sextus Empiricus:

> . . . for the true disjunctive announces that one of its clauses is true, but the other or others false or false and contradictory.[4]

Diogenes Laertius:

---

1. *Top.* xiv. 56–57. *Reliqui dialecticorum modi plures sunt, qui ex disiunctionibus constant: aut hoc aut illud; hoc autem; non igitur illud. Itemque: aut hoc aut illud; non autem hoc; illud igitur. Quae conclusiones idcirco ratae sunt quod in disiunctione plusuno verum esse non potest.*

2. *Noctes Atticae* XVI. 8. *Est item aliud, quod Graeci* διεζευγμένον *ἀξίωμα nos 'disiunctum' dicimus. Id huiuscemodi est: 'aut malum est voluptas aut bonum neque malum est'. Omnia autem, quae disiunguntur, pugnantia esse inter sese oportet, eorumque opposita, quae* ἀντικείμενα *Graeci dicunt, ea quoque ipsa inter se adversa esse. Ex omnibus, quae disiunguntur, unum esse verum debet, falsa cetera.*

3. *Inst. Log.* V. 1. . . . τῶν διεζευγμένων εν μόνον ἐξόντων ἀληθές, ἄν τ' ἐκ δυοῖν ἀξιωματων ἁπλῶν ἄν τ' ἐκ πλειόνων συγκέηται. (The translation is that of Kieffer 1964.)

4. *Outlines of Pyrrhonism* II. 191. τὸ γὰρ ὑγιὲς διεζευγμένον ἐπαγγέλλεται ἐν τῶν ἐν αὐτῷ ὑγιὲς εἶναι, τὸ δὲ λοιπὸν ἢ τὰ λοιπὰ ψεῦδος ἢ ψευδῆ μετὰ μάχης.

A disjunction is [a proposition] conjoined by means of the disjunctive conjunction "either" (ἤτοι). For example, "Either it is day or it is night." This conjunction declares that one or the other of the propositions is false.[5]

10.1.4 The question of arity

The first point to attend to is that three of the five admit disjunctions of more than two disjuncts, while two illustrate the construction with two-member disjunctions. No great importance is attached to this by the commentators, and it is unclear whether none of them thinks it significant. There need, of course, be no great importance in the fact that the earliest and the latest of the sources quoted define disjunction specifically with reference to two-termed disjunctions. In Diogenes' example, it may only be because the illustration is two-termed that the last comment is framed as it is. It is reasonable to surmise that neither Cicero nor Diogenes Laertius would have precluded three- or four-term disjunctions and that their account would coincide with those of Gellius, Galen, and Sextus Empiricus, according to which, in the three-term case, the disjunction is true if and only if exactly one of its disjuncts is true. Since none of the modern commentators explicitly addresses the issue of arity, one might have assumed that that is their view of the matter as well. Bocheński (1970, 91) mentions the greater generality of Stoic conjunction 'the [conjunctive] functor was defined by the truth-table "1110" [*sic*] as our logical product (only an indeterminate number of arguments was meant')', and one may assume that his omission of the corresponding remark about ἤτοι is an oversight. But some explain three-member disjunctions as though they nested a two-member disjunction. Commenting on the form

Either the first or the second or the third; but not the first; and not the second; therefore the third

which Sextus attributes to Chrysippus, the Kneales (1962, 167) surmise:

Here, it seems, we must think of the words 'the second or the third' as bracketed together in the disjunctive premiss; for the conclusion can then be obtained by two applications of indemonstrable 5. If this procedure is correct, the disjunction may be as long as we please, since the conclusion can always be proved by a number of applications of the same indemonstrable.

But though bracketing will have the required effect in the case of the fifth indemonstrable, its effect will be quite other in the case of the fourth. For correctly inferring from the truth of the first disjunct the falsity of the *disjunction* of the second and third will not then let us infer the falsity of the third from the truth of the second: the disjunction of the second and the third may be false because both the second and the third disjuncts are true. The conclusion must be that although we can in isolated instances treat three-term disjunctions as nestings, nevertheless if we are to give a unified account of Stoic disjunction, we may *never*

---

5. *Vitae* VII. 72. διεζευγμένον δέ ἐστιν ὃ ὑπὸ τοῦ "ἤτοι" διαζευκτικοῦ συνδέσμου διέζευκται, οἷον "ἤτοι ἡμέρα ἐστὶ ἢ νύξ ἐστιν." ἐπαγγέλλεται δ' ὁ σύνδεσμος οὗτος τὸ ἕτερον τῶν ἀξιωμάτων ψεῦδος εἶναι.

understand three-term disjunctions as understanding the second and third to be implicitly bracketed. Brackets are simply not permitted.

If this *arity*-free account is the correct and most general account of the Stoic notion of disjunction, several observations may be made: first that were we to symbolize such a connective it would be unambiguous and natural to do so in prefix notation as:

$$\vee_\sigma(\alpha_1, \ldots, \alpha_n)$$

where the subscript sigma serves to make the Stoic connection explicit. For the ἤτοι of Greek, like the 'or' of English, is not specifically a binary connective, and the Stoic practice of representing sentences by nominals (τὸ πρότερον, τὸ δεύτερον, τὸ τρίτον: the first, the second, the third) tends to mask the distinction which, when in a philosophical set of mind, we implicitly make in English between, say, a list of three nominals composed with 'or' and a three-term disjunctive sentence. In the former case, we do not — indeed, cannot — think of the *or*-list of two of the names as forming a new name and that disjoined to the third. In ordinary English we are not required to think of the or-composition of three sentences in this way either. No rules of well-formedness force us to parse a three-clause sentence composed with 'or' into a two-clause sentence one of whose clauses is a disjunction. Except for the exclusivity, the Stoic construction

ἤτοι τὸ πρότερον ἢ τὸ δεύτερον ἢ τὸ τρίτον
Either the first or the second or the third

alternatively,

$$\text{ἤτοι τὸ } \bar{\alpha} \text{ ἢ τὸ } \bar{\beta} \text{ ἢ τὸ } \bar{\gamma}$$

is more like the syntax of ordinary Greek than the modern symbolization

$$\alpha_1 \vee (\alpha_2 \vee \alpha_3)$$

is like the syntax of ordinary English. Now, to be sure, we could abbreviate a modern n-term exclusive disjunction analogously by:

$$\underline{\vee}(\alpha_1, \ldots, \alpha_n)$$

since exclusive disjunction is an associative operation. But although the ambiguity is not vicious, we would normally understand such a formula as associated to the left or to the right, since $\underline{\vee}$ is a binary connective, and well-formedness requires it. That modern exclusive disjunction is a binary truth-function and that the Stoic notion had no fixed arity should not be lost sight of when comparing the two. It will serve to remind us that the truth conditions of the two constructions are not in general the same, a fact on which none of the modern commentators seems to have remarked. Consider as an example the exclusive disjunction

$$\underline{\vee}((2 + 2 = 4), (2 + 3 = 5), (2 + 4 = 6)).$$

When it is disambiguated into, say,

$$(2 + 2 = 4) \veebar ((2 + 3 = 5) \veebar (2 + 4 = 6)),$$

it becomes evident that since the second disjunction is false (since both of its disjuncts are true) and the first disjunct is true, the whole disjunction is true in spite of (or rather *because* of) the fact that all its disjuncts are true. The Stoic disjunction

$$\veebar_\sigma((2 + 2 = 4), (2 + 3 = 5), (2 + 4 = 6))$$

is false since more than one of its disjuncts are true.

Since Stoic disjunction has no fixed arity, it would be suitable to regard it as a kind of restricted propositional quantifier, having, in prefix notation, the reading

Exactly one of the following is true:

Since exclusive disjunction is commutative and associative, a quantifier reading would be suitable for it as well. But as we have shown (Chapter 1), its quantificational rendering would be

An odd number of the following are true:

The two kinds of disjunction will, of course, coincide on the two-clause case, but will coincide for no *n*-clause case for $n > 2$. A three-clause exclusive disjunction, for example, will be true if and only if either exactly one or exactly three clauses are true, as will a four-clause exclusive disjunction. A five- or six-clause exclusive disjunction will be true if and only if either exactly one or exactly three or exactly five disjuncts are true, and so on.

A valid Stoic disjunction of two terms would disjoin a sentence α with a sentence equivalent to the negation of α. A true *n*-term Stoic disjunction would disjoin finite state descriptions. As an example, imagine the formulation of a row of a truth table, that is, the effect of conjoining propositional variables or negations of propositional variables accordingly as 1's or 0's appear under them in that row. A valid Stoic disjunction in *m* independent variables would be equivalent to the 2^m-term disjunction of the formulations of the rows of a table displaying all possible combinations of their truth values. Particularly if, as some of the early sources suggest, the Stoic notion of disjunction was that of an intensional operation, a sentence of the form

ἤτοι τὸ πρότερον ἢ τὸ δεύτερον ἢ τὸ τρίτον ἢ τὸ τέταρτον
Either the first or the second or the third or the fourth,

given such a technical use of ἢ would assert that the four sentences bore to one another a relationship akin to the relationship of the formulations of rows of a two-variable truth table:

ἤτοι $(p \wedge q)$ ἢ $(p \wedge \neg q)$ ἢ $(\neg p \wedge q)$ ἢ $(\neg p \wedge \neg q)$.

It is a consequence of this that if we seriously adopt the view that the disjunction that Chrysippus had in mind in the fourth undemonstrable is the present day 0110 disjunction, then the Stoics really had at least two different kinds of disjunction represented by the same piece of notation in their logical system. And having come this far, we could admit no grounds for regarding the disjunction of the fifth undemonstrable as anything but a third sort, namely, 1110 disjunction. The more plausible account would be that they had one sort of disjunction in mind, namely, the disjunction of no fixed arity that happens to resemble 0110 disjunction in the two-term case.

10.1.5 The consequences for the idea of form

The standard notion of form as applied to propositional argument schemata follows the lines set out earlier: let F be the set of sentences of a language L and S an argument schema expressed with constants of the language L and metalogical variables of the metalanguage ranging over F. Then the argument form F_S associated with S is the set of arguments which can be generated from S by uniform substitution of sentences of F for metalogical variables in S. This notion of form depends upon a fixed meaning for the constants of L. In the propositional case, for example, we assume that $\neg$, $\wedge$, $\vee$, $\rightarrow$, and the like, do not change their meanings as we uniformly substitute sentences for the metalogical variables flanking them. We do not account 'α; therefore α or β' an invalid form because from 'You may go or you may stay' it follows that you may stay. We say rather that 'You may go; therefore you may go or you may stay' is not of the form 'α; therefore α or β'. We might retreat, if pressed, to the claim that they share grammatical but not logical form. Or we might admit the argument to the form but insist that the conclusion must then be understood as a disjunction, from which 'You may stay' does not follow.

It seems certain that the Stoics never articulated a notion of argument form in these or equivalent terms. But, if we are to take into account the totality of evidence from early sources, according to which διεζευγμένον was understood in something like the quantificational sense outlined here, and the generally held view that they gave to the particle ἤτοι a technical meaning accordingly, then the Stoic schema [IV]:

ἤτοι τὸ πρότερον ἢ τὸ δεύτερον;
τὸ δε πρότερον;
οὐκ ἄρα τὸ δεύτερον.

Either the first or the second;
But the first;
Therefore not the second.

is insufficiently general to capture the inferential force of the connective ἤ in their technical sense. The three-term case is not obtainable from the two-term case by substitution of a two-term disjunction for one of the original disjuncts. Some such schema as

$\vee_\sigma(\alpha_1, \ldots, \alpha_i, \ldots, \alpha_n)$;
$\alpha_j \ (1 \leq j \leq n)$;
$\therefore \neg\alpha_k \ (1 \leq k \leq n) \ (k \neq j)$

would be required. So if the Stoic notion of disjunction was as general as the early commentators suggest, and we are to judge their conjectured position by standards of any rigour, then we must conclude that their understanding of the role of the fourth undemonstrable schema was something other than that of specifying a form in the modern sense.

Notably it is only the fourth undemonstrable that straightforwardly gives rise to such a problem of reinterpretation, since the other logical connections exhibited in the earlier undemonstrable schemata—*if . . . then . . .* and *not both . . . and . . .*—represent specifically binary connections, at least for the Stoics, and at least so far as the evidence tells us. Of these, only *not both . . . and . . .* readily admits of generalization to the *n*-ary case, and there is nothing in the sources to guide us in choosing between the generalization to *At most one of the following is true* and the generalization to *Not all of the following are true*, interpretations that again coincide only in the two-term case. If we suppose that they took conjunction seriously as a logical connection, perhaps the second is the more natural. For there is nothing to require the translation of the initial καί as *both* except in the two-term case. Even here a slightly dissimilar case would arise if we tried to construct the generalized schema. For in the two-term case, the connective *not both . . . and . . .* coincides in sense with the Sheffer stroke, which, since it is not an associative operation, cannot, in the *n*-term case, be straightforwardly thought of quantificationally. The sentence

$$\alpha \mid (\beta \mid \gamma)$$

would mean something like:

Either all of α, β, and γ are true, or α is false.

There would, however, remain the problem that the third undemonstrable schema

Not both the first and the second;
The first;
Therefore, not the second,

is insufficiently general in form to define the class of arguments that the general account of conjunction would license.

Now it is unfortunately convenient to treat Stoic logic, however fragmentary and indirect our understanding of it, as the outcome of deliberations illumined by the same general understanding of the issues that we ourselves are able to bring to bear, and to see our scholarly task as one of rational reconstruction in the light of that general understanding. In such a frame of mind, we might well agree with Josiah Gould (1974, 83) that

it is clear in each of our fragments that the author intends the adjective "undemonstrated" to qualify what we would today call "argument forms."

and that the examples given are 'what we would today call substitution instances' (84). But it would seem the more worthwhile approach to ask of the scraps of information available to us what stage the Stoics' general understanding might have reached, allowing the relics of their doctrines a reasonable degree of tentativeness without assuming that their approach, had it only succeeded, would have been our own. This would, admittedly, be a difficult task, not least because we could not know whether we had succeeded in it. But the cultivation of such an attitude would be salutary at least in freeing for a while our reading of the Stoics' work from our own present-day conceptions. And we could say, as need arose, 'They did not foresee this difficulty' rather than 'This view creates a difficulty on the modern understanding and must therefore not be attributed to them'.

As an exercise, one might ask whether, on the evidence, the Stoics had hit upon something like our notion of logical form. If they had, well and good, but if they had not, then we ought not to suppose that all of the undemonstrables were regarded as *formally* valid or correct schemata in any single sufficiently well-defined sense of 'formal' to be of use. We would not be compelled, as we are by the contrary assumption, to assert of them that their use of ἤτοι . . . ἤ . . . in the fourth and fifth undemonstrables was a technical one, according to which it meant what is meant by 0110 disjunction. As we have seen, unless they meant different things by ἤτοι . . . ἤ . . . in different contexts, 0110 disjunction is not what they meant anyway, even if there is something, in the relevant respects determinate, that they did mean.

In spite of what we have said about the notion of form, there is no harm in applying the word 'formal' to the Stoics' work. By some standards, it is not *informal*, and by those standards we may therefore call it formal where that is the contrast intended; and we may therefore distinguish their uses of ἤτοι and ἤ in formal contexts from their uses of them in merely expository ones, where by this we mean just to distinguish the ceremonial from the everyday.

10.2 What the Languages Can Tell Us

Was there something that ἤτοι and ἤ meant? What is the evidence? Quite apart from the remarks of the early commentators, there is the evidence provided by the Greek and Latin languages themselves. It is, we have seen, an urban myth that there is an exclusive sense of 'or' in English, and a suburban myth that Latin lexically marked the distinction between 1110 and 0110 disjunctions, in particular that it marked the distinction by *vel* and *aut*. It is unclear when these myths first arose. I have been unable to find them in any sources earlier than the twentieth century. They are comfortable clichés and are no doubt rather the product of innocence than of erudition howsoever insouciant. But they are false. Worse than that, they conceal the genuine puzzle about 'or', which, as we have seen, is also a puzzle about *aut* and to a lesser extent about *vel*, and are apt to mislead students of elementary logic and their instructors about the relationship between logic and discourse. Finally, the assumption that Latin marked the distinction lexically may support the conviction in some that Greek did as well, possibly by some other means.

Now it is true that the Latin commentators used *aut . . . aut. . .* to convey the Stoic use of ἤτοι . . . ἤ . . ., but we must not place too much weight upon this. Given what we have noted already, it was the best choice on grounds quite separate from the fictional one that *aut* corresponded to exclusive 'or'. We should recall that in the course of explaining the truth conditions of what he takes to be the Stoic notion of διεζευγμένον, Gellius uses *aut* in a long disjunctive antecedent clause of a conditional that is transparently intended to abbreviate a conjunction of conditionals:

> ... *si* aut *nihil omnium verum* aut *omnia plurave quam unum vera erunt,*
> aut *quae disjuncta sunt non pugnabunt,* aut *quae opposita eorum sunt*
> *contraria inter sese no erunt, tunc id disjunctum mendacium est.* . . .
> (*Noctes Atticae* XVI. VIII. 14)
> ... if none of them is true, or all or more than one are true, or the
> contrasted things do not conflict, or those opposed are not contrary, then it
> is a false disjunction. . . .

Evidently the choice of Latin vocabulary in which to cast the connective of the fourth and fifth undemonstrables was not dictated by the need to convey exclusivity formally. Had no Megarian or Stoic ever dreamt of the *fourth* undemonstrable, the most suitable Latin translation of the *fifth* undemonstrable and for the regimentation of ordinary language arguments of the corresponding grammatical cast would nevertheless have used *aut*. There is no reason to suppose that the mere use of *aut*, independently of ancillary discussion and explanation of what it was intended to convey, would have made the *formal* correctness of the fourth undemonstrable, or particular instances of it, transparent to Roman commentators.

What we have said about English and Latin may be repeated with flourishes about Greek. It possessed no special connective by which 0110 disjunction was distinguished from 1110 disjunction. The 'logical' sense of ἤτοι ... ἤ ... and its variants was essentially that of 'either ... or ...'; like 'either ... or ...', its use was indifferent as to the number of terms joined and as between exclusive and non-exclusive fillings; any additional imposition of an exclusive reading was through emphasis and intonation. In particular, the use of ἤτοι as an auxiliary had no special role as an indicator of exclusivity, that particle being a compound of ἤ meaning variously 'or' or 'than', and the enclitic τοι an etymological cousin of the second person singular pronoun. Its ordinary use was emphatic, akin to the use in English of 'now surely' or in Welsh English of 'Look you'. Galen reports ἤ as an alternative to ἤτοι in Stoic usage, although he himself uses the latter exclusively in the context of the undemonstrables (Frede 1974, 93–94). Certainly the use of ἤτοι ... ἤ ... in ordinary non-philosophical written Greek was uncommon by contrast with some philosophical writing and there is evidence that the philosophers have pressed into use a construction normally reserved as a spoken form. Thus Denniston:

> ἤτοι ... ἤ (often ἤτοι ... γε ... ἤ) is common in Plato and Aristotle. It is
> difficult to say what degree of vividness τοι retains here. On the one hand,
> Thucydides confines ἤτοι, like simple τοι, to speeches . . . this suggests
> that he felt τοι as vivid in the combination. On the other, the frequency of
> ἤτοι in the matter-of-fact style of Aristotle suggests that for him τοι did
> nothing more than emphasize the disjunction. (1966, 553)

But one ought not to infer from this that ἤτοι ... ἤ ... is more common than ἤ ... ἤ ... in Aristotle and Plato, or that either of them set aside the former for uses that prefigured the Stoic use. Neither is by any means true. In particular,

Aristotle uses ἤ . . . ἤ . . . in the overwhelming majority of cases, and in many which would have provided excellent examples of disjunction for the Stoics:

Πρῶτασις μὲν οὖν ἐτὶ λόγος καταφατικὸς ἢ ἀποφατικὸς τινὸς κατά τινος. οὗτος δὲ ἢ καθόλου ἢ ἐν μέρει ἢ ἀδιόριστος. (*Prior Analytic* 24ᵃ16)

A premiss then is a sentence affirming *or* denying something of something. This is either universal *or* particular *or* indefinite.

. . . συλλελόγισται ὅτι ἀσύμμετρος ἢ σύμμετρος ἡ διάμετρος (46ᵇ31)

. . . he has proved that the diagonal is either commensurate *or* incommensurate

and others where, if his understanding of the meaning of ἤτοι . . . ἤ . . . anticipated the Stoic use of it, we would expect ἤτοι . . . ἤ . . . :

. . . ἅπαν γὰρ ζῷον θνητὸν ἢ ὑπόπού ἢ ἄπουν ἐστι (46ᵇ15)

. . . every mortal animal is either footed *or* footless

However, Aristotle's uses of ἤτοι . . . ἤ . . . either give no evidence that he was after a distinction that anticipated the Stoics', or else provide evidence that he had no such intention. Thus, when in the course of explaining kinds of contrariety he denies that everybody must be black or white, he uses ἤτοι . . . ἤ . . .:

. . . οὐ γὰρ πᾶν ἤτοι λευκὸν ἢ μέλαν ἐστίν (*Categories* 12ᵃ13)

. . . not everyone is either white *or* black

but the reason for denying this is that there are intermediates between white and black, namely, all the other colours. It is in any case used here between predicates and not between whole sentences.

The relative scarcity of ἤ . . . ἤ . . . as opposed to ἤτοι . . . ἤ . . . in the logical setting does not of course indicate that the Stoics gave the word ἤτοι any special technical sense as distinct from a technical use. The thesis that it has a special sense is forced upon us only if we also adopt the view that their enterprise was a formal one in the substitutional sense. We have already seen that on any straightforward interpretation, it was not. A more plausible guess would be that that combination gradually gained favour in general philosophical practice and presented itself to the philosophical innovator, perhaps Theophrastus, casting about for suitably perspicuous notation as a construction already set apart for special philosophical applications. Compare the current use of 'It is not the case that . . . '. Again, it need hardly be said that there was no special *intensional* sense of ἤτοι or ἤ or ἤτοι . . . ἤ . . . in ordinary Greek, the necessity or contingency of a disjunction being entirely determined by its disjuncts. But insofar as intended exclusivity can be conveyed by emphasis, the intention is conveyed more easily with more syllables than with fewer. And on that score ἤτοι is more emphatic than ἤ.

Greek, like Latin and, come to that, like English, had a great variety of connectives, all of which could receive translation as 'or', but whose significance in discourse is best understood by immersion in the literature in which they occur. Like *sive . . . sive . . .* of Latin, Greek had εἴτε . . . εἴτε, which was common as a conjunctively distributive connective in the antecedents of conditional constructions. Homeric Greek sometimes has τε in place of a second ἤ, and ἤ καί, in place of a second εἴτε. Aeschylus sometimes answers εἴτε with εἴτε καί. But Greek was in general more fluid in its use of particles than Latin. There are recorded instances of ἤ ... καί ... where ἤ ... ἤ ... would be expected, and there are idioms in which καί occurs with the sense of ἤ, as in

ἀνθρωπίνη σοφία ὀλίγου τινὸς ἀξία ἐστίν καὶ οὐδενός
Human wisdom is worth little *or* nothing

χθὲς καὶ πρώην
yesterday *or* the day before.

In general, the use of particular particles in the Greek of the last several centuries of the old era varied, not only over time, but from author to author, even from work to work, and particularly from genre to genre.[6] As a symptom of this greater fluidity, there is evident a larger freedom in the use of particles in abbreviative constructions, especially favouring the use of constructions relying upon superficial grammatical ellipsis over those requiring (or rather, as my thesis demands, 'at least capable of receiving') a truth-functional logical transformation. This distinction between elliptic contraction and logical transformation can be made using conditional constructions of English and will seem familiar to anyone who has taught a course in introductory logic. Contrast the sentence forms:

(a) If A and B, then C
(b) If A, and if B, then C
(c) If A or B, then C.

They are, in the given order, increasingly easy for a person trained in logic to read as equivalent to

(d) If A, then C and if B, then C.

But to the inner ear of a beginning student more attuned to the ellipsis of colloquial speech, (d) may represent a possible reading of (a) even without contextual reinforcement, and the tiro, self-consciously fearful perhaps that what he naturally says is wrong, might well guess that, strictly speaking, (c) is an ellipsis for:

(e) If A, then C or if B, then C,

as some will say 'between you and I' to be impressively grammatic. Or she may, quite unselfconsciously, give precisely the same response understanding the 'or' of (e) conjunctively, as well she might. By contrast, the sentence

(f) If A, or if B, then C

particularly when the 'or' is given a good thump, naturally falls into a conjunction of conditionals as

---

6. For a detailed authoritative discussion, see Denniston (1966).

(g) The CN tower is taller than either the Eaton's building or the Royal Centre

falls into a conjunction of comparisons without truth-functional justification for doing so. The use of 'or' constructions in *if*-clauses to force a conjunctive reading is reinforced by the availability of a non-elliptical reading for an antecedent in 'and', particularly in a language that, like Latin, is less subtly variable than Greek in its use of particles. In Greek, for whatever reason, this tension between grammatical ellipsis and logical transformation was less insistent than in Latin, so that when the context demands it, an *if*-clause occurrence of 'καί' more readily accedes to a conjunctively distributive reading. And one finds καί sometimes following 'εἴπερ' and grammatically absorbed by it, producing something akin to 'if even . . .', as one finds them in the opposite order having the sense of 'even if . . .'. The 'logical' particles whose English counterparts we have been taught to think of as, to extend Ryle's colourful metaphor, importantly combat-ready, lived altogether more easily in one another's company. As Kitto (1951, 27) puts it, 'Greek is well supplied with little words, conjunctions that hunt in couples or in packs, whose sole function is to make the structure clear.' Somehow the work got done.

10.2.1 Form or distribution

This comparative fluidity in the Greek use of particles has given rise to some curious discrepancies in Old Testament translations. When the Septuagint scholars translated the Old Testament into Greek, they frequently translated the Hebrew אוֹ ('O = or) as καί, perhaps having in mind the distributive sense of what they were translating, perhaps indulging in what they regarded as permissible stylistic variation, but in any case certainly not providing what would have been the outcome of a strict truth-functional analysis. This is most evident in what would have become, in a literal translation, disjunctive *if*-clauses of conditional sentences. Of these there is a great fund in the laws of Moses in *Exodus* where, as one would expect, the Almighty's quirks and fancies are laid down in a characteristically irascible conditional form. The upshot of these liberties was that the Vulgate translators, who relied upon the Septuagint, have mainly translated these as *et* or *–que*. The King James translators, who relied principally upon Hebrew sources, and evidently set accuracy above style, have produced a truth-functionally distinct rendering. The wistful modern, taught by elementary logic textbooks to regard the Hellenistic period as the last golden age of disciplined truth-functionality, will doubtless find in these documents two distinct and distressingly inequivalent axiomatizations of the Will of God as to the disposition of such offenders as pushy oxen and sun worshippers. Here from Exodus 21: 31 to 32 are two examples:

Vulgate: *Filium quoque* et *filiam, si cornu percusserit.* . . .

KJV: Whether he have gored a son *or* have gored a daughter. . . .[7]

Vulgate: *Si servum ancillam*que *invaserit.* . . .

7. ' . . . the ox shall surely be stoned, and his flesh shall not be eaten.'

KJV: If [the ox] shall push a manservant *or* a maidservant . . . [8]

and an example from Deuteronomy 17: 2 to 3:

Vulgate: *Cum reperti fuerint apud te . . . vir aut mulier qui faciant malum in conspectu Domini Dei tui et transgrediantur pactum illius,* | *ut vadant et serviant diis alienis et adorent eos, solem* et *lunam* et *omnem militiam caeli.* . . .

KJV: If there be found among you . . . man or woman, that hath wrought wickedness in the sight of the Lord thy God, in transgressing his covenant, | and hath gone and served other gods and worshipped them, either the sun, *or* moon, *or* any of the host of Heaven. . . . [9]

Translators, guided by what they know of authors' intentions, must sometimes make adjustments in the opposite sense in translating Greek to English. For example, Edghill uses a conjunctively distributive *or*-list with quoted sentences to translate what Aristotle expressed with καί and no quotations:

From the proposition 'it may not be' or 'it is contingent that it should not be' *it follows that* it is not necessary that it should not be and that it is not impossible that it should not be.
(for: τῷ δὲ δυνατὸν μὴ εἶναι καὶ ἐνδεχόμενον μὴ εἶναι τὸ μὴ ἀναγκαῖον μὴ εἶναι καὶ τὸ οὐκ ἀδύνατον μὴ εἶναι.) (*De Interpretatione* 22ᵃ17.)

Of course, we need look no farther than English to find a language in which the so-called logical words are used in ways which are at variance with their logical uses. Consider only the conversationally equivalent 'You lose and I quit' and 'You win or I quit'. Or consider the 'but' in:

I have no money but I spend it

which is ambiguous between 'and' and 'or'. But it may be instructive to consider the standards of extreme parsimony by which classical Hebrew puts colloquial English in the shade:

וְ ['and'] is used very freely and widely in Hebrew, but also with much delicacy, to express relationships and shades of meaning which Western languages would usually indicate by distinct particles. In Hebrew particles such as אוֹ, אָז, אַךְ, אָכֵן, אוּלָם, בַּעֲבוּר, לְמַעַן, לָכֵן were reserved for cases in which special emphasis or distinctness was desired: their frequent use was felt instinctively to be inconsistent with the lightness and grace of movement which the Hebrew ear loved; and thus in AV and RV, words like *or, then, but, notwithstanding, howbeit, so, thus, therefore, that,* constantly appear, where the Hebrew has simply וְ. (Brown et al. 1907, s.v.)

---

8. '[. . . the owner] shall give unto their master thirty shekels of silver, and the ox shall be stoned.'

9. . . . then shalt thou bring forth that man or that woman, which have committed that wicked thing, unto thy gates . . . and stone them with stones, till they die.

10.2.2 The Stoics again

Any attempt to construct a useful formal system that still retains a connection
with the inferential practices that have inspired it cannot but sacrifice non-logical
distinctions, and the logic of the Stoics, arising as it did out of a language so
fluid in its particulate usages as the Greek of their period, was not to be
excepted. The abstraction of the logically essential into a simplified vocabulary
was part of the task, but refining their very conception of the task and what was
essential to it was all a part of the same continuing academic enterprise. As we
do not retain 'whether ... or ...', letting 'if ... or ...' do the work, and as
Roman logicians did not retain *sive ... sive ...* or *tum ... tum*, so Greek
logicians shed εἴτε ... εἴτε as they did the distinction between the suppositive
negating adverb μή and the absolute οὐ (οὐχ, οὐκ) since the retention of μή in
negated *if*-clauses would complicate conditionalization of arguments of the form
of the second undemonstrable.   In any case, however much greater fluidity there
may have been, and however much simplified the account of logical connection,
it remains true that the role of καί in Greek was *preponderantly* aggregative or
agglomerative. And the role of ἤτοι ... ἤ ... was *preponderantly* separative, as
that of 'either ... or ...' is in English. Its ordinary understanding was certainly
such as to support an inference schema such as the fifth undemonstrable. But the
use of ἤτοι ... ἤ ... in the fourth undemonstrable goes beyond simplification.
For, as we have noted, there was, in Greek as in Latin and English, no 'or' word
that indicated exclusive disjunction. If the Stoics intended that the fourth undemonstrable should be understood formally in the substitutional sense, they
could not have counted upon that *formal* correctness being evident from the
ordinary understanding of its logical vocabulary, as they could have in the case
of the first, second, third, and fifth. Consider, for example, a remark of Sextus:

> ... τὸ δὲ διεζευγμένον ἕν ἔχει τῶν ἕν αὐτῷ ἀληθέ, ὡς ἐαν ἀμφότερα ἤ
> ἀληθῆ ἤ ἀμφότερα ψευδῆ, ψεῦδος ἔσται τὸ ὅλον
> ... the disjunction has one of its clauses true, since if both are true **or**
> both are false, the whole will be false. (*Against the Logicians.* II. 283)

Evidently, the last occurrence of ἤ is not to be understood 'in an exclusive
sense', in spite of the exclusiveness of its disjuncts, but rather in the ordinary
sense that makes the conditional in whose antecedent it occurs elliptical for a
conjunction of conditionals.

The inequivalence of the conditional having an exclusive disjunctive
antecedent (in modern notation),

$$(\alpha \veebar \beta) \rightarrow \gamma$$

and the corresponding conjunction of conditionals

$$(\alpha \rightarrow \gamma) \wedge (\beta \rightarrow \gamma)$$

has consequences elsewhere. On a purely syntactic/semantic understanding of
διεζευγμένον by which it would mean just 'declarative sentences joined by ἤ
understood in the technical 0110 sense', that inequivalence would make it difficult to square the fondness for the dilemma, which was ubiquitous from pre-
Socratic through Hellenistic writings, with the acceptance of the principle of

conditionalization, which was generally accepted by the Stoics. Now the ordinary application of conditionalization as a test of validity would conjoin the premisses in the *if*-clause of a conditional, with the conclusion as *then*-clause. Presumably, in the particular application, an argument involving dilemma would yield a pair of conditionals whose validity would then be considered. The difficulty lies in the fact that the conditional

$$(\alpha \vee_\sigma \beta) \rightarrow \gamma$$

might be necessarily true because both α and β were necessarily true and $\alpha \vee_\sigma \beta$ therefore necessarily false, but both conjuncts of

$$(\alpha \rightarrow \gamma) \wedge (\beta \rightarrow \gamma)$$

false because γ was false. On those grounds alone, it is unlikely that διεζευγμέ-νον was a simple syntactic/semantic item in the Stoic conception of logic.

10.2.3 Cicero's clanger

There is further evidence of this tension between the normal use of ἤτοι . . . ἤ . . . and the Stoic use of it in the fact that there is a greater confusion sown in the accounts of διεζευγμένον than there is in the accounts of the other connections. If the fourth undemonstrable was intended as a *formally* admitted schema in the substitutional sense, the difficulty can only have been one of understanding a new technical sense being lent to the grammatical form ἤτοι . . . ἤ. . . . It cannot be confidently rejected that Cicero, whose faux pas in his *Topica* still costs him invitations, was among the victims of the confusion.

At least it must be said that a formal reading by which the fourth undemonstrable does represent a new technical use of ἤ ought to dispose us more charitably toward Cicero's curious augmentation in the *Topica* (XIII. 57.) of the standard five undemonstrables. Cicero claims there, so far as we know erroneously, that there was a Stoic undemonstrable, the Latin form of which would have been

> *Non et hoc et illud; non hoc; illud igitur.*
> Not both this and that; not this; therefore that.

When the undemonstrables are understood formally, this would seem on first hearing to represent a truly resounding logical clanger. Since the undemonstrables are almost universally regarded as formal, this estimation has been the conventional view.[10] There is no independent evidence that any Stoic logician ever included this kind of argument in his list of undemonstrables. On this point, we take it that Cicero was merely wrong. But could there have been such a kind of argument? If we are right about what inferences could be justified by reference to the meaning of ἤτοι . . . ἤ . . . in Greek, and if the undemonstrables are formal, then the use of ἤτοι . . . ἤ . . . in the fourth undemonstrable forces an exclusive reading that did not exist in the natural

---

10. The Kneales (1962, 179–181) are a notable exception, and offer a plausible and detailed alternative account. Bocheński has remarked (in conversation) that to ask Cicero about logic is about as sensible as to enquire of Sartre about the writings of Carnap. Calvin Normore has offered that the error may be imputed to Cicero's well known insomnia. Both may well have some bearing.

language. For there, the nearest we have to an exclusive ἤτοι . . . ἤ . . . is the use of ἤτοι . . . ἤ . . . with exclusive alternatives. But then the analogous *technical* use of 'not both . . . and . . .' would force a reading according to which from the falsity of one element the truth of the other would follow. Indeed, anyone whose understanding of Stoic logic was indirect and conjectural, and whose knowledge of Greek was not, might well have considered that given the eccentric character of the fourth undemonstrable, the Stoics could be expected to have a corresponding dual eccentricity of the sort embodied in Cicero's schema. It is true that the use of 'not both . . . and . . .' never implies by itself that both sentences cannot be false, but neither is there a use of 'or' that implies by itself that both sentences cannot be true. However, there are uses of 'not both . . . and . . .' with sentences that *cannot* both be false, just as there are uses of 'or' with sentences that cannot both be true. Understood as a formal theory, there is nothing more eccentric about Cicero's supplement than there is about the undoubtedly Stoic fourth undemonstrable. But suppose for the sake of argument that Cicero's addition were to be found extensively in Stoic logical writings and attributed, say, to Chrysippus. Any historian of Stoic logic finding himself unwilling to accept that undemonstrable as merely representing a technical usage ought to feel no more willingness to accept, on those terms, the Stoics' eccentric use of 'or' in the fourth.

Make the parallel more explicit. The formalist historian claims that the Stoics used   ἤτοι . . . ἤ . . .   technically   to   mean   'Either . . . or . . . and not both . . . and . . . '. In ordinary Greek, its meaning comprehended the former conjunct but not the latter. If Cicero were right, there would be a second pill to swallow: that the Stoics used 'Not both A and B' technically to mean the same thing. In ordinary Greek, its meaning comprehended the latter but not the former. Even on a formalist rendering, the mistake ought to seem on reflection no great logical howler. But when we consider, as we shall, the notion that the undemonstrables were not formally intended, we may also entertain among others, the possibility that Cicero's error represents at worst a merely historical error or a badly worded description, a wrong but not unreasonable reconstruction from memory of something he had read or heard from Diodotus or Philo, particularly bearing in mind that the account in the *Topica* is a reconstruction written, not in a library, but in the course of a journey. But again, on a nonformalist construal, especially given our complete ignorance of the teachings of minor Stoic teachers, it could well be an accurate recollection of something taught him (however erroneously) by Diodotus. It would not have been an impossible kind of argument, on a non-formalist view, for a Stoic to have noted. Consider what textbooks of this age say about *aut*.

10.2.4 The question of form

So we return to the question whether the Stoics regarded the undemonstrables as *formally* correct schemata in anything like the modern understanding of formal correctness. The evidence is clouded and there are many imponderables. We do not know with certainty to what extent the technical vocabulary, ὑγιής, *validus*, διεζευγμένον, and so on, had been freed from its etymological roots for Galen or Sextus, or with certainty what points of terminology and doctrine remained a matter of controversy into the Christian era. We do not know with what exactitude the logical vocabulary was defined by Chrysippus or others. But it would not be too pessimistic at least to lower our estimations of their capacity for logical description. As we have seen, the standard *substitutional* notion of valid form does not adequately provide for the Stoic account of disjunction in inference, since it does not accommodate connectives of no fixed arity. A relaxed, *descriptive* notion of valid form might come closer to theirs. The difference is this: a *substitution* account presents a schema and (perhaps implicitly) a rule of uniform substitution, or asserts that for every pair of sentences a and b, such and such a conclusion may be inferred from such and such promisses. Arguments of the same form retain the syncategorematic vocabulary and repeat sentences in the same pattern as the repetition of metalogical variables in the schema. One might say that the substitutional account stands for an abstract syntactic description applicable to any argument of the form. What I shall call a *descriptive* account would give an explicit description, saying what belongs in each premiss and what in the conclusion, perhaps illustrating by a schema or an example. Of the fourth undemonstrable it might say: 'An argument of the fourth type has a *diezeugmenonic* major premiss, and so on', and mention that a *diezeugmenonic* sentence is of the grammatical form

ἤτοι τὸ ᾱ ἤ τὸ β̄

(not 'a *diezeugmenonic* sentence is any sentence of the grammatical form

ἤτοι τὸ ᾱ ἤ τὸ β̄').

The class of valid arguments of that descriptive form would be the class of arguments satisfying the description, which might but might not coincide with the class of arguments obtained by uniform substitution in the illustrating schema. In the case of arguments with a *diezeugmenonic* major premiss, presumably the two notions would not coincide if the understood arity of disjunction were variable. If the distinction between the two notions of form were never explicitly stated, it is credible that discussions would sometimes vaguely have assumed the one and sometimes vaguely the other.

In the case of the fourth undemonstrable, a substitution account would offer the schema

Either α or β;
But α;
Therefore, not β.

A rule of substitution would license any argument obtained by substituting an occurrence of some declarative sentence A for every occurrence of α and an occurrence of some declarative sentence B for every occurrence of β as an argument of the form of the schema. Alternatively, a substitution account would say

For every sentence α and every sentence β, from α <u>or</u> β, and α, not-β may be inferred.

A descriptive account of IV (for the general case) would be this: 'From a disjunction together with one of its disjuncts, the negation of any distinct disjunct may be inferred'. What constitutes an argument of this description depends

upon what is meant by 'disjunction', but we may say that the simplest argument
of this kind would be of the form

> Either the first or the second;
> the first;
> therefore, not the second.

Now if, in addition, our notion of disjunction had as its foundation the notion of
a relationship between states of affairs or situations such that exactly one of
them must obtain (and only derivatively of a string of sentences alleging such
states, separated by 'or'), rather than *simply* any string of sentences separated by
'or', the puzzle about the 'technical meaning of ἤτοι ... ἤ ...' would be less
perplexing. Indeed there would be no puzzle. Both the fourth and fifth undemonstrables would represent valid *kinds* of argument, and the schemata
presented would represent the forms of the simplest arguments of this kind. Why
'Either ... or ...'? It is the obvious connective, since it permits the construction
of a true sentence out of contradictories and, in any case, the 'Either ... or ...'
construction is the one in which these contradictory alternatives are naturally
contemplated. That the fifth undemonstrable is justifiable solely on the basis of
the meaning of 'or' and the fourth only on the basis of the particularities of its
arguments, on such an account, does not matter. It is relevant only in the
presence of convincing evidence that they had in mind a substitution notion of
form. That is precisely what is lacking.

The evidence suggesting the less finely tuned notion of validity is by no
means unequivocal. The clearest case of a descriptive presentation of the undemonstrables is that of Ioannes Philoponous:

> The disjunctive syllogism proceeds on the basis of complete incom-
> patibles.[11]

But all of the early sources give, more or less, a descriptive account of the fourth
and fifth undemonstrables. Cicero, who gives barely more than schemata, feels it
necessary to add the comment that 'these conclusions are valid because in a disjunctive statement not more than one (disjunct) can be true', a remark more significant for having seemed necessary than for what it says. Much that is
otherwise puzzling is less so on the view that their notion of validity had, at least
not yet, become fixed upon a substitution account. If the notion of disjunction
was the descriptive one, meaning essentially sentences in a certain relation,
every disjunction that was ὑγιής or *validus* in the more etymological sense of
'proper' or 'sound' would also be ὑγιής or *validus* in the derivative sense of
true, even in the further derivative sense of valid. This would explain Gellius'
rejection of the premiss

> *Aut honesta sunt, quae imperat pater, aut turpia*
> A father's commands are either honourable or base

on the grounds that it is not what the Greeks call 'a sound and regular disjunction' ('ὑγιής et νόμιμον διεζευγμένον'). (*Attic Nights* II. VII. 21.) It would justify Favorinus' response to Bias' dilemma, that its major premiss (You will

---

11. Scholia to Ammonias, in Philoponous *Commentaria in Analytica Priora Aristotelis. Praefatio*
xi. The translation is Mates's (1953, 131).

marry either a beautiful or an ugly woman) was not a proper disjunction (*iustum disiunctivum*), since it was not inevitable that one of the two opposites be true, which must be the case in a disjunctive proposition (V. XI. 8). On the substitution account, the truth or falsity of a premiss ought not to affect validity. On the descriptive account, particularly in the case of a disjunctive premiss, its falsity cannot but affect at least the question whether it is of the particular valid kind, since if it is false, it is not a genuine disjunction. There are other, similar instances, as, for example, Sextus' rejection of the argument:

Wealth is either good or bad;
but wealth is not bad;
therefore, wealth is good

on the grounds that the first premiss does not state an exhaustive disjunction of the possibilities.[12] These 'extra-logical considerations' (Gould 1974, 165–166) and this 'serious confusion between a disjunction and a true disjunction' (Mates 1953, 52–53) have puzzled earlier modern commentators. But if the specification of form was thought of as being given descriptively rather than substitutionally, so that the distinction between disjunction and true disjunction was not present, then the inexhaustiveness of the major premiss would debar justification by reference to V as the incompleteness of conflict would debar justification by reference to IV. And notice the restricted claim Sextus Empiricus is, on one occasion, content to allow himself about the nature of disjunction:

τὸ γὰρ ὑγιὲς διεζευγμένον ἐπαγγέλλεται ἓν τῶν ἐν αὐτῷ ὑγιὲς εἶναι, τὸ δὲ λοιπὸν ἢ τὰ λοιπὰ ψεῦδος ἢ ψευδῆ μετὰ μάχης (*Outlines of Pyrrhonism* II. 191)
The true disjunction declares that one of its clauses is true, but the other or others false or false and contradictory.

It is a curious restriction if the distinction between a disjunction and a true disjunction is an important one.

Again, Galen's discussion of the distinction between διεζευγμένον and παραδιεζευγμένον makes it clear that he at least does not understand the claims of the fourth and fifth undemonstrables according to a substitution sense of validity. For he recognized what could be called paradisjunctive syllogism as a distinct type of syllogism, while evidently not regarding it as exhibiting a distinct form. Having given an account of Chrysippus' classification of the undemonstrables, he remarks:

In syllogisms of this sort [i.e., disjunctive and hypothetical] the major premisses determine the minor; for neither in the disjunctive do more than two additional premisses occur nor in the conditional, while in the case of incomplete conflict (ἐλλιπῆ μάχη) it is possible to make one additional assumption only. (*Institutio Logica* VII. 1)

But when earlier he discusses the distinction between complete and incomplete conflict, a single multitermed sentence does duty for both.

---

12. Sextus Empiricus [1933a] ii, 434.

For "Dion is walking" is one simple proposition, and also "Dion is sitting"; and "Dion is lying down" is one proposition, and so, too, "He is running," and "He is standing still," but out of all of them is made a disjunctive proposition, as follows: "Dion is either walking or is sitting or is lying down or is running or is standing still"; whenever a proposition is formed in this way any one member is in incomplete conflict with another, but taken all together they are in complete conflict with one another, since it is necessary that one of them must be true and the others not. (V. 2)

Notice that, as an example of conflict, Galen's is a good one in its listing states that cannot simultaneously obtain, but a bad one in providing a list that is not, as Galen suggests, genuinely exhaustive. (Dion might be crouching or signalling.) From an inferential point of view, its inexhaustiveness is unimportant, since given the truth of the disjunction it follows, solely in consequence of the meaning of the particle ἤ, that if one of the disjuncts is false, then one of the others is true.

Ian Mueller, in his discussion of the possible non-truth-functional status of the Stoic sentential combinations, says

We cannot be sure about 'or,' but I suspect that a disjunction was taken to be true only if the disjuncts were mutually exclusive and exhaustive of the alternatives. (1978, 20)

It is a more plausible conjecture that what was meant by 'disjunction' was what would be called 'true disjunction' on a substitution interpretation, that in the case of disjunction, the etymological sense of 'sound' suggesting the correct internal relationships among parts, was not absent from the understanding of ὑγιής. In an application to a very simple object, this sense would be tantamount to 'true' in the sense of 'genuine'. (For in a sufficiently simple kind of object, little in the way of internal relationships can fail before the object is not merely defective of the kind, but no longer an instance of the kind.) No disjunction that was true in the sense of 'genuine' could fail to be true in the sense of 'representative of how things are'. Now to say this is not to say that they were confused between form and content as we understand the distinction. It is to say that the boundary between the two had not yet been clearly drawn, let alone drawn where, at least in propositional logic, we now draw it. In fact, we can go further. One need only read De Morgan's Cambridge lectures to see how far much of the philosophical establishment of the nineteenth-century was from grasping our present understanding of form. The entrenched Kantianism of Sir William Hamilton and his followers was one of the most serious academic obstacles that De Morgan encountered in getting something approaching the modern notion accepted. One could argue that that struggle for liberation was one of the major contributions of nineteenth century logic. The battle will not be certifiably won until the day when logic textbooks no longer call 1110 disjunctions exclusive on the grounds that their disjuncts are incompatible. It is therefore a serious matter to suppose that the Stoics were in full possession of the notion, particularly when the historical evidence indicates so clearly that their conception of the nature and place of logic were fundamentally different from that of twentieth-century theorists.

Finally, when the matter is viewed in this light, one is tempted to speculate that it was precisely their preoccupation with the dilemma both as a form of argument and as a paradigm of moral predicament that fixed the attention of the later Peripatetics and the Stoics upon inference patterns such as IV, as having a fundamental place in a codification of academic inferential practice. If this were true, it would not be surprising that they would wish to exclude as improper those disjunctions of which both disjuncts could be true, for these are the just the instances that would defeat conditionalization of dilemmas. Since the substitution account of validity would not rule out such disjunctions and a descriptive account would, the descriptive account seems on that score to be the more likely candidate for the Stoic conception of validity.

10.3 What Stoic Disjunction May Have Been

Our interest in the technical Stoic use of ἤτοι . . . ἤ . . . and *aut . . . aut . . .* lies mainly in its possible relevance to misunderstandings about the meaning of *aut* and possible meanings of 'or'. For that reason I have concentrated upon disarming the prejudices that might suggest that they introduced a technical sense of ἤτοι . . . ἤ . . . and *aut . . . aut . . .* or relied upon senses of those constructions already present in Greek and Latin. But we have said little about what they did mean and have allowed, without comment, modern terms such as 'proposition' to creep into our account (albeit only descriptively), that might themselves create the false impression that the Stoics had some such notion in common with us. It would in particular be a serious misunderstanding to suppose that the Stoics had any notion corresponding to the Fregean proposition. But there is a Stoic concept which accords in some of its uses with the idea of propositional content in some of its uses. This is the idea of the *lekton*: what is (or could be) said or meant or signified.[13] An important difference is that certain parts of speech, particularly verbs and whole predicates, could have corresponding *incomplete lekta*. Complete *lekta* or *axiomata* correspond to declarative sentences. It is in the nature of the *lekton* that most recent commentators have based their arguments against the earlier assumption that the nature of Stoic logic could be well enough understood by comparison with modern calculi. Their arguments, to which may be added the arguments here, against the application to their work of a substitutional notion of logical form, have drawn their premises from quite a different source, namely, the nature of the relationship between Stoic logic and Stoic epistemology and physics. Resemblances between these later interpretations as applied specifically to διεζευγμένον and certain descriptive uses of 'either . . . or . . .' in English may shed a ray of light (albeit infrared) on the first myth, so a brief discussion is justified.

One account, which forcefully presents Stoic logic in a non-formalist interpretation, is due to Claude Imbert (1980). She takes as her point of departure the Stoic notion of φαντασία, usually translated as 'presentation', taken up as an alternative to Aristotle's theory of imitation and applied to the art of Alexandria. It is through an understanding of the nature of φαντασίαι and their relationship to the major premises of the undemonstrables that we understand why Stoic logic is conceptually incomparable with modern calculi.

---

13. For a discussion see Frede (1987, 303).

The conclusion of a Stoic syllogism is inferred from other sentences which translate natural signs apprehended in presentations, and which never presuppose the existence of transcendent forms or universals . . . Every logical structure rests on the possibility of translating presentations into discursive sequences, and each sequence must exhaust the scientific content latent in its presentation. Inference thus depends on a rhetorical function which maps utterances (*lekta*) on to contents of presentations (*phantasia*). (187–188)

The transition from impression, which all animals have, to a presentation characteristic of human apprehension, depends upon the capacity to grasp connections among the contents of experience. Complex utterances, hypothetical, conjunctive and disjunctive, represent three ways of grasping connections. The one that concerns us here is the way that corresponds to the disjunctive proposition: the recognition of alternative exclusive possibilities. The use of the language of φαντασία in this connection is suggestive, in one respect, of Aristotle's use of the same term in *De Anima*, where it designates an activity characteristic of common (as distinct from *particular*) sense. And other evidence has suggested to some commentators that the ideas of the logical connections were originally a Peripatetic innovation.[14]

Finally, a full understanding of the Stoic preoccupation with what appears to the present-day philosopher as a rather specialized and arcane notion of disjunction cannot neglect its connection with a theme that recurs as a leitmotif in one form or another throughout the history of Greek philosophy. The διεζευγμένον of the Stoics is a late practical refinement of the notion of the conflict of opposites, which can be traced through Heracleitus' doctrines of the unity of opposites to Anaximander's doctrine of the generation of opposites from the undifferentiated ἄπειρον, and is to be found in the central images of the mythic cosmogony of Hesiod. For the Stoics, it was at the heart of their ethics, physics, and logic, and its recognition was a necessary constituent of the rational unity to be made of the conduct of human affairs and the operations of nature. We can construct a simplified model that realizes some such conception as the one they seem to have had in mind. According to such a picture, each succeeding state of the world makes some atomic sentences true and the rest false. So each moment of time may be thought of as a function or rule that takes sentences to truth values. Coming to an understanding of the intelligent character of the world amounts to grasping the principles by which these functions are selected in their turn. And in a poetic or spiritual frame of mind, we might imagine such rules as competing for selection and thus, since they represent incompatible assignments of truth-values, we might imagine them as being in conflict. Moreover, the image comes equally to mind of nature selecting its way among these competing functions according to some rational principle. In the sphere of individual action, the notion will readily suggest itself to us that in minute part we each bear some responsibility through our choices for the successive states of the universe. The apprehension of the distinctness of these state-functions within the subdomain of alternatives presented to us would, in this admittedly fanciful reconstruction, correspond to the apprehension of διεζευγμένον. Like the rows

---

14. See Barnes (1985) for a discussion of the evidence suggesting that Theophrastus was one Peripatetic source.

of a truth table or the items of a menu, they would be represented as mutually exclusive alternatives; were we to articulate them, it would most naturally take the form of a string of alternatives separated by 'or': this set of atoms true or that or the other. . . .

Now this fancy is an anachronism, though the Stoics seemed to recognize something like the possibilities represented by the rows of a truth table. But if we cannot understand the Stoic use of 'or' in other terms than those of twentieth-century logical theory, it would be less misleading to bring the notion of διεζευγμένον into the light of such simplehearted model theoretic ideas than to associate it with the substitutional idea of a particular logical form.

As much as one might wish to complain to the Stoics that there are connections, such as non-exclusive alternatives, that are not provided for in their scheme, such objections are not to the present point, for what we have wanted is an explanation of the Stoic use of ἤτοι . . . ἤ . . . that accords with the evident fact that their technical *use* does not constitute a technical *meaning*. Understood as representing the most succinct way in which we reflect in utterance the connection between exclusive alternatives viewed as such, the use is surely unobjectionable. The fact that we and, for that matter, the Greeks had other less succinct ways of reflecting such connections and as well used the same connective for non-exclusive alternatives is neither here nor there. In any case, when such alternatives confront us, a complete analysis of the possibilities will always yield exclusive alternands, namely, those corresponding to the three 1's of the truth table of ∨. If α and β present themselves to us as non-exclusive alternatives, our choice, when fully and analytically apprehended, is seen to be among the three exclusive alternatives: pursuing both α and β, pursuing α but not β, and pursuing β but not α. Though the origins were different and the motives, the method need not be thought entirely unlike Boole's. He too took exclusivity, even the same arity-free idea of exclusivity, to be centrally important to his representation, but the exclusivity was constructed out of a non-exclusive disjunctive use of 'or'.

The Adverbial 'Or'

Omne verbum, quum desinit esse quod est, migrat in adverbium.
Every word, when it ceases to be what it is, betakes itself among the
adverbs.   SERVIUS

Sankara explains 'ten fingers' breadth' to mean infinity. Brahman permeates the
universe and extends into the boundless beyond. Or, he says, the passage may refer
to the heart, which is ten fingers above the navel.   SWAMI NIKHILANANDA

11.1 A Pragmatic Approach

11.1.1 The raw material of logical theory

Compound sentences are the stock in trade of propositional logic. Whether they
are properly regarded as a contribution of Stoic logicians and grammarians, or as
the outcome of an evolving philosophical acuity and its attendant linguistic
idiom, the fixed attention upon compound sentences roughly corresponding to
modern notions of conjunction, disjunction, negation, and implication and upon
their place in inference was nascent in the Hellenistic era. But though we catch
teasing glimpses of notions closely resembling modern truth functions, it would
be wrong to infer immediately that there was anything approaching the settled
attitudes of twentieth-century classical logicians as to the correct account of the
connectives. In any case, prudent good sense dictates that we try to draw our
inferences about what Stoic logicians were up to from a more general scholarship that will yield a point of view less sharply angled to their own. Again, there
is no reason to suppose that philosophers of the Hellenistic and Roman eras
were any clearer than their present-day counterparts about the relative places of
discovery, decision, and utility in the development of theories. They were not
above introducing a technical term and then fruitlessly debating what it meant as
though it were a matter of fact. In short, there is no warrant for the supposition
that they, unlike us, had a clear idea of what they were doing and why. But
without making detailed claims about the nature of their aims and accomplish-
ments, we can describe in a general way some of the theoretical notions that
were available to logical theorists at the end of their era, as compared to the raw

material available at the beginning of it from which those ideas were forged. Among these was the idea—however unsettled, however unfocused—of giving an account of the truth conditions for certain grammatical compounds of whole sentences. The programme, which fed upon concurrent advances in grammatical theory, involved the (possibly novel) idea of viewing compounds of whole sentences as themselves whole sentences, and that involved the subsidiary idea of sentences as whole individuals with a determinate internal structure, an idea already available from the work of Aristotle. The raw material of the programme was human discourse, spoken and written.

It is important to be reminded that the idea of compounds of sentences as themselves constituting sentences is the *product* of grammatical and logical theorizing and not its ultimate raw material, for it is the style of modern textbooks to suggest otherwise. As well, the reminder should tip us to pay attention to the contemporary reports, analyses, and criticisms of early logical theory that we might otherwise dismiss as attributable to fatuity or ignorance. Much of what we take for granted or suppose we have the means to think through for ourselves, Cicero and Galen and Sextus did not take for granted, and they were not drilled in the settled practice that makes matters seem obvious that ought not. In particular, the question of truth conditions for some compound sentences has *never* been settled to the satisfaction of all logical theorists, and we should not be surprised to find early criticisms of Stoic proposals expressed as objections to proposals rather than as arguments on matters of fact, even when the compound in question seems to us uncontroversial. Consider, for example, Sextus Empiricus on the proposed truth conditions for conjunction:

> . . . when they declare that the conjunction which has all of its parts true (ἀληθῆ) is valid (ὑγιὲς)—as for instance, "It is day and it is light,"—they are again laying down the law for themselves. For it should have followed at once that, if the compound with all its parts true is true, the compound with all of its parts false is false, but that which has some parts false and at the same time some true is no more true than false. For if it is open to them to make rules about these matters just as they choose, we must allow their assertion that the conjunction which contains one false clause is false; but it will be open also to others to make a contrary rule and assert that the conjunction with several true clauses and one false is true. But if we ought to pay attention to the real nature of these things, it is surely apposite to say that the conjunction which has one part true and one part false is no more true than false; for just as what is compounded of white and black is no more white than black (for the white was white and the black was black), so also the true is only true and the false is only false, and the compound of the two must be described as no more true than false.[1]

The tension still between the realist's preoccupation with the raw material of discourse and the theoreticist's need to explain his way of representing it is evident in the metaphors that Sextus cites and in the way the language of the metaphor is tugged one way by the one attitude and the other by the other. We are presented with three metaphors: digging a well, weaving a cloak, and

---

1. *Against the Logicians* II. 127-8. The translation is an adaptation of Bury's (1933, 2: 305).

building a house. If a portion of discourse, say, the utterance of a sentence, understood as an activity is likened to digging a well or weaving a cloak or building a house, then the object to which the logician wants to attribute properties should be associated with the product of the activity—the well, the cloak, the house—not the digging, weaving, or building of it. So although it is true that in the course of uttering a conjunction we may utter successively false conjuncts and true ones, when the whole is considered, the question of its truth and falsity can be viewed as a distinct matter, rather in the manner in which a cloak can acquire properties (such as tears), which are properly viewed as distinct in kind from the constitutive properties of its parts. But such a metaphor is mere massage, and Sextus is right to draw attention to the fact that a theoretical leap is required to get from the alleged parts to the alleged whole. Whether anyone can, at this remove, be persuaded against the logical enterprise by his observations is questionable, but he is surely right in his estimation of the distance between the given data and the theory that sought to comprehend them.

> For every speech, if it exists, is either coming to be or silenced; but neither does that which is coming to be exist, owing to its non-subsistence, nor that which is silent, owing to its not as yet coming to be. Speech, therefore, does not exist. Now that which is coming to be does not exist, as is shown by parallel instances; for a house when coming to be a house is not a house, nor is a ship, nor anything else of the sort; nor, consequently, speech. And that silent speech has no existence either is admitted. If then speech is either becoming or silenced, and at neither of these periods exists, speech will not exist. (131)

The problem for Sextus lay in finding a bearer for the properties of truth and falsity; the difficulties he raises bring home the fact that the concept of a truth bearer was a theoretical one, requiring, for its application to observable discourse, the adoption of a language that was not dictated by the ordinary experience of human speech.

> . . . if the true resides in speech, it is either in a minimal or in a long speech; but it is not in a minimal, for the minimal object is indivisible and the true is not indivisible; neither is it in long speech, for this is not really existent because, when the first part of it is uttered, the second does not yet exist, and when the second is being uttered, the first no longer exists. (132)

The raw material of logical theory in its most primitive description is sound emitted by humans. This description, essentially Sextus', is crude, but at the contemplated stage of logical theory-construction, we do not have an especially refined product, even when we describe it more generously as successions of clauses separated by 'and', 'or', 'then' and so forth. For we still do not have any observables that can be called compound sentences in the logical sense, or rather if we do find clearish cases, they are thinly seeded among the many more cases in which the connective vocabulary occurs but which requires considerable preprocessing of a generally sympathetic character before the theory can gain a purchase. (As an example, in Trollope's novel *Can You Forgive Her?* of more than 800 occurrences of the word 'or', only four join whole indicative sentences and require a disjunctive reading.) At the very least, logic texts neglect the evident fact that commas and full stops as well as connective words punctuate clauses in discourse, that frequently the connective words begin new sentences and are sometimes introduced by a different speaker

> The Cameron garden was a pleasing wilderness of old pear trees and lilac bushes growing out of shaggy grass. Or Lucy said it was pleasing and the boys used to play in it when they were younger. (Rendell 1985, 38)[2]

> After that, as he remarked to Dora while Sheila made a secret phone call, there didn't seem any more to be said. Or not for the present. (Rendell 1988, 52)

> " . . . We've a perfect right to offer suggestions."
> "If they're asked for," said Waring.
> "Or if they're not," said the Old Man. "It's a free country." (Balchin 1943, 117)

> If I'd been a bit sillier, or a bit more intelligent, or had more guts or less guts, or had two feet or no feet, or been almost anything definite, it would have been easy. (192)

An investigation of 'or' that does not prejudge its outcome will not assume that the truth conditions for disjunction were *discovered* in discourse, any more than that the truth conditions for conjunction were. It will go a little further than merely to suggest which features of 'or' (that is, ἤτοι . . . ἤ . . . or *aut*) made its adoption as disjunctive notation a natural course. That there was already a long history of philosophical uses of ἤ in the formulation of dilemmas is undeniable, and certainly there were also instances of its use in discourse which conformed closely enough to some logical uses of '∨'. But in the end perhaps we cannot say to what extent the regularities in the uses of 'or' and its ancestors reflect primordial or unreflective logical awareness and to what extent they merely coincided with, and in some measure also shaped, truth-conditional logic as it emerged.

11.1.2 Other etymological resources

It seems likely that there are phenomena of scope arrogation with origins in defunct meanings of 'or' involving physical and temporal relationships ('other', 'before'). But the application of the notion of scope to the implicit *else*-clause sheds such light as it does only where a verb phrase can be introduced. It will be of no obvious use in our understanding of conjunctively distributive *or*-lists in comparisons, and while it may be required as an element of our account of conjunctively understood sentential *or*-constructions (as 'You may go or you may stay'), it really does not of itself explain the conjunctive character of these constructions. Nevertheless, if we admit to our account of its uses that the English 'or' has inherited something of the character of *aut* as well, then the etymological title search, especially in the common ancestral territory of Latin

---

2. Notice that the 'and' of the second sentence is the principal connective in spite of the greater grammatical division before 'Or'.

and Greek, brings an unexpected benefit. In particular, the attempt to find the origins of the corresponding distinctions of Latin discourse in Greek etymologies suggests a plausible solution to the puzzles about 'or'.

As we have already noted, the Latin word *aut* has common ancestry with the Greek adverb αὖ, which spatially meant 'back' or 'backwards', temporally meant 'again', 'anew', 'afresh', 'once more', logically meant 'further', 'moreover', 'besides', but which then took on the adversative character of 'on the other hand', or 'on the contrary', much as 'again' gives rise to and figures in 'against'. The phonetically closer Greek cousin of *aut* is the word αὖτε, which adds the generalizing particle τε and which carried the same uses as αὖ in all but the spatial sense (Liddell and Scott 1864).

What is of note in this is that a part of speech that we all have learned in school to classify as a coordinating conjunction has its origins in an adverb, and an adverb that moreover had so obviously been propagated from root-stock of spoken as distinct from written discourse. The question that it suggests is this: how much of the behaviour of the connective words that logic has seized upon can be explained as residual or even essential adverbiality? To put it more plainly, is there any sense in which 'or' and perhaps other logical words are really adverbs? To put it less tendentiously, does that thesis provide a revealing angle from which to watch logical words at work and to understand what they are doing in ordinary speech and how?

11.1.3 Things adverbial

No one, I think, has so far made such a sweeping charge against all the standard logical connectives. But I am by no means the first to bring surprising things under the heading of adverbiality. As one distinguished grammarian (Mason 1918, 111n) has observed, 'when a man gets hold of a word that he does not know what to do with, he calls it an adverb'. Part of the reason for this is probably that adverbs may modify any of a wide variety of parts of speech (verbs, adverbs, adjectives, prepositions, nouns, and so on), but partly that so many words that normally play other grammatical roles also try their hands from time to time at playing the adverb. Even the form *the* can be adverbial, as in *the sooner the better*. Contrary to the remark of Servius' with which I began this chapter, in the case of logical vocabulary, it appears that it is rather from among a certain tribe of adverbs that these other parts of speech have sprung.

C. T. Onions (1932, 17–18) has taken the domain of adverbials beyond the modification of parts of speech, distinguishing a class of adverbs which he calls 'sentence adverbs'. Examples are: *therefore, however, nevertheless, yet, now, else, only, so, accordingly, hence, also, too, likewise,* and *moreover,* which 'qualify the sentence as a whole rather than any particular part of it'. He includes in this class other adverbs which are not always, but may be used in this way, such as *truly, certainly, assuredly, verily* and *undoubtedly.* His second group provides the clearest examples of the intended contrast between verb modification and sentence modification. His own illustration contrasts the pair of sentences

(1) This is certainly false

(2) I do not know certainly.

Presumably Onions would include *necessarily* (and *presumably*) among this class of adverbs, and adverbial clauses introduced by *if, because, when,* and so on would be sentence-adverbial clauses at least sometimes.

The distinction is apparent in many perplexing passages of the Authorized Version of The New Testament. The passages I have in mind are all those that end with some such adverbial clause as 'that the saying might be fulfilled . . .' Consider Matthew 21:2–4:

> (3) Go into the village over against you, and straightway ye shall find an ass tied, and a colt with her: loose *them* and bring *them* unto me. I And if any *man* say ought unto you, ye shall say, The Lord hath need of them; and straightway he will send them. I All this was done, that it might be fulfilled which was spoken by the prophet, saying, I Tell ye the daughter of Sion, Behold, thy King cometh unto thee, meek, and sitting upon an ass, and a colt the foal of an ass.[3]

There are several ways in which the construction can be taken. On one, Jesus is merely choosing courses of action that will optimize the fit between his activities and those prophesied of the messiah. On another, he is going about making honest propositions (in Anscombe's phrase) of as many prophecies as practicable.[4] On both of these, the adverbial clause 'that it might be fulfilled . . .' can be taken to modify the verb phrase 'was done'. But on the construal according to which these events were brought about by the prophecy, the clause modifies the whole sentence 'All this was done'. This I take to be the point of the comma after 'done'. In indicative cases the sentence can be recast as 'It was the case that all this was done'. The construal of the 'that' clause as a sentence adverb corresponds to its construal as modifying the former occurrence of the verb 'was'. I shall return to this later.

Two further examples from the Gospel according to St. John 20:28 and 20:24:

> (4) After this, Jesus knowing that all things were now accomplished, that the scripture might be fulfilled, saith, I thirst.

> (5) They said therefore among themselves, Let us not rend it, but cast lots for it, whose it shall be: that the scripture might be fulfilled, which saith, They parted my raiment among them, and for my vesture they did cast lots. These things therefore the soldiers did.

The former (verse 28), to my ear, seems actually to require a reading according to which the 'that' clause gives Jesus' reason for saying 'I thirst'. The latter (verse 24) seems to require a sentence-adverbial reading and to resist a reading according to which it is either a part of what they said, or a reason of theirs for saying what they said. What it supplies is a hybrid, partly causal, partly teleological explanation for their decision and their carrying it out.[5] For my

---

3. The italics indicate words added in the translation.

4. One could, of course, assign it to the *naïveté* of the author or to *his* incapacity to understand the relationship between prophecy and fulfilment.

5. Notice by the way that the prophecy is expressed in the past tense. Thereby surely hangs another essay, as much as by the force and the reference of the 'therefore'.

purpose, nothing hangs by the question as to which reading is correct; they serve only to illustrate the distinction.

11.1.4 Discourse adverbs

Now grammarians have sometimes shown a bias in favour of written rather than spoken language, and it is easy to lose sight of the fact that in discourse we not only offer connected sentences but we also must connect the parts of our discourse. The two activities usually coincide, and even when they do not, the same vocabulary is used for both purposes, so that even were it true that one was more primitive than the other, it would be difficult to tell. We might be tricked into assuming that the study of sentential connections will provide a sufficient account for every philosophical purpose or, worse, supposing that sentential connections are all that there are. Then, when anomalies arose we would leap to an explanation in terms of non-standard sentential connectives, and invent funny logics. Here is a pair of sentences (left unpunctuated) that illustrate the point:

(6) He is coming because he wants to see my new cello

(7) He is coming because I just saw him crossing the quadrangle.

The likely reading of the first one is as giving his reason for coming. But although some contexts might support a parallel reading of the second (perhaps he will request my discretion), on one possible reading (with a pause after 'coming') it provides my reason for believing, and so a basis for saying that he is coming. On this reading, the second *because* clause is not *sentence*-adverbial, but *assertion*-adverbial or, more generally, *discourse*-adverbial. (If you prefer, the *because* is not a sentence-sentence (s-s) connective, but an utterance-sentence (u-s) connective.)

The distinction is required sometimes with simple adverbs. In the sentence

(8) She is seriously ill,

the adverb modifies the predicate adjective. In the sentence

(9) Obviously she is ill,

the adverb modifies the sentence. But in the sentence

(10) Seriously, she is ill,

the adverb modifies the assertion.

When one thinks about it, some such distinction is bound to be required as soon as we lose our philosophical preoccupation with the indicative mood, because none of the usual sentence connectives and none of the sentence adverbs listed occurs exclusively with indicative sentences. So we are bound to give an account of, say, *and* and *or* that takes account of such sentences as

(11) Who are you and what do you want?

(12) Do you want information or do you want incivilities?

and we will certainly want to distinguish, more or less along u-s/s-s lines, between

(13) If the text has at last captured your prurient interest, Jenkins, please translate, beginning at '*utinam savium habeas*'

or

(14) Seriously now, if I may presume to advise you, get onto your solicitor immediately about it

and

(15) If you see Marty, tell him they're gunning for him;

between

(16) Is he coming because he is broke?

and

(17) Is he coming, because if he is I must hide the silverware;

and between

(18) For that reason, will you marry me?

and

(19) Will you really marry him for *that* reason?

For (13) and (14) are conditionally issued directives, but (15) is an issued conditional directive. (16) and (19) query a reason, whereas (17) and (18) ground a query in a reason.

It is difficult to accept the distinction and not see the so-called Austinian conditional as an example of an assertion-adverbial use. A sentence such as,

(20) There is *potage crème de* yester*jour* in the fridge if you are desperate.

is not an asserted sentence-adverbial modification, but an adverbially modified assertion. It is not an asserted conditional, but an assertion, some aspect of which is conditional upon your interest in it. Crudely, assertions provide the means by which attention is drawn to them, an implicit 'Pay attention to me', and it is this invitation that is conditional upon your interest. Other non-contraposing conditional constructions will be found to exemplify different kinds of assertion modification.

(21) If you think about it, he's really a very kind person.

There may be a temptation to say that this represents an unusual conditional in that it does not contrapose or that such examples prove that contraposition is not a universal property of the conditional considered as a u-s connective. But if we recognize the existence of u-s adverbial constructions, we have an alternative way of expressing this contrapositional peculiarity. We can no more expect a conditional assertion to contrapose than we can expect a conditional question or a conditional directive to do so. But, possibly because the main clause is indicative, one is tempted to disregard the fact that in its natural habitat it would be a conditioned assertion and not an asserted conditional. In captivity, they are not obviously distinct, except in the inapplicability of contraposition (and when one checks, other logical transformations).

Other authors have recognized the distinction between asserted conditionals and conditional assertions, even if they have not expressed the distinction in adverbial terms. Thus, Gilbert Ryle:

> [If] is often used in giving conditional undertakings, threats, and wagers. (1949, 123)

Dorothy Edgington puts the matter in these terms:

> It is worth remembering that any type of speech act can be performed within the scope of a supposition. There are conditional questions, commands, etc. as well as conditional assertions.
>
>> If he 'phones, what shall I say?
>> If I'm late, don't stay up.
>> If you're determined to do it, you ought to do it today.
>
> ... the double illocutionary force is *in*eliminable; there is no proposition such that asserting *it* to be the case is equivalent to asserting that **B** is the case given the *supposition* that **A** is the case. (Edgington 1990, 5)[6]

We must remark that Edgington's examples do quite not illustrate Ryle's point. Her first example is perhaps an example of an *interrogative* within the scope of a supposition, but it is not an example of an *interrogation* within the scope of a supposition. Contrast it with

> If you are legally of age, what would you like to drink?

We do not go far wrong in construing her example as an instruction in two parts. Suppose that he has just 'phoned, and I have taken the call; tell me what I should say. It is really a question to which the answer requires a supposition. By contrast, the grammatically parallel example cannot be construed as an instruction to the addressee to suppose himself or herself to be legally of age and to tell the interrogator what he or she wants to drink. In this case, the addressee is to understand the interrogation itself to be conditioned by the *if*-clause. We may contrast her second example in similar terms with

> If it is proper for me to order you about, don't stay up,

which asserts itself to constitute an instruction if the condition of the *if*-clause is fulfilled. Hers mentions no condition upon which it constitutes an instruction and is most naturally taken as a conditional instruction. Finally, compare her final example with

> If it is not too presumptuous of me to say so, you ought to do it today,

6. I am indebted to Dorothy Edgington for discussions on the subject of that paper and this chapter.

in which the *then*-clause is not claimed to constitute an issuance of advice unless the condition of the *if*-clause is satisfied.

The differences between (20) and (21) not only urge some such discourse-adverbial account upon us but also suggest that a finer-grained account can and, if the distinction is to be explained, must be given. We can consider first what responses are possible to them

(21′) I *have* thought about it, and you're quite right.

(21′′) I've thought about it more than I would admit to anyone but you, and I'm afraid you're quite wrong about him. It is precisely when you don't think very deeply that his goodness more or less comes off . . . .

(20′) I am indeed interested. Thank you very much. I'll warm some up when I've wiped Nigel's paws.

(20′′) I got a bite in town, thanks very much. But please have some yourself. Good God, man, you weren't waiting all this time for me!?

Of course, one may deserve thanks for a conditional offer as for any other, so polite responses may hold no clue. Nevertheless, it remains a puzzle what difference the truth or falsity of the antecedent is supposed to make to the way in which such an offer is to be received. What in general can we say? First, that from an act of speech, we expect certain information to be inferred, some but by no means all of which would count as a part of the 'content' of what is said. Many of those inferences can be forestalled, tempered, or otherwise manipulated or controlled by the use of adverbial devices. Among the adverbial devices available to us are discourse-adverbial *if*-clauses. What is, by intention, being controlled in this way must somehow be made clear, and how that clear indication of purpose is achieved will vary from speaker to speaker, hearer to hearer, occasion to occasion, and so on. There is no reason to suppose that a usefully definite and detailed, let alone exhaustive, account could be given of how it is done.

This does not entail that all uses of the conditional form are conditional speech acts. Such a claim, like any negative existential, would be difficult to prove. Moreover, there are plenty of considerations that make it prima facie implausible. Among these is the fact that we attribute truth and falsity to the conditional assertions of others. Against this, it is true that on some occasions the attribution of truth or falsity is merely a formulaic assent or dissent, an aligning of one's own sentiments on a subject with those of an earlier speaker, which may amount to a co-opting of an earlier set of remarks with all discourse-adverbial jots and tittles in place. But again, this is far from establishing the subsidiary negative existential claim that the attribution of truth is always an attempt to place one's mouth behind someone else's words, and is never to be understood as an assent to the conditional content of what was said. And again, neither point of view is gainsaid by the observation that there is no way of telling whether the assenter means the same thing as their author by the suppositive remarks that he is assenting to. This simply adds an index to an already mysterious account of the truth condition. Finally, the very fact that semantic accounts have been attempted provides something for conditionals to mean, a circumstance that, within the uses that are affected by those accounts, entails that they have truth values. In this respect, 'if' is not alone among the words that, in certain circles and in particular contexts, have come under the adoptive tutelage and regulation of an artificial formalism. 'Or', 'and', and 'not' are surely others. But a truth condition subsidized or wholly created in this way is nonetheless a truth condition, though monitory remarks about its artificiality and limited sphere of application may be in order, and an account of its real parentage desirable.

Now whatever general account emerges, it may be that the more primitive uses of *if*-clauses are discourse-adverbial uses. But even if only that much is true, there remains a multiplicity of distinguishable cases: think of the sentence as a conditional assertion. Consider the implicit constative frames in which any assertion is presented (the expression of belief and of the assumption that the hearer will believe, the invitation to hear, the invitation to believe, the invitation to accept the speaker's authority, the attestation of truth, and so on). Then ask with respect to which of these frames it is that the adverbial phrase qualifies the assertion. A similar experiment can be tried with assertion adverbs in general. An assertion is not only a theoretical entity consisting of information. It is also partly an information-conveying event. Assertion adverbs modify either or both in different measures. In educated speech we do not permit adverbs—call them *utterance adverbs*—which can be no more than stage directions, to masquerade as sentence or assertion modifiers. Speakers who care about such things (though their numbers dwindle) may shun 'hopefully' for this reason, just as they would 'hopelessly' or 'despairingly', but they do admit adverbs that qualify the relationship between utterance and information, such as 'crudely' and 'briefly', as well as adverbs that qualify the communicative aspect, such as 'confidentially'. These are all capable of assertion-adverbial use, but within the genus of assertion modification there is yet great variety in the qualificational range both of adverbs and of adverbial clauses. The essential point is that discourse-adverbial modification of an element of discourse yields a modification of the status of that element in discourse.

11.1.5 What can be adverbially modified and how?

In the course of making an assertion, asking a question, issuing an instruction, or performing any other act of speech, we perform many subtasks, among which we can distinguish a class of subtasks that come under adverbial as distinct from other kinds of control. One major distinction may be made in this way: among the things that we can do in discourse is to describe other discourse, that is, we say such things as 'Harry said that Hilda had left him', and among the subtasks of discourse description is the selection of constituent adverbs, as in 'Harry said, none too sorrowfully, I thought, that Hilda had left him'. We may distinguish then between controls on speech acts that the adverbs of a description may pick out, and controls on speech acts that may be accomplished by the inclusion of adverbials in the speech act itself. Thus it was in Harry's power to make his disclosure unsorrowfully, but he could not make the disclosure into an unsorrowful one by prefixing it with the adverb 'unsorrowfully'. Similarly, I may express myself hopefully on the subject of my next pay rise, for that represents a control that I can exercise over the way in which I utter the prediction. Someone describing my prediction may therefore choose the adverb 'hopefully' as a part of his description of my remarks, but 'hopefully' is not an adverb that can modify a remark or a sentence by inclusion in it.

Some of the subtasks of a speech act can be modified by the inclusion of other discourse-adverbials. A common discourse-adverbial construction takes the form of parenthetical *if*-clauses as in

Naming

Willem (if that is his name) says that the interview will have to be postponed,

Describing an action

Jaws argues (if you call a broken arm an 'argument') very effectively;

or Attributions

The line which you see there, if you *can* see it, marks a stress fracture;

This art, if art it be, deserves a more suitable setting.

Other forms of adverbial parenthesis can be introduced to mitigate the effects of a choice of expression or vocabulary:

'Well then, Mr. Mayble, since death's to be, we'll die like men any day you name (excusing my common way)'. (Hardy 1872, 109)

Sometimes an effect of studied exactitude or a suggestion of sensibilities finely tuned beyond the resolving power of one's native language is achieved by expressing part of a locution in a foreign language

The fact is, we have no great wish for each other—no spontaneous wish for each other, that is to say. This lack of *gout* makes us have to behave with a certain amount of policy. (Bowen 1938, 270)

Sometimes the effect is a delicate indirection.

I used to think that there was something rather admirable and enviable about being an *homme à bonnes fortunes*. (Huxley 1925, 64)

Adverbial modification occurs in allusive exchanges:

'Better to be a doorkeeper . . .'
'I don't think I'd care to live in a tent on a day like this',

and when we speak with self-mocking pedantry or with malicious ambiguity.

His is nothing if not a penetrating intellect.

All of these can be construed as ways of exercising discourse-adverbial control, a subject deserving fuller and more general study and which, when better understood, would set in a new light the distinction between natural and conventional meaning and the place of implicature in our understanding of discourse. Our interest here is just with connectives as they appear in this role.

Some distinctions between sentence-sentence (s-s) and utterance-utterance (u-u) connections can safely be collapsed, as when in speech two indicative sentences are connected with 'and'. Though no doubt there are interesting exceptions, it seems to make little practical difference whether we regard

(22) One dances and the other sings

as one conjunctive assertion or two assertions conjoined. (Note, however, that this not so in the case of sentences joined by adversative 'but'.) However, which of the two we say is the more primitive may make a profound difference to our detailed account of the origins of notions of logical form. We have seen that the falsity conditions of conjunction were not a matter of settled and uncontroversial doctrine at the time of Sextus Empiricus. Sextus himself wrote as though for him the u-u use of και was the fundamental one. The same consideration applies in spades to utterances joined with 'or'. In the cases we want to represent as disjunctions, the addition of the conjunction 'or' followed by the second sentence alters the conversational significance of the first. If it seemed straightforwardly an assertion before the 'or', its apparent status may nevertheless be greatly altered after it. And in those natural cases that seem most closely to fit the disjunctive mold, whatever status the first sentence is given, the second has been given similar status. The assertive or non-assertive status that an uttered sentence has, the conversational significance of an occurrence of a particular part of speech—any of these properties falls within a category of what may be loosely called discourse values. Discourse values are what I want to claim that discourse adverbials control.

11.2 'Or' as Adverb

11.2.1 Primary examples

Recall that our earlier gloss on

You may go *or* you may stay

had it rewritten as

You may go, and again, you may stay.

Notice two things about the transformation of the former into the latter: first, that it uses the adverb 'again', which, as we noted, is the etymological root of *aut*, and, second, that 'again' in that occurrence is an assertion adverb. Its use in the second sentence is to be distinguished from its use in

(23) You may go again

where 'again' modifies the verb 'go'. On the truth-conditional view, 'You may go or you may stay' represents an anomalous use of 'or' in that here 'or' joins whole sentences that are nevertheless both asserted. The discourse-adverbial view invites us rather to think of each clause as formulaically giving permission rather than asserting permissibility. (It would be more difficult though still not impossible to get a conjunctive reading for

(24) It is permissible that you go or it is permissible that you stay.)

In the primary example, the effect of following the first permission with 'or' is, as it were, to retrace conversational steps and give the second. As it happens, one could, from a purely truth-conditional point of view, have used 'and', 'but', a full stop, or a semicolon there to the same overall effect. However, it is to go in at the deep end of the problem to consider apparently conjunctive instances of whole clauses. The case is a little clearer where the 'or' occurs within the scope of the modal, as in

You may have tea *or* coffee.

The effect of the 'or' is to retrace and put 'coffee' in the position of 'tea', giving the second beverage, as near as can be, the same discourse value that was given the first. The effect of 'or' here is recombinative. We may think of its action as that of uncoupling from its antecedents the element that precedes it ('or') and coupling in its place the element that follows it ('or'). The effect in the last example is an approximation of simultaneous permissions having *ut nunc* or as-of-now status. What makes such permissions distinctive is that no guarantee is given that the taking up of one of them will not nullify the other (which, *contra* the textbook authors, is not to say that taking up one will effect a prohibition of the other). This *ut nunc* character is shared with certain *if*-clause uses of 'or' as

If Fred or George calls, I'll go along immediately

(offering no guarantee that, should the second one call, I will not have already gone). They represent, in one dimension, an extremity of the class of 'conjunctive' uses of 'or', in that the *ut nunc* character attaches still to the result of the transformation which yields whole sentences combined with 'or' or 'and' (If Fred calls, I'll go along immediately, or if George calls, I'll go along immediately; (don't bother to tell me if Harry calls). They are not, however, the most extreme examples of this recombinative role, which is more especially evident when the second phrase or clause or nominal is intended, not merely to have a similar discourse value to that of the first alternand, but rather to replace or correct or refine it or otherwise improve upon it.

You couldn't see the CitWest tower from here, or not from the ground. (Rendell 1987, 186)

'I know his wife-that-was-to-be personally', she said. 'Or I used to. We were at school together.' (1981, 20–1)

'. . . We'll have the room redecorated for you'. Or for someone, he thought but didn't say aloud. (1985, 223)

The same can be seen in successions of questions as

Got a grift brother—or just amusing yourself? (Chandler 1939, 53)

"No, why? Or is that an unnecessary question?" (Mair 1941, 185)

"How come your old man didn't leave you some money?" I sneered.
"Or did you blow it all?" (Chandler 1942, 43)

'What's so funny?' said Burden sourly. 'Or has that Mrs. Lake been
cheering you up?' (Rendell 1975, 40)

where the second, yes/no question, expecting as it does a positive answer, does
not so much put forward a plausible answer to the first as render the first
question otiose.

Altered comparative status of the two alternands can be indicated by finer-
grained discourse-adverbial constructions involving 'or rather', 'or at least', 'or
perhaps', 'or anyway', and so on:

. . . but she gave no sign that she was deeply moved by his death. Or
rather, that his death had left her with a sense of loss. (Lathen 1961, 154)

He was a good sixty, or rather a bad sixty . . . (Chandler 1940, 238)

Since neither my Papa
Nor my beloved Mamma
Hopes to be present
And open this bazaar—
Or rather concert—far
Be it from me to bar
This duty pleasant. (Waugh 1962, 167)[7]

He was in the presence of genius, or if that was journalist's extravagance,
of great talent. (Rendell 1967, 29)

'I've got that picture myself,' said Ethel. 'It stands by my bed. Or stood, I
should say, seeing that it's packed in the trunk I'm having sent on with all
my other little bits'. (1971, 72)

The words aren't the right ones; or rather, the right words don't exist.
(Barnes 1984, 161)

The terms or clauses that are successively introduced in *or*-constructions are
thus not always given equal weight or status, and devices exist for making their
comparative status explicit. As with any adverbial modification, the point can be
more or less clear, and there is room for ambiguity. Consider:

My sister, or rather my half-sister, has just failed all her exams

where the preferred 'half-sister' is placed in the discourse relations that 'sister'
would have been in, and the sentence as it stands is ambiguous between a
correction of reference and a correction of claimed relationship. We don't know

7. Waugh is quoting a poem composed by Knox for one of Lord Lovat's daughters who, having been
asked to open a concert, said she was unable to make speeches or sing anything except 'God Save
the King'.

whether the speaker has begun to make a claim about the wrong person and cor-
rected it, or is placing herself at safer collateral distance from academic misad-
venture. We can do much the same with whole clauses,

Dickie Baxter is our family doctor, or rather he was until this happened

effectively replacing the assertion that Dickie Baxter is our family doctor with
the preferred assertion that Dickie Baxter was our doctor until the occasion
mentioned. Sometimes the second clause is given equal or less weight than the
first by a weakening prefix such as 'possibly' or 'perhaps'.

> Extraordinary happinesses might present themselves and, finding her
> asleep and deaf to their calling, pass on. Or some one, perhaps, would be
> saying the one supremely important, revealing, apocalyptic thing that she
> had been waiting all her life to hear. (Huxley 1925, 60)

> The blonde was strong with the madness of love or fear, or a mixture of
> both, or maybe she was just strong. (Chandler 1939, 59)

> I guess it's just the way he is. Or right now he's working for the Indian
> and does whatever he's told. (Leonard 1989, 129)

Or, by setting the second clause in interrogative form as:

> As it turned out, the mixture . . . proved a panacea. Or (Lily pondered
> later) had her memory failed her? (Mo 1982, 86)

> A master-leaver and a fugitive, Wexford reflected, eyeing the alsatian who
> had abandoned Camargue to his fate. Or gone to fetch help? (Rendell
> 1981, 28)

Sometimes the second clause represents a mere throwing up of the hands. Philip
Marlowe:

> My face was stiff with thought or with something that made my face stiff.
> (Chandler 1942, 43)

In most of these examples it must be evident that questions of truth conditions
do not straightforwardly apply. They cannot even be raised until it is clear in the
particular case what has been said, and whatever that is, it will not be stated as a
disjunction without negotiation. Constructions such as 'or rather', 'or anyway',
'or at least', 'or else', 'or otherwise', 'or alternatively', 'or if . . .', 'or maybe',
'or perhaps', 'or even', and so on. are in any case frequently, perhaps usually
pleonastic, with the more explicitly adverbial portion serving to specify the
adverbial terms under which the 'or' has been surrendered into speech. In these
cases, the 'or' can be replaced with utterance-adverbial punctuation, a semicolon
or a full stop. We will certainly not, for example, want

$$P \vee (\text{Rather } Q)$$

or

$$(\text{a supposes that P}) \vee \Diamond Q.$$

Horn (1989, 379–380) has suggested calling some of these uses 'metalinguistic disjunction', but we may note as evidence that these are not straightforwardly *disjunctive* uses of 'or' since they are not reformulable in 'either . . . or . . .' form. We do not say 'Either α or rather β'. The modificative 'or' is at least stylistically, and usually in fact not anticipated before the initial foray. To tweak Sextus' metaphor, its adverbial uses are more akin to trimming a jib or hiking or even making running repairs or manning the pumps, than to building a boat. It is true that in some of the indicative cases the effect of treating the modification as rather the completion of a disjunctive claim does not yield truth conditions incompatible with the adverbial account. If, for example, I replace an intended strong claim with an inferentially subordinate one, I will be right if the weaker claim is correct as I will be if the stronger one is. And I will be wrong if in neither of my attempts have I got the matter quite right. So this fits with a representation of what has happened according to which I have replaced a strong claim with a weaker disjunctive one. If my replacement claim is weaker in the logical sense of being implied by but not implying the first, then the disjunction of the representation is truth-conditionally equivalent to my amendment. But seen in the broader context of amendments, some of which cannot receive such a representation, the artificiality of the representation is apparent. We have replaced a claim, α with another claim, β, not with the disjunctive claim α ∨ β. But there another sense of 'weaker' in which to replace one assertion with another, weaker one is to offer in the second assertion a claim that is more noncommittal or better attested to by the evidence.

> The lady was still in bed, or so I understood. (Lovesay 1992, 187)

> She was mentally unstable, or so it appeared at the time. (354)

The case is, if anything, clearer when we note that essentially the same effect can be achieved in the same circumstances without 'or':

> Mother's really crazy about Tommy, at least she used to be, and so was Dad. (MacDonald 1964b, 42)

> Susanna stopped going to parties, at least the ones I went to. (83)

> The girl was rather nice, at least my vanity thought so. (1953, 102)

In most of these examples, the discourse-adverbial modifications introduced by 'or' may be seen as actually nested modifications, as grammatical adverbial constructions often are. The order is fairly clear. In those roughly of the form 'α, or rather β', 'or rather' is an discourse-adverbial modifier of the utterance of 'β', and the whole of 'or rather β' is a discourse-adverbial modification of 'α'. The point is plainly seen where 'or' can be replaced by something recognizably adverbial such as 'alternatively'. Consider

> Go away; alternatively, sit and be quiet.

The first clause, unmodified, would be a categorical command to go away. 'Alternatively' modifies the second imperative utterance, and the whole of the second clause alters the status of the first.

If the discourse-adverbial account is correct, then the statement of the puzzlement about 'or' is only misleadingly expressed in terms of distribution. If truth values are to be given a central place in the statement of the puzzle, as the distribution description seems to require, then considerations of nuance of discourse value will be neglected. On the discourse-adverbial account, discourse values are the crux of the matter. Consider succeeding permissions punctuated by 'or':

You may have egg or you may have sausage.

The question is not, on this view, whether the truth value of that sentence is the same as that of the sentence

You may have egg and you may have sausage.

The question is rather, as in the case of what we have called 'conjunctively distributive *or*-lists', what would have been the effect of using 'and' instead of 'or' and why. The difference in this case is the difference between, on the one hand, giving one permission and then going *on* to give another, and on the other hand, giving one permission and then going *back* and giving another; between giving the second permission while the first is in effect on the one hand, and having the two of them coming into effect, as near as can be, simultaneously, between *ut nunc* and *cumulative* permission. There is in either case a tendency for the conjunctive word 'or' or 'and' to attach to the nearer verb rather than to the auxiliary, an effect that can be seen by replacing 'or' by 'or else' or 'and' by 'and as well'. In each case the anaphoric is naturally taken to refer to the nearer of the two verbs; that is, in the former case, the addition of 'else' does not tend to force a disjunctive reading of the sentence as a whole, but rather to make the second permission conditional: 'If you do not opt for egg, you may have sausage', or 'If you do not care for egg, you may have sausage', not 'If it is false that you may have egg, you may have sausage'. In the latter case (with 'and as well'), the addition suggests the reading 'You may have egg, and in addition to egg you may have sausage' rather than 'You may have egg and in addition to being permitted to have egg, you are permitted to have sausage.' A preoccupation with truth values may lead us to miss the significance in discourse of the fact that the second clause of an 'and' construction occurs after the first one and is understood in the light of it. It is that fact among others that makes a niche for 'or' in this as in other contexts. A preoccupation with syntax may obscure the fact that in many of these cases, the implicit *than*-clause is essentially discourse-adverbial rather than sentence-adverbial. The second permission ('If you do not care for egg, you may have sausage') is conditioned, as in 'There is fruit in the fridge if you want some' the assertion that there is fruit in the fridge is conditioned. But it is the permission and not the permissibility that is conditioned, as it is the assertion and not what is asserted.

I end this discussion of discourse-adverbial 'or' with an invocation of the motto: mainly we emit sounds. I have been serving up a distinction that makes sense only in the light of a theory that distinguishes the content of an utterance from the occurrence of it in a particular way. The fundamental distinction between the type of linguistic sound sequence in an utterance of 'A tree is falling' on the one hand and the non-linguistic sound sequence of a distant creaking then crashing tree on the other is not in their having different status as the basis for inference. It lies in the fact that we can make the latter sort a reliable basis for inferences only by refining the inferences that we make from them, whereas in the former case, we can try so to arrange things that sound sequences of that sort do not occur unless they provide reliable bases for inferences. We can exert influences on the world of linguistic events that we cannot hope for in the world of non-linguistic ones. The influences extend to the enforcement of Grice's maxims as well as to matters that more directly concern the truth conditions of sentences. But the inferences we make, as distinct from those we merely recognize, we make from linguistic events, and not from contents. If a colleague says, 'A tree, or rather a bush, is falling', I infer from features of the utterance, including that it is *his* utterance, that it is given *that* intonation, and so on, that a bush is falling. It is only from the point of view of a particular kind of theory, one that hypothesizes contents or form or both, that one class of uses of 'or' is here regarded as more primitive than another. But from such a point of view as that, discourse-adverbial uses of 'or' may be regarded as the most primitive uses.

11.2.2 Proto-disjunctive 'or'

We have so far emphasized one discourse-adverbial use of 'or', that of the modificative alternand, the effect of which is to enter an alteration of content or thrust of a previously uttered portion of discourse. To this we might have added that of the elucidative or exegetical alternand that merely offers or admits an alternative manner of expression, as

We make love. Or, if you prefer it, we copulate (James 1989, 138)

or

There is a statue of Cupid (or 'Eros') in Picadilly Circus.[8]

This family of uses may be supposed, on the basis of etymology at least, to represent a surviving primitive use of 'or', kin to 'otherwise', one adverbialized form of 'other'. Indeed that is the meaning of the adverb *alias*: 'at other times', 'in other places', 'in other circumstances'. But it is closely akin to a second use that takes us a step closer to the theoretical idea of the truth-functional 'or'. It too could be called a discourse-adverbial 'or' but its classification is problematic, and its account requires a brief digression for the purpose of making a boldface claim:

There is no reason to suppose that *any* of the central cluster of 'logical' vocabulary of English, including 'if', 'not', 'and', 'possibly', 'necessarily', and, if this account is correct, 'or', finds its origins elsewhere than in discourse-adverbial uses.

8. Latin would use *vel, sive* or *seu* in such cases:

  O Matutine Pater, seu Iane libentius audis?
  O, Father of the morning, or would you prefer to hear 'Janus'? (Horace. *Satires* II. vi.)

where, notice, 'Iane' is vocative. Greek, with quite a different but readily construable justification, would use what is called the exegetical καί.

For the present we need only note of the word 'possibly' that, in civilian life, the form 'Possibly α' sometimes just represents a formulaic mooting of α rather than an assertion that α is possible, and sometimes no more than a tentative non-rejection of α or a suspension of disbelief in α. 'Possibly' in these uses is akin, therefore, to 'perhaps', differing from it in having nominal and adjectival cognates that permit us to talk of possibilities and to form 'It is possible that', and that in their turn tempt us to ask questions of ontology and cast about for plausible truth conditions and corresponding logics. At any rate, the intermediate cases are those in which 'or' lists alternative possibilities presented as such

Perhaps she meant to settle in London or even return to America. (Rendell 1981, 50)

He hadn't told her but perhaps she had guessed she would be meeting Wendy again. Or Wendy herself had told her the evening before? (1985, 187)

They were behaving in the manner of house guests who have perhaps just got up or at least just put in an appearance. . . . (1981, 38)

It could, of course, have been a genuine boat trip, and a genuine accident. Or, their own side could have killed them both. (James 1989, 451)

Titus . . . had such winning ways, perhaps inborn, perhaps cultivated subsequently, or conferred on him by fortune—that he became an object of universal love and adoration. (Graves 1957, 287)

You may find, for example, that you have run out of formatted disks: use the DOS command and then run FORMAT. Or you may find a file you don't want to copy until you make a few changes. . . . (LapLink 1989, 62)

The difference between these intermediate cases and the earlier is that the weak assertional status of the first alternand (in the last example, the first and second) is made evident by its own discourse-adverbial modifier 'perhaps' or by the modal 'could have' and that of the last alternand by the use of 'or'. Notice here that the question of distribution of 'perhaps' over 'or'— even when it gives way to the question whether 'perhaps' applies to the unmodified alternand—remains idle. The last alternand clearly moots another possibility without the requirement that a prefaced 'perhaps' be understood. What is meant by the notion of a 'mooted possibility'? Only that if we think of the first alternand as offered in candidacy for a particular role, as a surmised intention, as an enlightening simile, as a workable hypothesis, or as a plausible explanation, then we are invited to think of later alternands as providing alternative candidates for that role.

But even with no occurrence of the weakening adverb 'perhaps', successions of principal clauses separated by 'or' can demand to be understood as a succession of mooted possibilities. And these examples represent the clearest contrast between the proto-disjunctive 'or' and its genuinely disjunctive uses. For in many of these cases, the truth-conditional account leads us astray.

Imagine an exchange in which I offer as an explanation of a third person's not having returned my greeting, 'She didn't see me,' whereupon my companion offers with jocular malice:

Either she didn't see you or she did.

From a truth-conditional point of view, he has said something trivially true. From a discourse-theoretic point of view, he has implicitly said something (however unseriously) that may be true and significant. I have offered one construal of the apparent slight; my interlocutor has counteroffered two.

It is with such examples as this, where the contrast is between vacuous disjunction and contentful alternation, that we find the clearest separation of actual use from the use that the truth-conditional account would predict. We also see illustrated a point introduced earlier, that the specification of *than*-scope cannot always be purely a syntactic task, but sometimes requires that we make the pragmatic point of earlier alternands explicit. In the case of the last example, the first alternand offers one explanation, and the force of the 'or' expressed in terms of *than*-scope is approximately 'else than that explanation serves . . .'. At least one linguist has noticed this. Mark Liberman (1973, 353), arguing that the syntactic form of a sentence is not a reliable indicator of presuppositional relationships, notes that some sentences with 'or' as principal connective sometimes behave like conjunctions rather than disjunctions, and that 'in some cases . . . adassertional qualifiers are clearly transparent to the force of connectives'. His example

I think that you had better leave, or I'm afraid that there'll be trouble

'is not a disjunction of states of mind, but of a course of action and the consequences of doing otherwise.' One might quarrel with the language of disjunction and place it syntactically in the more general category of scope arrogation, but the main point is surely correct: the proper understanding of such examples is a pragmatic one and recognizes them as presenting a pair of alternatives in some or another pragmatic category.

We find more workaday examples of constructions that, like the earlier examples, resist a vacuous truth-conditional, disjunctive reading, in favour of one that lists possibilities. Consider

In practice it is or is not according to local convenience (Orwell 1938, 177)

to be understood to mean that (during the Spanish Civil War) it was in some quarters asserted that everyone professing revolutionary extremism was in the pay of the Fascists; in others not, depending upon political expediency. The adverbial phrase specifies the terms of the alternation. Or consider Suetonius' account of Claudius' attempted emendation of his gladiators' customary salutation:

. . . but when the gladiators shouted: 'Hail Caesar, we salute you, we who are about to die!' he answered sarcastically: 'Or not, as the case may be.'

> They took him up on this and refused to fight, insisting that his words amounted to a pardon. (Graves 1957, 195)

Or consider Philip Marlowe's wry acknowledgment of his helpless attendance upon fact:

> There were a lot of bottles on the sink. Lots of bottles, lots of glass, lots of fingerprints, lots of evidence. Or not, as the case may be. (Chandler 1942, 486)

This I think is the proper explanation of the anomalously conjunctive 'or' occurring outside the scope of modal adverbs, as

> to call the dominant people 'Mycenaean Greeks', may be misleading or may not, but it is convenient, and by now unavoidable. (Andrews 1971, 21)

> The coin may or may not be here. (Chandler 1942, 393)

Even if we take such a sentence as the latter to be elliptical for a pair of sentences separated by 'or':

> The coin may be there or the coin may not be there,

the point of the sentence is still to offer two separate possibilities: of the possibility that the coin is there, *and* of the possibility that it is not. By the same token, even the occurrences of 'or' that lie inside the scope of modals as

> It might indicate contempt or envy or desire or simple hatred (Rendell 1981, 41)

may be regarded as elliptical for a sequence of whole clauses separated by 'or' as:

> It might indicate contempt or it might indicate envy or it might indicate desire or it might indicate simple hatred

and nevertheless be understood to moot four possibilities. It is only when the alternands are understood in such a way that uttered individually each of them would purport a modal fact, in the case of the first alternand, the fact that the impenetrable expression of Rendell's character, Zoffany, might indicate envy, rather than mooting the possibility that it does in fact indicate envy, that the resulting construction tempts us to treat it as a disjunction.

A similar construction may be put upon successions of conditional sentences separated by 'or' when they seem to demand a conjunctive construal.

> If you stay, you'll profit, or if you go you'll profit

is a list of options bearing the same reassurance. (You'll profit whether you stay or go.) The *than*-scope is 'you stay', not 'if you stay you'll profit'. Although the effect of the whole is to say you'll profit, this is the effect of neither of the alternands, each of which is merely a conditional assertion to that effect.

11.2.3 Getting it right and saying what is true

If I say, 'I think (suppose, guess, etc.) it's about to rain', and my accomplice says, 'I think you're right', I don't take her to be claiming to agree that I think (suppose, guess, etc.) that it's about to rain, but to be expressing agreement about the imminence of rain. This is so because my remark, though framed as if to state a fact about my thoughts, functions rather as an expression of my judgment that it is going to rain. Concurrence amounts here to being prepared to express the same judgment. But however clear we are about its status as a for-mulaically expressed judgment, the way in which it enters into practical deliberations may not be so crystalline in detail. The response 'If so, then we should put away the picnic things' may be a conclusion conditional upon a hypothetical expectation 'If rain is imminent . . .' or upon my actual expectation 'If Jennings thinks that rain is imminent . . .'. Similar though not quite parallel remarks might be made about formulaically weakened judgments as 'Probably (likely, perhaps, maybe , and so on) it will rain before we are ready to leave'. Agreement amounts to being prepared to contemplate the outcome with about the same expressed degree of expectation or hope. It is a little less clear in these cases what supposition is active in 'If so, we should pack up now', 'If there is a reasonable (any) expectation of rain . . .'. The same distinction between what a construction permits us to do on the one hand and what may be inferred from the use of the construction on the other may be applied to (occurrences of) succes-sions of portions of discourse, including parts of speech and whole clauses separated by 'or' in what I have been calling the intermediate cases. We use such constructions to take more than one run at getting things right.

> . . . there were quiet voices whispering of love, or ten percent, or whatever they whisper about in a place like that. (Chandler 1942, 437)

We have got things right if one of our attempts has succeeded, whether they were attempts at getting a matter of fact right, or the subjects of conversations or the relationships between things or the name of an object. But in cases constru-able as multiple attempts at getting a matter of fact right, the conditions for having been right bring us very close to an account of a discourse use of 'or' that is first cousin to a genuinely disjunctive use. Two elements are lacking in our manner of understanding *or*-strings of attempts. The first, which has already been mentioned, is the shift from considering conditions for one's having got matters right to consideration of the conditions for the truth of what one has said. This requires a representation of an *or*-string of attempts as a single (i.e., disjunctive) attempt and an understanding of truth conditions for that single entity. The way is prepared for the shift of viewpoint when inferences are made and decisions taken on the basis of the bare assumption that the speaker *has* got it right, without further assumptions as to which of the attempts succeeded. Those inferences are guaranteed only that allow for the possible success of each attempt. They are, in effect, discourse analogues of ∨-elimination inferences. The shift has been made when we understand 'That's true' in connection with an *or*-string of attempts, rather than 'You're right'.

The second element lies not only in the way that *or*-strings are understood, but also in the way that they are understood to be understood. This element may be called the implication (or 'implicature') of exclusivity. By this is meant, not the mythical exclusivity implication of the textbooks, but the implication, in the use of an *or*-string of sentences, for example, that one of the attempts has succeeded. It is the commitment to the exclusion of further possibilities, or, to put the matter positively, it is the element of commitment to the sufficiency of the slate of candidates and the understanding of that commitment on the part of the audience. It is this element of the use of 'or' that licenses the drawing of genuinely disjunctive syllogistic inferences, taking a speaker's *or*-string of sentences as the major premiss, and ruling out one of its members.

But it should be clear that much that goes on in intellectual life can go on with the proto-disjunctive 'or' alone, with the use of 'or' in which it punctuates mooted possibilities without a commitment to one's having got it right with at least one of them. Even something akin to disjunctive syllogism is left to us. If I contemplate exactly two hypotheses and then find grounds for rejecting one of them, I am left with the other as my only hypothesis. Reasoning goes on by force of gravity alone when the truth-conditional steam engine is not brought to bear. Consider

> Let us assume for the present that the drug was intended for Miss Jupp. It could have been put into the saucepan of milk, the Wedgewood beaker itself either before or after the drink was made, into the tin of cocoa, or into the sugar. You and Miss Bowers made your drinks from the milk in the same saucepan, and sugared them from the bowl on the table without ill effects. I don't think that the drug was put in the empty beaker. It is brownish in colour and would be easily seen against the blue china. That leaves us with two possibilities. Either it was crumbled into the dry cocoa or it was dissolved in the hot drink some time after Miss Jupp made it but before she drank it. (James 1962, 79)

Notice that the string 'It could have been put into . . .' is to be understood as distributed conjunctively over the succeeding *or*-list, so that the author presents initially five prima facie possibilities. Three of them are eliminated as incompatible with established fact. The two remaining are expressed in the final disjunctive claim of the passage.

Now, that there are such genuinely disjunctive uses of 'or' in natural discourse seems evident, and if there had not been such uses before the advent of modern propositional logic, there doubtless would be after it. But, in fact, the history of such uses in philosophical settings extends far into pre-Socratic times. What is significant for dispelling the mystery of the conjunctively distributive 'or' is the recognition of the elements already present in the proto-disjunctive 'or' and, it is arguable, present still in the properly disjunctive uses of 'or' in everyday discourse. This is that even in the proto-disjunctive cases, the role of 'or' is that of a separative conjunction. What distinguishes 'α or β' and 'α and β' in these uses is not a matter of truth condition; at least in the case of the *or*-string, the question of truth condition does not arise, except for α and β separately. What distinguishes them is rather the status of α and β in the two occurrences. In the *and*-string they are assertions; in the *or*-string they are mooted possibilities.[9]

9. It may be a significant fact that English provides the auxiliary 'either' for such *or*-strings, even those with more than two items, but no such auxiliary for *and*-strings. If the present analysis is

In the intermediate uses, those I have labelled uses of the 'proto-disjunctive "or" ', 'or' bears to 'and' a relationship that may be illuminated by comparing it, in one dimension, with the relationship that μή bears to οὐ. Both of these last are simple negatives, but the former occurs, roughly speaking, in non-assertive clauses (for example, in *if*-clauses) and the latter in assertive ones.[10] Proto-disjunctive 'or', at least in the relevant cases, joins non-assertive whole sentences; 'and' joins assertive ones. Historically, the comparison is also instructive. 'Or' found a place in the canon of logical connectives because its uses stringing non-asserted indicative sentences could be represented (if approximately) as producing something compound that had truth conditions, though it was many hundreds of years after the Stoics that the truth conditions were satisfactorily set out. (Recall that in the logic of terms, its use was still thought very close to that of 'and' even in the nineteenth century.) Mή, by contrast, did not survive as an independent item, because its personality was indistinguishable from that of οὐ at the truth-conditional level. In the simplifications of logical theory, that distinction went the way of the *vel/aut* distinctions of Latin.

I admitted earlier that the discourse-adverbial account was in one respect problematic, and the οὐ/μή distinction provides an illustration of the problem. In the primary discourse-adverbial use of 'or', it does seem to be the unanticipated occurrence of 'or' together with the following alternand that alters the status of the alternand that is overwritten. In the intermediate use, the claim is not that the 'or' alters the status of the alternands, but rather that the presence of 'or' is occasioned by the status, as the presence of μή rather than οὐ is occasioned by the suppositive status of the clause being negated and does not confer it. There seems no very satisfactory way in any such case of allocating responsibilities among the parts of speech for an effect that is already richly overdetermined. In any case no more is at stake than the retention of the language of discourse-adverbiality to the intermediate case. The relevant difference is that, in the primary case, the final discourse status of the first alternand is not anticipated, and in the intermediate case it is.

11.2.4 Disjunctive 'or'

Disjunctive 'or' is intermediate 'or' looked at through the normalizing constraints of a theory. The most fundamental innovative constraint of this theory is that it requires us to look at an *or*-string of indicative sentences as constituting a single sentence. This way of seeing such sentences (or rather their Greek and Latin counterparts) seems to have become explicit in the grammatical and logical theories of the Hellenistic era, and although by now it is difficult to see this as the artefact of a theory, rather than as a brute fact of language, it seems that it was at the time possible still to view the proposal suspiciously as an antirealist fiction. To view such constructions as single sentences naturally invites

correct, there is an advantage in having the non-assertive status of the first item of the string made explicit before its pronouncement.

10. Liddell and Scott (1864), without much conviction, hazard the οὐ/μή distinction in the following way: 'οὐ, *not*, the absolute or objective Negative Particle of the Greeks, used when a negative judgment is pronounced, whereas the negative of μή is dependent or subjective, so that οὐ declares that *the thing is not so*, μή that *one thinks it is not so*.' But that is quite unsatisfactory as an account of their distribution.

questions as to their truth conditions, and here the story becomes a little tangled. Although there are clearly uses of 'or' and of its counterparts in other languages that approximate to disjunctive uses, there is nothing in the data to distinguish the proto-disjunctive 'or' from the disjunctive one, except in certain cases. If I offer one construal, then offer an alternative construal preceded by 'or', I have got it right if and only if one of my construals is right, but in offering these construals I have not *said* that one of them is right; I have merely offered a string of alternative construals, not excluded the ones that I have not offered. The theory requires that I look upon the string of alternative construals as the single claim that one of them is correct.

Our earlier arguments against the mythical exclusive 'or' suggest that this question ought to puzzle us, for the argument against exclusiveness is an argument that no use of 'or' carries an implicit negation. But the transition from the proto-disjunctive 'or' to the disjunctive 'or' seems to require that 'or' in some of its uses carry just that, for the character of exhaustiveness no less than the character of exclusiveness requires an implicit negation. How should 'or' have been able to acquire the character of exhaustiveness in some of its uses if it has been unable to acquire the character of exclusiveness in any of them? In answer we must first remind ourselves that 'or' sometimes has this disjunctive character even in lists. In adopting the language of distribution, we may convince ourselves that it is the disjunction resulting from distribution that explains the disjunctive meaning that 'or' had in the list. We have no warrant for that supposition. The *or*-sentence resulting from distribution perhaps warrants the use of the label 'disjunctive' to the 'or' of the list, since the *or*-sentence can be *represented* truth-conditionally by a disjunction. And perhaps it enables us to distinguish the uses of 'or' that warrant the label from those list-forming uses that do not, but the role of disjunction here is as a representation. The 'or' of the list is at two removes from it. Second, it is well to bear in mind that the straightforwardly disjunctive uses of 'or' are comparatively rare, at least in written English, and among those already rather infrequent uses, the disjunctive use in lists is by far the more common.

The point of these reminders is that the answer to the puzzle is likely to be found by considering disjunctive *or*-lists rather than by dwelling on disjunctive *or*-compounds of sentences. In any case, since the language of exhaustiveness in this connection derives ultimately from term logic rather than propositional logic, its appositeness is more apparent in that domain. In the language of terms the sentence, 'All of Mrs. Brown's hats are red or blue' is taken (cumbrously) to claim that the set of things that are red taken together with the set of things that are blue *exhaust* the set of things that are hats belonging to Mrs. Brown. But that language fits less well for disjunctive singular attributions, such as 'The hat that Mrs. Brown is wearing is red or blue'. The language does not fit even as well as that onto the propositional cases. The tautologousness of $\alpha \vee \neg\alpha$ is sometimes expressed by saying that α and $\neg\alpha$ exhaust logical space, or that the set of α-worlds taken together with the set of $\neg\alpha$-worlds exhaust the set of all possible worlds. To say that a simple claim of the form $\alpha \vee \beta$ says something such as that α and β exhaust the possibilities for how the real world is, may be acceptable as a rough approximation, provided that the modal character of the claim is not taken seriously. But it is more straightforward in each case to adopt 'is one of these___: . . .' as a common terminology. Every one of Mrs. Brown's hats is one of these colours: red, blue. The hat that Mrs. Brown is wearing is one of these colours: red, blue. The world is one of these kinds: α-kind, β-kind. This is really to give a list-based representation for propositional disjunction, and to drop the language of exhaustion. Our question becomes: How does there come to be such a use of 'or' that the sentence 'Mrs. Brown's hat is red or blue' requires the reading 'Mrs. Brown's hat is one of these colours: red, blue.' rather than merely the reading on which the colours red and blue are successively mooted as possible colours for Mrs. Brown's hat: 'Mrs. Brown's hat is hmmm red hmmm or hmmm blue . . .'? One answer is that the 'or' would take on the *one-of-these* meaning if its meaning were derivative from its meaning in 'Mrs. Brown's hat is not red or blue'. On the assumption that the role of 'or' in the negated case is no more than that of a separative coordinator, in the language of the lexicographers, 'communicating the negation to a second term', the derivation of the disjunctive sense from this use requires that, in the example, 'red or blue' be treated as though it represented a single molecular predicate capable of negation, or of being denied of a subject. The Stoic innovation that permitted the negation to be represented as a wide-scope (that is, *sentence*- rather than *predicate*-) negation has made this move slightly less cumbrous to formulate. The disjunctive sense is got when we let the meaning of the denial dictate the meaning of the ascription; when we take the unnegated form to ascribe to Mrs. Brown's hat exactly what the negated form denies. It is worth reminding ourselves that this is not quite a trivial matter. In comparisons and ex- pressions of preference, we do not insist upon a consistent disambiguation of negations and affirmations. It is selective rigorism about consistency that has made propositional logic as close a fit as it is to that narrow range of ordinary uses of 'or'. As for the disjunctive use of English 'or' (and of Latin *aut*), it is plausible to suppose that consistency with the reading of negated instances played a role, but it is by now difficult to say with certainty what part the developments of logic have played in bringing the disjunctive force of 'or' into the intentions and expectations of native speakers. It seems unlikely that even the disjunctive uses have got entirely beyond the constraints of proto-disjunctive 'or'.

   This persistence of intermediate 'or' that colours even the disjunctive uses may cast newly angled light on a Gricean question of implicature and sense as applied to the meaning of 'or'

> Suppose that someone were to suggest that the word *or* has a single "strong" sense, which is such that it is part of the meaning of *A or B* to say (or imply) not only (1) that A ∨ B, but also (2) that there is some non-truth-functional reason for accepting that A ∨ B, i.e. that there is some reasonable (though not necessarily conclusive) argument with A ∨ B as conclusion which does not contain one of the disjuncts as a step. (Grice 1989, 44)

He goes on to produce arguments for rejecting this view by giving examples in which the suggestion of a non-truth-functional ground is cancelled:

> I can say to my children at some stage in a treasure hunt, *The prize is either in the garden or in the attic. I know that because I know where I put it, but I'm not going to tell you.* Or I could just say (in the same situation)

The prize is either in the garden or in the attic, and the situation would be sufficient to apprise the children of the fact that my reason for accepting the disjunction is that I know a particular disjunction to be true. (45)

He goes on to offer his hypothetical 'strong theorist', an alternative rejoinder, namely, that this example showed there to be two senses of 'or', the strong one and the weaker purely disjunctive one. (Grice does not remark at this point, as he might have, upon the oddity of a view according to which any of his children who believed his claim would, as a result, have acquired a stronger belief than the one he communicated.) He offers two possible responses to such a view. The first is the observation that if there is such a strong sense, one would expect it to be borne in such settings as *if*-clauses and negative environments (where it seems not to be).[11] The second is the available supposition that the stronger sense sometimes involves a conversationally implicated suggestion on non-truth-functional grounds, to be explained in terms of the requirement of his maxim of quantity that 'to say that A or B (interpreted weakly) would be to make a weaker and so less informative statement than to say that A or to say that B' (1989, 46). Grice's point in introducing his suppositious 'strong theorist' is to illustrate the utility of a larger methodological recommendation: that we should understand the significance of an assertion as contributed jointly by truth conditions and conversational implicatures, that we should not multiply senses beyond necessity.

This latter principle, which he labels his 'Modified Occam's Razor' makes a point that is well enough taken, but it has only a narrow application to our understanding of 'or'. What it is intended to curb is the proliferation of distinct sets of truth conditions for *or*-compounds of sentences. The class of uses we have labelled proto-disjunctive 'or' are not properly regarded as giving rise to *or*-compounds of sentences having truth conditions. So the proto-disjunctive 'or' does not represent a distinct 'sense' of 'or' in Grice's sense of 'sense'. And for application to proto-disjunctive 'or' uses, the Gricean stricture against making a weaker or less informative claim when a more informative one would be appropriate must be replaced by some such more likely rule as that we ought not to offer hypotheses or explanations or construals or the like without warrant. That conversational expectation, on the adverbial account would explain, in some instances though not in all, our disinclination to say 'α or β' when our grounds for saying that are just that α. That the infelicity can be felt both in the disjunctive uses and in the proto-disjunctive uses may be taken to point up the discrepancy between, on the one hand, the inference of the truth of one truth-conditionally understood item from the truth of another, and on the other hand, inferring the rightness of the conditions for performing one act from the rightness of the conditions for the performance of quite another. There is no warrant for mooting two possibilities in having already mooted one of them. The point has its truth-conditional analogue in the propositional commonplace that we do not infer $\Diamond\alpha \land \Diamond\beta$ from $\Diamond\alpha$.

Grice cites a hypothetical historical objection that, *mutatis mutandis,* is also germane. This is the objection that whether one sense of a word is derivative

---

11. Compare, in this respect, the menu 'or' that is preserved into these contexts: 'If it's tea or coffee, I'll have tea'. 'But it isn't tea or coffee. You can have cocoa if you want'.

from another sense should be treated as a question about the history of the language to which the word belongs.

> . . . but if I am right in thinking that conversational principles would not allow the word *or* to be used in normal circumstances without at least an implicature of the existence of non-truth-functional grounds, then it is difficult to see that research could contribute any information about temporal priority in this case. (47)

Now it is evident that Grice's confidence on this point is attributable to his assumption that the 'normal' use of 'or' is the disjunctive use, an assumption that no doubt would have been shaken by a simple statistical study of his own text, even of just the portion devoted to 'or'. But if we drop the restriction of the discussion to truth-conditionally given *senses* of the word, there is room for the historical supposition that the suggestion of non-truth-functional grounds is present in one sentential use of 'or' more primitive than its disjunctive use, namely, its proto-disjunctive, and more generally its arrogative occurrences. Thus when Grice tells us that he can say such-and-such to his children, and then adds, 'Or I could just say . . .', we may take him to have said this on the grounds that he can say the first thing and that he could have said the second. And if we consider the discourse-adverbial uses of 'or' to be more primitive still, then this is an even more primitive use in which the suggestion of truth-functional grounds is clearly present. When Flaubert says (according to Julian Barnes)

> I've long been meditating a novel on insanity, or rather on how one becomes insane (Barnes 1984, 119),

he says it on the grounds that he has been meditating a novel on how one becomes insane.

11.3 Conclusions

11.3.1 Discrepancies

We cannot admit that the natural language roles of the so-called logical words can change without allowing that the practices of logic have had some influence in the changes that have occurred. Throughout the history of philosophy, developments in logic have also influenced the ways in which philosophers have used the vocabulary of discourse description and possibly how they have understood the vocabulary as non-philosophers use it. So we distinguish, for certain philosophical purposes, between saying and uttering, where in non-philosophical contexts 'say' might be used more freely. 'What did you say?' 'I said, "How's your sister?" ' We do not feel obliged to say, 'I didn't *say* anything, I *asked* . . .' As applied to subordinate clauses of sentences, there is some philosophical point to denying that they are part of what we say. If I say, 'If you try it that way, you will destroy the threads', I do not say that you try it that way, though I utter the words, and so on. But logic suggests to us that in the sense of 'say' in which we deny that I have said that you try it that way, we do say that I have said that if you try it that way, you will destroy the threads. There is a competing non-logical point of view that invites us to disregard that suggestion in favour of another that describes what I have done as saying, though in a suppositionally dependent way, that you will destroy the threads. The same point of view might even, if pressed, let us regard the particular uttering of the *if*-clause as a *supposititious* saying that you try it that way. This idiom recognizes adverbially modified sayings of things, where the logical point of view finds unmodified sayings of compound and complex things. The logical idiom must furnish us with some standards by which to judge when the compound or complex things that we say are true. In the case of conditionals, the attempts to do this have been numerous, varied, and controversial. Though many of these have been ingenious and suggestive, none of them has gained anything like universal acceptance. By contrast, the competing idiom would have us rub along with good will and whatever pretheoretical standards or, in special cases, perhaps whatever theoretical models are used to judge suppositionally based sayings; it will not tell us under what conditions they are true, but only under what sorts of conditions they are said, and perhaps under what conditions, having been said, they find assent from those who hear them. In the case of sayings involving occurrences of 'or', in particular those that logic could justifiably have us represent as disjunctive sayings, the alternative account would ask:

Under what circumstances would such a form of speech occur, and what is it used to say?

This is not in general the same as asking for its truth conditions. Recall the familiar example involving saying of someone that he has money. A truth-conditional account of sayings might have this saying true if he has about him the smallest unit of negotiable currency, but that is not what it is used to say. If we think just of sayings that report beliefs, that is not typically the belief that it reports, not the view of the state of things that, with suitable other prompts, gives rise to the saying. In the case of a disjunctive saying, 'α or β', roughly we may say that it reports a view of some range of possibilities as exhausted by the possibility: α and the possibility: β. The difference between this account of what 'α or β' is used to say and the account that tells us the truth conditions, is that the truth condition will make 'α or β' true when α alone exhausts the possibilities, and when β exhausts the possibilities. But neither of these cases represents a view of the way things are which with the same additional prompts, will give rise to the saying that α or β, rather than a saying that α or a saying that β. So typically, the view of how things are that is reported in 'α or β' is one according to which α and β are both possibilities, one according to which neither has been ruled out; that is, both the sense of the proto-disjunctive 'or' and that of the truth-conditional 'or' are present.

We can distinguish, with this contrast in mind, between two kinds of logical principles: (a) those logical principles governing the disjunctive uses of 'or' that, when we reason in accordance with them, yield plausible successions of views of how things are and (b) those logical principles that, were we to reason in accordance with them, would yield successions that accord merely with the truth conditions of sentences. If we mark transitions between successive views of how things are by ‖, then the following represents a plausible succession of such views, the parenthesized '(α or β)' representing the bare truth-conditional remnant of 'α or β':

α or β ‖ (α or β), ¬β ‖ α.

So disjunctive syllogism is in accord with this conception of reasoning. *Or*-introduction is not, because

α ‖ α, α or β

does not represent an instance of reasoning that is also a plausible succession of views of how things are. There can of course be a succession of views:

α ‖ α or β

as when one supposes first that α, and then abandons the strong view of how things are in favour of the weaker, but it is not an inference. We see instances of this in passages where one character moots a possibility as though it were a certainty, and the others each add one, so that collectively, their final view recognizes three possibilities, representable as a three-term disjunction:

> "Well, then," said Parker, "Urquhart or somebody must have emptied it and dried it out. Now, why? What would one naturally do if one found one's water bottle empty?"
>
> "Ring the bell," said Peter, promptly.
>
> "Or shout for help," added Parker.
>
> "Or," said Miss Murchison, "if one wasn't accustomed to be waited on, one might use the water from the bedroom jug." (Sayers 1930, 175)

And the central cases of the adverbial 'or' are cases where the addition of a disjunct, in effect, replaces a simple assertion by a disjunctive one, replaces a confident assertion with a multiplicity of less confident hypotheses.

Now philosophers, psychologists, and linguists alike have recognized the oddity, in ordinary discourse, of asserting a disjunction on the basis of the truth of one of its disjuncts, though their account of the character of the oddity has varied. Tarski:

> . . . the usage of the word "*or*" in everyday English is influenced by certain factors of a psychological character. Usually we affirm a disjunction of two sentences only if we believe that one of them is true but wonder which one. If, for example, we look upon a lawn in normal light, it will not enter our mind to say that the lawn is green or blue, since we are able to affirm something simpler and, at the same time, stronger, namely that the lawn is green. Sometimes even, we take the utterance of a disjunction as an admission of a speaker that he does not know which of the members of the disjunction is true. And if we later arrive at the conviction that he knew at the time that one—and, specifically, which—of the members was false, we are inclined to look upon the whole disjunction as a false sentence, even should the other member be undoubtedly true. Let us imagine,

for instance, that a friend of ours, upon being asked when he is leaving town, answers that he is going to do so today, tomorrow or the day after. Should we then later ascertain that, at the time, he had already decided to leave the same day, we shall probably get the impression that we were deliberately misled and that he told us a lie. (1941, 22)

Compare Strawson:

If someone says: 'Either it was John or it was Robert—but I couldn't tell which', we are satisfied of the truth of the alternative statement if either of the alternates turns out to be true; and we should say that the speaker was wrong only if neither turns out to be true. Here we seem to have a puzzle; for we seem to be saying that 'Either it was John or it was Robert' entails 'If it wasn't John it was Robert' and, at the same time, that 'It was John' entails the former but not the latter. What we are suffering from here is perhaps a crudity in our notion of entailment, a difficulty in applying this too undifferentiated concept to the facts of speech; or, if we prefer it, an ambiguity in the notion of a sufficient condition. The statement that it was John entails the statement that it was either John or Robert *in the sense that it confirms it*; when it turns out to have been John, the man who said that either it was John or it was Robert is shown to have been right. But the first statement does not entail the second in the sense that the step 'It was John, so it was either John or Robert' is a logically proper step (unless the person saying this means by it simply that the alternative statement made previously was correct, i.e., 'it *was* one of the two'). For the alternative statement carries the speaker's uncertainty as to which of the two it was, and this implication is inconsistent with the assertion that it was John. So in this sense of 'sufficient condition', the statement that it was John is no more a sufficient condition of (no more entails) the statement that it was either John or Robert than it is a sufficient condition of (entails) the statement that if it wasn't John, it was Robert. (1952, 91)

Psychologists supposing themselves to have experimental evidence for the existence of an exclusive disjunctive 'or' in English have had this as an additional reason for rejecting *or*-introduction as a natural principle of inference, since it would not hold for exclusive occurrences of 'or', and hence is not universally applicable:

. . . the inference from *p* to *p or q* is intuitively not a natural inferential step: If *p* is already established, there is no reason to want to infer the weaker statement, *p or q*, which suggests doubt about *p* (Strawson, 1952). Second, G3[12] legislates the inclusive meaning of *or*, since it obviously is not valid for exclusive *or*. Thus we cannot accept it if we wish the system to capture the properties of *or*. Third, there is empirical evidence that subjects reject G3; for instance, the subjects in Osherson's (1975b) samples often rejected substitution instances of it, even though they had been coached that *or* was to be construed inclusively; without such coaching, the rejection rate would undoubtedly have been even higher. If one asks subjects why the conclusion does not follow, they say that *or* could

---

12. The Gentzen schema: $\alpha; \therefore \alpha \vee \beta$.

mean " . . . but not both," and in that case, the inference would not be valid. (Braine 1978, 14)

The empirical evidence of non-acceptance is, of course, different in character from such empirical evidence as we might have that people do not actually make this inference. And reasons given for not accepting hypothetical substitution instances of the scheme would of necessity be different from one's reasons for not making them ourselves. To be sure, if I thought that for every p and q, 'p or q' meant 'Exactly one of p, q is true', I should not make the inference except in special instances (such as when q is *not-p*). Conversely, if I did make the inference on occasions other than the special ones, it would be clear enough that I was under no such misapprehension about the meaning of 'or'. If, in the course of an experimental preparation, subjects are given to believe that there is such a sense of 'or' as the exclusive sense, by being told to disregard it, there must remain for them the possibility that a hypothetical reasoner might have intended the exclusive sense and reasoned incorrectly. By the same token, if it is part of an experimental preparation that I recognize that some people use 'if p, then q' to mean 'q only if p' then, within the experiment, and without access to the reasoner, I must not warrant instances of *modus ponens* as instances of correct reasoning.

We have seen instances of *or*-sentences ('I didn't see you or I would have waved', 'I must go or I'll be late', and so on) for which the question of inference of the sentence as a whole from one of its clauses does not arise, and these alone would be sufficient to rule out *or*-introduction as an inference pattern available for all *or*-constructions involving whole clauses. Even without these, the oddity of *or*-introduction as a principle of natural reasoning persists. It is not quite captured by the objection that 'p or q' is weaker than 'p'. So after all is 'q' weaker than 'p and if p, then q'. And we do, as Strawson remarks, want the truth of a disjunct to count as making a disjunctive claim true. One relevant difference between the cases that seem odd and the cases that do not is that in the latter, the second disjunct has already been introduced (in the conversational sense) in the original disjunctive claim. Someone has already said, 'It was John or it was Robert'; the two possibilities—its having been John, and its having been Robert—have already been mooted. In discovering that it was John, we have discovered that one of the attempts at saying who it was has hit its mark. But this presupposes that both disjuncts were attempts at some conversational goal, that the particular disjuncts were selected because of their supposed fit in this role. This is the feature of these uses of 'or' that the truth-conditional account of 'or' permits us to neglect, that in disjunctive uses of 'or', the disjuncts are chosen. They are also chosen in proof-theoretic uses of *or*-introduction, where a particular disjunction is an exigency of the proof, and as well in the confirmatory case cited. The point is made sharper when the specificity of the disjuncts is exaggerated. Imagine a detective saying that the crime was committed either by a tall right-handed person with a limp, or by a left-handed person attacking from above while lying atop a particular crate; then imagine the same detective, asked to explain his inferences, saying that he has deduced this from the facts (a) that Jacobsen committed the crime, and (b) that Jacobsen is tall, right-handed and has a limp. What is disappointed is our expectation that the selection of the particular disjuncts arises out of the evidence available, and that the specific detail of the second disjunct is intended to make its relationship to that evidence clear.

Now the notion of relationship of disjuncts to evidence is quite specific to the particular example, but the more general claim holds true, namely, that in naturally occurring disjunctive *or*-constructions, the disjuncts are chosen, and there is a presumption that their specificity is conversationally significant. A principle of inference that permits the introduction of arbitrary disjuncts will accordingly seem unnatural, since it invites us to discount the conversational significance of particularly chosen elements of speech.

Ultimately the oddity of *or*-introduction must be assigned to the truth-conditional account of 'or' that justifies it, and we will expect oddities to arise in other instances where the requirements of the truth conditions may seem to permit us to discount the specificity of the disjuncts selected. The distinction between the demands of the bare truth-conditional account of 'or' and those of an account of what *or*-constructions are used to say will be particularly apparent when indices occasioning particular of the disjuncts are introduced. Consider

> . . . his blue eyes were variously described as "poetic," "icy" or "hypnotic," depending upon his moods (Wambaugh 1987, 4)

where the adverbial phrase specifies the terms of the alternation, or

> In common language the stipulation is or is not made, according to the casual presence or absence of the necessity for it (Heath 1966, 226),

where De Morgan is evidently saying that the stipulation is made when necessary and not when not, not that the one tautology is true when the other is. Again when Ryle says:

> Now sometimes it is required to refuse such a licence to infer that something is not the case, and we commonly word this refusal by saying that it can be the case, or that it is possibly the case (Ryle 1960, 122),

he is saying that the refusal is, on some occasions by some of us, worded one way and, on other occasions by some of us, the other. Again what we are told of Mr. Pickwick when we are told

> . . . and in two minutes thereafter, Mr. Pickwick was joking with the young ladies who wouldn't come over the stile while he looked, or who, having pretty feet and unexceptionable ankles, preferred standing on the top-rail for five minutes or so, declaring that they were too frightened to move . . . (Dickens 1986, 390)

is that there were young ladies of each sort, and that Mr. Pickwick joked with some of each. There may be a school of literary criticism that would have us take from such a passage only what the bare truth-conditional account of 'or' will permit. It will not dismiss the possibility that there were only young ladies (and perhaps even only one of them) who would not cross while he looked, or the possibility that that young woman was a paraplegic or an amputee who would never cross the stile or who would die heroically in the attempt. The unsophisticated reader who thinks that there is a text, and that somehow the vivacious imagery of the second of the two alternatives figures in it other than as an elaborately depicted but perhaps unrealized eventuality, will take Dickens to be doing more than reporting the truth of a disjunction.

The inclination to assign a more exalted role to bare truth conditions than is their due is diminished somewhat by a consideration of instances of adverbially supplemented 'or'. These include instances of adverbial 'or', discourse-adverbial occurrences among them. In general, these constructions may be regarded as pleonastic, the supplemental adverb merely resolving the character of the alternation. In these cases, 'or rather', 'or instead', 'or perhaps (maybe, possibly, etc.)', 'or better', 'or if . . .', 'or alternatively', 'or sometimes', 'or occasionally' may, grammatically, be replaced, sometimes with 'or' *simpliciter*, sometimes with the supplemental adverb. In the former case, the context might make clear which adverbial resolution was intended, but it might not. For example,

Then the hills looked blue, or green

would be differently resolved by 'sometimes', by 'rather', and by 'perhaps', but pleonastically, so that having reformulated, we could excise the 'or'. Why not say in such cases that 'or' is ambiguous as among a variety of senses, particularly as embedded disjunction is not an essential constituent of our understanding of any of the contemplated substitutes? The matter is clear when adverbial supplements of frequency make it plain that all the list's cases are represented:

Senior trust officers and members of the Research Department convene in a glass-encased conference room on the fortieth floor for, with luck, a short round of self-congratulation, or occasionally, for a long session of disagreement and—because bankers are human—recrimination. (Lathen 1961, 8)

Priscian lists this use, within the wider category of *subdisiunctivae*, as signifying the discrete occurrence of more than one activity:

discrete utrumque tamen esse significat, ut 'toto die vel legit iste vel cogitat' (All day he reads or thinks); *significat enim et legere et cogitare, sed non simul utrumque facere, sed aliis horis legere, aliis cogitare. similiter 'remex vel expellit remum vel attrahit'* (An oarsman pushes the oar or pulls it), *cum simul paene utrumque fieri, sed distincte. Alius enim motus pellentis, alius trahentis.* (Keil 1961, 3: 98)

Again, the case can be made that the sentence 'All day he reads or thinks' would be true if all day he reads or all day he thinks. Nevertheless, an apprentice speaker of the language, asking how, succinctly, to say of someone that his day is filled with the two activities, now one, now the other, will be told to say 'All day he reads or thinks'. Furthermore, the truth-conditional reading will defeat any requirement of compositionality when the terms of the alternation are adverbially made explicit by such a phrase as 'as the fancy takes him' or 'according to the casual presence or absence of the necessity for it'; and in such cases it will typically be clear that the fancy or the necessity toggles between alternatives, and not between the truth and falsity of a disjunction. We find 'or' even when the presence of the adverb 'alternately' would, by disallowing a combinative reading, permit 'and' instead of 'or', as

> She was a rich man's only child, alternately overindulged or neglected . . .
> (James 1989, 484)

and understand, even in the absence of toggling adverbs, as when Yeats admits:

> I have passed with a nod of the head
> Or polite meaningless words,
> Or have lingered awhile and said
> Polite meaningless words,
> And thought before I had done,
> Of a mocking tale or a gibe ('Easter 1916')

or when we are told of two characters

> He and Lyn knew most people in the Three Towns either to speak to or by
> sight or had heard of them or knew their relatives. (Rendell 1982, 120),

that there were representatives, in the Three Towns, of each of the four categories of acquaintance. It is plausible to see in such cases a surviving trace of the ancestral 'other'. We are being told that they knew some townfolk to speak to, *others* by sight, *others* by hearsay, and *others* through relatives. Notice that distribution over the list is not in question here. The subclassification is of that majority of the townfolk known to the subjects. And the implication that all categories of the classification are represented would be present if 'most' were replaced by 'all'. It is present in the following construction using 'any':

> His mother's calm response to any event was either 'very nice', equally
> appropriate to an enjoyable dinner, a royal engagement or birth, or a spec-
> tacular sunrise, or 'Terrible, terrible, isn't it? You wonder what the world's
> coming to', which covered events as diverse as Kennedy's assassination, a
> particularly gruesome murder, children abused or violated, or an IRA
> bomb. (James 1989, 286)

Even in twentieth century logic texts the recognition of this feature is not entirely absent. Witness H.W.B. Joseph (1916,)

> A disjunctive judgment affirms alternatives: bees are either male, female
> or neuter. (footnote: For any given bee these are alternatives; for bees col-
> lectively, there are three forms which are all realized.)

When such an interpretation seems to be precluded, the construction is puzzling on any but a superficial reading:

> Alice had only once before spoken of her family or her past life . . . (James
> 1989, 147)[13]

---

13. On this occasion, Alice has said something about each.

Why, we want to know, is it not divulged which of the two it was on that earlier occasion? And we are left with an impression that whatever it was, in some measure it probably touched both topics.

The discrepancies between what a bare truth-conditional account of 'or' would let us infer from these uses and what we actually take such sentences to say do not arise because in conversation we go, by implicatures, beyond what is strictly justified by the meaning of our 'logical' vocabulary. They arise because the truth-conditional account represents a particular, simplified abstraction from the historically evolved uses to which the vocabulary is put. There is no precise truth-conditional semantics for these sentences independently of their representation in an artificial language whose sentences have precise truth-conditional semantics. Independently of such a representation the distinction between entailment and implicature will not provide an adequate account of our extraction of information from such sentences. And an account according to which the English sentence entails what follows from its first-order representation and merely implicates the rest of the information that we extract from its occurrence gives an oversimple view of discourse.

11.3.2 A unified account?

What unity is bought for an account of 'or' by the recognition of its discourse-adverbial uses and its origins in physical relationship? In the long run, what we want is a correct account, and the degree of unity or disunity that that dictates. As for the middle distance, if we cannot have The Good, then we must settle for The Not-so-bad; one looked-for improvement is that our account should afford one common language of description that is suited to all of the cases. How does the adverbial account fare on that score? In a global sense, it fares none too badly if its assumptions are more or less correct. For the same general approach is applicable to all of the so-called logical vocabulary of English: 'and', 'or', 'if', 'not', 'necessarily', 'possibly', and so on; if it is false that, for all such vocabulary, its logically represented use has its origins in discourse-adverbial controls, then a measure of doubt is cast upon the account of 'or' that I have given. Locally, as applied to particular pieces of logical vocabulary, to 'or' in particular, it will seem at first blush both to fare better and to fare less well. It is a better account than a truth-functional one in that it applies to uses of 'or' with non-indicative sentences, including those where it can receive something like a conjunctive reading, and it is better as well in that it applies autonomously to uses of 'or' between non-sentences, including occurrences in conjunctively distributive *or*-lists. But the adverbial account would also seem to involve greater complication and variety than the truth-conditional account. For unlike the language of truth conditions, the language of adverbiality suggests indefinite variability of use, nuance, and subtlety of effect. It would seem to deny the possibility of a single description that will adequately fit all classes of uses of 'or'. But while this is true, the account in its detail does give us a single question that is askable of every apparently distinct use of 'or', namely, What would have been the effect of using 'and' instead of 'or'? If it is a denial of the existence of absolute disjunctive colour, it is also an affirmation of the importance of something like inferential *chiaroscuro*. It asserts that in discourse the differences between 'and' and 'or' are not fundamentally truth-conditional differences, but differences in the status of the portions of discourse that they separate. 'Or' is as much a 'conjunctive' word as 'and'; we should not expect it never to have what logic teaches us to regard as 'conjunctive' uses, but only that the conjunctive uses should be different in crucial central cases from those that a substituted 'and' would have. This claim requires perhaps the most radical alteration of viewpoint. It invites us to think of the natural language predecessor of the disjunctive ∨ of logic as differing from the immediate predecessor of ∧ quite otherwise than the truth-conditional semantics of those connectives would suggest. According to it, we are to think of 'or' and 'and' neutrally as two alternative ways of connecting portions of discourse, except that the portions of discourse that 'or' joins have a discourse status different from that of the portions of discourse joined by 'and'. This point of view is not incompatible with a truth-conditional account where truth conditions apply; it is in fact crudely representable in classical propositional logic, where a disjunction is truth-functionally equivalent to a conjunction of conditionals. That natural language 'or' is fundamentally additive rather than, as the truth-conditional account would suggest, subtractive suggests as a rule of thumb that the work that 'or' does in a particular use will be illumined by the contrast with what 'and' would do in the same context.

We have seen one such distinction already, that between distributive and combinative lists, which makes for a possible distinction between

Hilda is heavier than Mary and Clyde

and

Hilda is heavier than Hilda or Clyde,

and have confronted the apparent difficulty that *or*-lists seem to permit conjunctive distribution even in comparisons where no combinative interpretation is available for an *and*-list. Here the adverbial account ought to suggest that the *or/and*-distinction will attach itself to other related distinctions as required. One such is the distinction due to difference; another the difference due to respect. That is, if Sarah and Sally are of the same height, but Sarah noticeably taller than Hilda, we might expect

Mary is taller than Sarah and Sally

but

Mary is taller than Sarah or Hilda.

We might expect

Mary is different from Sarah and Hilda

when some single respect is understood, but

Mary is different from Sarah or Hilda

when she differs in one respect from Sarah, in another from Hilda, or again as in the previous case, when the respect is constant but the difference is more marked in the one case than in the other. Compare T. S. Eliot:

> And I will show you something different from either
> Your shadow at morning striding behind you
> Or your shadow at evening rising to meet you. ('The Waste Land', 27–29)

Notably, it is a distinction that, should it be made explicit, could be made by a difference in the scope of a quantifier. But we should by now feel no temptation, on that account, to bring the notion of quantificational scope into the explanation for our making the distinction by selecting between 'or' and 'and'. 'And' and 'or' are simply available for the job.

11.3.3 Logical disjunction

Logical disjunction is an invention. Or, if the point is insisted upon, it is a discovery—but not principally a discovery about the 'or' of English, about the *aut* or *vel* of Latin, or about the ἤτοι or ἤ of Greek. The various kinds of arguments that the modern device of logical form enables us to represent using ∨ and other artificially introduced connectives have, to be sure, their counterparts expressible in natural language, but the word 'or' need figure in none of these. We may say, for example, 'At least one of these two is true, but the former is not; therefore the latter is'. In fact, however, most of these valid forms are consonant with natural uses of 'or'. The falsity condition for disjunction is also consonant with the fact that negative elements of discourse, without contextual inhibitors, will naturally distribute conjunctively across *or*-lists. These facts make it convenient to read ∨ as 'or' and to represent the rules governing the introduction and elimination of ∨ as useful for the study of natural language arguments in which 'or' figures. But we must bear in mind two considerations in judging the significance of this consonance. The first is that if it represented a significant contribution to the realization of logical theory, it did not do so for the first sesquimillennium of logical history; for the distribution of negative elements over *aut* is actually at odds with the earliest official logical use to which *aut* was put. The second is that the uses of 'or' in the applications of formal logic to natural language argument may reasonably be regarded as a distinct class of uses of 'or'. The methods that logic makes available permit a principled understanding of arguments of any finite length involving sentences of any finite complexity. It becomes possible, with the help of formal theory, to construct and assess unambiguously sentences and arguments unmanageable without it. At the same time, students of logic replace one set of ill-formed intuitions with another, sometimes less ill-formed.

The deliberate architectonic of logical theory belies the rough and ready free-market economy of natural language, tricking us into seeing symmetries where none are. No feature illustrates the fact better than the equivalences noted by Petrus Hispanus and named for De Morgan. It is true that something like these equivalences hold for English constructions in 'and' and 'or'. But the conjunctive distribution of negation over 'or' is an instance of a fundamental separative conjunctive function of 'or', not a consequence of an alleged primarily disjunctive meaning. The disjunctive distribution of negation over 'and', by contrast, is a discoverable consequence of its primary combinative use.

We learn the equivalence of '. . . not F or G' with '. . . not F and not G' as a use of 'or', along with a great diversity of other instances of the same idiomatic practice. The one is one of the ways of conveying the other. We learn the equivalence of '. . . not F and G' with '. . . not F or not G' by having it drawn to our attention. The one is not merely the form in which we idiomatically express the other.

The invention of logic, or rather the many inventions of logic, for it has been invented many times, has always involved the suspension of some regularities governing the uses of 'and', 'or', 'not', 'if', 'possibly', and so on in favour of others. In general, those governing the formal simulacra of those English words have been those dictated by the adopted truth conditions. The notion of grammatically compound sentences as representations of entities having truth conditions is the central invention. The idea is therefore partly the inherited invention of grammatical theory. But having stressed the inventive aspect of logical theory, we must acknowledge that there is also an element of discovery. This is also partly an inherited discovery of grammatical theory. It consists in the discovery of a language in which to couch systematic judgments about human discourse, and it embodies the fundamental theoretical apparatus that collectively makes truth-conditional logic possible. But to understand the relationship between logic and discourse, it is necessary to bear *that fact* in mind and not another. Traditional grammar and its late offspring represent *one possible way* of describing and representing discourse, howsoever fragmentarily. Our understanding of discourse ought to be measured, not in our understanding of that isolated path, but in the multiplicity of other possible paths that we are also capable of recognizing.

The Evidence of Empirical Research

An impressive harvest of experimental findings has accumulated under the general heading of the development of reasoning in young and adolescent children, and much of the resulting literature has, in one way or another, purported to concern itself with the development of children's comprehension of 'or', as well as adults' settled understanding of the word. Unhappily, although doubtless the researchers have had their own clearly understood objectives, it need hardly be said that none of their experiments was designed to test comprehension in ways that agree in detail with the main theses of this book. So the relevance of these discoveries to the present work is not direct. No comprehensive survey of the work will be useful here, and none will be attempted. Nevertheless, since as might have been expected, the experimental psychologists have presumed, or at any rate adopted, essentially the simple taxonomy of the logic textbooks as the correct classification of the uses of 'or', one might expect some indirect evidence or relevant observation concerning its adequacy. At any rate the field of research has afforded opportunities for thoughtful consideration of the place of 'or' in discourse, and it is worth setting some of these investigators' suggestions alongside our own.

The experiments have been intended to shed light upon understanding, at various stages of development, of 'or' as it occurs in the offering of choices, as it is used in constructions we represent by set-theoretic operations, and as it occurs in premises and conclusions of arguments involving propositional disjunction. Unfortunately, in much of the literature, the uses of 'or' that actually figure in the experiments reported lie in more than one of those categories, and frequently the way in which the use is taken by the experimentist to represent the category is not fully explained. Thus, for example, in an early study by Patrick Suppes and Shirley Feldman (1971, 306), the instruction they include to test comprehension of exclusive 'or' is:

6. Give me the green things, or, the round things.

They used eighteen wooden blocks, each with two salient properties, shape (star, circle, or square) and colour (red, green, or black), there being two representative blocks for each combination of colour and shape. The study was conducted with 32 children between the ages of 5.7 and 6.7 years. The expected correct response to their instruction (6) was that the child should do exactly one of: (a) give to the experimentist every block that was green regardless of its shape and (b) give to the experimentist every block that was round regardless of its colour. Nine percent of the children gave the experimentist the intersection; six percent gave the union; sixty-eight percent gave the expected correct response, twice as many giving the green blocks as giving the round blocks. Seventeen percent gave collections of blocks that bore none of those set-theoretic descriptions. The results are compared for responses to their command intended to test understanding of inclusive 'or':

11. Give me the things that are green or square,

where responses were as follows: forty-seven percent gave the intersection, three percent the union (the expected correct response), twenty-five percent gave the green blocks, six percent the square ones, and nineteen percent apparently set-theoretically unstructured collections.

Two initial points suggest themselves. The first is that we should not take the large percentage of correct responses to instruction 6 as an indication that the children of the study had command of an exclusive sense of 'or' in the sense of 0110, since the occurrence was imperative, not indicative. But neither should we take the result as an indication that they understand 'or' as Boole understood it, that is as representing a union of differences; for the categories of green things and round things had a non-empty intersection, in spite of which forty-five percent gave all the green things including the round green things, and twenty-three percent gave all the round things including the green round things.

More important, we are in a position now to venture a plausible classification of the interpretations that the children put upon the two instructions. Those who proffered the intersection may have understood themselves to be giving over all those things that could be called green or round (green or square), that is, all those things that could be called green and could be called round (square). Those who proffered the union may have understood themselves to be giving over all those things that could be called green or round (green or square), that is, those things that could be called green or could be called round (square), that is, all those things that could be called green and all those things that could be called round (square).[1] Those who offered all the green things may, in either case, have taken themselves to have been given an instruction that offered a choice between modes of compliance, a larger number in each case taking the first option. None of these possible explanations calls into question the correctness of the experimentists' judgment about the correct understanding of the two instructions, but their availability offers us an alternative account of the kind of understanding that is still imperfectly developed in some of the experimental subjects. It would be better described as the development of an understanding of how those different uses of 'or' are cued in discourse. We may add, with less charity to the experimentists, that the children have not yet learned, as undoubtedly the experimentists have, the oversimplified taxonomy of undergraduate logic textbooks.

Remarkably, some researchers, in their experimental preparations, actually presuppose a more sophisticated understanding of 'or' on the part of the children than their experiments themselves are designed to detect or their experimental presuppositions admit. Consider Osherson:

---

1. Notice the difficulty, which successive paraphrases diminish, in forcing a *union* interpretation in the presence of the modal 'could'.

An important concept with the logic that we are investigating is inclusive disjunction. To keep the wording of the argument familiar, the natural-language word "or" is employed to represent it. But often the word "or" in English has an exclusive sense. An example is the admonition to a child: "You can have either cake cake or icecream." Because of situational factors "not both" is implicit. We do not wish to determine whether subjects typically interpret "or" inclusively. Commonplace observation indicates that they do not. Instead, the experiment concerns deductive abilities with a few key concepts, among them, inclusive disjunction. It would thus defeat the purpose if subjects uniformly interpreted "or" exclusively. The obvious precaution is to explain to subjects that "or" is used inclusively in the experiment, and to explain the inclusive sense. (Osherson 1975, 59)

Now, it is a fair bet that adolescents, in their everyday speech, have unselfconscious command of most of the *or*-constructions that we have distinguished in this book, and although they may accept the authoritative word of a psychologist that they will be 'using this word in a slightly different way than it is ordinarily used' (67), it cannot but be confusing for them to have this explained to them in the following terms:

If a problem says: 'There is either a *T* or a *Q*,' that means that at least one of *T* and *Q* on the board, maybe both; that is, the sentence, 'There is either a *T* or a *Q*' is true if there is a *T* but not a *Q* **or if** there is a *Q* but not a *T*, **or if** there is both a *T* and a *Q* (67)

for they will not be able to understand its occurrences of 'or' (in boldface) either in the way they are told is normal or in the way those occurrences are being used to explain. In fact, it is likely that such uses of 'or' would seem quite unremarkable even to a young speaker of the language, and may well have been understood by many of the subjects in just the way that the experimentist intended. But they are not disjunctive occurrences of 'or', there is no transformation of the construction into a conditional sentence having a disjunctive antecedent, exclusive or inclusive, and there is no *logical* transformation by which it can be made to yield the conjunction of conditionals that represents its ordinary idiomatic construal. A subject who took the *or if* construction to mean

the sentence, 'There is either a *T* or a *Q*' is true if there is a *T* but not a *Q* or the sentence, 'There is either a *T* or a *Q*' is true if there is a *Q* but not a *T*, or the sentence, 'There is either a *T* or a *Q*' is true if there is both a *T* and a *Q*

and interpreted that to mean that at least one of the constituent sentences was true rather than that all of them are, would have got the experimentist's meaning wrong, but his misunderstanding would be a misunderstanding of idiom rather than logic. A child who had not yet sorted out the nuances distinguishing the places in discourse where 'either' is called for and those where 'both' is would sometimes find himself using 'either . . . or' to conjunctive effect where 'and' would be idiomatic. Asked which of the properties *green, round* apply to a round green block, he might say 'either', which by itself would convey correct information unambiguously if unidiomatically. Required to complete the construction, he might say, 'Either *green* or *round* applies' which in the context, though a doubtful use, would not be misunderstood. Habits in such adjacent areas of discourse, we may suppose, are what inform the subjects' choices when they participate in experiments where an artificially simplified taxonomy is insisted upon and virtually schematized forms are the fare. One may well wonder how De Morgan, Boole, or Venn would have responded in similar studies, given their observations of the near synonymity of 'and' and 'or' in such forms. The authors themselves unselfconsciously use 'or' in the usual variety of idiomatic conjunctive ways in the course of drawing their conclusions and describing their experimental procedures and, as we have seen, even in their instructions to their subjects. Consider Osherson:

> One of the experimentists will confer individually with the student (or, if the question arose during the instructions, it was answered publicly). (65)

Hatano and Suga use conjunctive 'or' in the course of puzzling over why subjects tend to give intersections when the expression 'A or B' is used of overlapping classes A and B:

> It will lead him to make intersection instead of union if he does not pay much attention to conjunction or disjunction, treating both connectives the same. Or, even when he recognizes the two connectives as being different, applying the operation which is not implied in the context will tend to produce errors. (Hatano and Suga 1977, 396)

But they do not recognize the related phenomenon as normal or derivative from a normal use in the case they are considering.

Not all experimentists have failed to make the distinction between truth-conditionally based uses of 'or' and its other coordinative functions in language, though they cling to the myth of the exclusive/inclusive distinction in its logical uses and, with Osherson, do not always draw the distinction between the logical and non-logical uses with more care than the authors of logic texts have managed. Bo S. Johansson, influenced by Dik (1968), has studied young children's comprehension of 'or' in contexts rather than uses that offer choices. That is to say, the child was told a story in which a character wanted to drink lemonade *or* milk, and asked at that point to put up a picture showing what the character drank (Johansson & Sjölin 1975, 235). He makes the distinction more crisply than most:

> ...the logical *and* and *or* can be used only between assertive sentences to which truth values can be assigned, and the context of the sentences is not allowed to affect the meaning of the logical expression. (Johansson 1977, 311)

Such an account would make it clear that there is no exclusive 'or' in English that satisfies it. Nevertheless, his logical test is once more one that requires the subject to respond to imperative sentences in which 'and' and 'or' occur between adjectives as

3. Encircle all figures that are blue *or* square (312)

and his explanation once more blurs the distinction:

> Take, for example, command 3, this command may either be interpreted to mean that all figures with at least one of the attributes should be encircled (a response identical with inclusive disjunction), or that only figures with one of the attributes should be encircled (a response identical with exclusive disjunction). (314) [Note the conjunctive 'or'.]

And again, the second alternative, which one naturally understands (given the association with exclusive disjunction) as requiring the encircling of figures with exactly one of the attributes, is, in the event, taken as Suppes and Feldman take it, to require the encirclement of all blue figures or all square figures, a response labelled '*exclusive*' (315).

In general, the reports of comprehension experiments that I have read take account of too few distinctions to have much detailed relevance to any careful study of the role of 'or' in discourse, and its relationship to propositional disjunction. Doubtless the results have some significance for the direction of psychological research, but such philosophical use as they might be given is diminished by the absence of philosophically significant detail in the reports of procedures. In some cases such details as are provided inspire rather philosophical misgivings than hope. Consider, for example, the account of the method by which Braine and Rumain (1981) test for the order in which children acquire comprehension of 'or' as used in formulae offering choices, and as used in specification of classes of objects.

> Subjects were introduced to two puppets, Mary and Jane, each of which concealed a tape recorder. On one tape recorder, the voice of one 5-year-old acquaintance was recorded to be that of Mary; on the other tape recorder, the voice of another 5-year-old was recorded to be that of Jane. In front of the puppets was a closed box. Subjects were told that Mary would say something about what was in the box, then Jane would say something about what was there, and they were to listen carefully to each of the puppets. (49)

For another test:

> After the pretesting, the subject would be told that Jane would look into the box and say something about some of the animals there. The contents of the box were plainly visible to the subject, who was to determine whether Jane was right or not. We used a puppet with a 5-year-old voice to make it eminently plausible that she might be wrong. Jane's statements were all of the form "Either there's a (NAME OF ANIMAL) or there's a (NAME OF ANIMAL) in the box." Jane made four such statements in total, one corresponding to each of the truth forms, TT, TF, FT, FF, each of which was tested by a different one of the four boxes. . . . The box used for the FT truth form contained a duck and three other animals, but no horse, and Jane said "Either there's a horse or there's a duck in the box." After each sentence, the subject was asked "Is Jane right?" (50)

The question that naturally arises for the philosophical reader is the question whether the subject received, as the experimentist clearly intends, and the experiment requires, a *de dicto* understanding of the clause 'Jane would look into the box and say something about some of the animals there', an understanding that the wording could not have been better designed to defeat. One wants to ask what might the significance be of their almost certain *de re* reading of that clause upon the significant number of subjects who said that Jane was partly right in the intermediate cases. For that matter, the reader might well care to ponder what would be the correct truth value for the disjunction 'Either you are reading this page or the present king of France is reading this page' in the face of a prefatory 'I am about to say something about some of the people reading this page'. The answer to that question must surely attend the answer to the more general one: what to say about truth-functional combinations when the referential presuppositions of only one component are met.

In spite of the oversimplified taxonomy, the enthusiastic adherence to the inclusive/exclusive distinction sometimes misapplied, and the general persistence in drawing conclusions about comprehension of propositional disjunction on the basis of experiments concerning imperative sentences where 'or' joins terms, there are intriguing speculations and suggestions to be found in the literature, which it would be philosophically rewarding to explore. Martin Braine, of all the researchers canvassed, has best preserved the distinctions among the uses of 'or' in choice-offering formulae, set-theoretic constructions, and genuinely sentential inferences. And even if one occasionally disagrees with his reasons, which sometimes arise out of a respect for the alleged inclusive/exclusive distinction between disjunctive uses of 'or', his practical conclusions are consonant with the theoretical ones of this book. In his essay on natural logic already quoted (Braine, 1978), he offers a set of inference rule schemata that offers as primitive essentially the propositional rule schemata for 'or' that earlier conclusions of this book would permit. It does not go quite far enough. For it would require the inference from 'If either **a** or **b** φ's then α' to 'If **a** φ's, then α' to be recast as the inference from 'If either **a** φ's or **b** φ's, then α' to 'If **a** φ's, then α'. In fact Braine's natural language illustration of the utility of the corresponding schema (his N4) has non-propositional 'or':

> Thus from sentence 14 [Either it was John or it was Robert, but I do not know which] we can say *If it was either John or Robert, then Smith was right*. Whence we obtain, by Schema N4, *If it was John, then Smith was right*. (15)[2]

Braine then seems to accept without question the grammaticological account of the correctness of that inference pattern while taking the inferential analogue of the distribution of 'then' over antecedent 'or' as a primitive. But his system purports after all only to be a natural *propositional* system of inference and cannot be expected to represent natural non-propositional inference patterns or those involving, say, modal vocabulary.

Johnson-Laird and Byrne (1991) report experimental evidence for a psychological theory of inference that postulates a representation of logical disjunction as a set of mental models, one for each state of affairs capable of verifying the disjunction. As for other connectives in their study, they distin-

---

2. Since Braine's system contains no material conditional, intermediate premisses and conclusions separated by subsidiary inference lines must serve to represent natural language conditional premisses and conclusions.

guish between implicit and explicit models. For disjunctions, implicit models contemplate a state of affairs for each disjunct and explicit models that realize a state of affairs corresponding to each verifying row of the truth table, in effect, one model for each disjunct of a perfect disjunctive normal form.

As in our approach to other psychological theoretic approaches already canvassed, it is important not to demand more of the theory than its author intends it to contribute, and the authors evidently have intentionally restricted their attention to patterns of inference involving 'or' that parallel those for '∨' and ∨ in truth-functional logic. Nevertheless, it is fair to compare Johnson-Laird and Byrne's approach with that of Braine in its fit to what we take to be the natural inferential behaviour of 'or'. On this score, a notable difference lies in Johnson-Laird and Byrne's acceptance of *or*-introduction (α /∴ $\alpha \lor \beta$) as the only plausible means of admitting the inference of γ from α and $\alpha \lor \beta \rightarrow \gamma$, an inference pattern taken as primitive by Braine, who rejects *or*-introduction because it presupposes a non-exclusive 'or'. Now an adequate sorting out of the issues that separate Johnson-Laird and Byrne from Braine requires more detailed discussion than we can give here, but a few general remarks are in order. First, we may set to the credit of the Johnson-Laird and Byrne approach that the intermediate uses of 'or' could happily enough endure representation by their mental models. But on the debit side, we must remark that those uses of 'or' will not happily accept *or*-introduction, and this, contrary to Braine's account, for reasons that have nothing to do with exclusive disjunction. By contrast, the desired inference,

$$\alpha; \text{ if } \alpha \text{ or } \beta \text{ then } \gamma; \therefore \gamma,$$

does seem to be licensed, as Braine suggests, by a primitive characteristic of 'or'. And again, *or*-introduction will not help that inference along if the conditional is in general not left-downward monotonic. Of course, as we have already admitted, a theorist who wants a *systematic* account may find this intolerably ad hoc, for the explanation of the cited inference does not draw upon the mental models that seem to work nicely for some autonomous occurrences of 'or'. But researchers who take themselves to be studying the human capacity for reasoning within the framework of an explicitly artificial formalism need not concern themselves with what is primordial in the natural 'or'. And they may provide unexpected insights about human reasoning and draw valuable practical conclusions. Nevertheless, they may also rely at many points in the exposition of their theory upon the natural capacity of 'or' to trigger inferences of which their theory does not take account. So, for example, in understanding what Johnson-Laird and Byrne mean by

One is at liberty to introduce or to exclude the joint contingency of circle and triangle (46),

we infer that one is at liberty to introduce the joint contingency of circle and triangle. But that inference is licensed by an understanding of the inferential role of 'or' that does not depend upon anything truth-functional, just as, on the account that I have given, the last cited inference schema is licensed.

Dictionaries and Grammatical Texts

Brown, Francis, S. R. Driver, and Charles A. Briggs.
    (1907)   *A Hebrew and English Lexicon of the Old Testament*. Oxford.

Crystal, David
    (1987)   *The Cambridge Encyclopedia of Language*. Cambridge.

Glare, P. G. W.
    (1982)   *Oxford Latin Dictionary*. Oxford.

Hedericus, B.
    (1832)   *Lexicon Manuale Graeco-Latinum et Latino-Graecum*. Rome.

Lewis, Charlton T., and Charles Short
    (1879)   *A Latin Dictionary*. Oxford.

Liddell, H. G., and R. Scott
    (1864)   *A Greek-English Lexicon*. 5th ed. Oxford.

Murray, James A. H., Henry Bradley, W. A. Craigie, and C. T. Onions
    (1933)   *The Oxford English Dictionary*. 13 vols. Oxford.

Rey, A. et al., editors
    (1970)   *Le Petit Robert: Dictionnaire Alphabétique & Analogique de la Langue Française*. Paris.

Schrevelius, Cornelius
    (1805)   *Lexicon Manuale Graeco-Latinum et Latino-Graecum*. 18th ed. Edinburgh.

Skeat, Walter W.
    (1911)   *Etymological Dictionary of the English Language*. Oxford.

Smith, William
    (1855)   *A Latin-English Dictionary*. London.

Other Works

Abelard
    (1956)   *Dialectica*. Edited by L. M. de Rijk. Assen.

Alexander of Aphrodisias
    (1883)   *Alexandri in Aristotelis Analyticorum Priorum Librum I Commentarium* in *Commentaria in Aristotelem Graeca*, Vol. 2. Edited by M. Wallies. Berlin.

Anderson, A. R.
   (1967)   The Formal Analysis of Normative Systems. In *The Logic of Decision and Action*, edited by N. Rescher. Pittsburgh.

Andrews, Anthony
   (1971)   *Greek Society*. Harmondsworth.

Arnauld, A., and P. Nicole
   (1662)   *La logique, ou l'art de penser*. Paris.

Barnes, Jonathan
   (1985)   Theophrastus and Hypothetical Syllogistic. In Fortenbaugh et al. (1985).

Barrett, Robert B., and Alfred J. Stenner
   (1971)   The Myth of the Exclusive 'Or'. *Mind* **80** (317): 116–121.

Bekker, Immanuel, editor
   (1960)   *Aristoteles Opera*. Berlin.

Bocheński, I. M.
   (1963)   *Ancient Formal Logic*. Amsterdam.
   (1970)   *A History of Formal Logic*. 2d ed.   Translated and edited by Ivo Thomas. New York.

Boethius
   (1987)   *Commentarii in Librum Aristotelis*. Edited by C. Meiser. New York.

Boole, George
   (1854)   *An Investigation of the Laws of Thought*. Reprint. Dover Publications, New York.

Bosanquet, Bernard
   (1911)   *Logic or the Morphology of Knowledge*. 2 vols. 2d ed. Oxford (First published 1888).

Bradley, F. H.
   (1922)   *The Principles of Logic*. 2 vols. 2d ed. Oxford (First published 1883).

Braine, Martin D. S.
   (1978)   On the Relation between the Natural Logic of Reasoning and Standard Logic. *Psychological Review* **85**: 1–21.

Braine, Martin D. S., and Barbara Rumain
   (1981)   Development of Comprehension of 'Or': Evidence for a Sequence of Competencies. *Journal of Experimental Child Psychology* **31**: 46–70.

Broadie, Alexander
   (1985)   *The Circle of John Mair: Logic and Logicians in Pre-Reformation Scotland*. New York.

Bury, R. G., translator
   (1933)   *Sextus Empiricus*. 4 vols. Cambridge, Mass.

Carlson, Greg N.
(1980)   Polarity *any* Is Existential. *Linguistics Inquiry* **11**: 799–804.

(1981)   Distribution of Free-choice *Any*. *Papers of the 17th Regional Meeting of the Chicago Linguistics Society.*

Cicero, Marcus Tullius
(1942)   *De Fato*. Translated by H. Rackham. Cambridge, Mass.
(1949a) *Topica*. Translated by H. M. Hubbell. Cambridge, Mass.
(1949b) *De Inventione*. Translated by H. M. Hubbell. Cambridge, Mass.
(1975)   *De Officiis*. Translated by Walter Miller. Cambridge, Mass.

Couturat, Louis, editor
(1966)   *Opuscules et fragments inédits de Leibniz*. Hildesheim.

Dahl, Ö.
(1979)   Typology of Sentence Negation. *Linguistics* **17**: 79–106.

De Morgan, Augustus
(1846)   On the Syllogism: II; On the Symbols of Logic, the Theory of the Syllogism, and in Particular of the Copula. *Transactions of the Cambridge Philosophical Society* **8**: 379–408. (Reprinted in Heath 1966).
(1847)   *Formal Logic*, edited by A. E. Taylor, London 1926.
(1862)   On the Syllogism: IV; and on the Logic of Relations. *Transactions of the Cambridge Philosophical Society* **10**: 331–358. (Reprinted in Heath 1966).

Denniston, J. D.
(1966)   *The Greek Particles*, 2d ed. Oxford.

Dik, Simon C.
(1968)   *Coordination: Its Implications for the Theory of General Linguistics.* Amsterdam.

Diogenes Laertius
(1925)   *Lives of Eminent Philosophers*. Translated by R. D. Hicks. Cambridge, Mass.
(1964)   *Vitae Philosophorum*. Edited by H. S. Long. 2 vols. Oxford.

Dudman, V. H.
(1983)   Tense and Time in English Verb Clusters of the Primary Pattern. *Australian Journal of Linguistics* **3**: 25–44.
(1984)   Conditional Interpretations of *If*-Sentences. *Australian Journal of Linguistics* **4**: 143–203.
(1985)   Toward a Theory of Predication for English. *Australian Journal of Linguistics* **5**: 143–197.
(1986)   Antecedents and Consequents. *Theoria* **52/3**: 169–199.
(1989)   Interpretations of If-Sentences. In Jackson (1991).

Edgington, Dorothy
(1990)   Do Conditionals have truth conditions? *Critica* **18** (52): 3–30. (Reprinted in Jackson 1991).

Fauconnier, Gilles
    (1979)   Implication Reversal in a Natural Language. In *Formal Semantics and Pragmatics for Natural Languages*, edited by F. Guenthner and S. J. Schmidt, Dordrecht.

Fillenbaum, S.
    (1974)   *OR*: Some uses. *Journal of Experimental Child Psychology* 103: 913–921.

Fortenbaugh, William W., Pamela M. Huby, and Anthony A. Long, editors
    (1985)   *Theophrastus of Eresus: On His Life and Work.* New Brunswick.

Frede, Michael
    (1974)   *Die Stoische Logik.* Göttingen.
    (1987)   *Essays in Ancient Philosophy.* Minneapolis.

Galen
    (1896)   *Institutio Logica.* Edited by Karl Kalbfleisch. Leipzig.

Geach, P. T.
    (1962)   *Reference and Generality.* Ithaca.

Gellius, Aulus
    (1903)   *Noctium Atticarum.* Translated by Carolus Hosius. Leipzig.
    (1977)   *The Attic Nights.* Translated by John C. Rolfe. New York.

Geulincx, Arnold
    (1662)   *Logica Fundamentis suis a quibus hactenus collapsa fuerat Restituta.* In Land (1891).

Gould, Josiah
    (1974)   Deduction in Stoic Logic. In *Ancient Logic and Its Modern Interpretation*, edited by John Corcoran. Dordrecht and Boston.

Grice, Paul
    (1989)   *Studies in the Way of Words.* Cambridge.

Hamilton, Sir William
    (1860)   *Lectures on Logic.* Edited by H. L. Mansel and J. Veitch. Edinburgh.

Hatano, Giyoo, and Yasuko Suga
    (1977)   Understanding and Use of Disjunction in Children. *Journal of Experimental Child Psychology* **24**: 395–405.

Heath, Peter, editor
    (1966)   *On the Syllogism and Other Logical Writings by Augustus De Morgan.* New Haven.

Hilpinen, Risto, editor
    (1981)   *New Studies in Deontic Logic.* Dordrecht.

Horn, Laurence R.
    (1989)   *A Natural History of Negation.* Chicago.

Humbert, J.
  (1960)   *Syntaxe Grecque.* Paris.

Imbert, Claude
  (1980)   Stoic Logic and Alexandrian Poetics. Translated by Jonathan Barnes. In
           Schofield et al. (1980).

Jackson, Frank, editor
  (1991)   *Conditionals.* Oxford.

Jennings, R. E.
  (1966)   Or. *Analysis* **26**: 181–184.
  (1967)   *Topic-neutral Expressions.* Ph.D. thesis. University of London.
  (1969)   *Punctuation and Truth-functionality.* Unpublished mimeograph.
  (1974)   Utilitarian Semantics for Deontic Logic. *Journal of Philosophical Logic* **3**:
           445–456.
  (1985)   Can There be a Natural Deontic Logic? *Synthese* **65**: 257–274.
  (1986)   The Punctuational Sources of the Truth-functional 'Or'. *Philosophical
           Studies* **50**: 237–259.

Jespersen, Otto
  (1917)   Negation in English and other Languages. *Historisk-filogiške Meddeleser,* 1
           (5). Reprinted in Jespersen (1934).
  (1934)   *Selected Writings of Otto Jespersen.* London.
  (1949)   *A Modern English Grammar on Historical Principles.* Phototyped edition.
           Copenhagen.

Johansson, Bo S.
  (1977)   Levels of mastery of the coordinators *and* and *or* and logical test
           performance. *British Journal of Psychology* **68**: 311–320.

Johansson, Bo S., and Barbro Sjölin
  (1975)   Preschool Children's Understanding of the Co-ordinators 'And' and 'Or'.
           Journal of Experimental Child Psychology **19**: 233–240.

Johnson-Laird, P. N. and Ruth M. J. Byrne
  (1991)   *Deduction.* Hove.

Jungius, Joachim
  (1957)   *Logica Hamburgensis.* Edited by Rudolf W. Meyer. Hamburg (Originally
           published 1632).

Kamp, Hans
  (1974)   Free choice permission. *Proceedings of the Aristotelian Society* **74**: 57–74.

Katz, J.
  (1977)   *Propositional Structure and Illocutionary Force.* Cambridge, Mass.

Keil, Heinrich
  (1961)   *Grammatici Latini.* Hildesheim.

Kenny, A.J.
  (1963)   *Action, Emotion and Will.* London.
  (1966)   Practical Inference. *Analysis* **26**: 65–75.

Kieffer, John Spangler, translator
(1964)   *Galen's Institutio Logica*. Baltimore.

Kitto, H.D.F.
(1951)   *The Greeks*. Harmondsworth.

Kneale, W., and M. Kneale
(1962)   *The Development of Logic*. Oxford.

Ladusaw, William A.
(1980)   *Polarity Sensitivity as Inherent Scope Relations*. Bloomington, Indiana.

Land, J. P. N., editor
(1891)   *Arnoldi Geulincx Antverpiensis Opera Philosophica*. Volumen Primum. The Hague. (Republished Stuttgart-Bad Cannstatt, 1965).

Lane, G. M.
(1899)   *A Latin Grammar for Schools and Colleges*. London.

Legrand, Jean Ehrenkranz
(1975)   Or *and* Any: *The Semantics and Syntax of Two Logical Operators*. Doctoral dissertation, the University of Chicago.

Liberman, Mark
(1973)   Alternatives. *Papers from the Ninth Regional Meeting, Chicago Linguistic Society.*

Lindsay, W. M.
(1894)   *The Latin Language*. Oxford. (Reprinted New York, 1963).

Long, H. S., editor
(1964)   Diogenes Laertius. *Vitae Philosophorum*. 2 vols. Oxford.

Łukasiewicz, Jan
(1967)   On the History of the Logic of Propositions. In *Polish Logic 1920—1939*, edited by Storrs McCall. Oxford.

Mabbott, J. D., G. Ryle, and H. H. Price
(1929)   Symposium: Negation. *Aristotelian Society Proceedings Supplement* (1929): 67–111.

Makinson, David
(1983)   Stenius' approach to disjunctive permission. *Theoria* **50**: 138–147.

Mason, C. P.
(1918)   *English Grammar*. 42d ed. London.

Mates, Benson
(1953)   *Stoic Logic*. Berkeley and Los Angeles.

McCawley, James D.
(1981)   *Everything That Linguists Have Always Wanted to Know about Logic but Were Ashamed to Ask*. Chicago.

Mill, John Stuart
(1867)   *An Examination of Sir William Hamilton's Philosophy. Collected Works of John Stuart Mill*, Vol. 9. Edited by J. M. Robson. Toronto.

Mueller, Ian
(1978)   An Introduction to Stoic Logic. In Rist (1978).

Mutschmann, Hermann, editor
(1914)   *Sextus Empirici Opera*. Leipzig.

Onions, C. T.
(1932)   *An Advanced English Syntax*. 6th ed. London.

Osherson, D. N.
(1975)   *Reason in Adolescence: Deductive Inference*. in *Logical Abilities in Children*, Vol. 3. Hillsdale.

Parkinson, G.H.R.
(1965)   *Logic and Reality in Leibniz's Metaphysics*. Oxford.
(1966)   *Leibniz: Logical Papers, A Selection*. Oxford.

Pelletier, F. J.
(1978)   Or. *Theoretical Linguistics* **4**: 61–74.

Philoponous, Ioannes
(1905)   *Commentaria in Analytica Priora Aristotelis*. Edited by Maximilian Wallies. Berlin.

Pott, A.
(1859)   *Etymologische Forschungen*. Halle.

Quine, W.V.O.
(1960)   *Word and Object*. Cambridge, Mass.

Reichenbach, Hans
(1947)   *Elements of Symbolic Logic*. New York.

Rescher, Nicholas, and John Robison
(1964)   Can One Infer Commands from Commands? *Analysis* **24**: 176–179.

Richards, T. A.
(1978)   *The Language of Reason*. Rushcutters Bay, N.S.W.

Rist, J. M., editor
(1978)   *The Stoics*. Berkeley.

Rohlfs, Gerhard
(1960)   *Vom Vulgärlatein zum Altfranzösischen*. Tübingen (Translated into English by Vincent Alamzan and Lillian McCarthy. Detroit, 1970).

Ross, G. R. T.
(1903)   The Disjunctive Judgment. *Mind* **12**: 489–501.

Russell, Bertrand
  (1937)   *The Principles of Mathematics*. London.
  (1940)   *An Inquiry into Meaning and Truth*. London.

Ryle, Gilbert
  (1949)   *Concept of Mind*. Harmondsworth, 1973 (First published London, 1949).
  (1960)   *Dilemmas*. Cambridge.

Schofield, Malcolm, Miles Burnyeat, and Jonathan Barnes, editors
  (1980)   *Doubt and Dogmatism: Studies in Hellenistic Epistemology*. Oxford.

Schotch, P. K. and R. E. Jennings
  (1981)   Non-Kripkean Deontic Logic. In *New Essays in Deontic Logic*, edited by R. Hilpinen. Dordrecht.

Sextus Empiricus
  (1914a) *Outlines of Pyrrhonism*. In Mutschmann (1914).
  (1914b) *Against the Logicians*. In Mutschmann (1914).
  (1933a) *Against the Logicians*. Translated by R. G. Bury. Cambridge.
  (1933b) *Outlines of Pyrrhonism*. Translated by R. G. Bury. Cambridge.

Small, George William
  (1924)   *The Comparison of Inequality*. Baltimore.

Stoothoff, R.
  (1964)   'Any' and 'Every'. *Analysis* **24**: 153–159.

Strawson, P. F.
  (1952)   *Introduction to Logical Theory*. London.

Suppes, Patrick, and Shirley Feldman
  (1971)   Young Children's Comprehension of Logical Connectives. *Journal of Experimental Child Psychology* **12**: 304–317.

van Dijk, Teun
  (1977)   *Text and Context. Explorations in the Semantics and Pragmatics of Discourse*. New York.

van Fraassen, Bas
  (1972)   The Logic of Conditional Obligation. *Journal of Philosophical Logic* **1**: 417–438.

Vendler, Zeno
  (1962)   Each and Every, Any and All. *Mind* **71**: 145–160. Reprinted in expanded form in Vendler (1967).
  (1967)   *Linguistics in Philosophy*. Ithaca.

Venn, John
  (1894)   *Symbolic Logic*. 2d ed. New York (First published 1881).

von Wright, Georg Henrik
  (1957)   *Logical Studies*. New York.
  (1963)   *The Logic of Preference*. Edinburgh.
  (1981)   On the Logic of Norms and Actions. In Hilpinen (1981).

Wittgenstein, Ludwig von
   (1953) *Philosophical Investigations.* London.

Zandvoort, R. W.
   (1957)   *A Handbook of English Grammar.* London.

Zeller, Edward
   (1895)   *Outlines of the History of Greek Philosophy.* London.

Logic Texts

Ambrose, Alice, and Morris Lazerowitz
   (1962)   *Fundamentals of Symbolic Logic.* Revised edition. New York.

Barker, Stephen
   (1985)   *The Elements of Logic.* New York.

Basson, A. H. and D. J. O'Connor
   (1960)   *Introduction to Symbolic Logic.* New York.

Baum, Robert
   (1975)   *Logic.* New York.

Bergmann, Merrie, James Moor, and Jack Nelson
   (1990)   *The Logic Book.* New York.

Bosanquet, Bernard
   (1911)   *Logic or the Morphology of Knowledge.* 2d ed. 2 vols. Oxford (First
            published 1888).

Brody, Baruch
   (1973)   *Logic Theoretical and Applied.* Englewood Cliffs, N.J.

Chi, R. S. Y.
   (1969)   *Buddhist Formal Logic.* Delhi.

Churchill, Robert Paul
   (1990)   *Logic: An Introduction.* New York.

Copi, I. M.
   (1961)   *Introduction to Logic.* New York.
   (1979)   *Symbolic Logic.* 5th ed. New York.

Fogelin, R. J.
   (1982)   *Understanding Arguments.* 2d ed. New York.

Georgacarakos, G.
   (1979)   *Elementary Formal Logic.* New York.

Govier, Trudy
   (1988)   *A Practical Study of Argument.* Belmont.

Hacking, Ian
(1972)   *A Concise Introduction to Logic.* New York.

Harrison, Frank R.
(1992)   *Logic and Rational Thought.* St. Paul, Minn.

Hodges, Wilfred
(1977)   *Logic.* Harmondsworth.

Hurley, Patrick J.
(1982)   *A Concise Introduction to Logic.* New York.
(1985)   *A Concise Introduction to Logic.* 2d ed. New York.
(1988)   *A Concise Introduction to Logic.* 3rd ed. New York.
(1991)   *A Concise Introduction to Logic.* 4th ed. New York.

Jeffrey, Richard C.
(1967)   *Formal Logic: Its Scope and Limits.* New York.

Johnson, Robert M.
(1986)   *A Logic Book.* Belmont.

Joseph, H.W.B.
(1916)   *An Introduction to Logic.* 2d ed. Oxford.

Kahane, Howard
(1990)   *Logic and Philosophy: A Modern Introduction.* 6th ed. New York.

Kalish, Donald, Richard Montague, and Gary Mar
(1980)   *Logic: Techniques of Formal Reasoning.* 2d ed. New York.

Kaminski, Jack and Alice Kaminski
(1974)   *Logic: A Philosophical Introduction.* Reading, Pa.

Kegley, Charles W., and Jacquelyn Ann Kegley
(1978)   *Introduction to Logic.* Lanham, Md.

Kelly, David
(1988)   *The Art of Reasoning.* New York.

Keynes, John Neville
(1906)   *Studies and Exercises in Formal Logic.* 4th ed. London (First published 1884).

Klenk, Virginia
(1983)   *Understanding Symbolic Logic.* Englewood Cliffs, N.J.

Lambert, Karel, and Bas van Fraassen
(1972)   *Derivation and Counterexample.* Encino, Calif.

Langer, Susanne K.
(1967)   *Symbolic Logic.* 3d revised ed. New York.

Lemmon, E. J.
(1965)   *Beginning Logic.* London.

Manicas, Peter T.
  (1976)   *Logic: The Essentials.* New York.

Massey, Gerald J.
  (1970)   *Understanding Symbolic Logic.* New York.

Mates, Benson
  (1965)   *Elementary Logic.* New York.

McKay, Thomas J.
  (1989)   *Modern Formal Logic.* New York.

Mellone, Sydney Herbert
  (1905)   *An Introductory Text-book of Logic.* Edinburgh and London.
  (1934)   *Elements of Modern Logic.* London.
  (1945)   *Elements of Modern Logic.* 2d ed. London.

Nolt, John
  (1984)   *Informal Logic: Possible Worlds and Imagination.* New York.

Pospesel, H.
  (1984)   *Propositional Logic.* 2d ed. Englewood Cliffs, N.J.

Purtill, Richard
  (1979)   *Logic for Philosophers.* New York.

Quine, W. V. O.
  (1961)   *Mathematical Logic.* Cambridge, Mass.
  (1972)   *Methods of Logic.* 3d ed. New York.

Rennie, M. K., and R. A. Girle
  (1973)   *Logic: Theory and Practice.* Brisbane.

Rescher, Nicholas
  (1964)   *Introduction to Logic.* New York.

Resnick, Michael
  (1970)   *Elementary Logic.* New York.

Richards, T.A.
  (1978)   *The Language of Reason.* Rushcutters Bay, NSW.

Rubin, Ronald, and Charles M. Young
  (1989)   *Formal Logic: a Model of English.* Mountainview.

Salmon, Wesley C.
  (1984)   *Logic.* New York.

Schagrin, Morton L.
  (1985)   *Logic: A Computer Approach.* New York.

Simco, Nancy D.
  (1982)   *Elementary Logic.* Belmont.

Strawson, P. F.
    (1952)   *Introduction to Logical Theory*. London.

Suppes, Patrick
    (1957)   *Introduction to Logic*. Princeton.

Tapscott, Bangs L.
    (1976)   *Elementary Applied Symbolic Logic*. Englewood Cliffs, N.J.

Tarski, Alfred
    (1941)   *Introduction to Logic and to the Methodology of the Deductive Sciences*.
          New York (Revised 1946 edition).

Thomason, R. H.
    (1970)   *Symbolic Logic*. London.

Vernon, Thomas S., and Lowell A. Nissen
    (1968)   *Reflective Thinking: The Fundamentals of Logic*. Belmont.

Whately, Richard
    (1834)   *Elements of Logic*. London.

Yanal, Robert J.
    (1988)   *Basic Logic*. St. Paul.

Sources of Quoted Examples

Andrews, Anthony
    (1971)   *Greek Society*. Harmondsworth.

Balchin, Nigel
    (1943)   *The Small Back Room*. Oxford, 1985.

Barnes, Julian
    (1984)   *Flaubert's Parrot*. London. 1985.

Baum, Robert
    (1975)   *Logic*. New York.

Bowen, Elizabeth
    (1938)   *The Death of the Heart*. New York, 1955.

Chandler, Raymond
    (1939)   *The Big Sleep*. New York, 1986.
    (1940)   *Farewell, My Lovely*. New York, 1986.
    (1942)   *The High Window*. New York, 1986.

Cornificius
    (1981)   *Ad C. Herennium*, translated by H. Kaplan. Cambridge, Mass.

Deus, Omnipotens
    (1959)   *Bibliorum Sacrorum*, New Edition. Vatican.

Dickens, Charles
  (1986)   *The Pickwick Papers*, edited by James Kinsley. Oxford.

Graves, Robert, translator
  (1957)   Suetonius (Gaius Suetonius Tranquillus). *The Twelve Caesars*, Harmondsworth.

Hardy, Thomas
  (1872)   *Under the Greenwood Tree*. London, 1950.

Huxley, Aldous
  (1925)   *Those Barren Leaves*. London, 1978.

James, P. D.
  (1962)   *Cover Her Face*. Harmondsworth, 1989.
  (1989)   *Devices and Desires*. Harmondsworth, 1990.

LapLink
  (1989)   LapLink Release III Manual.

Lathen, Emma
  (1961)   *Banking on Death*. New York.

Leonard, Elmore
  (1989)   *Killshot*. New York.

Lovesay, Peter
  (1992)   *The Last Detective*. New York.

MacDonald, Ross
  (1953)   *Meet Me at the Morgue*. New York.
  (1958)   *The Doomsters*. New York.
  (1962)   *The Zebra-striped Hearse*. New York.
  (1964a)   *The Chill*. New York.
  (1964b)   *The Far Side of the Dollar*. New York.

Mair, John
  (1941)   *Never Come Back*. Oxford, 1986.

Mo, Timothy
  (1982)   *Sour Sweet*. London.

Neely, Henry M.
  (1989)   *A Primer for Star-Gazers*. New York.

Orwell, George
  (1938)   *Homage to Catalonia*. New York, 1980.

Paretsky, Sara
  (1987)   *Bitter Medicine*. New York.

Priestley, J. B.
  (1969)   *The Prince of Pleasure and His Regency*. London.

Rendell, Ruth
    (1967)   *Wolf to the Slaughter*. London, 1982.
    (1971)   *One Across, Two Down*. London, 1983.
    (1975)   *Shake Hands Forever*. London, 1976.
    (1981)   *Put on by Cunning*. London, 1982.
    (1982)   *Master of the Moor*. New York, 1983.
    (1985)   *An Unkindness of Ravens*. London, 1986.
    (1987)   *Talking to Strange Men*. London, 1987.
    (1988)   *The Veiled One*. London, 1989.

Sale, George, translator
    (1734)   *The Koran*. London.

Sallust
    (1930)   *Catilina*. Translated by J. C. Rolfe. Cambridge, Mass.

Sayers, Dorothy L.
    (1930)   *Strong Poison*. London.

Simco, Nancy D.
    (1982)   *Elementary Logic*. Belmont.

Terence
    (1965)   *Phormio*. Translated by John Sargeaunt. Cambridge, Mass.

Trollope, Anthony
    (1857)   *Barchester Towers*. New York.
    (1864)   *Can You Forgive Her?* London.

Wambaugh, Joseph
    (1978)   *The Black Marble*. London.
    (1987)   *Echoes in the Darkness*. New York.
    (1990)   *The Golden Orange*. New York.

Waugh, Evelyn
    (1962)   *Ronald Knox*. Glasgow.

I N D E X *of* N A M E S